THE NECESSARY NATION

D0217340

GREGORY JUSDANIS

THE NECESSARY NATION

PRINCETON UNIVERSITY PRESS

PRINCETON AND OXFORD

Copyright © 2001 by Princeton University Press
Published by Princeton University Press, 41 William Street,
Princeton, New Jersey 08540
In the United Kingdom: Princeton University Press,
3 Market Place, Woodstock, Oxfordshire OX20 1SY
All Rights Reserved

Library of Congress Cataloging-in-Publication Data

Jusdanis, Gregory, 1955-
The necessary nation / Gregory Jusdanis.
p. cm.
Includes bibliographical references and index.
ISBN 0-691-07029-6 (alk. paper)
1. Nationalism. 2. Culture. I. Title.
JC311.J87 2001
306—dc21   00-056513

This book has been composed in Sabon

The paper used in this publication meets
the minimum requirements of
ANSI/NISO Z39.48-1992 (R1997)
(*Permanence of Paper*)

www.pup.princeton.edu

Printed in the United States of America

10 9 8 7 6 5 4 3 2 1

10 9 8 7 6 5 4 3 2 1
(pbk)

For Adrian, Alexander, and Clare

CONTENTS

ACKNOWLEDGMENTS

I BEGAN THIS PROJECT some years ago with the hope of understanding certain political, social, and economic problems faced by the world at the turn of the twentieth century. In a previous work I sought to investigate the development of a national literature. I realized, however, that if I really wanted to gain insights into nationalism, I had to undertake research beyond literary texts and aesthetic artifacts.

The generous support of a number of institutions has given me time to read in fields beyond my own area of specialty, modern Greek literature. I would like to thank the John Simon Guggenheim Memorial Foundation for a one-year fellowship (1992–93) which made it possible for me to start the project in the first place. A year later I was fortunate to receive a fellowship from the Woodrow Wilson International Center for Scholars at the Smithsonian Institution, which allowed me to do further research in Washington and write the first draft of the manuscript. The College of Humanities of The Ohio State University has been very supportive of my work throughout the years with grants and released time for research. I am indebted to all three institutions for believing that a modern Greek literary critic could undertake a conversation between the humanities and social sciences.

My project has benefited greatly from the efforts of a number of assistants who worked with me for periods ranging from one academic quarter to a year. I would like to thank for their efficiency and dedication Gerasimus Katsan, George Anagnostu, Michelle King, Cynthia Hohlfelder, Eric Ball, Sophie Forbes, Lee Papouras, and Aletheia Pallam. I am grateful to Brian MacDonald for his careful copyediting.

I had the good fortune to present portions of this work at The Ohio State University, the Woodrow Wilson Center, Harvard, Cornell, Stanford, Oregon, San Francisco State, and the Bilar Institute in Istanbul. I am grateful to colleagues for their invitations and members of the audience for their questions.

This study would not have been possible without the help of certain friends and colleagues. Eugene Holland went over with me some of the French material. Abiola Irele and Isaac Mowoe offered references for nationalism in Nigeria and Joseph Zeidan for Egypt. Artemis Leontis discussed many of these issues with me over years of close collaboration. Carole Fink and James Sheehan read chapters 5 and 3 respectively and made many useful comments. Peter Murphy read a substantial portion of an earlier draft, having jotted countless remarks along the margins, which often continued on the back of the page. Two anonymous readers of

Princeton University Press helped me rethink and sharpen my argument in a fundamental way. I am grateful to them for their commitment to scholarship and its evaluation. Mary Murrell of Princeton University Press believed in the manuscript and promoted energetically its publication.

Nick Howe read the entire manuscript twice and encouraged me to revise it, delete many portions, and recast my thoughts. I very much appreciate his comradely advice and rigor. My father-in-law, Carl Anderson, also read the manuscript two times with a fine eye and an ear well attuned. I cannot thank him enough for all his help over the years. As in my previous works, so in this one, Vassilis Lambropoulos shared selflessly his thoughts and his work with me. His critical skills and his friendship emboldened me to continue at those crucial moments.

My wife Julian Anderson has read each word of the book. Over the years she has taught me that writing is as important as the ideas it conveys. "It is not often," to quote from E. B. White's *Charlotte's Web*, "that someone comes along who is a true friend and a good writer." Julian is both. My children Adrian, Alexander, and most recently Clare have seen me writing this work at various stages. It has been written between naps, feedings, park visits, trips, the assemblage of toys, and cooking. They have demonstrated to me that public identity, one topic of this book, is meaningless without a home. And, of course, the national home is the main subject of this study.

THE NECESSARY NATION

INTRODUCTION

AN APOLOGY for the nation? It is necessary and overdue. The nation has been maligned today, charged with xenophobia, fascism, and genocide. Journalists and academics, conservatives and liberals, Marxist and cultural studies critics seem to hold the nation responsible for the most odious crimes. Although they differ in their political and epistemological orientations, these writers launch their attacks on the nation from primarily two camps, cosmopolitanism and particularism— paradoxically the two forces that have led to the rise of the nation in the first place. On the one side are those who reject the nation as a betrayal of universal, rational reason. Looking at the ethnic cleansing, the bloodletting, and general interethnic strife around the globe, these commentators are horrified by nationalism's destabilizing potential, its chthonic, backward-looking energy. For them, nationalism abroad and at home is a historical cul-de-sac, an error, or a plague. On the opposite front are those who denounce the nation for oppressing the tribes within its borders, who regard national culture as a weight imposed on minority groups, crushing them with the stamp of the dominant ethnicity. They long instead for a utopian world of scattered diasporas, open borders, and hybrid identities.

In a sense, the case against nationalism had been argued forcefully more than a century ago by Lord Acton, the British historian and Liberal member of Parliament, who lamented the potential this doctrine had to wreak violence in the world. For this very reason the social theorist Elie Kedourie in an influential work dismissed postcolonial nationalism as the "opium of the masses," an irrational ideology built on "resentment and impatience, the depravity of the rich and the virtue of the poor, the guilt of Europe and the innocence of Asia and Africa" (1970: 146–47). Looking at the ethnic conflicts around the world in the 1980s and 1990s, the journalist Michael Ignatieff recoiled with understandable horror. People fooled themselves, he averred, into believing that humanity had moved beyond tribalism. "The repressed has returned, and its name is nationalism" (1993: 5). But this "repressed" is for Eric Hobsbawm at variance with history. Thus he characterizes Quebecois nationalism, for example, as a "headlong retreat from historical forces which threaten to overwhelm it" (1990: 164). Many commentators in the United States, such as Arthur Schlesinger, E. D. Hirsch, and Sheldon Hackney (the chairman of the National Endowment for the Humanities in Bill Clinton's first term) have pointed to the politics of "blood and belonging" in places like Bosnia-

Herzegovina, Azerbaijan, Ireland, and Quebec, in order to awaken Americans to the dangers of "the politics of difference" at home.

The most caustic vitriol against nationalism, however, has been poured by poststructuralist critics who see this discourse as the ultimate attempt to impose upon a heterogeneous people an essentialist identity. Thus, even though from a different perspective, the critic Neil Larsen comes to a conclusion similar to Ignatieff's: "Postnational" consciousness has not really banished nationalist thinking. "Nationalism, in fact, *unless confronted and repudiated in all its ideological ramifications*, can find any number of ways to reassert itself within the thinking that claims to have abjured it" (1995: 142). Poststructuralists renounce nationalism because they find in its core the search for origins, mimetic representation, the narratives of myth, and the logic of identity. Because they associate nationalism with a Western, imperialist, logocentric reason, they promote what David Lloyd in his own rejection of nationalism has characterized as "anti-identitarian thinking" (1993: 55). Indeed, one of the most visible academic movements of the past twenty years has been an attempt to investigate the "writing of the nation" in order ultimately to "unwrite" it. What has gained favor is a critique of the nation, a hermeneutic of negativity, or, in the words of Lauren Berlant, a "counter–National Symbolic" (1991: 34). Because poststructuralist criticism wishes to free humanity from the constraints of the nation, it places great emphasis, as the work of Paul Gilroy, Homi Bhabha, and Arjun Appadurai has shown, on border writing, transcultural formations, and syncretic forms. Only rarely does one encounter any opposition to this stance in the way, for instance, Timothy Brennan ends his study of cosmopolitanism with the pronouncement: "Nationalism is not dead. And it is good that it is not" (1997: 317).

This vilification of nationalism is shortsighted, to say the least. That most of the world's nationalist struggles resounded with the call for freedom from foreign rule rather than for freedom of speech, women's rights, or protection for minorities is no reason to denounce the whole enterprise. Was it not noble to end colonial domination, establish a republic, and set up a society of citizens? Those critics who identify the nation with oppression forget that nationalism has inspired people over the past two centuries to fight collectively against the illegitimacy of foreign occupation.

In contrast to its dominant representations in currency today, I argue that the nation should be perceived as a positive institution in human society. More important, I wish to restore history to the study of nationalism, a dimension shockingly missing in poststructuralist approaches to the subject. The concentration on the present, both in terms of scholarship and current events, has led to the demonization of nationalism as a procrustean force restraining difference. This presentism is particularly evident in literary and cultural studies, manifesting itself in the way, for instance, that theorists depict the nation as an invention, a fantasy, or a narration. The defamation of the nation goes hand in hand with its portrayal as an ideological construct. Both processes occlude the long political developments leading to the emergence of the nation-state as a body of citizens, making it seem inevitable, a matter of writing. The emphasis on the present, however, has the effect of highlighting the role of literary and cultural critics as slayers of the malevolent nationalist dragon.

My aim is neither to celebrate the nation nor to gloss over its crimes, but rather to evaluate its contribution to historical developments over the past two centuries. Nationalism appeared in Europe at least as early as the destruction of the ancient regime and the industrialization of the economy; however, it cannot be reduced to these developments. The undertaking to build nations is an autonomous process that seeks to unify a particular people in a hostile world, to give them a realm of emotional attachments in the face of continuing change, and, above all, to propel them on a path of progress. Rather than sliding back into darkness, nationalism actually is an attempt to interpret and participate in modernity.

The inescapability of Western progress had made itself felt in the past two centuries to societies in central, eastern, and southern Europe as well as to its colonies overseas. The original nationalists in the latter part of the eighteenth and early nineteenth centuries, fearing that their own societies had been left behind by early modernizers, placed enormous value on a self-enclosed national culture as a way of pushing their compatriots toward a more sanguine future. The great challenge to nationalists has always been to take part in modernization while at the same time preserving traditional identities. They have been able to persuade their populations to enter the modern age by promising them that what was dear to them would be safeguarded. While people stepped diffidently into a competitive, heartless world, nationalists assured them that the road ahead was paved with ancestral materials. From the beginning nationalism has incorporated the tensions between tradition and progress and between a full past and the sketchy future.

I argue that nationalism developed in the latter eighteenth century for two reasons. First, the far-reaching transformations accompanying modernity brought about a profound interaction among populations. Although cultural and economic exchanges had always been part of human history, in the modern age this intercourse began to threaten the ethnic identities of regional groups more than had been the case with the polyethnic empires of antiquity and the Middle Ages. Capitalism, colonialism, and new means of communication and transportation pulled distant places closer together and mixed their populations, endangering thereby their cultural existence. The intensity and scope of contact among the world's peoples engendered a deep interest in the collective self and in the separation of this self from others. The more people confronted groups beyond their frontiers and borrowed from them, the more the differences between those inside and those outside were emphasized. Elites conceived ideologies, like nationalism, which promised to save autochthonous traditions threatened by a seemingly ceaseless penetration of foreign ideas, capital, goods, and people. To the forces in modernity pushing toward sameness and standardization, nationalism responded by defending difference.

The safeguarding of identities became a political objective in modernity because a centralized, omniscient, and omnipotent state could infiltrate and affect the minutiae of daily life in ways inconceivable in the past. Invading armies could bring about not only physical destruction and plunder but also the dissolution of traditional folkways, which had become increasingly meaningful for reasons already noted. The possibility of such a loss became real to Europeans, for instance, in the Napoleonic Wars. Confronted by an aggressive state bent upon imposing the universal values of the French Revolution upon the world, Germans and Scandinavians sought in culture a way of preserving their identities and of repelling their foes. This was true of Europe's colonies as well. Edward Said has shown that colonialism had a distinct cultural dimension, seeking to know the people of its territories, to transform their societies, and to use this knowledge in the aid of its administration.

In other words, social, economic, technological, and political developments in modernity directed attention to collective identities and endowed them with a materiality they had not had before. Starting at the close of the eighteenth century people began to believe that their ethnicity, once as transparent as the water they drank, was a vital possession that could be harmed by ruling groups, aggressive neighbors, or colonial masters. They began to associate consciously their sense of their own well-being with that of their national culture rather than, say, their religion or their king. In other words, they politicized their identity. National culture began to signify those practices and social relations which, expressing the difference of one nation from others, formed the foundation of the new states.

Culture became political when it became national–that is, when people began to justify political rule on the basis of ethnic unity. It acquired this political status, however, in the interaction of groups. National culture is a relational concept that has gained its significance in the struggles of groups and states for representation, land, and resources. Ethnicity was nationalized when people began to feel that they could best protect their identities in their own unitary state rather than in the province of other states or empires. The justification of the new states, as to both their genesis and continuing life, was the preservation of a certain uniqueness. The experiences of the stateless Palestinians and Kurds show that the principle of cultural survival is as much alive at the end of the twentieth century as it had been for the Greeks at the beginning of the nineteenth. Nationalism has brought together two originally separate ideas: power resides with the people, and a people sufficiently different from others has a right to govern itself. In modernity an attack on the political liberty or the cultural integrity of a nation is tantamount to ethnocide.

That nationalists look to culture as a safe haven from foreign aggressors does not mean, as is often asserted, that nationalism promotes a purely defensive posture, one hostile to the outside world. Rather than advancing a narcissistic concern with the self, nationalism actually mediates in the interaction between the self and the other, between the individual and the universal, the old and the new. Nationalism fosters an interchange among groups by promoting self-confidence among them, by encouraging them to find strength in their own cultural resources, and ultimately to fight against oppression and for independence.

Nationalism has been an extraordinary force over the past two hundred years because it has permitted groups to maintain their differences while ensuring their survival in modernity, to seek justice and self-respect while becoming members of a transnational world of states, to form a polity on the basis of a (presumed) homogeneous identity. National culture itself serves as both the manifestation of uniqueness and its guardian, a process of creation and its end product, a result of and determinant of intergroup dialogue. In short, it provides an unfolding map for the nation's future as well as an archive of its history.

My second argument is that nationalism is born out of a theory of progress and that nationalists appropriate culture in their projects of modernization. I do not mean that human society has been moving resolutely toward an unlimited future but rather that a significant impulse for the emergence of nationalism has been the discovery by intellectual and political elites of the tardiness of their societies. Nationalism therefore is in part a response to a condition of belatedness. European modernization produced its first successes industrially in England and the Netherlands and politically in France. The advances made by these countries in modernizing themselves put all other societies, not least their neighbors, in a situation of "backwardness." This was so because the theory of progress, another specifically European value now universalized, accentuated forward movement and unlimited material improvement. It divided the world into pioneering and successful societies, on the one hand, and follower and failed communities, on the other. Those left behind had no choice but to catch up with the winners of the race. Ever since they were co-opted or had inserted themselves into the narrative of Western progress, they have been striving to catch up.

In the colonial situation, Partha Chatterjee contends, nationalist thought "asserts that the superiority of the West lies in the materiality of its culture, exemplified by its science, technology and love of progress. But the East is superior in the spiritual aspect of culture" (1986: 51). In other words, nationalists of postcolonial societies recognize the inevitability of Western modernity, the inescapability of progress, and the necessity of copying its models. But the need to imitate Western skills has been accompanied by the greater urgency to preserve ethnic distinctiveness. Anticolonial nationalists divide the world of institutions and practices into two domains, the material and the spiritual. The first consists of the economy, statecraft, science, technology, "a domain where the West has proved its superiority and the East had succumbed." The spiritual sphere, containing the marks of cultural distinctiveness, is declared sovereign, beyond the control of the colonial power (Chatterjee 1993: 6).

Chatterjee rightly argues that the aim of this nationalism is to create a new, modern, national culture, but one not Western. He is mistaken, however, to see this as a feature of only "anti-colonial nationalisms in Asia and Africa" (1993: 6). Nationalist thought has always given priority to cultural survival and the pursuit of progress at the same time, as the cases of Germany and Greece indicate. Germany, where the theory of cultural nationalism first appeared and received its most comprehensive treatment, presents an interesting example because it is now regarded as a Western country. Yet German poets, artists, and scholars developed an imagined nation in response first to French cultural hegemony and then to Napoleon's invasions of their territories in the name of Enlightenment universality. Greece offers a fascinating twist to the postcolonial situation. Although viewed today as a European nation, it was ruled until 1821 by the Ottoman Empire, an Oriental society. Greek elites, residing in European cities, launched a project of modernization once they discovered the progress of Europe. Persuaded that their nation had fallen into "backwardness" in the hands of the Ottomans, they saw in culture a way of making their society modern. This pattern can be seen in Egypt, which had been an Ottoman province but was invaded by Napoleon in 1798, occupied by Britain, and ruled as a protectorate from 1882 until 1922. In response to these invasions Egyptian nationalist intellectuals began to see the national state as a way of acquiring the benefits of modernity in order to strengthen Egypt. They assumed a direct "correlation between the realization of Egyptian authenticity and the attainment of modernity" (Gershoni and Jankowski 1986: 130). All three cases, German, Greek, and Egyptian, show that, contrary to the claims of postcolonial theory, nationalism has resisted political and cultural universal systems from the beginning and has sought in national culture the resources for moderniza-tion. The nation-state itself has always been seen both in Europe and in its colonies as a vehicle to modernity.

Thus, R. Radhakrishnan mistakenly claims that the nationalist project is complicit with the European Enlightenment. It is complicit only if we understand by this that it reacted against the Enlightenment. The earliest European nationalisms, for instance, fought against the attempt of the French to create a new world order, to extend the principles of the French Revolution across the rest of Europe. Ironically, when Radhakrishnan criticizes nationalism for continuing the "baleful legacies of Euro-centrism," he calls, in fact, for more nationalism. Echoing Chatterjee, he enjoins postcolonial subjects to produce "a genuine subaltern history about themselves and not merely replicate . . . the liberal-elitist narrative of the West" (1992: 86).[1] In so doing, of course, he is promoting a Herd-erian and ultimately nationalist proposition, as German thinkers had done in the latter eighteenth century. For it was Herder who first insisted that nations should desist from copying others, look for strength in them-selves, and value their own unique qualities. Each historical period, he wrote, "has in itself the center of its own happiness" (1992: 45).[2]

The prominent position given culture and progress in nationalist thought accentuates the roles of elites in modernization, making this proj-ect, in the words of Chatterjee, "an elitist program" (1986: 51). Tradition-ally those promoting modernization have been intellectuals who usually have come into contact with modernity before the general population and who, as a class, have had much to gain from this program. As a result of the devastating comparisons they made between their own society and western Europe, out of which their own society emerged as inferior and backward, they undertook a project of social reconstruction. Their proj-ect was and is to a great extent cultural, as it places emphasis on identity, language, antiquity, and the nation. The "passionate search for a national culture" by intellectuals in colonial societies, Frantz Fanon wrote, has to do with the "anxiety" of being "swamped" in Western culture, and of

---

[1] Basil Davidson makes the same argument. While he understands the need of African nations to modernize, he asks: "But why then adopt models from those very countries or systems that have oppressed and despised you? Why not modernize from the models of your own history or invent new models?" (1992: 18). Although postcolonial nations adopt these models of modernization, they also attempt to defend the integrity of their cultures.

[2] Like Herodotus, Herder believed in a dogged particularism. He attacked the evils of ethnocentrism: "People who are ignorant of history and know only their own age believe that the present taste is the only one, and so necessary that nothing else besides it is think-able; they believe that everything they find is indispensable for all ages. . . . Commonly, this ignorance is also joined by pride . . . that their age is the best of ages, because they dwell within it and other epochs did not have the honor of their acquaintance" (1992: 66).

"becoming lost to their people" (1963: 209). The fear of cultural loss has motivated intellectuals to preserve their ethnic heritage ever since national culture in the eighteenth century began to take shape as an object of political concern.

Culture has figured prominently in plans for modernization because it allows elites in postcolonial and belated societies to understand their "backwardness" as well as to try to overcome it. Insofar as modernization entails a process of catching up, it requires recourse to models, copying, imagining, representation, interpretation—the very devices of culture. Modernization in these societies necessitates the work of intellectuals to imagine, fabricate, and self-consciously formulate what is considered lacking. Intellectuals thus serve not as movers of heaven and earth but as revolutionaries, poets, interpreters, and teachers. Although they do not create the conditions for their actions, they play an extraordinary role in imagining the possibility of a unified nation, often decades before its realization.

Rather than constituting a compensatory prize of victimized people in search of absent ideals, nationalism acts as a dynamic power, pushing societies into a modern, global world. It is a revolutionary, progressive, and utopian doctrine, seeking the transformation of the inherited, and quite often, unjust and oppressive order. Nationalism promotes modernization by reassuring the *Volk* that its way of life will survive because it, rather than the monarchy, the church, or the colonial ruler, now forms the life and structure of the state. The nation is modern insofar as culture legitimates political sovereignty.

I propose, in short, that nationalism is ultimately a cultural phenomenon. In contrast to a dominant trend in political theory, and one ignored by cultural studies, I put into question the possibility of a purely civic (noncultural) conception of nationalism—that a nation-state can be based on an idea, that it can flourish in a purely political sense, that it is held together by its constitutional documents and democratic institutions. Through a discussion of specific states I show that cultural and political nationalisms are intertwined and that the distinction between ethnic and civic nations, itself carrying a long tradition, is false and ultimately Eurocentric. For it reduces the history of the past two centuries into a morality tale, a struggle between "good" nationalisms (those of the United States, France, and England) and "bad" nationalisms (those of eastern Europe and of Asia and Africa). Differences in nationalisms exist. Some may be open and accommodating to foreigners and minorities, whereas others can be hostile, repressive, and downright murderous. Others still may attempt to suppress emergent nationalist movements at home or in colonies. But these differences cannot be expressed solely in terms of ideology. Each nationalist movement must be seen as a product of historical conditions of the nation, class relations, and the concurrent development of constitutional forms of government and of civil society that can check the excesses of the state.

Culture has been implicated in the development of even the most political of nations, the United States—which has been portrayed traditionally as a country built on political ideals rather than on common blood ties, on enlightenment ideas rather than notions of uniqueness, on republican principles rather than cultural values. Culture, I argue, has in varying degrees been involved in all projects of nationalism, and even in those most actively denying it. This does not mean that culture works like a magician, conjuring nations out of thin air, nor that nationalism alone is responsible for the emergence of nation-states. I claim, rather, that nationalists exploit the resources of culture (interpretation, rhetoric, symbols, myths), its institutions (art, literature, the academy), and its ideology (the fantasy of a homogeneous identity) in order to promote the creation and maintenance of a nation.

The workings of nationalism provide proof of the impact that culture and, by extension, intellectuals can have in daily life when conditions are right. Nationalism highlights the capacity of culture to serve as a means for political action and, ultimately, social change. Cultural nationalism enables a people to see itself as separate from others, to pursue a political program of justice and autonomy, and to promote a program of modernization. In this sense nationalism is a creative force, allowing social movements to imagine themselves achieving greatness, pursuing self-government, and building a society of citizens.

A central strand running through these pages is an investigation of how people use culture to bring about social change. In contrast to social and political theory, which has portrayed nationalism as a secondary, derivative phenomenon, a response to social change or uneven development, I regard it as a force capable of shaping our world. That is, I see nationalism as part of the modernizing process, as neither subservient to the economy nor an extension of the state. In this, I follow the traditions of Weberian sociology and cultural studies that seek to show the impact ideas can have in society. At the very least I examine the connection between ideas and historical developments in the way Weber analyzed the link between the genesis of capitalism as an economic system and the birth of the Protestant ethic. I have in mind studies like Colin Campbell's *The Romantic Ethic and the Spirit of Modern Consumerism* (1987) and Paul Gilroy's *The Black Atlantic: Modernity and Double Consciousness* (1993). Whereas Campbell explores how beliefs can affect conduct, Gilroy looks at the "cultural force" of modernity, specifically the artistic expressions of slave society, and examines how these expressions serve as media for the self-fashioning of individuals and of collective liberation (Gilroy 1993: 40).

In a similar way I am interested in discussing the impact the practices and institutions of nationalism have had on people over the past two centuries. My study is based on the assumption that modernity constitutes the separation of society into a series of autonomous but interrelated spheres of thought and activity: religion, law, the economy, bureaucracy, and, of course, culture. This process is, as Emile Durkheim noted, part of the general division of labor as various social functions, "whether political, administrative, or judicial, are becoming more and more specialized" (1984: 2–3). As a functionally differentiated domain, national culture is a constitutive part of modernity rather than a reaction to it. In other words, it is not a case of what sociologists call dedifferentiation—an escape from modernity or a strategy to provide comfort in time of ceaseless change and social differentiation.[3]

To argue that culture has been functionally differentiated is obviously not the same as saying that it has been freed from social, political, and economic forces. Nor does it mean that national culture serves as the causal agent in the construction of nation-states. When I claim that national culture exists as an autonomous domain, I mean that ethnicity has been politicized and endowed with institutions and practices unique to itself. I conceive of it in the way writers like Howard S. Becker and Peter Bürger see art as an "art world" or institution respectively—a sphere with its own rules and regulations, discourses, symbolic forms, and social spaces. This institutionality portrays national culture as a real structure that people can see, hear, and feel, rather than as a relational construct, which has acquired its historical significance in the past two centuries.

The challenge in any study of national culture involves the examination of how this phenomenon came to be seen as a justification of political authority and how it gained an institutional framework in this process without reproducing the "myths" of culture spawned by nationalism. In this I am mindful of Peter Murphy's caution that it would be "a mistake to confuse a culture's significance with the ghoulish or romantic attention paid to it" (1997: 275). At the same time, it would be wrong to avoid a positive evaluation of culture for fear of essentializing or reifying it. The trap of essentialism can be dodged through historical analysis of specific

---

[3] If differentiation refers to the creation of separate spheres of human activity, informed by their own logic, dedifferentiation alludes to the collapse of these autonomous spheres. In *The Division of Labor* Durkheim observed that the division of labor is brought about by pressure exerted upon social units, "which forces them to develop in more or less divergent manner. But at every moment this pressure is neutralized by a reverse pressure that the common consciousness exerts upon every individual consciousness" (1984: 226). Yet the division of labor "unites at the same time as it sets at odds; it causes the activities that it differentiates to converge; it brings closer those that it separates" (217). See Parsons 1975 and Alexander 1988.

nationalist projects. Such an analysis would show, as I attempt to do in chapter 5, that national culture cannot be understood in isolation from the development of the state. The aim of this historical approach is ultimately to demonstrate that national culture is both a manifestation of and participant in social change.

This diachronic approach differentiates my study from recent attempts in political theory to look at the nation as a beneficial institution. Thus unlike recent defenses of nationalism such as David Miller's *On Nationality* (1995), Yael Tamir's *Liberal Nationalism* (1993), and Will Kymlicka's *Multicultural Citizenship: A Liberal Theory of Minority Rights* (1995), which consider nations as ethical communities, seeing membership in them as morally and rationally sound, my approach to nationalism is historical rather than ethical. It seeks to explain, for instance, why culture has been regarded as a site for social strife during the past two centuries by examining the roots of the impulse to link ethnicity with political sovereignty, to imagine culture as a means of achieving progress, to regard cultural tradition as a refuge of values in a hostile world. Although my study deals with the past, its ultimate concern is with the present and with the question of how people can live in a peaceful world while maintaining their collective identities. It begins and ends with this question in mind.

This study is also comparative and interdisciplinary. In order to consider the capacity of nationalism in generating social change over the past two centuries, it has to excavate resources from a number of mines. Thus, in addition to the disciplines of cultural and literary studies, I borrow insights from sociology, anthropology, political science, and history. Although sociology has provided adequate theories of social change, it has until recently neglected nationalism, especially research in this area conducted by cultural critics. Similarly, although much exciting work on culture has been conducted by cultural studies, this field has ignored questions of historical development and the relationship between national culture and the state. In bringing together research from the humanities and social sciences, my intent is to facilitate a dialogue between the historical analysis of the nation-state and the study of culture. This dialogue is most audible in chapter 5, which puts into question the possibility of both a purely civic nationalism and a political nation.

While I am interested in defending nationalism from those who associate it exclusively with xenophobia, ethnic cleansing, and genocide, I do not celebrate it, however. I am aware of nationalism's dualistic nature, its capacity to confer benefits to humanity as well as wreak havoc. It is both Pandora's box and Hephaestus's hammer, capable of unlatching evil and chaos while also creating novel forms of social life. Nationalism may inspire groups to seek dignity, justice, or political autonomy, but it can also incite them to murderous violence. This double heritage of nationalism has constituted our social and political reality for some time. An assumption underlying my study is that ethnic identities, which over the past two hundred years have become nationalized, are not an ephemeral phenomenon. They have made and will continue to make their presence felt in human societies. Although no one can make predictions about the close of the twenty-first century, we can say with certainty that its dawn will find ethnic conflict throughout the globe.

This being the case, the challenge we all face is how to cope with two conflicting tendencies: on the one hand, the legitimate demands made by groups for cultural and political autonomy and, on the other, the need for peace and neighborly coexistence. Some writers like Liah Greenfeld and Michael Ignatieff, respond to this dilemma by extolling the virtues of civic nationalism, a nationalism cleansed of longing for blood and soil and inspired by constitutional documents and institutions. Distressed by the threat of social and political fragmentation, other commentators like E. D. Hirsch, Samuel P. Huntington, and Arthur Schlesinger point to America's model of cultural pluralism by which identities become privatized and thus devoid of political consequence. Such a model, they believe, has preserved peace in the United States and could be promoted as a solution abroad. They paint the United States as a utopia of ethnic calm in a century of bloodshed. On the other hand, cultural critics like Homi Bhabha, and Arjun Appadurai, and philosophers like Martha Nussbaum and Kwane Anthony Appiah fear not social heterogeneity but the assimilationist policies of states. They thus raise the banner of diversity for people to follow. Believing in the superior value of a polyethnic society, they advocate the philosophy of cosmopolitanism, diaspora consciousness, hybrid identities, or various forms of soft or radical multiculturalism as models for today and the future.

The culture wars of the 1990s have been fought to a certain extent by these two groups, the former predicting doom for the nation, the latter apotheosizing difference. Many political thinkers, however, such as Yael Tamir, Will Kymlicka, Michael Lind, and David Miller refuse to see work on identity and nationalism as an absolute choice between Hephaestus and Pandora. Believing that the uncompromising attack on nationalism is unjustified and ahistorical, they aspire to a liberal nationalism that reconciles support for cultural identity with respect for individual autonomy. In this way Maurizio Viroli speaks of a republican nationalism and Jürgen Habermas of a *Verfassungspatriotismus* (constitutional patriotism).

I consider these positions in the last few chapters. But rather than closing with critique, the traditional strategy of cultural studies, I conclude with a discussion of federalism as a solution to the challenges posed by social diversity. Whereas my study begins with the investigation of national culture, it ends by restraining this culture in a web of constitutional agreements. In contrast to many theorists of globalization who foresee the demise of the nation-state and a new era of open borders, I assume that states will coexist with other transnational structures. Moreover, I believe that globalization will promote unceasing ethnic differentiation and the maintenance of ethnic boundaries, as it has since the daybreak of modernity. Nationalism will continue to agitate the next century as a twin-headed force, releasing chaos into the world and leading to internecine strife but also allowing peoples to look for collective inner strength, to preserve their identities in the face of perennial change, and to strive for justice. In short, there is no proof to Bill Readings's contention that culture no longer "matters" with the decline of the nation-state (1996: 117). In fact, the explosive events around the world and within the United States show how much culture does matter for people.

Because groups will continue to identify their well-being with the condition of their culture and rationalize their sovereignty on the basis of their ethnic difference, culture will in the foreseeable future act as a fault line for conflict. Any solution that, in the name of cosmopolitanism, civic nationalism, or diaspora, does not recognize the need people feel for their identities and their connection to the native soil, will fail. This holds true for proposals for the creation of commonwealths of privatized identities. The history of the past two hundred years has shown that identities—ethnic, racial, national, religious—have an impact on governance and cannot be checked in the cloakroom. The key should be neither the suppression of identity nor its glorification. We need no longer be bound by the false dilemmas between a winsome hybridity or a dour national culture.

Our goal should be to reconsider the link established two hundred years ago by nationalism between culture and polity, ethnos and topos. We then have to devise political arrangements that can best mediate between the need for identity, nation, and locality with the necessity of universality, peace, and security. Federalism is a political system that can allow people to participate in their identities without regressing into internecine strife. It is thus best suited to reconcile the ongoing tug of war between universality and particularity, between the urgency for unity with the tonic of heterogeneity, between the necessity for amicable coexistence and the call for cultural rights.

In proposing federalism as a practical solution to the challenges confronting our postcolonial and multicultural world, I put myself at variance with the dominant tendency in humanistic study, which portrays intellectuals as commentators or censurers of political authority but never its practitioners. Literary and cultural critics, as Vassilis Lambropoulos contends, "have in general insisted on treating questions of power in a Manichean way that precludes any consideration of authority whatsoever." They continue to believe that "the hands of the intelligentsia will never be dirtied by the concessions and compromises of government as they wield the holy sword of the pen and cut a swath through the corruption of the age" (Lambropoulos 1996b: 859). They rejoice in seeing themselves as members of an opposition, never having to contemplate the qualities of a government that would enable people to pursue the good life and to live with other groups within and outside their state. The critical reflection on governance is related to one of the oldest philosophical questions, namely, how we should run our society (Lambropoulos 1996a: 851). The history of nationalism shows that cultural and literary critics have in the past engaged with these issues. They can do so again.

If one of my aims in this study is to show how ideas are implicated in social change, it goes without saying that a corollary aim is to demonstrate that intellectuals themselves are involved in this process. One of the unfortunate by-products of contemporary theory on the left is the belief that intellectuals are outside of power and hence incapable of influencing events or debates beyond their specialties. This is a curious situation because, as Said notes, those who "view us with antipathy" actually believe in the power of the intellectual (1999: 4). More curious still is the diffidence among left intellectuals to deal with culture in a positive light. One can speak authoritatively of culture, it seems, only if one represents it as an instrument of oppression or imperialism. Or one does not consider it at all for fear of essentializing it. Thus intellectuals are put in the unenviable—and professionally untenable—situation of not being able to talk about the subject from which they derive their livelihood. They address all manner of interests except the matter of professional self-interest. It is not an accident that in a collection of essays concerned with the relevance of comparative literature "in the age of multiculturalism," most commentators do not consider the value of teaching literature itself (Bernheimer 1995). They leave unanswered the question of why anybody should study literature. Why should students register for classes on culture? Why should these classes be funded?

The examination of nationalism reveals, first, the interrelationship of culture and politics and, second, the impact intellectuals can have under proper conditions. If the practitioners of culture find themselves at an impasse today over their public relevance, the task before them should be neither to celebrate nor to denigrate culture but to reconsider its significance in society and history.

Chapter One

ON NATIONALISM

THE RETURN of nationalism surely counts as one of the most
stunning occurrences of the past quarter century, having baffled
politicians, journalists, diplomats, and academics alike. Most of
them felt that the anticolonial struggles in Asia and Africa had ushered in
a postnational world, a global order never to be shaken again by nationalist tremors. This conclusion was strengthened by the speed with which
capitalism was creating an interconnected web of cultural, economic, and
technological exchanges. There was much talk about the end of history,
the death of the nation-state, and the twilight of national culture.

Nationalism—for many, a vestigial form of identification—was
thought to have been swept up by the whisk of modernization. But the
ethnic cleansing in the Balkans, bloodletting in the Caucasus, genocide in
Rwanda, autonomy movements in western Europe, civil war in Sri Lanka,
rebellions and invasions in West Africa, and multiculturalism in North
America proved that nationalist sentiments had not at all disappeared.
Their resurgence even in industrially advanced countries, where they were
least expected, shows once again that these "premodern" elements form
the pattern of the carpet of modernity and cannot be brushed away.

Why are nations rejecting the gifts of progress? Why are they not revel-
ing in the openness of cosmopolitanism? Why do they come increasingly
to fear the messages of global optimism beamed to them from the skies?
Conservative newspaper columnists or liberal politicians wish to know
why individuals and groups want still to maintain their borders. Poststructuralist critics, who routinely praise boundary crossing and mongrel
identities and who systematically denounce Enlightenment universalism,
condemn nationalism and the dogmatism of the *Heim*. The one question
they rarely pose is why individuals should not be happy with their homes
or not keep their traditions. Because they are preoccupied with the present and because they portray nationalism as an irrational force, these
writers cannot understand why people should still hold on to seemingly
senseless values. Nationalism is really an affront to their cosmopolitan
sensibilities.

Yet nationalism has reproduced itself around the world as have few
ideologies. John H. Ehrenreich has rightly concluded that in much of this
century and much of the world "it has been *nationalism*, not socialism,
that has been the dominant ideology of movements for social change"
(1983: 1). Having adapted itself to local situations, it has given rise to

capitalist, socialist, liberal, fascist, and theocratic nations. In order to understand its appeal, it is necessary to go beyond the cautionary tales that seek to distinguish falsely between a tolerant transnationalism and a doctrinal nationalism.

First, what is nationalism? Although patriotism and nationalism are often used interchangeably, particularly in the media, they are different. Patriotism refers to the feelings of affection and attachment of a people toward the nation. Nationalism, however, is a discourse that tries to foster a collective sense of belonging among a population with the aim of declaring and maintaining political sovereignty.[1] Although I often portray nationalism metaphorically as a movement or a force, I mean by it a set of statements, documents, opinions about the nation, national identity, autonomy, cultural survival. A group adopts a nationalist program when it seeks to establish an independent nation-state on a particular territory and endow it with the attributes associated with statehood: government, bureaucracy, army, education system, flag, anthem, and so on. Nationalism, as Anthony Smith has shown, contends that the world is divided into nations, each with its own character, that the nation is the sole source of political power, that everyone must belong to a nation, and that nations must be free and secure (1994: 379).

THE UNION OF NATION AND STATE

What is unique about nationalism is not that, as Benedict Anderson has claimed, it fosters an ideological (i.e., imaginative) connection among a large-scale population, for world religions have to some extent promoted such relationships in the past. The singularity of nationalism rests in its tenet that a marriage must take place between culture and politics and that this union must be sanctified on a native land. This proposition is both radical and exceptional in human history. At no other time had it ever been proposed that the identity of the governed must somehow coincide with the institutions of government. That the hoped for homogeneity is largely an ideological construct and that few enterprises have attained an overlap between nation and state have not robbed nationalism of its power. The attraction of nationalism lies in its promise of self-rule to the oppressed. But this promise, based on the unity between identity and political authority, has come at a great cost.

---

[1] The word *nationalisme*, G. de Berteir de Sauvigny writes, was first used in 1798 by Augustin Barruel, an exiled French priest, in his *Mémoires pour servir à l'histoire de Jaconinisme* who defined it as "l'amour national [qui] prit la place de l'amour général" (1970: 155).

If national self-determination means the right of people who regard themselves separate from others to establish their own state, this goal cannot be realized by every group. With very few exceptions, those aspiring to this aim necessarily tread on the rights of others. This indeed has been the experience in Europe where Woodrow Wilson's doctrine of self-determination was first declared.[2] In reality the new states ended up enclosing sizable minority populations within their borders, a situation that created the potential for conflicts in the 1990s.

Wilson in a sense underwrote what nationalism implicitly had established in the previous century—the right to culture. The idea of cultural rights has been forgotten in the discourse of nationalism and has only become apparent in the 1980s with the advent of multiculturalism in North America. But the significance of nationalist thought is that it added the prerogative of collective difference to the already established list of individual franchises: liberty, equality, and security. It tied the happiness of a people to the well-being of its culture. By rendering ethnic distinctiveness into a right, nationalism gave it shape and substance, endowing it with an essence it had not had before. In other words, it rendered these distinctions into a positive entity, national culture.

What do I mean by this shaping of culture? I do not claim that culture had actually become a real thing, a cement house within which one lived and against which one bumped. Rather, ethnic, linguistic, and racial differences, *hitherto politically inconsequential*, acquired an ideological force and institutional weight. In short, nationalism politicized ethnic divisions, making them represent a specific group. Although national culture is usually perceived as embracing a whole people, whereby Albanian or Brazilian culture actually stands for Albania or Brazil respectively, it really represents the perimeter separating one group from another. Rather than being a property of this group or a primordial feature, it signifies, as Arjun Appadurai notes, a set of differences "that has been mobilized to articulate the boundary of difference" (1996: 13). Appadurai rightly argues that groups mobilize these differences in the pursuit of greater political interests. But his reluctance to look at this phenomenon historically leads him to conclude that this is a peculiarity of today's ethnic movements —the Tamils, Serbs, Sikhs, and Malaysians—rather than a feature of nationalism (139, 146–47). For how are the Bosnian Serbs of the 1990s different from those Serbs who fought against Ottoman authority in the

[2] Because Wilson's principle has been enshrined in the United Nations, it has been forgotten that Wilson posed it as a way of disbanding the Austro-Hungarian and Ottoman Empires in Europe, never intending it to be applied to Europe's overseas colonies. It was invoked in the peace settlements of 1919 to guarantee the independence of Albania, Austria, Czechoslovakia, Estonia, Finland, Hungary, Latvia, Lithuania, Poland, Romania, and Yugoslavia but not to justify the establishment of non-European states.

nineteenth century to win their own state? The presentism characterizing current research on nationalism frustrates attempts to explain why and how nations emerge. Moreover, it cannot see the rebellions of Greeks, Serbs, and Bulgarians against Ottoman rule as postcolonial, reserving this appellation exclusively for Ireland or Europe's overseas colonies.[3]

The political dimension given to ethnicity is what distinguishes the nation from other forms of political organization. As Walker Connor has observed, the nation is "a self-aware ethnic group" (1978: 388). Although ethnic groups have been "conscious of their distinctiveness centuries before the popular grafting of ethnicity to political legitimacy occurred," only in modern times have these groups been transformed into nations (Connor 1973: 4). This self-awareness becomes a premise for political power. J. S. Mill had made this very point more than a century ago when he wrote that a "portion of mankind may be said to constitute a Nationality if they are united amongst themselves by common sympathies, which do not exist between them and any others—which make them co-operate with each other more willingly than with other people, desire to be under the same government, and desire that it should be government by themselves or a portion of themselves exclusively" (1958: 229). Lord Acton acknowledged the novelty of this phenomenon when he remarked that in the old European system "the rights of nationalities were neither recognized by governments nor asserted by the people" (Dalberg-Acton 1948: 169).

The nation is product of both the social exchange among members within the group and the erection of boundaries between these members and those outside. Research on ethnic identity in the United States has brought attention to this interactional aspect of identity: groups delimit themselves internally on the basis of "inherent" characteristics while also comparing themselves with outsiders.[4] Groups define themselves and are also defined by others. Frederik Barth's work has highlighted the significance of boundaries that clusters of human beings set up to separate themselves from others (1969: 9). Where there are groups, Manning Nash argues, there are boundaries and mechanisms to maintain them—that is, index features of membership visible to insiders and outsiders alike (Nash 1989: 10). The most common form of boundary marker is kinship, a

---

[3] Although it would be historically and epistemologically wrong to lump all struggles against colonial control into one group, the classification of the Balkans as postcolonial—European societies ruled by a Moslem state—would at the very least enrich the concept of the postcolonial itself. See chapter 4.

[4] Herodotus had an insight into this aspect of identity. He saw the relationship between Greeks and foreigners as polarities, regarding the Scythians, for instance, as the opposite of Greeks (Hartog 1988).

presumed biological tie to other members of the group which implies a continuity with the past and a connection to ancestral land.

Physical features, religion, speech, dress, cuisine, accent are highlighted in the interaction among people. Identity is always a hybrid phenomenon despite the claims of nationalists to the contrary. The nation is a modern manifestation of the human propensity to devise shared identities and to divide the outside from the inside. Nationalism itself believes that political fences make good neighbors. It transforms the human urge to make distinctions into a self-conscious project of outlining a national culture.

Although the nation is a recent invention, ethnicity is not. Forms of ethnic identification have been recorded since early antiquity. Ancient Egypt saw itself as "separate, chosen and central, the community of inhabitants of 'the land' " (Anthony Smith 1984: 287; 1994: 383–86).[5] Up to half a million people may have thought of themselves as Sumerians in the third millennium B.C. Not having regarded themselves as a *Volk*, they did have a "weak but nonetheless real sense of collective identity, buttressed by language, foundation myths, and invented genealogies" (Mann 1986: 92). This concept most certainly applies to the Jews of ancient Palestine. Before the capture of Palestine in 63 B.C. by the Romans, "the national symbols of temple, territory, army, and kinship (or rulership) emerge very clearly as political entities, and the literature of the time shows that a new nationalistic phase in Judaism was dawning" (Mendels 1992: 6).[6]

These societies, hierarchical in character, were built on the divisions of people into ranks based on family, education, and caste. They thus never aspired to a congruence between *Volk* and *Reich*. But even if elites of polyethnic empires had ever wanted to create a homogeneous society, they lacked the technical means by which to impose their own "imperial" identities on the vast majority of the population divided into estates, millets, or castes. Moreover, because communication over long distances was difficult, language could not have served as an agent of unity. If anything, culture seemed to make visible and confirm unequal social relationships.

Literacy, a tool in the production of national consciousness and cultural homogeneity in modernity, served the interests of political, pedagogical, and clerical elites in the premodern past. In late antiquity, for instance, classical learning (*paideia*) emphasized social distance. The acquisition of

[5] A word "ethnic" exists in early languages such as Hittite, Veric, Sanskrit, and Mycenaean Greek (Hinsley 1973: 20). John Armstrong's *Nations before Nationalism* (1982) analyzes the long record of ethnicities in Europe and the eastern Mediterranean.

[6] Although Mendels makes a fascinating case for the existence of Jewish nationalism in antiquity, he does not pay enough attention to the crucial differences between modern and ancient manifestations of identity and state formation, often using the word nationalism anachronistically.

its skills, based on rhetoric and classical texts, was time-consuming and difficult and hence became the property of privileged groups who could communicate in Greek and Latin and read the same texts. Thus a new Roman governor would have expected a shared cultural knowledge from the local elites but not from the general population. Genuine diversity at the time was a result of social divisions as well as the physical segregation of groups within cities, two conditions anathema to liberalism. Because culture was not invested with political authority, it was possible to have structural heterogeneity—many ethnic and racial groups in one empire—rather than the symbolic diversity of the multicultural nation.

Social divisions were accepted as natural, with subject peoples assuming their place in the unequal order. In these hierarchical contexts, Fred W. Riggs adds, the word *ethnic* came to be associated with the connotations of "heathen, infidel, goy, barbarian, outcast, outsider, eta, pariah, nigger" (1991: 293).[7] It was applied to outsiders rather than to those who enjoyed power, status, and wealth, very much in the way race still functions today in the United States. Race, as I show in chapter 6, enforces hierarchical divisions, whereas ethnicity does not.

The nation, however, tries to undo these distinctions at least in the realm of ideology. In this imaginary forum everyone is one. The nation promulgates Saint Paul's populist message: "There is neither Jew nor Greek, there is neither bond nor free, there is neither male nor female, for ye are all one in Christ Jesus" (Gallatians 3.28). Able to communicate to the masses as well as intellectuals, women and men, blacks and whites, the rulers and the ruled, nationalism promises people that they participate in a community more appealing than class and more durable than earthly power. This inclusivity in meaning has been borne out, for instance, in France where until the revolution *nation*, as the elite, was contrasted to *peuple*. After the Revolution it began to refer to all citizens of the state (Zernatto 1944: 361; Fischer 1995: 93–93).

But the real difference between ethnic groups and nations is the political interpretation nationalism gives to ethnicity. Nationalism enables a population to transform its perception of difference from other groups into a political project. With some justification John Breuilly writes that the

---

[7] Interestingly the Latin *natio*, from which the word "nation" stems, referred to a group of people bound together by similarity of birth. The Romans, however, never applied it to themselves but to foreigners who lived among them, contrasting these *nationes* to themselves as *populus Romanus* (Zernatto 1944: 352). In ancient Greece the word "ethnos" denoted a population thinly scattered over a territory without urban centers yet politically united (Snodgrass 1980: 212). It thus signified either large kingdoms, such as Macedon or the Persian Empire, or the "backward" regions of Greece like Aitolia (Hansen 1991: 355). "Ethnos" was usually juxtaposed to the polis—a state based on an urban center and the only place where democracy could take place (Ehrenberg 1960: 24; Runciman 1982: 370).

hope expressed in Greek ballads during Ottoman rule (1453–1821) for God to help Greeks retake Constantinople did not constitute a political program (1982: 3). That is to say, the sentiment of ethnic cohesiveness does not by itself make a nation. They must first be incorporated into a political plan.

Positive feelings of ethnic solidarity do not always lead to nationhood, as the examples of Wales and Scotland indicate. Macedonians have seen themselves as a separate group since the latter part of the nineteenth century but their identity has become politicized since the creation of the Macedonian Republic in Yugoslavia and especially since the republic's declaration of independence in 1992. African Americans have had a clearly defined sense of identity but, not concentrated in one particular region, have not made claims to political autonomy.

NATIONS AS SELF-INSTITUTIONS

In most cases, however, nationalism advocates political autonomy, seeking to bind people together on native soil. It combines two separate impulses, the right to a collective difference with the right to self-government. And it is this union that makes the nation modern. The idea of a self-constituting polity is itself another process of social differentiation through which political power is separated from other spheres of human activity such as economy and religion. The state, in the words of Gianfranco Poggi, "unifies and makes distinctive the political aspects of social life, sets them apart from other aspects, and entrusts them to a visible, specialized entity" (1990: 20). The nation-state is a self-positing form of civil association, like the ancient Greek city-states. But unlike them, it rationalizes its existence by recourse to national culture.

The idea of self-institution goes a long way in helping us define the nation, for one of the greatest challenges facing the student of nationalism is how to circumscribe the nation without becoming ensnared in the terms and language of nationalism itself. That is, one can accept the validity of the nation's self-institution without believing its myths about its own natural birth.[8] One can say then a nation is that which regards itself as

---

[8] Most recent studies of nationalism have falsified this claim as even a glance at the etymology of "nation" can show. The Latin word reappeared in the medieval period, referring to university students from similar countries of origin who formed networks of support known as *nati17nes*. Resembling professional organizations rather than ethnic groups, they designated "a community of origin, a union of purpose, and a *community of opinion*" (Zernatto 1944: 354). Similar *natiznes* arose among representatives attending the great ecclesiastical meetings of the period, such as the Council of Lyons (1274) and Council of Constance (1414–18).

such or is so seen by others. Ernest Renan made an early attempt at such a delineation in the nineteenth century. He sidestepped the positivism implied in the question, "What is a nation?" by answering that a nation defines itself: "It presupposes a past; it is summarized, however, in the present by the tangible fact, namely, consent, the clearly expressed desire to continue a common life. A nation's existence is, if you will pardon the metaphor, a daily plebiscite" ([1882] 1990: 19). A nation believes that, because of common features (language, territory, history, myths, blood, institutions), it has the right to govern itself. It is a product of self-invention, made by mortals rather than by gods, a result of earthly struggle rather than divine revelation.

Although this voluntaristic description occludes the historical factors implicated in the building of nations, making it seem that they are simply a product of individual desire, it undermines the essentialist attempt to posit language, blood ties, or territory as the basis of nationhood.[9] Max Weber rightly stressed that it is impossible to define a nation in "terms of empirical qualities common to those who count as members of the nation" (1968: 922). The nation cannot be identified with the state because most states contain more than one nation. Neither is a shared tongue identical with the nation. People in Great Britain, the United States, and India speak English yet belong to autonomous states. Although it does not presume nationhood, language since Herder has been regarded as the heart pumping the blood of the nation. Yet, while his idea may have been applicable to Germany, it proves untenable in Nigeria with over three hundred languages.

Cultural critics often ignore the self-institutional, hence political aspect of the nation, concentrating instead on the way nationalism naturalizes identity, specifically the way culture can slide into biology. They reject the nation as evil because of its claim to common blood ties. That nations can cast themselves as organic entities, born deep in history, goes without saying. Max Weber wrote that the concept of nationality, like the notion of *Volk*, is based on the belief that whatever is held to be distinctively common must derive from common descent (1968: 395). In other words, people suppose that the cultural bonds they share flow from one wellspring: "We shall call 'ethnic groups' those human groups that entertain a subjective belief in their common descent because of similarities of physical type or of customs or both; . . . it does not matter whether or not an

[9] Renan's conception of nation as a "daily plebiscite" had political implications. Like other French citizens of his day, he was incensed at the annexation of Alsace-Lorraine by Germany after the Franco-Prussian War in 1871. Renan was implying here that, because the people of Alsace and Lorraine felt themselves French, the provinces should be repatriated as, indeed, they had been following the Treaty of Versailles of 1919.

objective blood relationship exists" (389). Even though no direct blood connections can actually persist after centuries of interbreeding, nations see their identities as genetic in nature.

Nationalism emphasizes primordial loyalties, what Clifford Geertz has referred to as the givens of social existence: "blood, speech, custom, faith, residence, history, physical appearance" (1993: 58). In the formation of identities these congruities can acquire an ineffable coerciveness of their own. "One is bound to one's kinsman . . . as the result not merely of personal affection, practical necessity, common interest, or incurred obligation, but at least in great part by virtue of some unaccountable absolute import attributed to the very tie itself" (1969: 259). These social ties attain such an "absolute import" because they have been turned into a relationship of common ancestry. Blood relations, David Schneider explains, are conceived as permanent, objective facts of nature. "A blood relationship is a relationship of identity. People who are blood relatives share a common identity, they believe. This is expressed as 'being of the same flesh and blood' " (1980: 25).[10]

But nationalism does not always foster the essentialization of identity. Loring Danforth's work (1995) on Australian immigrants from Florina, a prefecture in northern Greece, shows that, depending on their position in the conflict over Macedonian and Greek ethnicity, people resort to biological arguments to bolster their own claims to their own ethnicity while showing the constructed, "artificial" nature of the identity of their opponents. At the same time, however, these very same people could, if they found it rhetorically necessary, argue that identity was also a matter of socialization, the adoption of the customs and life-styles of another society. Even though these immigrants prefer to see their ethnicity as natural, they may regard it as a matter of social construction.

This type of research shows that, at the very least, it is not always possible to differentiate between conventional and natural conceptions of identity. Yet in an influential work Rogers Brubacker bases his whole theory of citizenship on this distinction. Specifically he compares the French and German conception of citizenship as an example of the differences between cultural and political nation building. Because the French perception of nationhood, he argues, is state-centered and assimilationist,

---

[10] In a later study Schneider looks at Judaism and Christianity from this perspective. In the Jewish tradition state and kinship group are identical, the relationship of kinship to nationality being a clear one. "To be a Jew one's mother must be Jewish even if one's father is not." While there is a code of conduct attached to the act of birth, the latter takes precedence as the defining feature. With Christianity the basis for membership changes from "birth to volition," shifting away from a "particularistic, bio-genetic criterion of substance as the defining feature" to a code of conduct. One is or becomes a Christian through baptism or an act of faith (1969: 122).

France defines citizenry expansively as a territorial community. The German understanding of nationhood, on the other hand, is ethnocultural; hence, Germany regards citizenship restrictively as a community of descent (1992: x). Brubacker states that German citizenship is restrictive to non-Germans but expansive to ethnocultural Germans (114). Surely the latter applies to Germans in the former Eastern bloc. The ancestors of Germans in Manitoba or Minnesota are not entitled to automatic German citizenship. The categories are more blurred than he allows. Canada, for instance, like the United States, ascribes citizenship to all those born in Canada. But children born to Canadians abroad are entitled to Canadian citizenship, a necessary and humane policy for obvious reasons but one that recognizes relationships of blood.

Be that as it may, the real issue here is the often simplistic association of nationalism and identity in general with xenophobia or racism. Nationalism to many writers reveals the dark side of the human soul, its proclivity to worship ethnic and racial purity. For Étienne Balibar racism is a supplement of nationalism. "Racism sees itself as an 'integral' nationalism, which only has meaning (and chances of success) if it is based on the integrity of the nation, integrity both towards the outside and on the inside" (Balibar and Wallerstein 1991: 54, 59). Even if not bent on seeking domination over others, the nation is regularly represented as a totalization. Although Homi Bhabha acknowledges the symbolic ambivalence of the nation, he associates "the deep nation" with other "justifications of modernity," such as progress, homogeneity, and cultural organicism, "that rationalize the authoritarian, 'normalizing' tendencies within cultures in the name of the national interest or the ethnic prerogative" (1990a: 4).

Because cultural and literary critics regard the nation as an ideological totalization, they recognize the urgency of deconstructing its narratives, of seeking the nation's "transgressive boundaries" and "interruptive interiority" so that, in the words of Bhabha, an "anti-nationalist, ambivalent nation-space" can become the "crossroads to a new transnational culture" (4). Having characterized the nation as a matter of narrative, they seek to uncover the "counter-narratives of the nation that continually evoke and erase its totalizing boundaries . . . and disturb those ideological maneuvers through which 'imagined communities' are given essentialist identities" (Bhabha 1990b: 300). It is not surprising that, having located the nationalist devil in the cultural space of identity, they choose to fight him with the weapons of aesthetic modernism.

Indeed, the dominant poststructuralist approach to nationalism can be characterized as literary modernist. Regarding nationalism as a relentlessly mimetic discourse, it hopes to subvert the fullness of the nation with the fragmentariness of modernist techniques. Thus David Lloyd turns to the writings of Beckett, finding in his oeuvre "the most exhaustive dismantling we have of the logic of identity" (1993: 56). He discovers in Beckett, Joyce, as well as the Irish street ballads "processes of hybridization" that deconstruct the "aesthetic politics of nationalism" (114). His modernist approach to nationalism seeks to juxtapose an "anti-identitarian" hybridity to the monologic nation.

Along these principles the nation in Bhabha's work becomes the ultimate realist novel, ruthless in its metonymic logic but carrying in itself the germs of its own metaphoric deconstruction. This modernist approach to nationalism has in the 1990s been established as a critical pedagogy seeking to show the ambivalence of the nation. It is not difficult to translate these ideas into a practice: in *Border Writing: The Multidimensional Text*, Emily D. Hicks focuses on border literature from South America in which the "subject is decentered and the object is not present or immediate but displaced" (1991: xxiv). For Ian Chambers the lyrics of Yousou N'Dour, sung in Wolof (a Senegalese dialect) in Naples, open up "the differentiated territories in which the imaginary is being disseminated" (1994: 15). Frederick Buell discovers in Asian American literature "the development of boundary violation, heterogeneity, hybridity, and border crossing as a means for transformation of ethnic and national identity into globalist America" (1994: 211).

Although such oppositional criticism is laudatory, it stands on a pile of unexamined assumptions. For one thing this approach cannot imagine that its modernist antirepresentational strategies can themselves turn into a totalizing system. We should not forget that the antitraditional rhetoric of modernism did not prevent this literary movement itself from setting up a tradition. Moreover, deconstruction, the antirepresentational discipline par excellence, was effortlessly institutionalized in the North American academy. Derrida's radical ideas of the undecidability of language were transformed into a critical strategy of uncovering undecidable texts. The book was about nothing other than its own inconsistency.

Beyond this, one wonders how oppositional this writing actually is. For in seeking to open up within the nation a space for a "counter–National Symbolic" (Berlant 1991: 34), these writers continue, rather than break, a tradition going back to romanticism that has seen culture as the Other of modernity, a domain of charged negativity. Most cultural criticism, Lawrence Grossberg observes, "focuses on culture's critical relation (negativity) to the dominant positions and ideologies. Politics becomes defined as resistance to or emancipation from an assumed reality; politics is measured by difference. . . . Opposition may be constituted by living, even momentarily, within alternative practices, structures, and spaces, even though they may take no notice of their relationship to existing systems of power" (1988: 170).[11]

But unlike the romantics, who saw in culture a utopian sphere to withdraw from the dry, instrumental, and competitive values of industrial society, today's cultural critics regard it as a means of undermining totalizing structures. Thus, in contrast to Shelley ("Defense of Poetry") or Wordsworth (preface to the "Lyrical Ballads") who regarded culture as an alternative space to capitalism and industrialization, they celebrate culture as a site of opposition. Nearly two centuries after romanticism critics have not been able to look beyond that movement's representation of the aesthetic as the asylum of the counterculture. Although claiming to have deconstructed the aesthetic domain, they continue to use its language, strategies, and concepts.

Their aesthetic predisposition leads them to glorify the hybrid and the cosmopolitan and to devalue the home and nationalism. In so doing, they accept the false assumption that the nation is actually monologic. Although they display the poststructuralist penchant for the metaphoricity of discourse, their approach to nationalism is remarkably literalist, taking this discourse at its word. Just because nationalist thought depicts identity as uniform does not mean it is or has ever been homogeneous. Identity is hybrid at all times, constantly changing due to movement of people, the exchange of ideas and products, and the passing of time. Finally, in representing the nation as an imagined community only, cultural critics continue to see solutions to the excesses of nationalism in terms of cultural resistance. Rarely do they look at political resolutions to social conflict, such as federalism, to complement their important ideological critiques.

EMOTIONAL ATTACHMENTS

The demonization of nationalism makes it almost impossible for cultural critics to understand why people value local identities. To a certain extent their modernist stance to the nation expresses a high-culture distaste for provincial values. For in its most basic form, nationalism has the capacity to make individuals believe that they are related to one another. But it makes them feel connected not only to one another but also to the homeland itself, its history, language, traditions. These attachments constitute what we understand as national identity, which to cosmopolitans seems straitlaced, illiberal, and vulgar.

---

[11] John Fiske writes that the "culture of everyday life is best described through metaphors of struggle or resistance" (1989: 47). Ian Hunter (1996) has shown, however, that the effortless political claims of cultural studies are untenable.

Although this identity cannot alone hold a society together, as has been often assumed, it promotes bonds of affection and loyalty among members. As W. S. Gilbert (1836–1911) wrote in *H.M.S. Pinafore* ([1878] n.d.: 135–37).

> For he might have been a Roosian,
> A French, or Turk, or Proosian,
> Or perhaps Ital-ian!
> But in spite of all temptations
> To belong to other nations
> He remains an Englishman.

In face of inducements to join other nations or even to reject their nationality, people abide with their own nation, even dying for it. It is for reasons of identity that, say, Anglo-Canadians choose to remain within Canada despite the sirens of economic union with the United States. This does not mean that national culture single-handedly keeps Canada sovereign. One has to look to additional factors such as a common market, mass media, state mechanisms, and so on to explain national solidarity. A national culture, however, makes it possible for a vast population to think of itself as a unified body even though most of the people, as Anderson has argued, never meet one another. It fosters this attachment in the absence of clear face-to-face contact or direct kinship ties of smaller social entities (1983).

The only reason Canadians can give to justify an independent Canada is that their country is sufficiently different from the United States that its absorption into the latter would represent a cultural tragedy. What other reason could they provide? They do not argue for autonomy on the basis of class loyalties, political ideology, or the protection of their welfare state.[12] This also applies to Kosovo, Timor, or any other nation in modernity. A particular group may strive for independence because it feels that its way of life and its social and political institutions make it distinct from its neighbors, that it has been oppressed by them, and that this way of life can be best protected within a sovereign state. If this demand clashes, as it often does, with the rights of other groups, the most effective solution for us is not just to criticize nationalism as a totalizing discourse but to

---

[12] The problem for most Anglo-Canadians is that this identity is relatively undefined, especially in contrast to the robust cultures of Quebec and the United States. The nebulousness of this identity can be seen in a list of values, compiled by a federal commission, allegedly held in common by Canadians: a belief in equality and fairness; a belief in consultation and dialogue; the importance of accommodation and tolerance; support for diversity; compassion and generosity; attachment to the natural environment; a commitment to freedom, peace, and nonviolent change (Kymlicka 1995: 187). There is nothing distinctively Canadian about these liberal values, shared, as they are, by a host of different nations.

conceive of political arrangements that can reconcile the right to culture with the realities of demographically heterogeneous territories.

The success of nationalism is that it makes political attachments a personal process. The transfer of a person's loyalties to the nation is an intensely psychological dynamic, which is why we speak of nationality as a form of identity. When an individual says, "I am Eretrian" or "I am American," she is describing something about her person. She points to aspects of her personality. It goes without saying that the phrase "I am American" coexists with numerous others, such as "I am black, gay, a parent, a conservative, a teacher, an ecologist, a soccer player." Nationality, the Russian philosopher Vladimir Solovyof observed at the end of the nineteenth century, "is an inner, inseparable property of the person—is something very dear and close to him. . . . if we love a man we must love his nation which he loves and from which he does not separate himself" ([1897] 1918: 297).

Although hardly a political novel, Edith Wharton's *The Age of Innocence* gives us an insight into the intensely personal aspect of nationality. M. Rivière, the emissary sent by Count Olenski to persuade his estranged wife, Ellen, to return to Europe, refuses to carry out his mission when he discovers that the countess is "American." As he informs Newland Archer, the countess's lover: "if you're an American of *her* kind—of your kind—things that are accepted in certain other societies . . . become unthinkable, simply unthinkable" ([1920] 1966: 218). Being an American, it seems, says something about the person, marking her like an invisible tattoo. A similar link comes out in one of the earliest English novels, Daniel Defoe's *Robinson Crusoe*, published in 1719. Disgusted and horrified by what Crusoe sees as evidence of cannibalism on the island, he concludes that he cannot change such practices because they were "national," the features of certain groups. So he resolves to leave these to the justice of God, "who is the governor of nations, and knows how by national punishments to make just retribution for national offenses" (1982: 179). Although not referring to nation-states at this point, Defoe believes that certain practices are characteristic of national groups.

By sharing objects of sympathy, such as language, tradition, and territory, individuals become somehow linked together, sensing that they belong to a particular nationality. William Bloom interprets national identity as a process by which a people identifies with and internalizes national symbols to such a degree that it acts as one psychological body (1990: 52). This does not mean, as Bloom assumes, that the internalization of social values automatically guarantees social solidarity. Identity by itself cannot account for national unity. Other factors beyond culture—such as the economy, state bureaucracy, schooling—help bring this about. The emotional and psychological aspect of identity is acquired and conditioned in social niches over which people have little control. Specific individuals participate in the operations of unification but do not determine them.

But references to sentiment, attitude, and loyalty underscore the very visceral dimension of identity. Nationalism works through people's hearts, nerves, and gut. It is an expression of culture through the body. This bodily and (seemingly) irrational dimension may explain the hostility to nationalism shared by cosmopolitan writers. But their attempt to deny the insistent corporeality of nationalism reduces it to dreary thoughts. Men and women are willing to sacrifice their lives for their native land as for few ideals. This is nationalism's rebuke to us all.

The singing emotionality of nationalism can be traced back to the German spiritual movement at the end of the seventeenth century known as Pietism. While Pietism promoted personal inwardness, it began to stress the importance of the nation a century later, enjoining people to love the nation with Christian devotion.[13] Its teaching advocated, among other things, egalitarianism and self-respect in the masses, perhaps Pietism's most lasting contribution to nationalist thought. For the idea of self-esteem has become the most potent message of all identity politics, binding the fervent lectures delivered by Fichte to a vanquished Berlin and the fiery speeches of civil rights leaders in the United States in one common exhortation: despite humiliation, discrimination, and anguish a people must find inner strength, stand tall, and be proud. It ties the self-regard of the individual to the majesty of the nation.[14] Few ideologies, outside religion, have perfected this link.

The nation-state is more deeply fastened to the inner life of people than was the multiethnic empire of the past or today's common markets. By associating the nation and the state, nationalism has integrated the emotional life of people with political life. In his monumental—but now largely ignored—*The Nationalization of the Masses* (1975), George L. Mosse explores this psychological function of nationalism. Looking into the political symbolism and mass movements in Germany from the Napoleonic Wars to the Weimar Republic, he investigates festivals, parades, music societies, monuments, and athletics groups, as sites of mass involvement in politics. Mosse thus demonstrates how nationalism has affected the lives of ordinary people involved in ordinary activities: sports, choirs,

---

[13] On Pietism, see Pinson 1934 and Lambropoulos 1993: 49. Weber discusses Pietism in reference to the Protestant ethic (1958: 131).

[14] Pietists stressed intuition, feeling, and spontaneity—later to become essential features of the Sturm und Drang and romanticism—as opposed to reason. The irrationalist, antiphilosophic, and antispeculative ideas of Pietists entered nationalist thought, endowing it with a chthonic, Dionysian potential to whip up the passions of the faithful. In addition to emotionalism, it bequeathed to nationalism the notion of uniqueness.

athletic events, workers' organizations, music. Often Mosse displays organicist assumptions about culture, believing that rites, festivals, myths, and symbols can effortlessly and successfully "draw the people into active participation in the national mystique." He argues, for instance, that "the unity of people was not merely cemented by the idea of common citizenship; rather, a newly awakened national consciousness performed this function" (2). Nationalism alone, as I noted earlier, cannot achieve such mobilization. Despite these assumptions, Mosse is able to demonstrate that participation in nationalist politics actually takes place in distinct nooks and arenas of society, involving the internalization and expression of ethnic values.[15]

His investigations of fascism led Mosse to conclude that nationalism is a "secular religion." In the failure of Christianity to supply a unifying myth, nationalism filled the empty "sacred space" with "parades, marches, gymnastics exercises, and dances, as well as ritual speeches" (1975: 208). This explanation, however, is reductive for two reasons. First, it posits culture as a reactive agent, always responding to changes outside of its realm. Second, it sees culture, in this case nationalism, as the glue of social life. This second position is based on the assumption that societies always require collective ideologies so that when one disappears another takes its place. While it is possible to argue, as I show in chapter 3, that nationalism originally emerged out of the religious civil wars in the seventeenth century, whereby faith began to be identified with a particular territory, it is simplistic to regard nationalism as a unifying myth. Nationalism may be seen as religious only in the extended sense given to this term by Durkheim: "when a conviction of any strength is held by the same community of men, it inevitably takes on a religious character" (1972: 222). The French Revolution "established a whole cycle of holidays" in order to keep itself alive forever in the memory of citizens (Durkheim 1915: 476). These public events and rituals acquire a religious character, a fact that demonstrates Durkheim's belief in the ultimate continuity between the sacred and the profane. This translation of everyday practices and events into the sacred and vice versa itself shows the dialectical relationship between tradition and modernity and the presence of one in the other.

If nationalism promotes an ideological unity within the nation, it accomplishes this not mystically but through actual practices, events, and rituals. For, as Durkheim argued, a religion unites all believers into a "sin-

[15] Fascism pushed nationalist symbols and rituals toward a radical extreme. But contrary to common belief, Mosse notes, the aim of fascism was not to stir the crowd into wild ecstasy but to direct and discipline it, thereby avoiding the "chaos which defeats the creation of a meaningful movement" (1975:16).

gle moral community" through compulsive acts, rules, and regulations (1915: 62). People reaffirm these "common sentiments" through "re-unions, assemblies and meetings" (475). By speaking the same language, living in the same place, sharing an experience of colonization and oppres-sion, or participating in the same political institutions, people feel them-selves to be in some form of union. The effect of national rituals and symbols is to strengthen even further the bonds attaching the individual to the society. The public nature of national culture allows it to demand obligations from its members. Because these compulsions stem from out-side and inside the individual, they have a greater sanction than physical coercion.

To say that nationalism promotes cohesion among members of the na-tion through bonds of debt and association is not the same as saying that it serves as society's adhesive. Montserrat Guibernau, adopting some of Durkheim's conclusions, argues that nationalism has the "capacity to re-strain and instill cohesion within any one community as a means to obtain co-operation and communication" (1996: 28). Guibernau's argument treats nationalism as a grand agent of social determinacy. Yet evidence indicates even Durkheim himself did not believe that shared beliefs and values themselves bring about social integration directly. Nicholas Aber-crombie, Stephen Hill, and Bryan S. Turner contend that Durkheim actu-ally attempted to locate social stability in modern societies at three levels: "a system of economic ties arising out of social differentiation, a network of intermediary occupational associations linking the individual and the state, and an emergent system of moral restraints generated by profes-sional bodies."[16]

Rather than postulating national culture as an overarching system of norms and sentiments bringing about social regulation, it is more accurate to see this regulation a result of moral restraint, social coercion, economic practices, professional associations, class loyalties, and state policies. Shared rituals can create bonds of solidarity among members of the na-tions because they emphasize similarities among them and differences from those outside the nation. Collective experiences, rituals, and sym-bols promote feelings of fellowship, distinguishing in this way those peo-ple who belong from those who do not.

Although at the practical level nationalism promotes social solidarity by differentiating the self from the other, its overall force and appeal stem from its metaphysics—the assurance of salvation. The symbolism of a particular nation can enable individuals to experience an emotional com-

[16] In *Professional Ethics and Civic Morals*, for instance, Durkheim does indeed claim that the division of labor produced occupational groups and professional organizations that prevent the state from tyrannizing over individuals (1957: 63, 103, 206).

munion with others and to imagine a victory over their own mortality. Linked to one another they become part of an entity greater than themselves. To the insistent question, "Who are we?" nationalism answers, "You are a people fighting to be free, to be happy, to be great." It ties the individual who asks, "Who am I?" to the fate of a national body, which transcends contingency, humiliation, and death. Ultimately, nationalism is a form of self-worship, the adoration by the nation of its own uniqueness. For nations are very much like people. National pride is insulted when a nation is told that it lacks originality, that it has a weak character, that it is mediocre. No one can love a nation without qualities.

The idea of uniqueness is at the heart of the national project. Nations come into being and continue to exist because they are believed to be immaculately conceived. The call to nationalize ethnicity is based on this presumption of ethnic distinction. Indeed, nationalism posits the universal value of culture by validating the existence of the nation in the name of its uniqueness, which is itself a product of culture. Max Weber understood this self-referential nature of nationalist thought when he remarked that the mission of nationalists is to cultivate the singularity of the group aspiring to become a nation. He rightly referred to their goal as a "culture" mission insofar as it justifies nation building by positing the "contents" of the nation as an absolute value. The reasons for creating a nation lie within the nation itself: "The significance of the 'nation' is usually anchored in the superiority, or at least the irreplaceability of the culture values that are to be preserved and developed only through the cultivation of the peculiarity of the group" (Weber 1968: 925). In other words, national culture is revered as a holy relic because it contains the indivisible distinctiveness of a people—itself the keeper and expression of this distinctiveness—whose loyalty to the nation-state is cultivated in the name of its originality. The group must survive to preserve culture, which in turn must preserve the identity of the group in order to survive. The message of nationalism is succinct: because the nation is exemplary, the state and its subjects must preserve its exemplariness.

The idea that the identity of each people is both original and special explains why nationalism began its odyssey two centuries ago. Ethnic groups declare their sovereignty by recourse to the globally accepted values of nationalism, which portray the nation as archetypal and political independence as self-evident. Each nascent nationalism is idealistic, justifying itself before the tribunal of world sympathy with the argument that political autonomy represents the fulfillment of its destiny. It claims that it is entitled to statehood, because it is uncommon, and that its very survival is dependent upon its attaining statehood.

Nationalism is a metaphysical discourse less because it traces the origin of groups in nature than because it is a self-justifying discourse. Having elevated the nation as an absolute good, nationalism defends the necessity of a state on the grounds that it safeguards the nation. In other words, nationalism proclaims the self-sufficiency of culture through self-grounding sophistry. Insofar as it demonstrates the distinctiveness of the nation through culture, nationalism renders culture as its goal (i.e., national identity) as well as the means of attaining that goal (i.e., narrative, interpretation, metaphor). In affirming the uniqueness of the group, nationalism shows that it is ultimately the product of and contributes to a historicist understanding of the world. On the one hand, nationalism strives to escape contingency by resorting to the self-justifying arguments but, on the other, it affirms the nation's specificity. In responding to universalist discourses and colonial regimes, nationalism promotes the Herderian idea of the equal validity of incommensurable cultures. Rather than judging individual nations according to the measuring stick of one ecumenical and often imperialist ideology, it looks into each nation for the measure of its own ideal.

We are all products, Johann Gottfried von Herder (1744–1803) argued, of a particular time, place, and culture (1877–99: 2:275). Human perfection is determined by social, cultural, and physical environments. "We develop only that which is occasioned by time, climate, necessity, world, or accidents of fate" (1989: 41). Mining this insight from Johann Joachim Winckelmann's (1717–68) magisterial *Geschichte der Kunst des Altertums* (1764)—which saw Greek art as a product of environment, people, and nationality—Herder applied it to all societies in general (Ergang 1966: 251).[17] Thus, in an influential essay on Shakespeare, he noted that Greek drama "emerged in Greece in a way it could not have in the North" (Herder 1877–99: 2:209–10).[18] Because Greek drama could only have arisen in Athens, it was pointless to look for it elsewhere. Because a nation could make drama solely out of its own history, the cultural products of Elizabethan England are bound to be different from those of fifth-century Athens (5:217). The effect of Herder's insight was revolutionary for it allowed him to propose the incommensurable, unique, and authentic nature of nations. We are all still living in the shadow of this interpretation of nationhood.

[17] Unlike the Moderns, however, who rejected the worth of antiquity, Herder recognized the usefulness of previous ages: "The Egyptian could not have existed without the Hebrew; the Greek built on the work of the Egyptian; the Romans lifted themselves on the shoulders of the whole world" (Herder 1989a: 45). From his point of view, the Moderns seem rather chronocentric. The multicultural denunciation of Greek antiquity evinces an equally blind chronocentrism. See my discussion in the following chapter on the struggle between Ancients and Moderns in seventeenth-century France.

[18] All translations, unless otherwise identified, are my own.

ANCIENT ROOTS

Although nationalism is a product of this historicist tradition, nationalists often forget that nations are born out of specific conditions. Quite often even students of nationalism seem to overlook the nation's history. In order to undermine the nation's claims to natural status, for instance, recent studies have emphasized their manufactured nature. Critics argue that nations are not old but modern fabrications; the words "invented" and "imagined" recur repeatedly in current work. Insofar as he regards nations as imagined, Benedict Anderson sees them as primarily conceptual entities. His entire theory of nationalism "is based on the premise that the power holding individuals in the embrace of the community of the nation is at bottom narrative" (Holquist 1996: 111). The prominence given to narrative is not surprising in light of the conspicuous position that two literary theorists, Erich Auerbach and Walter Benjamin, occupy in Anderson's book.[19] Anderson, however, does not explain how other identities, such as those bestowed by universal religions, which united populations spread over continents, were not imagined. And were the mythical origins of ancient societies not invented?

Furthermore, the current emphasis on design and innovation presumes that nations are novel entities. A case in point is the interpretation given to Scottish Highland tradition. Although it seems distinctly Scottish today, Trevor-Roper shows it was of minor significance before the seventeenth century. Having largely been created in the late eighteenth and early nineteenth centuries, the Highland tradition was later accepted by Lowland (Eastern) Scotland (Hobsbawm and Ranger 1983: 16).[20] In accentuating the constructedness of these symbols and myths, Trevor-Roper gives the impression that they are entirely new, artificial, fashioned by the intelligentsia and foisted upon an unsuspecting public. Evidence indicates, however, that Scottish identity emerged in the Middle Ages, having been fashioned out of several ethnic groupings (Foster 1989: 37, 44).

Nations are indeed modern and manufactured but they have been built on an old, often centuries-old, foundation.[21] The history of nation build-

---

[19] Nicholas Howe (1977) discusses Anderson's debt to Auerbach.

[20] His essay is found in *The Invention of Tradition* (1983) edited by Eric Hobsbawm and Terence Ranger. In the same volume David Cannadine explains that the pageantry associated today with the royal events in Britain goes back to the period between the 1870s and 1914. Before that time royal marriages and coronations—made for the era of mass communication—were of limited appeal. They became splendid spectacles when the monarch became a largely symbolic figure (1983: 120).

[21] Nationalists themselves portray this act of fabrication as novel. Note a confidential memorandum written in 1933 by King Faisal I (1921–33) concerning the need to cultivate among Iraq's diverse groups a feeling of unity: "In Iraq there is still . . . no Iraqi people but

ing shows that there are as many staircases as floors between prenational and national identities. The separation of modernity and tradition implied in the idea of invention does not stand up to scrutiny, as Lloyd Rudolph and Suzanne Rudolph's work in India demonstrated three decades ago (1967: 10). It was the unilinear view of time and progress, proposed by the Enlightenment, that made tradition and modernity such polar opposites and saw religion as an obstacle to change. But tradition can be modernized and an invention can become a tradition, as the case of literary modernism shows. The use of inherited symbols can promote innovation by ensuring a sense of continuity and providing a legitimating authority (Werblowsky 1976: 103). Religion can act as a catalyst to reform. One need only point to the instrumental role played by the church in bringing about political reform in Poland, South America, and South Africa. Tradition can thus serve as a modality of innovation. Marilyn Waldman argues that some "of the world's greatest movements of change—often reform—were associated with the founding of major world religions or their offshoots" (1991–92: 89).

Nationalism has itself introduced such transformation. But it has done so by using already available raw materials. When the nation proclaims itself as new, it does not really spring ex nihilo, like Athena from the head of Zeus. Anthony Smith has rightly argued that nationalism as both "ideology and a structure of specific identities would be inconceivable and unintelligible" without the antecedents of premodern identities (1984: 284). This stuff of nationalism is the collective name, language, religion, association to a territory, memories of former statehood, shared texts, sentiments, symbols, and myths. The formation of nations incorporates common stories and symbols despite the fact that the idea of shared biological ancestry is imaginary. It is not surprising, Seamus Dean argues, that a modernizing program in Ireland was accompanied by a "cultural annexation of the distant past." This return to the past, he explains, makes sense if we understand modernity as a sequence depending on a "paradigm of rebirth, renaissance, recovery of which the modern becomes both the beneficiary and the culmination" (1997: 51).

Like all historical work, the creation of a national tradition necessitates the recovery of the past, the removal of shameful or distressing incidents, and the glorification of illustrious individuals or events. This reworking of tradition allows the nascent nation to appear old and legitimate, to deny the fortuity of its own fabrication while at the same time pointing

---

unimaginable masses of human beings, devoid of any patriotic idea. . . . Out of these masses we want to fashion a people which we would train, educate, and refine" (Batatu: 1978). The king's wish echoes Massimo d'Azeglio's celebrated pronouncement at the first meeting of the Italian Parliament in Turin in 1860: "Italy is made, but who will now make the Italians?" (Latham 1970: 234).

to the conventionality of subgroups desiring the same autonomy. Recent history offers many examples of creative appropriations of historical events. Two cases in point are the commemoration in modern Israel of the Battle of Masada fought against the Romans in A.D. 66 and the celebration in Iran of the founding of the Persian Empire some 2,500 years ago. Having been largely forgotten, both events were introduced into the public consciousness initially through the efforts of scholarship, particularly archaeology.[22] The celebration of Cyrus's anniversary in Persepolis by the Shah of Iran in 1971 was meant to represent the transformation of the Persians from a religious community to a secular nation, with the core of the identity no longer referring to Islam but to Iran (Lewis 1975: 101). It goes without saying that, from the perspective of the Islamic Revolution of 1978, the Shah's project to unearth pre-Islamic glories seems to have persuaded a small section of the population only.[23]

Yet the Shah's failure should not be generalized to include all similar enterprises, as the dramatic resurrection of Hebrew in Israel demonstrates. One of the most noteworthy examples is, of course, the resuscitation of ancient Hellas in modern Greece. The construction of Greece upon the ruins of a classical civilization shows how successful such efforts can be. The endeavor worked, however, not because it was the fanciful creation of scholars and artists but because it incorporated memories, stories, and ideas already in circulation.[24]

The practices of cultural remembering, reconstruction, and fabrication are not new. Many regimes have challenged the representation of the past or associated themselves with illustrious mythological or historical figures and states.[25] But the process of invention has been augmented in the age

---

[22] Neil Asher Silberman (1989) explores the relationship between archaeology and the building of nations in Israel, Egypt, Cyprus, Turkey, Yemen, the former Yugoslavia, and Greece.

[23] There is a twist to this story, however. In April 1992 President Hashemi Rafsanjani made a public visit to Persepolis, the first by an Islamic revolutionary leader, where he announced: "Standing in the middle of these centuries-old ruins, I felt the nation's dignity was all-important and must be strengthened. Our people must know that they are not without a history" (New York Times, May 8, 1992). A. A. Duri (1987) has shown that the pre-Islamic patrimony, rather than disappearing, actually contributed to the creation of the new cultures.

[24] Popular memory preserved many traditions, the most notable being the ritual lament, which, according to Margaret Alexiou, has persisted from Homer to the present (1974). See the discussion in chapter 4.

[25] As countries try to reconceive themselves, they find that many of the artistic treasures are in the museums of Europe and North America. The most notorious such case is that of the Parthenon Marbles, removed from the Acropolis by Lord Elgin in 1806 and now housed in the British Museum. Melina Mercuri relentlessly lobbied for their repatriation, arguing that the marbles represent "a part of the deepest consciousness of the Greek people." Nigeria seeks restitution of the Benin treasures, most of which are found outside the country.

of nationalism because the nation-state as a new form of polity is more fully defined as a cultural entity than its predecessors. Cultural values and practices are overwhelmingly deployed in the creation and maintenance of a nation-state to justify its existence and guarantee its rightful place in the transnational order.

This fact is often ignored by social scientists who see nationalism purely as a program for the acquisition of power and as an extension of the state's development.[26] While nationalism does seek political autonomy and the creation of a republic, it simultaneously attempts to give a cultural interpretation to this mission. We see this, for instance, in the attachment it seeks to foster among people for their territory. Of course, groups, like the Jews, have always had a mystical connection to their land. But nationalism appropriates these feelings for native soil into a cultural and political project.[27] What differentiates the nation-state from other forms of social organization such as multinational corporations, labor unions, and volunteer associations is the belief that it must occupy its own piece of land without overlapping jurisdictions. Nationalism, Artemis Leontis has shown, is in a way a project of "mapping a homeland." It is a topographical undertaking of outlining boundaries, assigning names to places, endowing them with meaning. "In this sense, a homeland emerges not when it has been inhabited but when it has been mapped" (1995: 3).

NATIONAL INTEGRATION

But let me repeat the emphasis nationalism gives to culture does not make nation building solely an act of conceptual fabrication. The enterprise of invention is accompanied by practical, mechanical, down-to-earth practices that help bring about national integration. All the cultural fabrication imaginable would be useless without the school, the army, the train, the newspaper, the market, the bureaucracy to put it into practice. France illustrates this very well for it emerged as a political unit while expanding into and incorporating adjacent territories. Having achieved unification

---

Upon its independence in 1945 from Denmark, Iceland requested the return of manuscripts of medieval sagas taken to Denmark in the seventeenth century; they were returned in 1971. Even the two-million-year-old fossil remains of "Proconsul Africanus," removed by Mary Leakey, were restored to Kenya in 1982, as a national treasure. These examples are discussed in Greenfield 1989.

[26] See, for instance, Breuilly 1982: 19.

[27] A case resembling the Jews is that of the Gujaratis, originally from India, who settled in large numbers in East Africa. Expelled from Uganda in 1972, the majority has settled in Britain. Yet they still "express attachment to India, and explain that this is the place most strongly associated with their religious and cultural roots" (Kalka 1990: 258).

from the core out, it was established by 1488 as one of the earliest states in Europe.[28] Although this centralization was an exercise in absolutism rather than nationalism—it strengthened the power of the king as opposed to the people—it achieved its results, making France in the eyes of Europeans a model of political consolidation. Indeed its neighbors, particularly the Germans, suffered in the subsequent comparisons they were to make between themselves and the French. Yet this unification, as Eugen Weber has demonstrated in *Peasants into Frenchmen* (1976), left the majority of the rural population largely untouched until the last quarter of the nineteenth century. In fact, the whole infrastructure enabling national solidarity was lacking until the nineteenth century.

Weber narrates an astonishing story about rural France that seems out of sync with the image that contemporaries had of that country. In the 1870s France was "neither morally nor materially integrated; what unity it had was less cultural than administrative. Many of its inhabitants, moreover, were indifferent to the state and its laws, and many others rejected them altogether" (1976: 484). The distance between peasants and the state is best expressed by the attitude prevalent in the provinces that to be French meant to be ruled by French officials (486). Statistics show that even as late as 1863 8,381 of France's 37,510 communes, representing about half of the population, used dialects rather than standard French as the main medium of communication (67). Linguistic diversity was so pronounced by the end of the eighteenth century that it was taken by political elites as a threat to the solidarity of the state.

The program of national integration emerged in response to this social fragmentariness and the state attempted to bring the peasants in the "national society, economy, and culture" (5). A new nationalist ideology had come into being that "embraced unity as a positive good and recognized language as a significant factor in achieving it" (72). At first the elites of large towns (burghers, clerics, and lawyers) became bilingual, a skill subsequently copied by others. Education was an essential means in the dissemination of French and its subsequent elevation into the national tongue. In schools children learned this language as well as French history, geography, and hygiene. The fact that French was the language of the school (as well as of the administration, economy, and high culture) made the patois useless beyond the local region. Improvement of the transportation system and postal systems by the 1880s facilitated the circulation of people, goods, and ideas throughout the national realm and enabled

---

[28] Noteworthy were the policies of Francis I (1515–47), who initiated a campaign of centralization. He assembled in his court writers and artists and supported the French language. Moreover, by ordering that all laws be written in French, he established the idea that unity of law be based on unity of language (Kohn 1956: 129–30).

representatives of the state to reach the regions in a way not possible before. World War I, with its mass conscription and the large number of refugees, brought large numbers of people together from different areas of France whose only common bond was their sense of Frenchness.

The case of France shows that, rather than being an ideological operation alone, unification involves the incorporation of people into a national economy, administrative system, and political framework. Individuals attach their loyalties to the nation-state but they also become connected to it and to one another through education, taxation, the army, the welfare system, labor unions, the professions, and so on. The relationship citizens have to their country and to each other is therefore both ideological and institutional.

The state itself attempts to even out local conditions for all its subjects in two ways: by enforcing a conformity in economic and social environments and by enacting citizenship with an attendant set of rights valid for all (Watkins 1991: 171, 176). One cannot, however, underestimate the power of a common language for the diffusion of state ideologies.[29] This type of cultural and institutional integration, which began to take shape in Europe in the latter part of the eighteenth century, differentiates the nation-state from previous polities in the history of humanity. The division of the world into recognizable plots of land, represented on the map by different colors, may seem so natural that it is hard for us to believe it to be only a few centuries old.

It is the result of the modern tenet that politics and culture must overlap. It is also an unworkable ideal. For a true nation-state, one in which the extensions of the nation match perfectly with the borders of the state, is rare indeed. Ironically many countries have the ethnic, racial, and religious heterogeneity of an empire while claiming the homogeneity of a village. The exclusiveness of territorial possession—that it cannot be occupied by another nation—as well as the link between culture and land has led to the seemingly endless eruption of nationalist struggles.

In light of this experience the understandable impulse has been to reject the nation and nationalism. I believe this is shortsighted. For, as I demonstrate in the following chapters, the nation emerged in modernity under specific conditions that obtain today: an intrusive and unitary state that unceasingly claims the private (i.e., cultural) dimension of individuals under its purview; the possibility of an invading army to threaten the public identities of a captured people; the even greater menace stemming

---

[29] Watkins points to the correspondence between language and demographic behavior. Once new information or new attitudes about fertility control within marriage entered a particular community, its adoption was likely to proceed from the innovators to those closest to them in geographical and social space (1991:176).

from the implacable forces of globalization. Nationalism emerged in part because the armies of a Napoleon and the machineries of the state could endanger the very existence of a nation in a way that Alexander's pha-lanxes could never have. In fact, the issue of cultural survival has become all the more critical today because the great peril stems from invisible chariots in the skies: the satellite, e-mail, and the World Wide Web.

The nation is necessary to counteract these forms of universalism and imperialism. Despite the sirens of cosmopolitanism and global capitalism, we should keep in mind that the peace and prosperity that these ideologies promise come at the expense of small societies. This was understood by Origen (A.D. 185–255), an early Christian author and defender of Roman imperium. In his rebuttal to the attack on Christianity by the pagan Cel-sus, he justified the unification of the Roman Empire this way:

> It is quite clear that Jesus was born during the reign of Augustus, the one who reduced to uniformity, so to speak, the many kingdoms on earth so that he had a single empire. It would have hindered Jesus' teaching from being spread through the whole world if there had been many kingdoms . . . because men everywhere would have been compelled to do military service and to fight in defense of their own land. This used to happen before the times of Augustus and even earlier still when a war was necessary, such as that between the Pelo-ponnesians and the Athenians. . . . Accordingly, how could this teaching, which preaches peace and does not even allow men to take vengeance on their enemies, have had any success unless the international situation had everywhere been changed and a milder spirit prevailed at the advent of Jesus. (*Contra Celsum* 2.30)

Origen knew that the propagation of Christianity and defeat of paganism required the political stability enforced by the empire. Moreover, Jesus' exhortation to his disciples to "make disciples of all nations; baptize them in the name of the Father and of the son and of the Holy Spirit, and teach them to observe all the commands I gave you" (Math. 28.19–20; Mark 16.15; Luke 47; Acts 1.8) had been made possible by the transportation system and the urban centers of Rome. The emperor Constantine enabled the realization of Jesus' mission when in A.D. 310 he issued the Edict of Milan, proclaiming Christianity a lawful faith. From then on there would be one God, one empire, one emperor.

Origen, Garth Fowden observes, speaks for all apologists of imperial systems in history as he applauds the peace their victory has brought to the world and "the limitless prospects for propagating their particular ideologies" (1993: 172).[30] The praises of ecumenicity have been always

[30] Fowden shows that the relationship between universalism and particularism, so crucial to the rise of nationalism, was an important philosophical opposition even in antiquity.

sung by these winners, be they Alexander, Augustus, Constantine, Sultan Mehmet the Conqueror, Napoleon, Coca-Cola, or NATO. They always seek to affirm the global validity of their own values and institutions. This is most certainly true today with the spread of global capitalism and Euro-American global culture.

The nation continues to serve as one of the places of resistance to these universal systems. Rather than destroying it, the challenge before us today is to question the unity forged two centuries ago between culture and politics and between culture and territory. We should devise alternate modes of political organization that claim jurisdiction over nations and not land and which thus allow people, who share the same territory but not the same nation, to coexist. It is within these federal structures that it would be possible to have a workable reconciliation of strong local identities with cosmopolitan ideologies and practices.

Chapter Two

THE AUTONOMY OF CULTURE?

BY MAKING ethnicity the raison d'être of the state, modernity has given cultural identities a prominence they could not have had in earlier periods. Because it has accentuated the significance of ethnic identity, it steadily creates more ethnicity. By this I do not mean that modernity fashions ethnic groups, but that it promotes the conditions in which they become self-conscious entities—nations. National culture is, as I noted earlier, an ethnicity that has been politicized, given an essence, and made to justify the existence of the state. The emergence of national culture exemplifies the emphasis put in modernity on autonomy and self-awareness of people and institutions.

One of the most pressing issues in a study of nation building is how to theorize about national culture. Does it serve as an autonomous force in its own right? Can it hold a society together? Does it react to social transformations, or is it itself implicated in these transformations? Is national culture a product of disaffected groups, the sour grapes of modernity's losers, or is it a means these groups use both to understand their situation in the globe and promote modernization?

Our own thinking about national culture comes at the end of more than two centuries of philosophical reflection on this concept. This reflection in itself is part of a longer tradition that goes back to the Renaissance, when scholars began to look at connections among the various arts and disciplines.[1] It can also be traced to the Battle of the Books in the seventeenth century in France. In this conflict there seem to have been two interconnecting discourses, Joan DeJean has argued, one seeing society as an interrelation of activities and thought and the other as a culmination away from a state of barbarism (1997: 130). The words normally used to refer to these two conceptions were "culture," stemming from the Latin *cultura* (cultivated land), and "civilization," deriving from the Latin *civilis* (of the citizens). Although there was much overlap between the two terms, it is clear that in the eighteenth century both were linked to the discourse on manners, civility and taste. For Enlightenment thinkers the concept civilization was universalist in scope. Although they claimed to integrate all peoples into civilization, they discriminated between the civilized and the savage, and they, of course, celebrated France as the epitome of

---

[1] The literature on the subject is vast. See, for instance, Burke 1991.

civilization. Even for German writers such as Kant, Schiller, and Goethe—who preferred the word *Kultur*—this idea indicated the perfection of society and implied a climb from barbarism toward refinement (Bénéton 1975: 37).[2]

Both terms—civilization and *Kultur*—signaled the material and technical progress of humanity, which was seen as evolving from primitivism to modernity, and reflected the hopefulness and universalism of the Enlightenment. In other words, they were simultaneously optimistic and imperialistic—ideals to be spread and imposed all over the world. Inevitably, they invited their own counterresponse. The cosmopolitanism of "civilization" was rebutted philosophically and militarily. The Herderian conception of culture as a particular society, for instance, emerged as a rebuke to the argument that humanity constituted one ecumenical society. Indeed, culture for Herder embodied and expressed human difference (1989b: 6:160). Nature, he noted, placed in our hearts the disposition towards diversity (*Mannichfaltigkeit*) (1877–99: 6:509). His notion of equally valid but incommensurable societies was meant as a corrective to the ethnocentric philosophy equating Western culture with enlightenment. He argued, for example, that even the indigenous inhabitants of California or Tierra Del Fuego had acquired the ability to think, speak, and hunt. They were therefore "cultured" and "enlightened," though not to the same extent as Europeans (1887–99: 13:348).[3] For Herder a "chain" of culture (*Kultur*) and enlightenment (*Aufklärung*) extended to the ends of the earth.

French universalism was refuted also on the battlefields by the wars that broke out between 1803 and 1815 against Napoleon. Although many Europeans had originally welcomed the French Revolution, they came increasingly to see the imposition of its political values by Napoleon's troops as threats to their own societies. These battles themselves gave practical proof that the world, far from constituting one catholic civilization, was made up of separate communities, each valid unto itself, and each striving to preserve its own uniqueness.

---

[2] Beneton provides a useful discussion of the appearance of "civilization" and "culture" in Europe, particularly in France. Raymond Williams's *Culture and Society* (1958) illuminates the origins and subsequent permutations of the idea of culture in British thought. J. S. Mill had acknowledged early in the nineteenth century the significant philosophy of society and human culture produced by "the Germano-Coleridgean school" ([1838] 1980: 129–30).

[3] We see the presence of this philosophy in a passage from Madame de Staël's *De l'Allemagne* (1813): "The Italians, the French, and the Spaniards, received their civilization and language from the Romans; the Swiss, the English, the Swedes, the Danes, and the Dutch are Germanic peoples. . . . The nations whose intellectual culture is of Latin derivation became civilized earlier than the other nations" (1956: 39). Civilization here signifies a particular society.

The response of Europeans to Napoleon's mission has much relevance to the debates on nationalism today. New universalisms are struggling for authority in the world be they in the form of liberal cosmopolitans, NATO peace-keepers, or the bankers of the International Monetary Fund. Nations today, much like the Russians resisting Napoleon's forces, perceive the new ecumenical doctrines as representing the ways of life of particular societies. The basic mode of resistance to cosmopolitanism, whether that of the Enlightenment or global capitalism, still remains the revolutionary idea that the world contains independent societies each sharing its own characteristics. People justify opposition to imperialism in the name of a nation that is culturally, politically, religiously, or economically extraordinary.

CULTURE AS A TOTALITY

Implied in the conception of national culture is the proposition that the various components of society somehow cohere and are represented in its culture. The historical development of this belief has been amply studied;[4] my purpose here is to consider how the idea of society's coherence became connected with the idea of national culture. For the roots of this connection we have to go back to the writings of the earl of Shaftsbury (1671–1713), David Hume (1711–76), and Adam Smith (1723–90), who formulated a theory of ethical conduct. Unlike the philosophers of the baroque era with their emphasis on ritual, privilege, and honor, these thinkers stressed gentility, moderation, tolerance, and, of course, civility.[5]

Adam Smith devoted *The Theory of Moral Sentiments* to investigating society as a product of shared sentiments, which served as points of linkage in the social system. To the question, "What makes human societies cohere?" Smith answered, "custom." Specifically Smith regarded feelings and sentiments as the conjoining ties in society, binding people together and enabling their existence as social beings. Human society, wrote Smith, appears like a "great, immense machine, whose regular and harmonious movements produce a thousand agreeable effects. As in any other beautiful and noble machine that was the production of human art, whatever tended to render its movements more smooth and easy, would derive a

---

[4] See Herbert 1991.

[5] Jane Austen (1775–1813) herself explored these social virtues in her novels. In *Pride and Prejudice* (1813), for instance, Elizabeth Bennet discovers her own prejudiced nature from her conflicts with Charlotte Lucas and learns the benefits of good behavior: "The recollection . . . of my conduct, my manners, my expressions . . . has been many months inexpressibly painful to me." When she finally accepts Mr. Darcy's renewed proposal, she says: "We have both, I hope, improved in civility" (1966: 253).

beauty from its effects, and, on the contrary, whatever tended to obstruct them would displease upon that account." Smith, for instance, traced the origins of our sense of approbation and disapprobation in this "immense machine," ultimately deriving from our regard "to the order of society" ([1759] 1982: 316).

What had emerged by this time was a philosophy of moral conduct that regarded social cohesion as a result of sentiments and affections as opposed to obeisance to tyrannical laws. In Smith, for example, virtue stemmed from one's inner self, from one's desire for approbation rather than the fear of the law.[6] These ideas, however, were applied not just to society but also to the nation.

Writing about twenty years after Smith, Edmund Burke (1729–97) referred in *Reflections on the French Revolution and other Essays* (1790) to the relevance of customs for national coherence. "These public affections, combined with manners, are required sometimes as supplements, sometimes as correctives, always as aids to law. The precept given by a wise man, as well as a great critic, for the construction of poems, is equally true as to states—*Non satis est pulchra esse poemata, dulcia sunto*. There ought to be a system of manners in every nation, which a well-formed mind would be disposed to relish. They make us love our country, our country ought to be lovely" (1910: 75).

A few years earlier than Smith, David Hume had analyzed—in an essay tellingly entitled "Of National Characters" (1742)—how these links of sympathy, binding originally those within a kinship group, could in time entwine a whole nation. "Where a number of men are united into one political body, the occasions of their intercourse must be so frequent, for defense, commerce, and government, that, together with the same speech or language, they must acquire a resemblance in their manners, and have a common or national character, as well as a personal one, peculiar to each individual" (1898: 248). The predisposition to "company and society" is so intense among humans that the interchange among them produces a likeness of manners leading ultimately to a society relatively distinct from that of their neighbors. The critical words for Hume are "communication" and "social exchange." Thus even people living outside their native lands, such as the Jews and Armenians, can maintain

---

[6] Terry Eagleton rightly sees in these developments the emergence of an aestheticized theory of social conduct that refashions "the human subject from the inside, informing its subtlest affections and bodily responses with this law which is not a law" (1990: 32–43). We see this expressed in Matthew Arnold nearly a century after Smith. We want authority, Arnold wrote, but find nothing but checks and deadlocks. Culture thus is the "most resolute enemy of anarchy" because of the great hopes and designs for the state, which culture teaches us to nourish (1971: 170). Rules become imperative because they lie buried deep within the self.

their sense of difference from their host societies as long as they have a means of interaction with each other. Although inhabiting the same space, "any accident, as a difference in language or religion" keeps these people "from mixing with one another" (250).[7] That these characteristics are what differentiate one populace from another would become the central message of nationalism. For nationalism politicized these ethnic differences, gave them shape and form, and made them constitute the essence of the new, unitary state.

Although Hume had not used the term culture, this word would come to signify the ensemble of collective features typical to each nation. Thus J. S. Mill could assert nearly a hundred years later that all peoples regardless of their level of development, be they civilized or "unmitigated savages," possessed a culture. "Every form of polity, every condition of society, whatever else it had done, had formed its type of national character" ([1838] 1980: 130). He provided his own definition of a nation. A portion of humanity, he claimed, "may be said to constitute a nationality if they are united amongst themselves by common sympathies, which do not exist between them and any others—which make them cooperate with each other more willingly than with other people, desire to be under the same government, and desire that they should be governed by themselves or a portion of themselves, exclusively." This feeling of nationality, according to Mill, was generated by a number of causes: the belief in common descent, community of language and religion, geography, political antecedents, memories of shared history, collective pride, and humiliation ([1860] 1958: 229).

Mills's definition indicates that by the middle of the nineteenth century there had emerged a conception of the nation as a unified domain of shared feelings, symbols, history, language, and blood. The problem, however, is that it represented the nation as a homogeneous, self-contained society, sharply delineated from other societies by clearly visible borders. David Hume expressed this belief when he asserted that "national character follows the authority of government to a precise boundary; and upon crossing a river or passing a mountain, one finds a new set of manners" (249). This idea would become one of the central tenets of nationalist thought. But it never corresponded to reality, for in no nation could there ever be such an orderly overlap of culture, territory, and state. Thus, when multiculturalists today point to the heterogeneity of the nation, they are not really making a startling discovery about human society. They are correcting the hyperbole of nationalist rhetoric.

---

[7] Hume often buttressed his remarks with ethnic generalizations. Thus, in order to show how groups living alongside each other can nevertheless preserve their separate traditions, he pointed to the Greeks and Turks. "The integrity, gravity, and bravery of the Turks, form

CULTURE AS A WAY OF LIFE

But it has not been a simple correction to make, because this conceptualization of the nation is embedded in the way we conceive of social coherence in general. A whole tradition of sociological and anthropological thinking has incorporated two interrelated assumptions about culture: first, that culture is a way of life and, second, that it is a patchwork of customs, symbols, beliefs, and laws. We can see this in one of the founding texts of anthropology, E. B. Tylor's *Origins of Culture*. Tylor delineated his object of study as follows:

> Culture or civilization, taken in its wide ethnographic sense, is that complex whole which includes knowledge, belief, art, morals, law, custom, and many other capabilities and habits acquired by man as a member of society. The condition of culture among the various societies of mankind, in so far as it is capable of being investigated on general principles, is a subject apt for the study of laws of human thought and action. ([1871] 1958: 1)

Culture for Tylor designated the institutions, practices, and artifacts of one specific society that differentiate it from its neighbors. As such, culture imposes a certain uniformity on society ensuring that "our thoughts, wills, and actions accord with laws as definite as those which govern the motion of waves" (2). The fact that human will and conduct are subject to a particular code meant for Tylor that all societies are bound by it.[8] Customs, beliefs, and institutions become techniques making social life possible, just as the tools and methods of agriculture make it possible to satisfy the human need for food (Lévi-Strauss 1963: 357).

After Durkheim demonstrated that social phenomena should be studied as things, Bronislaw Malinowski argued that things themselves (weapons, tools, ritual articles) could be conceived as social phenomena. For Malinowski culture "is an integral composed of partly autonomous, partly coordinated institutions. . . . Each culture owes its completeness and self-sufficiency to the fact that it satisfies the whole range of basic, instrumental and integrative needs." Malinowski saw culture in the widest context of human behavior as an "organized system of purposeful activi-

---

an exact contrast to the deceit, levity, and cowardice of the modern Greeks" ([1742] 1898 250).

[8] It also meant that culture could be studied scientifically. "Just as the catalogue of all the species of plants and animals of a district represents its Flora and Fauna, so the list of all the items of the general life of a people represents that whole which we call its culture" (Tylor 1958: 8). Activities such as wood chopping, fishing , cooking "repeat themselves with wonderful uniformity in the museum shelves which illustrate the life of the lower races from Kamchatka to Tierra del Fuego, and from Dahome to Hawaii" (6). This line bears many similarities to the comments of Herder cited earlier in this chapter.

ties" whose ultimate goal was the satisfaction of human wants (1944: 40, 5, 52).[9]

By investigating the general characteristics of all religious life, Durkheim wanted to show that "the most primitive religions do not differ from the most recent and the most refined" (1915: 468). Moreover, he argued not only that religious behavior determined the lives of "primitives" and civilized alike but also that many essentially modern institutions like science were religious in origin (477). All human societies, notwithstanding their level of development, were enmeshed in a net of norms, beliefs, traditions, and feelings, which ensured that human beings were bound together by an internalized mesh of coercion. In other words, every act, any insignificant gesture, each facial expression was determined by laws, norms, and customs. All societies thus had a culture.

These ideas on the ubiquity of culture were eventually transferred to studies of industrialized societies, which, social scientists feared, were being destabilized by ever-increasing functional differentiation. These theorists were worried that the tendency toward professional specialization would yield more and more autonomous spheres of human activity, each subdividing into even additional areas of skill and knowledge. What could prevent or stop this process of particularization? Could such form of association maintain its internal coherence, or would it break apart into a myriad of unconnected domains? Social scientists wondered, in other words, how humanity could withstand the pressure of unceasing change in the absence of an unwavering tradition. One answer they gave was culture.

The definition of culture as an assemblage of shared sentiments and beliefs has thus figured throughout modern thought, manifesting itself in various attempts to understand human societies, including the idea of national culture. Underwriting this conception, Margaret Archer believes, are two sorts of arguments: the first contends that culture acts as a code enforcing unity on disparate parts. The second claims that culture can be imposed by one people on another to contrive a homogeneous community, such as a nation, or by a ruling elite on subordinate classes in order to enforce the former's ideological hegemony. Although both strands of the theory are related, they are logically distinct: the first, the imposition of order on chaos, is a function of ideas, whereas the second, the ordering of other people, is a property of human beings (1988: 4). The effect of

---

[9] At its core, the holistic approach sees culture as a unity of customs and beliefs. Interestingly, it emerged (in England at least), as Christopher Herbert concludes, during the late nineteenth century out of discussions concerning desire and restraint, chaos and order, freedom and control. Anthropologists arrived at the idea of culture as an ensemble of feelings, affections, and habits in a time when they perceived social disorder around them (1991: 60). Its origins, as we have seen, are much older.

this approach has been to treat societies as harmoniously integrated and to emphasize their deep meaning.[10] If societies exist, the assumption goes, then they must be held together by shared values and beliefs.

Only recently has culture's capacity to legislate our lives through the rules and customs we internalize come into question. The main weakness of this approach to social reproduction is that, by highlighting the necessity of consensus, it downplays the possibility of resistance to the imposition of these values. It also deflects attention from other institutions in society that bring about coherence, such as the state, labor and professional organizations, religious institutions, volunteer associations, the market, education, and so on. Furthermore, by placing emphasis on ruling ideologies, as Abercrombie, Hill, and Turner argue, it necessarily exaggerates the power of elites to compel lower classes to adopt their belief system.[11] The theory of a shared national culture cannot be applied to premodern societies in which, as I have shown, elites strived to distance themselves from the peasants rather than integrate with them.

The recent criticism of the holistic thesis of culture in studies by Archer and by Abercrombie, Hill, and Turner has been important. But in rejecting this thesis, such studies have devalued the significance of culture per se in society. The understandable questioning of the extraordinary authority with which scholars had endowed culture in the past has now robbed it of any relevance in the process of nation building. In short, theorists have thrown out the grain with the chaff, presenting a skewed theory of social change. It is impossible to grasp the emergence of nation-states over the past two centuries without addressing issues of identity, language, ethnicity, race, tradition, and the very necessity of preserving difference. This does not mean that cultural factors have miraculously created nations and kept them together. They alone can never be responsible for a society's integration or disintegration, for example, leading either to the uniting or "disuniting" of America.

Yet, as I have argued in the preceding chapter, the idea of a national culture has an integrative potential. Although French culture does not

---

[10] The search for hidden meanings, a preoccupation of philosophical hermeneutics and psychoanalysis, has become the dominant methodology of the social and human sciences in the last half of the twentieth century. Structuralism, having alerted us to the underlying system of all human artifacts, sought this code in language, poems, and fairy tales. Clifford Geertz brought these insights into ethnography by naming all social practices texts to be decoded. "I take culture to be those webs, and the analysis of it to be therefore not an experimental science in search of law but an interpretive one in search of meaning" (1963: 5).

[11] This is the critique leveled on the Marxist "dominant ideology thesis" by Abercrombie, Hill, and Turner. Patterned on the notion of a shared culture, the thesis sees social compliance as a factor in the ideological control of a population by elites or the state. It maintains that capitalist society reproduces itself through a system of common beliefs that ensures the subjugation of the working class to the bourgeoisie (1980: 2–3).

magically maintain the integrity of France, like cement holding mosaic pieces, it does signify the major differences between the French and the Germans. These sets of distinctions have acquired enormous symbolic value and motivate people of one nation to consider themselves closer to one another than to their neighbors in the way Hume and Burke had explained. They are worth dying for. Social scientists, who justifiably place in doubt the holistic approach to culture, do not address these differences, seeing societies neutrally as dry amalgamations of institutions and practices. One does not have to subscribe to the excesses of nationalism to believe that nations cannot be reduced to a bloodless nexus of overlapping power relations. One of the main reasons the Kurds choose the path to sovereignty is to preserve their identity in an autonomous state. This reason is good enough for them. In this way nationalism has promoted social unity: by placing a premium on a group's ethnic uniqueness and on safeguarding this uniqueness from other nations. A social theory that does not take this into account cannot provide a satisfactory explanation of social change nor can it explain the historical appearance of national culture.

ABSOLUTE STATES AND RELIGIOUS WARS

The link that was drawn in the late eighteenth century between ethnicity and politics was not just a product of philosophical speculation. It had to do with the emergence of the modern state out of the religious wars in the sixteenth century. Unleashed by the Reformation, these wars showed the consequences of multiple powers exercising authority within one territory. From the second half of the sixteenth century the pressing problem of rulers had been to secure an end to the unbearable state of *bellum omnium contra omnes*. People had recognized that a solution had to be found to the "intolerant, fiercely embattled, and mutually persecuting churches" (Koselleck 1988: 17). A temporary reconciliation was reached through the Peace of Augsburg in 1555, the maxim of which, *cuius regio eius religio*, declared that henceforth whoever governs a territory would determine its religion. Each ruler would decide whether Catholicism or Lutheranism would be the faith of his land. Those not wishing to live there were allowed to emigrate. This exercise of religious cleansing, however, would have important consequences for the formation of nation-states and for our contemporary understanding of national culture and cultural diversity.

As a result of the Augsburg formula, religion (and morality in general) was henceforth subordinated to politics, eventually becoming a personal affair of individuals rather than matters of state. More important, this formula "was the beginning of the specifically modern view that a political order must be based on articulately affirmed beliefs" (Shils 1962: 195). In the age of nationalism the Augsburg formula led to the conviction that those residing within political borders should all share not the same religion but the same culture. Indeed, whereas religion was thought to divide, culture was believed to unify. This conviction was given practical consequence by the policies of the unitary state, which promoted the diminution of differences among those living within its borders and their increase from those outside.[12]

Detached from one particular church, the state no longer advocated one creed over others. It gradually began to promote ethnicity as the justification of political authority. But the politicization of ethnicity rendered it a source of conflict. It has remained an arena of struggle ever since—from the wars of national liberation to the culture battles in the United States. The institutionalization of national culture took place in relationship to the growth of the unitary state. Nationalism went hand in hand with statism.

The ever-growing power of the state finally brought the end of the civil wars. The solution came about when the sovereign began to demand subjugation of all his subjects. The fear of personal injury or brutal death, Thomas Hobbes (1588–1679) believed, motivated people to build a state and surrender their freedom and defer to the absolute power of the monarch. The ongoing threat of civil conflict, as he outlined in *Leviathan* (1651), made them cede their rights to the state in exchange for its protection. For "during the time men live without a common Power to keep them all in awe, they are in that condition which is called Warre; and such a warre, as is of every man, against every man" (1991: 88). In such a time of general warfare, "there is no place for Industry; . . . and consequently no Culture of the Earth; no Navigation; . . . no Arts; no Letters; no Society; and which is worst of all, continually feare, and danger of violent death; And the life of man, solitary, poore, nasty, brutish, and short" (89). This state of injustice was the result of the lack of a "common Power" without which there is "no Law" (90). For Hobbes the state developed from the experience of this civil strife. Consequently, he himself promoted the idea of the state as a structure in which personal beliefs would forfeit their political consequence.

---

[12] Ultimately the solution of Augsburg introduced to Europe the idea of religious tolerance, which undermined the public consequence of religion. Having been freed from official function in society, it withdrew into private spaces and exerted its influence from there. "The experience of Germany and France and Britain forced the state and then society to recognize first reluctantly and later freely, the 'right' of the individual to profess the faith he found to be true" (Chadwick 1975: 23). Political liberalism has its roots in the notion of

In response to a host of political, economic, and sociological developments in the sixteenth and seventeenth centuries, power began to consolidate in states as they expanded their control over people and land through the creation of standing armies and bureaucracies. Not least of their attributes was their ability to reinforce their claim through their nearly exclusive control over physical coercion. War itself, Reinhart Koselleck writes, was expelled from the territory of the state, having come to characterize the relationship between states rather than citizens (43). The war of all against all was translated into an interstate conflict.

The Peace of Westphalia, signed in 1648, recognized the reality of these states. It brought to a formal end the Thirty Years' War (1618–48), a pan-European struggle of cataclysmic proportions whose causes were territorial, dynastic, and theological. This treaty, having revealed the Holy Roman Empire to be bereft of political clothes, effectively crowned the state as a supreme power.[13] Unlike the empire with its overlapping authorities and interconnected polities, the state declared its own sovereignty, which, in theory at least, entailed the "assertion of final authority within a given territory" and control over the "transborder movements of people, goods, capital, and culture" (Krasner 1989: 89). The Peace of Westphalia in a sense institutionalized the maxim introduced by the Peace of Augsburg.

The Peace of Westphalia gave validity to a secular European system, which emerged from the disintegrating *respublica Christiana*. This new global order made the possession of states desirable and mandatory. It bequeathed to modernity an international system of interconnected states, which still constitutes reality for the world's population at the turn of the century. This system itself, as Hedley Bull rightly observes, is united in the belief that states are the "chief actors in world politics and the chief bearers of rights and duties within it" (1977: 16–17).[14] Critics of nationalism tend to ignore this system and the history that created it, holding the nation itself responsible for the ills of the nation-state. In disregarding the

---

religious tolerance. For the right to hold a dissenting political view evolved from the privilege to hold a dissenting religious opinion.

[13] The Peace of Westphalia paralyzed and ultimately destroyed the Holy Roman Empire, having undermined the delicate system of constitutional balances established over the centuries of its existence. "The vastly expanded prerogatives of territorial supremacy which it conferred meant that a consistently pursued policy of dynastic self-strengthening in any of several larger territories could, over time, produce something resembling modern states whose power would be greatly disproportionate to that of the vast majority of the other imperial territories" (Gagliardo 1980: 45). This, of course, is exactly what happened as several states built standing armies and sophisticated administration systems, causing others to copy these measures.

[14] See also Bull 1984.

state, as the second member of the "nation-state" epithet, literary and cultural critics misrepresent the power of nationalism itself.

Culture as Secondary Agent

Paradoxically, these critics underestimate the significance of national culture, seeing it as either compensatory, a reaction to the ailments of modernity, or as a malady itself of modernization. They conceive it in this way partly because they themselves are responding to the way nationalist thought has represented national culture as an agent of social transformation. The tendency to exaggerate the social effects of identity goes back, as I mentioned earlier, to Herder, who placed priority on culture as opposed to politics in his explication of historical change. He argued, for instance, that the nation actually precedes politics, the primeval form of humanity being the *Volk* rather than the state. The state, according to Herder, has to grow out naturally from the *Volk* rather than be brought about through the will of politicians or institutions. He defined the *Volk* in cultural terms, that is, with reference to national language and culture (1877–99: 13:384, 258). To be sure, language was for him the primordial manifestation of national difference from which the *Volk* itself emerges (1877–99: 2:67; 18:387).[15]

That Herder made these essentially culturalist and ahistorical arguments—contradicting in this way his own historicist position—does not mean that culture actually antecedes politics. This could never be the case—not even in Germany, the quintessential cultural nation. Although the act of imagining a national Germany took place nearly a hundred years before its unification by Bismarck in 1871, it occurred within the state structures of the Holy Roman Empire, which had been in existence for centuries. Culture does not have some kind of metaphysical priority vis-à-vis the polity even though this was the belief shared by thinkers in the late eighteenth century.

Class reasons account for the organicist position adopted by German intellectuals at this time. They were engaged in a struggle, as I show in chapter 3, to undermine the hegemony of French culture in the German aristocratic courts and gain cultural capital for themselves. By arguing for the ontological primacy of the German nation, they could demonstrate that it was authentic; hence it did not require imitation of French models for its justification. At the same time, they hoped to gain class advantages, having been until then excluded from the courts. By disabling French cultural authority, they, as producers and interpreters of German language

---

[15] On Herder's influence, see the studies by Ergarg (1966) and Berlin (1976).

and literature, could consolidate their own social position. Their insistent question, "How German is it?" was intended in part to consolidate their place as experts of German culture in the new national order. In so doing, they offered both a fresh discourse (nationalism) and a new system of values (an ethic of originality and naturalness). The politics of authenticity has been used by intellectuals since then, most recently in the culture wars in the United States, to pursue a policy of social justice and their own class interests.[16]

Whatever the specific reasons for the excessive emphasis given to national culture in Germany, there is no doubt that nationalism itself exaggerates the significance of national identity as an instrument of social cohesion. And critics of nationalism seem to be reacting to this rhetorical overstatement. Taking nationalist rhetoric at face value, they end up denying a function that questions of language, tradition, and ethnicity could have in the process of nation building. It is not that they dispute the existence of national culture. Rather they devalue it by representing this social domain as a reaction to the great transformations of modernity, such as urbanization, industrialization, and functional differentiation. Culture in contemporary theories appears as a reparatory agent, providing people with ways of coping with the pathologies of modernity.[17]

This particular understanding of national culture follows, on the whole, paradigms in the conception of culture established over the past two centuries. I argued earlier that humanists and social scientists have perceived culture as a synthesizing force in part because they have regarded society as undergoing a process of unceasing differentiation. They found evidence of this destabilization in the division of labor, the formation of classes, accelerated specialization, and growing social complexity. Culture, as the realm of identity and the aesthetic, was supposed to provide the necessary social glue but also a means of contending with the ravages of modernity, such as alienation, the dissolution of local communities, and environmental degradation. The aesthetic realm, Jochen Schulte-Sasse has argued, "emerged in the second half of the eighteenth century as a privileged space of cultural activities; it is increasingly viewed as a realm of reconciliation and redemption that is able to suspend the negative side effects of the functional and social differentiation of society" (1989: 87).[18] Culture, in other words, became a domain separate unto

[16] See my discussion in chapter 7 on how cultural studies has established itself by ushering in novel methodologies and how its rise must be seen in connection to the emergence of a new information class.

[17] Wuthnow examines this conception of culture in the social sciences (1992).

[18] One of the intents of poststructuralism was to end the separation of science, art, and morality into autonomous, self-governing spheres. This was also one of the hallmarks of the historical avant-garde and, most recently, of postmodernism. The original avant gardist

itself among other domains in society but the only one invested with the capacities to identify and reconcile the distance among them. Its purpose in such circumstances could only be restitutive because, by making sense of and alleviating the burdens of fragmentation, it could not change the structure of this system (93).[19] For this reason those romantic poets and philosophers (and their heirs) who sought salvation in art found the experience only palliative and short-lived. Since then writers have invoked the unifying powers of culture in response to the perceived breakup of the world and the consequent Weberian disenchantment—the routinization of life, the subjection of the world to instrumental reason, and the domination of experience by material needs. They have also summoned culture as a means of condemning these developments.

In the hands of post-poststructuralists, however, culture becomes a hermeneutics of negation rather than a safety net against anomie. This is not surprising, for cultural studies is a successor to a two-century-long tradition that has considered the two primary aims of culture as critical and compensatory. Instead of offering the "superior" cultural values of love, intimacy, and aesthetic contemplation, as was the case of humanism, cultural studies provides radical critique. Despite its revolutionary rhetoric, cultural studies has not really departed significantly from its humanist ancestors. Although it has brought attention to hitherto neglected manifestations of human creativity, giving them value in their own right, it still treats culture primarily as a response to developments outside its realm. Thus in one of the founding texts of cultural studies, *Culture and Society, 1780–1950,* Raymond Williams wrote that the "development of the word culture, is a record of a number of important reactions to . . . changes in our social, economic, and political life" (1958: xvii). Culture for Williams constitutes a "general reaction to a general and major change in our common life" (295). In other words, it emerged not only as a "response to industrialism alone" but also "a response to the new political and social developments, to *Democracy*" (xviii). Culture is both a chronicle of change and itself an outcome of it. Indeed, *Culture and Society* narrates how the realm of ideas and feelings reacted to political, economic, and industrial transformations.

For Williams culture signified not just elite aesthetic forms but also the artistic creations of the working class. He understood culture in the extended sense as an assemblage of all features of a particular society,

---

project failed because, as Habermas has noted, life could hardly be saved by the shattering of one realm only, art (1981: 10). Unlike other poststructuralist thinkers, however, he favors the continuous separation of these fields but has striven to formulate a theory that would permit more effective communication among them (1984).

[19] The bibliography on this development is extensive. In addition to Schulte-Sasse, see Lambropoulos 1993 and Eagleton 1990.

from manufactured goods to songs. "Where *culture* meant a state of habit of the mind, or the body of intellectual and moral activities, it means now, also, a whole way of life" (1958: xviii). In *The Long Revolution* (1961), which focused on England in the 1840s, he described his project as "the study of relationships between elements in a whole way of life. The analysis of culture is the attempt to discover the nature of the organization which is the complex of these relationships" (1961: 46–47).

In *The Uses of Literacy* Richard Hoggart strove for a similar goal, seeking to describe the speech, beliefs, lore, songs, texts, and attitudes of the working class. "To live in the working-classes is even now to belong to an all-pervading culture, one in some ways as formal and stylized as any that is attributed to, say, the upper classes" (1957: 31). Hoggart took it upon himself to "listen to working-class people at work and at home," and then narrate the story of their houses, their parents, and their way of life (27). Fearing, however, that massification would rob the working class of its distinct identity, he undertook, like an artist, to rescue its experiences by recording and analyzing them.[20]

But Hoggart and Williams accomplished something more.[21] They saw the cultural production of the working class and its study as being engaged in power struggles against capitalist hegemony. Both writers thus were bound by an ethics "of resistance and opposition to the instrumental reduction of the human" (Slack and Whitt 1992: 576). Cultural studies has continued this tradition. On the one hand it affirms the significance of (popular) culture, showing that it is a necessary tool for understanding society. But on the other, it undermines this significance by positing it as a reactive agent in history.

NATIONALISM AS A REACTIVE FORCE

This very same pattern occurs in studies of nationalism, where culture either serves as a unifying ideology, is a by-product of economic developments, or responds to social transformations taking place around it. We see the latter, for instance, in Immanuel Wallerstein's world-system theory.

---

[20] Like many other Marxist humanists of his generation, he found the products of the culture industry inferior: "Most mass-entertainments are in the end what D. H. Lawrence described as 'anti-life.' They are full of a corrupt brightness, of improper appeals and moral evasions" (Hoggart 1957: 277).

[21] By augmenting the range of culture's signification they also opened up the space for cultural studies. Grossberg, Nelson, and Treichler explain that in "cultural studies traditions culture is understood *both* as a way of life—encompassing ideas, attitudes, languages, practices, institutions, and structures of power—and a whole range of cultural practices: artistic forms, texts, canons, architecture, mass-produced commodities, and so on" (1992: 4, 5).

To the extent that he examines culture at all, Wallerstein portrays it primarily as evolving out of the historical development of the capitalist world economy. "Culture," he argues, "the idea-system of this capitalism world-economy is the outcome of our collective historical attempts to come to terms with the contradictions, the ambiguities, the complexities of the socio-political realities of this particular system" (1990: 38). Culture in Wallerstein's work becomes derivative. His model, based almost exclusively on political economy, cannot really explain why nationalism appeared in the world and continues to maintain its hold on people's imagination and hearts.

Many theorists of nationalism, insofar as they emphasize culture's cohesive and legitimating function, regard national culture as a bystander to historical transformations. In his pathbreaking *The Break-Up of Britain* Tom Nairn represents nationalism as a phenomenon "determined by certain features of the world political economy in the era between the French and Industrial Revolutions and the present day" (1977: 332).[22] Although on the whole very nuanced, Nairn's study explains the appearance of nationalism as a by-product of industrial development. On the one hand, he rightly sees its emergence as an "aspect of progress," but, on the other, he depicts it as a function of failed modernization, a project promoted by elites in Greece, eastern Europe, and South America who realized that their countries were largely shut out of modernity.[23] Pushed to the periphery of the world economy and unable to "copy the advanced lands (which would have entailed repeating the stages of slow growth that had led to the breakthrough), the backward regions were forced to take what they wanted and cobble it onto their own native inheritance of social forms." The only resources available to the elites to fight back were the populace and its culture: "its inherited *ethnos*, speech, folklore, skin-color" (339–40). In his scheme of things national culture itself becomes important only because it helps the elites mobilize the masses. To accomplish this they require a "sentimental culture sufficiently accessible to the lower strata now being called to battle" and the demotic language with which to "invite the masses into history" (340). This converts nationalism to a "compensatory reaction on the periphery" against foreign domination and imperialism. In the absence of modern structures culture is transformed into an "ideological weapon" (343). Nationalism represents the "pathology of modern developmental history, as inescapable as 'neurosis' in the individual" (359). It becomes another sickness, a human reaction

[22] It is "pathbreaking" because it discussed British nationalism in 1977 when so little was written on this subject.

[23] See Ehrenreich 1983 for a similar argument. Ehrenreich sees nationalism as being "rooted in the uneven process of capitalist development" (1983: 25).

to a problem of modernity's own making, manifesting itself in its most deadly form in the fascism of Germany, Italy, and Japan (346).

Nairn's theory also forces him to argue that nationalism is a product originally of the periphery that is transferred back to the center. Although nationalism does indeed appear in societies dominated by foreign powers such as Greece, India, or Mexico, it also takes hold in countries like England, France, and the United States very early in their history. More often than not people enlist culture (identity) and its resources (literature, fiction, imagination, interpretation) into nationalist movements in the hopes of modernizing their societies, perceived by them and foreigners as backward. The principal goal of nationalists has always been to acquire the accouterments of nationhood and gain recognition for their country on the world stage.

Perhaps the most uncompromising portrayal of nationalism as a result of economic conditions is James M. Blaut's *The National Question: Decolonizing the Theory of Nationalism*. While Blaut criticizes Nairn for his conception of nationalism as the reaction of frustrated elites in backward countries to uneven development, he depicts it as a form of class struggle for state power.[24] The issues of language rights, religious freedom, even civil equality and equal opportunity are for him "embraced within the idea of class struggle" (1987: 24–27). Therefore he rarely discusses cultural matters such as ethnicity or tradition let alone language, literature, or music. He does not consider them because they are epiphenomena, manifestations of deeper economic and social transformations. By refusing to take culture into account, Blaut's theory is incapable of explaining many of today's nationalist struggles. How, for example, can the conflict between Greece and Macedonia over the name "Macedonia" or between the Palestinians and the Israelis be reduced to class struggle? What possible economic advantage can there be for the Chechnyan, Abkazian, or Kosovar elites to seek sovereignty in what would amount to impoverished protectorates? Can the lot of Quebecois bourgeoisie improve in an independent Quebec caught between two economic giants, Canada and the United States? Blaut's theory cannot appreciate how nationalism enables a populace to posit itself as a unique body, fit to govern itself in an autonomous republic. Moreover, it cannot make sense of the absolute import people grant to their ethnic and national affiliations because it portrays this significance as false.

In denying the weight of culture, Blaut ends up denying that cultural struggle has been part of all political struggles for independence. Fanon

---

[24] Blaut's position is doctrinaire for he seeks to show that "theories of nationalism are wrong if they do not reduce national struggle in the last analysis to class struggle" (1987: 26).

understood this when he wrote that in colonized countries national culture "falls away and dies. The condition for its existence is therefore national liberation." Therefore the search for national culture reaches "at the very heart of the struggle for freedom" (1963: 233, 244). As so many recent postcolonial studies have shown, cultural domination has been "a major aspect of imperialist domination," and culture always therefore serves as "a major site for resistance" (Ahmad 1992: 8). In the realm of literature this feature has amply been explored by an earlier generation of postcolonial intellectuals: Chinweizu and Imechukwu (1983), Ngugi Wa Thiong'o (1981), and José Carlos Mariátegui (1971). More recently and with reference to India, Sara Suleri notes that British imperialism was predicated "on an act of cultural looking," that is, a strategy of classifying, categorizing, and constructing racial and gender inventories (1992: 18).[25]

Imperialism took a cultural dimension because nationalist and statist ideologies had posited in eighteenth-century Europe a direct relationship between power and politics, the nation and the state. National identity had emerged at this time as a necessary medium to maintain and to possess political authority. And the state took it upon itself to invade the cultural, private domain of social life. As I have shown, however, premodern empires did not conceptually and institutionally isolate the cultural lives of their subjects. Only in the past two centuries have groups turned to culture in their fight for liberation, in part because culture had already been targeted by their colonizers.

As Declan Kiberd demonstrates, Irish political leaders drew on ideas of poets and playwrights in their nationalist enterprise. In Ireland, he argues, the "cultural revival preceded and in many ways enabled the political revolution that followed" (1996: 4).[26] The problem is that social scientists have ignored issues of culture in their study of nation building. For this reason it is possible for John Breuilly to argue that ethnic nationalism was "the product rather than the cause of the Greek nation-state" (1982: 110). It is best, as I note later, to avoid the chicken-and-egg question of whether the nation or the state came first. But in answer to Breuilly's contention I think one can demonstrate that Greek nationalism, like examples in Germany, Ireland, and the Third World, actually preceded by decades the founding of the Greek state. Literary and cultural critics have been making this argument for years. With justification Kiberd contends that stu-

---

[25] As Said notes, "Orientals were rarely seen or looked at; they were seen through, analyzed not as citizens, or even people, but as problems to be solved" (1979: 207).

[26] Kiberd assumes that this makes the Irish case unique. A more comparative analysis could show that Irish cultural nationalism came nearly a century after similar efforts in eastern Europe and the Balkans.

dents of imperialism, colonialism, and nationalism have until recently "devoted most of their attention to the economic and political ramifications and have tended to underestimate the cultural factors" (5). It is this stance toward culture that allows Blaut to see nationalism as a derivative phenomenon to be swept under the carpet of class relations.

Even in studies sympathetic to nationalism the appearance of national culture is represented as an indirect function of modernization. The basic tenet, for instance, of Ernest Gellner's influential *Nations and Nationalism* is that the workings of industrial society depend on a common culture. Ethnicity, he argues, "enters the political sphere of 'nationalism' at times when cultural homogeneity . . . is required by the economic base of social life" (1983: 94). Culture in modern societies becomes the "necessary shared medium, the life-blood or perhaps the minimal shared atmosphere within which alone the members of the society can survive" (1983:38). Moreover, with the breakdown of traditional guarantors of state loyalty, such as dynastic legitimacy and divine ordination, nationalist feelings came to serve as a means of underwriting political authority.[27]

"It is not that nationalism imposes homogeneity out of a willful *Machtbedürfnis*," Gellner insists, "it is the objective need for homogeneity which is reflected in nationalism" (1983: 46). Because modern society requires certain shared qualifications such as literacy, numeracy, and basic work and social skills, it has devised institutions, like schooling, to bring about the desired homogenization.[28] Gellner explains the conspicuousness of culture in nation building by pointing to the inner demands for cohesion of modern society, so unceasingly shaken by change and internal division. In the absence of traditional means of support (rigid class divisions), capitalist society must rely on a uniform mode of communication (language) and popular education, which teaches both this demotic as well as the skills indispensable to the functioning of the nation-state. His thesis turns out to be a liberal version of the legitimization theory already examined, which regards national culture as providing the social mortar in the face of crumbling ideologies like religion. Ethnic identity and its

---

[27] Gellner's position has some similarities with Lenin's who saw a causal relationship between capitalism and nationalism. "Unity and unimpeded development of language are the most important conditions for a genuinely free and extensive commerce on a scale commensurate with modern capitalism, for a free and broad grouping of the population in all its various classes and, lastly, for the establishment of a close connection between the market and each and every proprietor, big or little, and between seller and buyer. Therefore, the tendency of every national movement is towards the formation of *national states*, under which these requirements of modern capitalism are best satisfied" (Lenin 1964: 396–97).

[28] Gellner rightly observes that, although modern society is functionally differentiated and hence the most highly specialized, its education system is the least specialized and most standardized. In premodern societies, whose social system is highly stratified, its education requires training of a minority of individuals.

subsequent transformation into national culture are the result of social transformations, being derivative phenomena.

Gellner, however, does not really explain why inherently a modern, industrial society should be a secular nation-state and not an empire or a theocracy. He seems to argue not capitalism per se but modern society needs the nation-state. As modernization sweeps around the world, Gellner writes, it makes everyone feel unjustly treated, usually by another nation; if enough victims identify themselves within one group then nationalism is born. The claim, however, that capitalism requires a homogeneous population is unconvincing and has been disproved by the late phase of global capitalism, which, if anything, taunts the nation-state by bringing attention to the irrelevance of its borders and its pretensions to economic independence.

Will Kymlicka in his *Multicultural Citizenship: A Liberal Theory of Minority Rights* follows Gellner in representing common culture as a product of modernization. He argues that a common culture is a "functional requirement of modern economies." It both reflects the need for solidarity within modern democratic states and is necessitated by the modern commitment to freedom (1995: 76). E. J. Hobsbawm similarly sees culture as a mere outcome of social, political, and economic developments in modernity. In his *Nations and Nationalism since 1870* he traces the origins of nationalism in the legitimation crisis of modernity. As traditional guarantors of loyalty like dynastic legitimacy, divine ordination, and historic right had become severely weakened, states "required a civic religion ('patriotism') all the more because they increasingly required more than passivity from citizens" (1990: 84). Hobsbawm understands national culture as the invisible threads of society. In overemphasizing its capacity to foster social and national cohesion, he also portrays it as a response to social change.

This bias against culture shared by many social scientists we see in the way John L. Comaroff represents ethnicity as a derivative form. While stressing that ethnicity constitutes a set of relations that have to do with the human need for classification, Comaroff traces the origins of ethnicity "in the asymmetric incorporation of structurally dissimilar groupings into a single political economy" (1987: 307). For Comaroff ethnic groups themselves as well as their ethnic consciousness arise when historical forces produce structures of inequality between social entities. They emerge when these entities come to experience their asymmetrical "we-them" relations (309). Comaroff emphatically argues that the forces that create consciousness (ethnic or totemic) lie in the "transformations of economy and society." Ethnicity thus constitutes a secondary set of social relationships. Experientially, however, people perceive it as a primary, autonomous, and primordial force, capable of determining social life. Comaroff does grant that ethnicity may have "a direct and independent impact on the context in which it arose." But those initial conditions must lie in the division of labor. Thus he is quick to characterize this "independent impact" as a "reification" which enables ethnicities to have a "pervasive functionality" for individuals "who share them" (313). He insists that the "structures and signs of inequality" continue to give ethnicity even today the "appearance of an objectified force" (318).[29] For this reason people seem to believe that it is ethnicity that "orders social status, class membership and so on—and not class or status that decides ethnic identities." Hence, according to Comaroff, "working class black Americans do not view their blackness as a function of their class position, but their class position as a function of their blackness" (312–13).

Ethnicity, of course, cannot determine class relations. No one seriously believes this. But the example of black Americans exposes Comaroff's reductive analysis, which regards both ethnic groups and their sense of difference as the results of social hierarchies. But by what measure is it possible to argue that class has created the sense of blackness in the United States? After all, were Africans enslaved because of their class or their color? While economic dictates prescribed the need for cheap or free labor and hence the importation of slaves, the subsequent emergence of a black consciousness was a complex phenomenon involving issues of race, culture, and class. A black culture could only configure itself in contrast to white colonists who brought Africans of disparate tribes and enforced upon them a collective experience in the United States. The interplay between cultural and economic forces explains the emergence of not only an African American culture but also of other American panethnicities such as Indian, Latino, and Asian, which have taken or are taking shape today. It is simplistic to look for the point of origin of ethnicity and give credit to class positions.

Comaroff speaks confidently about the possibility of explaining the general roots of ethnicity. Although this explanation might indeed be possible in the modern period, how could one trace the origins of those groups whose genesis lies in the deep past, often in prerecorded history? If we assume, however, that Comaroff's thesis could determine the point of birth of any ethnicity, how could it explain, say, the emergence of today's so-called symbolic ethnicity among whites of European extraction as a function of unequal relations? This form of identification is seen as a matter of personal choice to be changed in the course of an individual's life. Existing on the surface of people's lives, it rarely stipulates whom

---

[29] See Zubaida for a similar position: "common ethnicity and solidarity are not the product of communal factors *given* to modernity but are themselves the product of socio-economic and political forces" (1989: 320).

they will marry or where they will live, as was true of their ancestors' identity. His thesis, insofar as it needs to represent culture as derivative, cannot deal with such questions.

Beyond these questions, however, there is a point where Comaroff's argument can be neither proved nor disproved. This is so for two reasons. First, his model has a built-in safeguard. The notion of ideology serves as an invincible force field shielding it from inquiry. Although at the "experiential level of subjects" ethnicity appears as a dynamism governing their lives, in fact—as the unmasking tools of the social scientist tell us—unequal social relations do so. Any empirical evidence brought forth by individuals about their lives is shown by the anthropologist to be false. The social scientist thus makes it impossible for anyone to breach his theory. Second, Comaroff's characterization of ethnicity as a consequential aspect of social life has to do less with verifiable data than with foundational assumptions about society, the consequences of which I explore here.

THE CHICKEN OR THE EGG?

I have presented a set of arguments that depict cultural identities themselves as secondary phenomena to either economic or political developments, in other words, as products of external transformations. Depending on the theory, national culture is viewed as a guarantor of class domination, a mode of resistance to it, a means of coping with or compensating for the consequences of modernization, or an agent legitimating state authority. Yet it cannot have a creative role in the building of nation-states, as an instigator of social change rather than simply a reaction to it. Thus, those who wish to highlight national culture's constitutive potential are faced with a quandary. The knee-jerk reaction might be, in answer to reductive formulations of national culture, to prove its very autonomy. Whatever its merits, such a strategy might end up fetishizing culture. But it also might be futile.

Roland Robertson rightly argues that it is fruitless to engage in a purely theoretical debate with "anti-culturalists" because it would be conducted on their territory and, hence, in their ineluctable favor. He observes that those wishing to show the productive power of culture have a steeper hill to climb than others since, by entering this particular discussion, they have agreed upon the "anti-culturalist" rules of argument. "The 'culturalist' agrees to try to prove that culture explains more than the anti-culturalist about allegedly non-cultural matters" (1992: 46). Moreover, the debate might also be ultimately unverifiable as it involves groundwork assumptions about society itself and social change. Because the argument has to do with rudimentary theoretical principles, no amount of raw data can really help one side or the other. Comaroff, for instance, may claim that ethnicity is a secondary phenomenon, but ultimately there is no way that his contention can be proved other than by sheer belief in the theory itself.

This debate is, to be sure, one strand of an age-long and vexing shoving match between materialism and idealism. The influential social thought inaugurated a hundred years ago dealt in part with this conflict: Max Weber's work on how the emergence of a modern ethos facilitated the rise of the capitalist spirit and Durkheim's attempts to show the relationship between faith and social structures. Although these thinkers themselves never reduced their work to a choice between opposites, subsequent schools have. For more than a century each side has steadfastly planted its feet on opposite sides of this tug-of-war between autonomy and determinacy. On the one side are those who claim that culture has an integrity of its own and, on the other, those who argue that culture is an epiphenomenon.

This is still the case today. The poststructuralist theory of culture, Michael Ryan writes in a study tellingly entitled, *Politics and Culture*, poses a series of questions:

> Is culture a secondary representation or embodiment of a group's life substance that is assumed to be prior and that is expressed through culture, or does culture, defined as shape, form, representation, embodiment, and objectification play a more primary constitutive role in the making of group life?. . . Can group life even be said to be at all possible prior to cultural embodiment or form? (1989: 21)

New participants continue to pull on the same ideas. Although divided by their ontological conception of culture, both sides of the contest paradoxically are held together by a rope of dichotomous thinking.

It might be more profitable to forgo the either- or structure and ascribe to culture and society "some measure of autonomy as well as a degree of mutual influence" without reducing the one into the other (Griswold 1987: 1080, 1115). By avoiding this Manichaean face off completely, one can examine the position of culture in society while highlighting its affirmative power. It is not a question, Janet Wolff argues, "of counterposing to a mechanistic, deterministic view (economism) a 'better' account, stressing the 'relative autonomy' of culture, or emphasizing the effects of culture in social change. Nor is it a question of investigating 'cultural response' to economic factors" (1991: 171). As I show with specific case histories in chapters 4 and 5, historical analysis of *actual* nationalist projects demonstrates that the dilemma of the chicken or the egg, implicit in the culture-society dichotomy, is irrelevant. For the idea that nations constitute unique groups appeared in tandem with the rise of modern political structures. Trying to find out which came first, the state or the nation, is like trying to determine the initial boiling point in a pot. What is the purpose ultimately, since it is impossible, as I show in chapter 5, to separate culture from the state? What is at issue here is to understand that culture occupies an integral place *in* social processes and *in* social change. The answer may be simpler because "people don't live materially and then add culture; they live and have culture at the same time" (Ryan 1989: 21).

National culture is part of society, a participant in historical development and interwoven with all social practices. Culture represents, as Stuart Hall explains, "the meanings and values which arise amongst distinctive social groups and classes" and the lived traditions and practices through which these meanings and values are "expressed and in which they are embodied" (1986: 39). Culture is simultaneously the mode of representation and the represented object; it is a territory of codes, symbols, norms, and the signifying practices like texts, tropes, rhetoric, discourse. My own perspective here owes in part to work in cultural studies that has demonstrated that narratives, texts, metaphors, and codes of representation can produce meaning and that this meaning can have an impact on social developments.

It also is based on the Weberian approach to cultural change, so little followed today outside sociology. Weber's work, despite its reliance on the teleological transition of societies from tradition to modernity, has offered a paradigmatic example of how ideas can have an influence on social life. Weber showed that culture can bring about social change, albeit not in a "vulgar," unmediated manner. He never claimed, for instance, that religious transformations actually led to the emergence of capitalism. Indeed, he categorically stated that he had no "intention whatever of maintaining such a foolish and doctrinaire thesis as that the spirit of capitalism . . . could only have arisen as the result of certain effects of the Reformation, or even that capitalism as an economic system is a creation of the Reformation. . . . On the contrary, we only wish to ascertain whether and to what extent religious forces have taken part in the qualitative formation and the quantitative expansion of that spirit over the world" (1958: 91). He wanted to see what aspects of capitalism could be traced back to religious motives. Wishing to examine the parallels between modes of conduct characteristic of Protestantism and those of early capitalism, he explored the extent to which religious forces conditioned the emergence of capitalism. Thus he could conclude that one of the "fundamental elements of the spirit of modern capitalism, and not only of that but of all modern culture: rational conduct on the basis of the idea of calling, was born . . . from the spirit of Christian asceticism" (180).[30]

---

[30] For a useful discussion of Weber, see Schluchter 1996.

A useful adaptation of Weber's insights is Colin Campbell's *The Romantic Ethic and the Spirit of Modern Consumerism* (1987), which investigates broadly the effect ideas can have on conduct. Drawing lessons from Weber's thought, namely that a cultural ethic is connected to the emergence of a modern form of economic practice, he came to conclusions somewhat different from Weber's. Whereas Weber, for instance, explained how Protestant beliefs promoted the rise of an ethic favorable to a capitalist orientation, Campbell examined how "an ethical code served to justify consumption." Thus he analyzed how the nature of conduct issues from acceptance of a given belief. His aim was to trace "the manner in which changes in society's conceptions of the true, the good and the beautiful influence patterns of conduct, not in any direct prescriptive fashion but through the way that ideals give direction to character-confirming conduct" (12). These epistemological assumptions allowed Campbell, for instance, to speculate on how the development of modern hedonism—so essential to the rise of mass consumerism—lay in the shift of primary concern from sensations to emotions, for only through the latter could prolonged stimulation be connected to autonomous self-control (69). In short, Campbell was interested to see how romanticism and the cult of sensibility made hedonism possible and, in turn, gave rise to "further outbursts of romantic fervor" (216). Campbell's study is one example of a work that seeks to show the productive potential of ideas and beliefs.

In the context of literary studies Ian Hunter has examined current critical theory as a set of discourses seeking to develop a set of techniques of personal comportment rather than uncover truths about literature. He thus regards literary theory as an ethical exercise in the hermeneutics of the self. In order to understand the success of this discourse, Hunter maintains, one has to examine what it says about the self rather than about literature. Thus, if theory contends that literature is "inscrutable," one has to ask not why literature is inscrutable but rather "what kind of relation to or comportment of the self is formed by teaching that the operation of literature is inscrutable." The unexplainable nature of literature thus arises from "its pedagogical . . . use as a discipline shaping the comportment of the one who reflects" (1996: 1103).

For Hunter academic theory is the tradition of aesthetic education of the past two centuries, a way of creating the self as an object of ethical concern: "an autonomous set of techniques and practices by which individuals continuously problematize their experience and conduct themselves as the subjects of an aesthetic existence" (1992: 358). The principal characteristics of this aesthetic ethos are inwardness, attentiveness to subjective states, intensification of imaginative experience, disregard for "public" appearances, and dialectical thinking. Culture, it was felt, enabled human perfection and refinement through study and aesthetic contemplation. One became a better human being by becoming intimately acquainted with the masterpieces of scholarship and art drawn from all the ages.[31]

I have referred to the works of Campbell and Hunter, and earlier to those of Gilroy, Chatterjee, and Appadurai, as examples of current research that seeks to indicate the subtle relationship between literature and politics, culture and society. The tradition of Weberian cultural sociology and the discipline of cultural studies demonstrate that ideas can have an effect on life. This impact is not simple, like the collision of two billiard balls, because national culture is not like a ball, perfectly spherical with a hard outer shell. Its autonomy should be seen more heuristic than real. That is to say, it is necessary to conceive of national culture as a sovereign entity not because it can be touched and seen as an actual thing but because this metaphor allows us to understand a series of practices and institutions that are organized in its name. The domain of national culture is intersected by other domains—politics, the market, the law, education, the army, the bureaucracy—in the same way that the realm of literature is linked with publishers, agents, librarians, editors, and readers. All these practices and individuals are brought together within the space of the literary. To say that culture has been functionally differentiated is not at all the same as saying that it has been freed from social, political, and economic forces and left hovering in an aestheticist heaven, much like Flaubert's idea of art. It means, rather, that it has been separated symbolically and institutionally from society, endowed with its own rules and logic.

I regard national culture as a specifically modern manifestation of a social tendency toward collective identities. National culture, as I noted earlier, is an ethnic identity that has become politicized. This politicization separates it from previous modes of group identification and makes it both a desirable quality and a site for social strife. For the past two hundred years culture has been involved in the social contest for political authority, for the right to representation, for prestige, and for justice. The history of nation building shows that culture can in various circumstances become a site for agency by enabling a people to posit itself as a special community worthy of sovereignty, to resist imperialism, but also to oppress marginalized groups.

---

[31] Poststructuralism has denounced this ethos for being grounded on a too narrow, exclusive conception of culture that emphasizes higher values and privileges works of learning and art. Ironically, its formulation in the nineteenth century was enabled, as I have explained, by a different assumption, namely, that the arts themselves are interrelated and that culture in general constitutes a way of life.

In representing the act of nation building as a dynamic operation in itself, one not necessarily subservient to economic or political institutions, I am *not* proposing a culturalist theory of either nation building or social change, one that would elevate culture as superior to the market or the state. Nationalism, having arisen alongside capitalism and the state, cannot be understood independently of them. My intention is to direct attention to the role of culture in the construction of nation-states because in the past this role has either been ignored by social scientists or has been demonized by cultural and literary theories. As a result, the reasons for the original appearance of and continued appeal of national culture have been occluded.

From one point of view, any examination of culture, insofar as it investigates culture per se—from the study of literary texts to the investigation of cultural nationalism—risks the accusation of essentializing or reifying this concept. There can be no answer, as I noted earlier, to satisfy the purist and doctrinaire position that every conceptual isolation of culture is by definition culturalist. But, I think, there is a difference between an examination of the social effects of culture and one that sees culture exclusively as a causal agent. Although I conceive of national culture as autonomous for analytical reasons, my examination is not abstract. On the contrary, I wish to rescue nationalism from the ahistorical speculations of this topic in cultural studies. Thus my discussion of culture is situated in specific enterprises of nation building over the past two centuries. Ultimately, it is by accounting for nationalism as a distinct historical development that one can bypass the dead end of the autonomy and determinacy argument.

National culture is not the police force invented in modernity to maintain order within the boundaries of the state. Yet it does have definite social consequences. While it can be used to unify a nation, it often promotes resistance to this nation among those excluded from that group. In its most basic form, national culture is not a primordial, ontological feature of human beings, but a product of the human necessity to classify and to differentiate one set of objects, people, and ethnic groups from another set.

Chapter Three

THE BASTION OF NATIONAL CULTURE

CULTURAL NATIONALISM appeared two centuries ago and is still a vibrant force today because it is seen as a blueprint for modernization, a sentinel of ethnic identities, and a spark to postcolonial struggle. Nationalism arose as a result of the interaction of peoples in modernity through war, imperialism, and trade. Although groups have always fought with one another and exchanged goods, in modernity this interchange has been intensified as never before by capitalism and by new technologies in the fields of transportation and communication. Moreover, conquering states and colonial powers had at their disposal the bureaucratic, military, and technical means to infiltrate the social fabric and threaten indigenous identities as never before.

While England, Spain, France, Portugal, and Holland were establishing overseas empires, France was attempting to conquer Europe itself. Nationalist movements, for instance, appeared throughout Europe in the early eighteenth century partly in response to the French Revolution and Napoleon's campaigns (1803–15). The political revitalization of France demonstrated not only the success of the new kind of state—integrated, centralized, and legitimated by popular sovereignty—but also its potential to extinguish local identities. French political and military achievements in the late eighteenth and early nineteenth centuries demonstrated that the main road to modernity was propelled by a machine powered equally by culture and politics. We normally think that the real message of the French Revolution was the universal call for freedom, equality, and fraternity, but its explicit linkage of ethnicity and polity may be equally, if not more, profound. It emerged as a model to be copied because a growing number of Europeans began to see that the nation-state was showing "the way to reach the future, to progress toward a good (or better) society, or . . . to modernize" (Shafer 1972: 83). This model was also exported to Europe's colonies abroad during their independence movements.

In this drive to modernization cultural identities were conceptually and institutionally isolated in ways unthinkable before modernity. Culture began to be seen as a source of political power and as something precious to be saved from the thrust of this power. Jean Jacques Rousseau had associated political sovereignty with nationality as early as 1765 when he wrote that those formulating the constitution of a state should keep in mind its "caractère national." "Every people," he argued, "has, or should have, a national character; and if a people did not, the first thing to do would be to provide it with one" (1915: 319). Reacting to the cosmopolitanism of the *philosophes* and their dislike of state boundaries, he wanted to show, first, that groups were united by their language, customs, and social interaction and, second, that their political institutions were legitimated by their national character.

Rousseau's position, however, was not just philosophical. He was also reacting to political events of his day, such as the invasion of the newly established Corsican republic by French troops in 1768 and the partition of Poland by Russia in 1772. In response to these actions he wanted to accentuate the political significance of "national character" because he saw it as a shield in the preservation of both political freedom and a distinctive way of life. Insofar as Poland possessed a national consciousness, he argued, it also had a mechanism to resist its enemies: "The virtue of its citizens, their patriotic zeal, the particular form that national institutions can give to their spirit, that is the only rampart always ready to defend it [Poland], and which no army could breach. If you arrange things such that a Pole could never become a Russian, then I can assure you that Russia will never subjugate Poland" (1915: 431). Even though the Poles were not free at that time, he insisted, they were obligated to maintain their difference as a way of preventing their cultural extinction. By keeping their Polishness distinctive, they could ensure that, in the future, they would be independent. In these statements we discover the representation of national culture as a site of opposition to foreign rule, which Chatterjee associates only with twentieth-century postcolonialism. From Rousseau we see that the hostility to imperialism has been the raison d'être of nationalism from the beginning. That he enjoined the Poles to preserve their identity so as to achieve their freedom later shows that he made a connection between politics and culture.[1]

The French Revolution played an important role in further establishing this connection. It "politicized the cultural concept of nationality" (Heater 1990: 57) as an act in itself and internationalized this politicization. As France began its conflicts with much of Europe after 1792, the originally cosmopolitan outlook of the eighteenth century gave way to the intense preoccupation with the French self. And the civic concept of citizen came gradually to be associated with a cultural nation. The sentiments expressed by the Dantonist Robert in 1793 captures this new exaltation of the nation: "I desire that the Legislator of France forget the

[1] We should remember that Rousseau advocated the coexistence of cultural homogeneity with constitutional forms of government. To be free a people needs a nation and a republic. See Viroli (1995: 78–92), who also discusses the republican patriotism of eighteenth-century British thinkers.

universe for a moment and occupy itself with its own country. I wish that kind of national egoism without which we betray our duties. . . . I love all men, I love particularly all free men, but I love the free men of France more than all the others of the universe" (in Shafer 1972: 110). These kinds of statements, stemming from the mouths of the victors, would increasingly be uttered by the losers, be they in Germany, Greece, the Philippines, or Nigeria. It took little time for the Rhinelanders, for instance, to develop their own sense of patriotism in response to the French invaders. National love proved infectious.

This should not be understood, however, to mean that nationalist ideas spread consistently from the west to the east, as this movement has been traditionally understood. Elie Kedourie, for instance, has written that "nationalism is a doctrine invented in Europe at the beginning of the nineteenth century" (1993: 1). Kedourie is right if we see nationalism as a self-conscious theory that did emerge in Europe. But if we see it as an assemblage of ideas and events, his observation does not hold. Franco Venturi has demonstrated that the end of the old regime in Europe was brought about originally by rebellions in the periphery. The first reforms and revolutions occurred in unexpected places: the Peloponnese, Corsica, Poland, Behemia, and Montenegro. The revolt of the Greeks in 1770 against Ottoman rule (organized by agents of Catherine II) along with other insurrections of the time seemed "disquieting" to Europeans who sought to understand the significance of these events for their own societies (1989: ix). Anderson has shown that the creole peoples of North and South America had created a sense of nationhood by the late eighteenth century, often earlier than many European societies (1983).

At the onset liberal thinkers all over Europe enthusiastically endorsed the French Revolution, believing it to be the realization of Enlightenment ideals of freedom and happiness. From their perspective the revolution was a triumph of universalist thought, which now was spreading victoriously throughout Europe. It served as a model for intellectuals seeking political sovereignty for their own societies.[2] For instance, the poets and intellectuals of the Ionian Islands, then the possessions of Venice, looked at Napoleon as a political savior. Napoleon himself dreamed of liberating mainland Greece from the Ottomans. While in exile he confessed that "Greece still awaits its savior. And what glory awaits the one who succeeds in this endeavor! His name will be engraved alongside that of

---

[2] In a novel dramatizing the life of Novalis (Friedrich von Hardenberg, 1772–1801), Penelope Fitzgerald captures the idealization of the Revolution by artists and intellectuals. In a morning conversation about the upheavals in France at the Hardenberg household, Novalis's younger brother, Erasmus, says: "The revolution is the ultimate event . . . what is certain is that a republic is the way forward for all humanity" (1995: 26).

Homer, Plato, and Epaminondas. . . . I myself had conceived of such an idea, when, fighting in Italy, I had come to the shores of the Adriatic. I wrote then to the Directorate [in France] that I was facing the kingdom of Alexander" (in Koukou 1983).[3] The Revolution remained an inspiring symbol for liberals and radicals[4] although many had become disenchanted by its grisly turn in the years 1793–94. They reacted against it in greater numbers, however, when Napoleon sought to foist upon Europe its universalist values.

We can see this in the response of the Rhineland, the area occupied the longest by French troops, from 1792 to 1802—a reaction that points to the ever-present struggle between nationalism and universalism. In his study of the French occupation T.C.W. Blanning claims that the original French aims of forcibly liberating Europeans from despotism backfired because the methods used were brutal, without their bringing any benefits to the population.[5] There is ample evidence of rape, murder, robbery, and vandalism by the troops. The army, ill-disciplined and unpaid, survived by exploiting the people it was supposed to free from the evils of the old regime. Troops, for instance, had to be billeted in private houses, generals had to be fed and entertained lavishly in a manner befitting their elevated rank, labor was conscripted for special projects such as the building of fortifications (1983: 88, 118, 123.) Significantly, in addition to economic mistreatment, the occupied lands were subjected to cultural degradation. In 1794, for example, the French authorities began to requisition a vast amount of valuable books, scientific instruments, and works of art (110).[6]

The scale and scope of repression ensured that the population of the Rhineland, as elsewhere in Europe, began to revolt against the occupation. The French policy makers were astonished by these rebellions because they had hoped that the horrors of the wars would be offset by the benefit they would bring—the destruction of feudal oppression. Rather than creating a new transnational order, the Napoleonic Wars actually brought about the opposite effect, resistance. The forced imposition of universal principles provoked the effort to protect local cultures and

[3] Giorgos Andreiomenos examines the literary reception of Napoleon by Ionian poets (1997).

[4] In Puccini's Tosca, set in Rome in 1800, the jailed revolutionary, Cavaradossi, shouts out "Vittoria! Vittoria!" upon hearing news of Napoleon's victory. Like many of his contemporaries, he had many hopeful expectations from Napoleon's campaigns.

[5] Andreiomenos (1997) and Koukou (1983) investigate this very reaction among the Ionian Islanders as well.

[6] The Louvre was named the Musée Napoléon to commemorate the vast number of plundered works of art that Napoleon had brought back from his conquests. The museum became a symbol of national aggrandizement.

oppose foreign rule as would happen again and again in the next two centuries.

This national remonstrance was given grand historical sweep in Tolstoy's *War and Peace* (1869), which dramatizes, in its latter half, Napoleon's invasion of Russia. In one epic scene Tolstoy has the French emperor proclaim the civilizing mission of the Enlightenment as he stands at the gates of Moscow, observing in awe: "From the heights of the Kremlin—yes, that's the Kremlin, yes—I will dictate to them the laws of justice, I will teach them the meaning of true civilization, I will make the generations of boyars to enshrine their conqueror's name in love" (n.d.: 814). When Napoleon entered the "Asiatic city," he found it, to his dismay, empty. But he should not have been surprised, given the opposition offered him by Russian forces (and guerrilla units) described so memorably by Tolstoy.[7]

The Napoleonic invasions allowed various European nations to see that the ecumenical ideas of the Enlightenment had become localized, serving the ambitions of the French state. Fearing for their ethnic survival in a French empire stretching from Portugal to Russia, they sought strong states and vigorous cultures capable of withstanding such foreign assaults. They responded to the possibility of such an empire in the same way colonized peoples of Asia and Africa reacted to European colonialism.

The stand against the French took a decidedly nationalist turn as Europeans began to search for self-respect in their own traditions. The French sense of national selfhood and superiority, for instance, strengthened by the Revolution, helped the Germans develop their own feeling of collective consciousness. As in all forms of identity, the formation of a national culture involved the making of comparisons. Pride in German achievements and unique character, now goaded by a fierce Francophobia, transformed the conflict into a struggle between Teutons and Gauls. The clash with a political and cultural enemy helped make the ever-developing sense of German identity into a political phenomenon.[8] Insofar as the French Revolution nationalized culture, it contributed to its nationalization elsewhere.

[7] Napoleon was right, however, to expect an enthusiastic welcome from the aristocracy, given the hegemony enjoyed by French culture among the nobles. Tolstoy himself emphasized the love of French ways in a scene at the house of Prince Nikolay Andreitch, when Count Rastoptchin, one of the guests asked: " 'And how should we, prince, fight against the French!' . . . 'Can we arm ourselves against our teachers and divinities? Look at our young men, look at our ladies. Our gods are the French, and Paris—our Paradise.' . . . 'Our fashions are French, our ideas are French, our feelings are French!' " (n.d.: 509).

[8] This example goes to show how essential war is in the formation of identities because, by differentiating friend from foe, it affirms ethnic boundaries. Nicole Loraux, reflecting on war in the classical polis, writes that it is a "political institution" ensuring the "internal functioning of the city" (1991: 38). When confronted by an enemy, internal unity is vital.

It lobbed culture into the political arena, like an apple of discord in the banquet of the gods, making it an object of desire and source of conflict for all mortals.

The unitary state, with its powers of surveillance, could threaten the ethnic survival of captured peoples.[9] We have seen that polyethnic empires or dynastic kingdoms did not purposefully impose an ethnic *Weltanschauung* upon their possessions. Even if ethnic absorption had been desired, the logistics of enforcing an identity on a foreign population or even of intensive military control would have been staggering. It has been estimated that throughout ancient history the maximum unsupported march of an army was about ninety kilometers. Thus a military force located about three hundred kilometers away from a city could compel a population to supply annual tribute or recognize the suzerainty of its leader, but it would leave everyday behavior unconstrained (Mann 1986: 26, 328).

The modern state, in contrast, can infiltrate systematically the private lives of people. It exercises unchallengeable jurisdiction over its citizens through explicit and implicit coercion. It alone, Max Weber has argued, is allowed to claim a *"monopoly* of the *legitimate* use of force in the enforcement of its order"* (1968: 54).[10] But the modern state is more than an organization that can mobilize the means of violence to maintain its rule. It affects ordinary people daily by insinuating itself in their lives through the acts of certifying, counting, reporting, registering, classifying. Michel Foucault has shown how the bureaucracy can identify and document each individual according to sex, age, gender, race, ethnicity, class—totalizing and individualizing at the same time.[11] The state represents its citizens as members of a national community but also identifies them individually as taxpayers, employees and employers, draftees, students, consumers. Only a hermit could avoid contact with the state's agents: police officers, postal carriers, tax collectors, teachers, soldiers.

This capacity of the state or invading army to affect the language, customs, and symbols of a people makes it very menacing to minorities and

[9] Foreign invasion could also lead to the physical ruin of a nation as when the overthrow of the Inca Empire by the Spanish resulted in the cataclysmic destruction of the previous social order. See Guilmartin 1991.

[10] See also Weber 1946 and Giddens 1985.

[11] See Foucault 1979. This form of intervention, as Foucault said of all power, can be both tyrannical and liberating. The all-providing state helps and prods while it monitors and controls. Only in the state, for instance, can citizens be free and have rights. "It is the State," Durkheim reminds us, "that has rescued the child from patriarchal domination and from family tyranny; it is the State that has freed the citizen from feudal groups . . . ; it is the State that has liberated the craftsman and his master from guild tyranny" (1957: 64). As the state provides for the welfare of its subjects, it accumulates more power over them, having extended its scope during the liberal and socialist phase of its development.

to captured groups.[12] In possession of advanced means of communication, the state aggressively pursues a policy of homogenization, of bringing its lands and people under the same laws, institutions, and culture. The possibility of being swallowed by the national culture of a hegemonic power has made ethnic self-preservation an extraordinary public issue in modernity. Rule by foreigners has come to be regarded as horrible and illegitimate.

Because invasion and colonization take a cultural dimension, it goes without saying that resistance by the captured populations will also incorporate cultural values and measures. In modernity groups enter into conflict with each other not just over economic resources but also over culture. Contrary to the modernization theories of Karl Deutsch and W. W. Rostow, modernity ignites ethnic distinctions rather than extinguishing them insofar as it politicizes them. Be they the Germans of the nineteenth century, the Algerians of the twentieth century, or the African Americans of today, people turn to culture as a means of fighting against military defeat or discrimination. They ally politics with identity in the struggle for self-esteem, autonomy, and a brighter future. We are modern in that we believe that our ethnic or national identity is a vital part of our personal and public happiness, that we should preserve it at all costs, and that its potential destruction would constitute a global shame.

FORTRESS CULTURE

Captured groups politicize culture in order to gain agency, in order, as Rousseau said of Poland, to fortify a domain untouched by colonial rulers so as to gain freedom in the future. We can see how culture had been transformed into a national bastion when we look at Scandinavian nations in the early nineteenth century, particularly Finland. National culture became a public concern during the Napoleonic Wars after the country—ruled by Sweden since the thirteenth century—was invaded by Russia in 1808, conquered, and annexed a year later. Many Finns, fearing that this union would lead to their absorption into the Russian Empire, believed that the possible disappearance of Finland could be kept at bay

[12] Ethiopia and Thailand, with their histories of statehood, illustrate how the problem of ethnic survival has intensified in modernity. Walker Connor notes that "ethnic groups were able to coexist for a lengthy period within each of these two states because the states were poorly integrated, and the ethnic minorities therefore had little contact, with either the (mostly theoretic) state government or each other" (1994: 36). By the middle of the twentieth century, however, with improvements in communication and transportation, groups had become more susceptible to the influences of the central government. Both countries were faced with separatist movements.

"only if the people were set off sharply from the Russians by the possession of a distinct national culture" (Wuorinen 1931: 1).[13]

Alarmed by the imminent disappearance of Finnish life, patriots sought a defense against it. They found this safeguard in the creation of a distinct nationality, which would form the foundation of an independent state. Convinced that their political autonomy was subject to the vagaries of the great powers, they sought to protect their own distinctiveness as Finns. Although impotent to prevent union with Russia, they could withdraw within the sanctuary of culture and preserve there a sacred flame until it was safe to light it outside. They began to regard ethnicity, now politicized into a national culture, as both the space to cultivate a sense of uniqueness and the means to safeguard it. This was so because in modernity a people's existence has been linked to their survival as Finns, Eretrians, or Latinos. The possibility of ethnic dissolution has become even more real under conditions of globalization. Nations fear being sucked down by a global Charybdis.

What remains apparent in the Finnish case is the prominent role nationalists assigned to culture in bringing about national integration. For them culture served both the goal of nationalism as well as the tool of attaining it. This response is also true of neighboring Norway for, when it declared itself independent from Denmark in 1814, it was forced into another union with Sweden.[14] In response to this thwarted bid for autonomy, Norwegian intellectuals undertook the nationalization of culture, particularly language.[15] This was a novel development, for before 1800 the written language in Denmark-Norway was felt to be shared and called *Fælles-sproget* or the common language (Haugen 1966: 29). Neither government nor the general population was sensitive to its national implications because, being a written medium, it was used by a literate minority. The challenge for reformers lay in devising a written demotic. This mission

[13] Finland had been part of Sweden for six centuries. Wuorinen asserts that before the nineteenth century Finns had not thought of themselves as a unified ethnic group. Complaints, largely economic having to do with taxation, trading privileges, and the like, were not translated into a political program until the middle of the nineteenth century (1931: 2, 27).

[14] Norway had a prehistory of statehood whose roots lay in the Middle Ages. Miroslav Hroch (1985) provides a useful study of "smaller European nations" such as Norway, Bohemia, Finland, Estonia, Lithuania, and Slovakia.

[15] European languages had been studied for centuries but had only become nationalized in the end of the eighteenth century. Academies, for instance, had been inaugurated in Italy (1589), France (1635), Spain (1713), Sweden (1739), and Hungary (1830) to stave off linguistic corruption by cleansing language of foreign elements. The puristic pastime of grammarians however, was a far cry from the politicized struggles of the nineteenth and twentieth centuries in which language was winnowed in the name of national authenticity.

necessitated the codification and use of Norwegian in schools and the search for the history of this language.[16]

In Norway and its neighbors, intellectuals enjoyed a leading role in the consolidation of the nation. The poet, the historian, linguist, and folklorist came before the machine, factory, and the train. "At their hands there had emerged attractive conceptions of Norwegian, Swedish, Finnish, and Danish 'national characteristics,' and in them they and their followers took immense pride" (Wuorinen 1950: 464). But cultural politics, as Chatterjee shows in the case of India, was not enough. Convinced that their project could succeed only if in association with organs of the state, language reformers had to affiliate themselves with the nationalist and democratic party to realize their aims. Such a union was necessary because the state, whose existence is legitimized by culture, becomes the ultimate protector of ethnic uniqueness and a vehicle for modernization.

Although nationalism becomes appropriated by the state, initially it has served as a cultural project, having appeared as a response to universalist thinking and foreign occupation. This is certainly true in Europe's former colonies but also in the case of Germany. German nationalism serves as a paradigmatic example of an invented nation, of a country whose birth and development were seen by contemporaries as a cultural project, integration having been experienced textually before being achieved politically.

When I say Germany is a cultural nation, I am not at all claiming that the consolidation of Germany as a nation-state in 1871 was a discursive phenomenon. On the contrary, it was a historical act of state building. The struggle for liberation from the French was also a political event. So were the rebellions of 1848. These revolts, the first mass manifestation of German nationalism, broke out in the cause of a liberal, constitutional polity. The failures of the revolts in 1848 dissipated hopes for an all-German state founded on parliamentary rule.[17] Disappointed idealists turned their attention away from politics, and the state gradually gained prestige as both the carrier of nationalism and harbinger of progress. Thus the cultural interpretation of nationality was superseded by the ideal of the strong state. The dream of a modern centralized nation-state built on popular sovereignty floundered, giving way to Bismarck's *kleindeutsch*

[16] In their search for oral traditions stemming ultimately from the formation of the Norwegian kingdom in the ninth century, scholars returned to Old Norwegian manuscripts and Old Icelandic written sources, which had disappeared a century after the union with Denmark in 1397 in the absence of support from a Norwegian court (Haugen 1966: 30).

[17] Although German nationalism in the late nineteenth century grew obsessed with the purity of the German character, in the early nineteenth century it was more liberal, striving for a progressive polity based on constitutional guarantees. There was a lively discussion of constitutionalism, for instance, in the last decade of the eighteenth century (Fischer 1995: 107–8).

solution (Germany under Prussian control but excluding Austria), a state constructed from above.

But this unification would have been unthinkable without the cultural work of the previous two centuries. The guiding principles for the legitimation of the German Reich in 1871 were found in literature rather than in politics, wherein the Prussians, Saxons, and Würtenbergers hardly had a fund of common experience (Hohendahl 1989: 196). For nearly a century cultural nationalism drew up blueprints for modernization, making it possible for people to depict and desire a united Germany.[18]

The German case highlights how nationalism, in making the distinction between inside and outside, differentiates between political institutions (controlled by foreigners) and the domain of culture (controlled by locals). Chatterjee has shown that postcolonial nationalism separates the material sphere (statecraft, science, technology) from the spiritual sphere (cultural identities), declaring the latter sovereign territory (1993: 6). But Germany, Greece, and the Scandinavian countries indicate that such a division has been emblematic of nationalism since the latter part of the eighteenth century. German elites saw nation building as a moral rather than a political enterprise, an act of persuading fellow Germans that they were bound by a shared consciousness. For them the authentic German character had little to do with politics, transcended petty squabbles between states, and would survive the destruction of the Holy Roman Empire.

This belief comes out in a passage from Schiller, written in 1801 after the Peace of Lunéville which reorganized the empire. Although the Germans had been defeated in battle, Schiller observed, they had not lost their most valuable quality. This is so because

> the German Empire and the German nation are two separate things. The majesty of the German people has never depended on its sovereigns. The German has established his own worth independently of politics. Thus, even if the empire were to fall, German dignity would remain untouched. The strength of this dignity is a moral nature. It resides in the culture and the character of the nation that are independent of its political fortunes. This realm blooms in Germany and is in its full growth. (Schiller 1844: 386–97)

It would be wrong to see in this passage—as Liah Greenfeld sees German nationalism in toto—an expression of *resentiment*, a consolation for

---

[18] That Germany is invented does not at all mean that it appeared miraculously out of thin air. A distinct form of the German language began to coalesce in the eighth century. Around the ninth century distinctions were made between Latin peoples west of the Rhine and the Germanic-speakers to the east. A passive awareness of German identity began to take shape around the next two centuries (Hughes 1988: 18). The first glimmer of "national" consciousness appeared in the fifteenth century (Borchardt 1971: 95–96).

the loss of a particular battle between France and Austria. Schiller attempted to define here the national character of the Germans, beyond the temporal affairs of states. For him their moral strength was superior to political power, now in decline at home but in ascent among their enemies. Schiller's assertion, while not strictly speaking nationalist, certainly manifests a feature of nationalist thought—its tendency to locate the majesty of national culture beyond the clutches of foreigners.

Schiller expressed the general belief in the capacity of Germans to excel in "morality and creativity" (Gagliardo 1980: 137–39). This ideological position only intensified in the last years of the empire, more so after the abdication of Emperor Francis in 1806, which signaled the collapse of the only political structure the German nation had known. While the empire was crumbling, France was capturing German territories, and French learning and manners were in possession of court society, German intellectuals were aspiring to produce a spiritual domain autonomous of foreign control.[19]

That this endeavor was intensely cultural can be seen in Schiller's famous essay, "Theater Considered as a Moral Institution" (1784). The stage, he explained, had a national mission: determining the spirit of the nation. He defined the people's national spirit "as the similarity and agreement of its opinions and inclinations concerning matters in which another nation thinks and feels differently." Only the stage was capable of uniting all classes and strata. "If we could witness the birth of our national theater, then we could truly become a nation" (1985: 212). The creation of a national culture was a project of ethnic survival in modernity. "Self-defense," Herder asserted "is the root of all human and national worth." A Volk that does not defend itself culturally would become like powerless Italy (1877–99: 18:345).

As in all nationalist enterprises, the effort to fashion such a cultural armor was motivated in part by comparisons Germans were making between themselves and their neighbors. Comparisons, as I shall show, are the engines of nationalism. For by 1800 Britain, France, Spain, the Netherlands, Sweden, Prussia, Austria, and Russia had solidified their control over their territories. Germany, with the exception of Italy, was the only major power without strong state structures. The success by which other countries had integrated themselves made many Germans aware of their own failures. Moreover, other countries seemed to have distinguished themselves in all areas of cultures, most especially literature.

---

[19] They also hoped to save the universal values of the empire. In the latter part of the eighteenth century German nationalism was expressed in cosmopolitan principles of both the Enlightenment and the empire. Those who defended these ecumenical ideas could never have foreseen the turn to a narrow, racial, and genocidal nationalism in the twentieth century.

This comparison that Germans made between themselves and other peoples emphasized their belatedness. Poets, scholars, and philosophers began to look for reasons and solutions to their tardiness and found them in culture. By the end of the eighteenth century the search for a German culture had become a practical and philosophical problem, at least among the intelligentsia. The question they increasingly posed, "What is German?" launched an anguished odyssey for the authentic attributes of Germanness. This ontological quest, however, was motivated by a more agonizing question: "Why are our neighbors ahead of us?"

This question was posed emphatically by Johann Gottlieb Fichte (1762–1814) in his famous, "Address to the German Nation," delivered in Berlin in 1807–8. He gave these lectures after the French defeat of Prussia in 1806, an event resulting in the dissolution of the Holy Roman Empire. The Treaty of Tilsit forced Prussia to cede significant territory to France, pay it enormous reparations, and reduce its army to forty-two thousand men.[20] Smarting from the crushing defeat, Fichte gave this spirited series of lectures, calling for cultural renewal and unity. They stand now as exemplary nationalist documents because for the first time they make culture and politics confront each other so directly, a confrontation that releases the energy of nationalism.[21]

Lecturing in a capital city vanquished and humiliated, he wanted to rekindle a sense of pride among his listeners and endow their developing sense of nationality with a political commitment. This has become a classic strategy of all nationalists whether they are exhorting their audience in the eighteenth or at the end of the twentieth century. Many critics of multiculturalism, such as Arthur Schlesinger, William Bennett, and Dinesh D'Souza, forget this function of nationalist rhetoric when they decry calls to revise school curricula as no more than ploys to stimulate minority self-regard. Even a cursory glance at the past two centuries shows nationalism has been deep down a visceral endeavor to raise consciousness. Nationalists must persuade their fellow patriots that, despite their miserable situation, they are capable of surpassing their oppressors in greatness. They have to deliver their speeches in the hortatory subjunctive.

For Fichte the challenge before the German nation, so ruined and devoid of optimism, was to "find an entirely different and new binding tie," one that could link up the welfare of the nation with the self-interest of

---

[20] The subjugation of Prussia aroused men such as Wilhelm von Humboldt (1768–1835) to reform the state along the principles of the Enlightenment. This enterprise, largely a product of administrators, stressed organization, military power, and the education of the general public.

[21] Even though Fichte is considered a precursor of a cultural German nationalism, early in his life (as Kant's disciple) he supported the cosmopolitanism of his peers. The outbreak of war, however, between France and Prussia in 1806 forced him to abandon this position.

its members (1979: 11).[22] This binding tie was, of course, the national culture that had been gradually forming for decades. For him the superiority of the Germans lay in their being "held together as a common whole almost solely by the instrumentality of the man of letters, by speech, and writing" (217). Faced by the overwhelming strength of a centralized and predatory France, Fichte invoked the powers of culture to politicize the Germans. He wanted to persuade them that, insofar as they were held together by the same identity, they had the right to call themselves a people (108). He, like thinkers before and after, located German distinctiveness in language, tradition, and literature. But this uniqueness was not an aesthetic judgment but a fact entitling Germans to political autonomy. "Whenever a separate language is found, there a separate nation exists which has the right to take independent charge of its affairs and to govern itself" (217). Culture was the basis for self-governance.[23] Critics of nationalism forget that a national identity enables people, who are not bound by immediate ties of kinship, to imagine themselves as belonging to the same republic. It makes them feel, as Habermas argues, "politically responsible for each other" (1996a: 286). Relationship by culture leads to relationship by citizenship.

NATIONAL CULTURE IN ASPIRATION

When Germany was finally liberated after a short war of one-and-a-half years, it remained still a country in aspiration. Even foreigners like Madame de Staël (1766–1817) referred to the heterogeneity within the German territories as a problem. In *De l'Allemagne* (1813) she wrote: "Only a few major traits pertain equally to the entire German nation, for this country is so diverse that there is no way to unite religions, governments, climates, even peoples that are so different under a single rubric" (1956: 55). This political decentralization, reflected in the economic realm as well, had in her opinion a direct consequence on culture, making it paro-

---

[22] This does not mean that resistance to the French troops was conducted through poetry. In order to give practical effect to their ideas, intellectuals formed organizations through which to disseminate nationalist ideas. During the wars of 1813–14 and afterward, these private societies were useful for this purpose. Typical was the gymnastic society founded by Friedrich Ludwig Jahn (1778–1852). By 1818 there were about 150 gymnastic societies with twelve thousand members (Düding 1987: 24). Singing clubs also proliferated.

[23] Although he called for self-governance, Fichte, like his contemporaries, distrusted government. "The State . . . cannot be built up by artificial measures from whatever material may be at hand. . . . Only the nation which has first solved in actual practice the problem of educating perfect men will then solve also the problem of the perfect State" (1979: 102). The state came to take a greater importance for Fichte though he supported a republic, not "a bureaucratic machine of Frederician Prussia" (Sheehan 1989: 376).

chial. In *De la littérature* (1800) she maintained that an aesthetic sensibility could not develop under conditions of fragmentation: "Since the separation of states precludes [the possibility] of a single capital where all the resources of the nation can be concentrated, where all distinguished men can meet, the formation of taste is more difficult in Germany than in France." One does not judge, one does not criticize with severity, she added, "when each city wishes to have superior men of its own" (1959: 244). Madame de Staël offered the example of centralized France where institutions could legislate aesthetic standards.[24]

It is true that political and demographic decentralization defined the Germans for centuries. Lacking a centralized, political apparatus, the Holy Roman Empire sprawled out like a web of overlapping and interconnected legal and political relationships whose goal was to preserve both general peace as well as the autonomy of individual polities. Under such circumstances of demographic fragmentation, it is not surprising for Herder to write that "geographical boundaries alone do not constitute the totality of the nation" (1877–99: 7:276). This statement, however, can really be applied to a majority of nations before nationalism.

For reasons of history, geography, and empire, German elites turned to culture as a way of modernizing the nation. The enterprise took on a more pressing direction, as I mentioned earlier, with the French Revolution. While there is little evidence of German nationalism in 1776, the Revolution taught the Germans the value of possessing a strong state founded on popular will. This lesson was underscored by the Napoleonic campaigns, which demonstrated the impuissance of the imperial system. In a world of standing armies, political boundaries, voracious states quite ready to absorb a territory, the way of life specific to each people became all the more valuable and, hence, worthy of preservation. The confrontation with the enemy and the destructiveness of the war forced Germans to think about their common characteristics.[25]

By the late seventeenth century signs could be seen of national identity greater than that of each individual *Heimat*. Limited to the elites at this stage, it was national only in an optative sense, yet it aspired to tear down

[24] Having painted a picture of chaotic Germany, she came to the conclusion that political decentralization was incompatible with literature because the latter required the concentration of power to legislate standards. While federalism, she added, is a system favorable to the attainment of liberty, "it harms the greater development of the arts and talents, for which the perfection of taste is necessary. Habitual contact amongst all the distinguished men, their gathering in a shared central location, establishes a kind of literary legislation which leads all minds in the best direction" (Staël 1959: 244).

[25] At this time the word *Heimat* (homeland) reentered the language. Originally conveying the sense of being rooted in a rural community, *Heimat* had become the focus of a moral discourse for two centuries about place, belonging, and identity (Applegate 1990: 4).

the physical, linguistic, ethnic, political, and economic fences dividing the Germans. Moreover, it was literary in both the narrow and extended connotations of the term. First, identity was conceived through the genres of literature such as poetry, the novel, and the stage and associated largely with the writings of Herder, Kant, Lessing, Klopstock, Goethe, and Schiller. Second, national identity was an indirect product of print, which made possible new channels of communication between authors and readers spread beyond their own locality. Books, periodicals, and newspapers allowed people to form loose networks of reading and interpretation, facilitated by growing number of libraries, reading societies, discussion groups, and publishing houses. It is in this respect, Wolfgang Kaschuba argues, that in Germany bourgeois aspirations and identity formation found a common mode of expression first in culture (1988: 19).

The use of German in publication had been steadily increasing since the sixteenth century. While in 1518 only 10 percent of all books in the empire were printed in German, by 1681 books in German actually surpassed those in Latin (Fischer 1995: 92). One periodical alone, the *Allgemeine deutsche Bibliotek,* reviewed eighty thousand titles between 1765 and 1805.[26] The growing use of a demotic in print was essential in the subsequent rise of both nationalism and a more inclusive public realm.[27] For print (along, of course, with a sound transportation and communication system) facilitates the quick spread of ideas, allowing people to see their shared characteristics and interests. Literacy, Benedict Anderson has argued, in creating "unified means of exchange," makes it easier for nationalists to "arouse popular support" (1983: 47, 77). Tom Nairn's pithy observation that the "new middle-class intelligentsia of nationalism had to invite the masses into history . . . in a language they understood" is entirely justified (1977: 340). Nationalism attempts, at least in theory, to overcome all social differences in the name of the nation. As Herder asserted: "There is only one class in the state, the *Volk* . . . and the king belongs to this class as well as the peasant" (1877–99: 18:308).

The signs of a national culture become evident in the following passage from Goethe's epistolary novel, *The Sorrows of Young Werther* (1774), which describes a scene in a ball involving the novel's two protagonists, Werther and his beloved Lotte. On the window Lotte "stood leaning on

[26] The eighteenth century witnessed an astonishing rise of print material. In 1700 the Leipzig Book Fair catalog contained 978 titles but eighty years later the number of entries expanded to 2,600. In the 1770s over 700 periodicals were being published, in comparison to only 58 at the turn of the century. Criticism itself blossomed at this time (Sheehan 1989: 153).

[27] Daniel Moran discusses the role of the press in the creation of a public sphere, focusing on Johann Cotta, publisher of the great authors in the early nineteenth century, and the first person to convert cultural prestige into political power (1990: 2).

her elbows, her gaze searching the landscape; she looked up to the heavens and then at me, I saw her eyes fill with tears, she put her hand on mine and murmured, *Klopstock*!" (1929: 23) Contemporary readers, Sheehan writes, knew that Lotte could only have been referring to Klopstock's ode, "Die Frühlingsfeier," written in 1759 (1989: 160). Lotte and Werther understood each other and their surroundings by reference to a poem that both they and the novel's readers knew. Werther actually saw Klopstock in Lotte's face. "And looked up again into her eyes—Noble poet! would that thou hadst seen thy apotheosis in that gaze."

When I say that national culture creates new bonds of attachment, I have in mind these references in Goethe's novel. They indicate the emergence of a literary culture at least among an educated public. The configuration of such a culture could be seen around the 1770s, even though it touched only a small percentage of the population. By this time, Friedrich Schlegel (1772–1829) observed in his *Lectures on the History of Literature, Ancient and Modern* (1812) that it was hardly a paradox "to talk of German nationality, its genius and character, its aspirations and its wants" (1882: 348). Although this literary discourse could not on its own have enabled social coherence, it and supporting institutions (libraries, reading societies, universities, coffee clubs) bound readers in networks of shared interest and aesthetic perception. Friedrich Schiller had this in mind when he defined the "spirit of the nation," as the "similarity and agreement of its opinions and inclinations concerning matters in which another nation thinks and feels differently." He added, however, that only the "stage is capable of eliciting a high degree of such agreement, because it ranges throughout the entire domain of human knowledge . . . and because within it, it unites all classes and social strata" ([1784] 1985: 217, 218). The issue here is not that the theater by itself brought about German unity. It could not in such a crude way. But these philosophers and poets foregrounded the capacity of culture to transform society in an attempt to enhance their own class positions. Nationalism is promoted partly by the self-interest of elites.

INTELLECTUALS AND CLASS INTEREST

Unless independently wealthy, the philosophers, poets, and scholars of the eighteenth century required the patronage of aristocratic courts, which were dominated by French neoclassicism. Often denied social privileges in an order ruled by blood lineage, they turned against it and its French pretensions in the name of German genuineness. The instrument they used to undermine the influence of French manners and writing was historicism, ironically a by-product of the French Battle of the Books.

Taking a central tenet of historicism that all values were products of specific circumstances, they sought to prove that, because all cultures are
genuine and unique, German culture was as good as the French.[28] Culture
was to them, as Robert Musil writes in *The Man without Qualities* of
the Austrian middle class at the beginning of the twentieth century, an
"invisible weapon" to "trounce" the aristocracy ([1951] 1995: 292).[29]

German intellectuals denounced the servility of the aristocracy to
French manners, arguing that such mimicking of foreign ways perverted
the German spirit. Fichte, for instance, complained that the upper and
educated classes loved "everything foreign" (1979: 109). Influenced by
Pietist doctrines on egalitarianism and authenticity, they posited the *Volk*
as the keeper of German character. Herder, for instance, celebrated the
songs, epics, and customs of agrarian peoples as treasure chests of purity.[30]
He also exhorted Germans to be themselves, to be unique, to be true. In
calling for national self-realization, he appealed to their sense of authentic
experience. Because nations, like people, had an identity, they had to be
faithful to this experience in order to be happy. Perhaps no other principle
stemming from German romanticism has made its influence felt today
more distinctly than the elevation of personal experience as a focus of
public and individual concern.[31]

Herder and fellow writers represented themselves as spokesmen of the
nation, even though they were socially distanced from and were sometimes uneasy with it (Blackbourn 1990: 22). Often considering themselves
liberal, they belonged to what contemporaries referred to as the *Bildungs-
bürger,* in contrast to the *Stadtbürger,* the merchant bourgeoisie. Defined
by education, they institutionalized the university as counterbalance to
the court and as a site of modernization. The university disseminated both

---

[28] Ironically they used classical Greece as a weapon in their struggle. By positing Hellas as
the most authentic of all cultures, they could reject neoclassical French poetics as inauthentic
(Nisbet 1985: 2, 6). In Winckelmann's idealized description of the Greek polis, they found
an attractive solution to political absolutism. The idea, however, that they may have been
interested in Athens for its democratic institutions is not seriously entertained by Martin
Bernal (1987).

[29] Musil's novel treats with irony a patriotic campaign undertaken by the protagonist
Ulrich (the man without qualities), his cousin, Diotima, and a host of aristocrats and bourgeois bureaucrats in 1913 to celebrate the seventieth jubilee of the ascension to the throne
of the emperor Franz Joseph. Very much like Cavafy satirizing pompous Hellenistic rulers
who were in fact beholden to Roman authority, Musil focuses on this campaign to celebrate
"global Austria" just a few years before the collapse of the Austro-Hungarian Empire.

[30] He celebrated the poems of the legendary Gaelic poet Ossian, which had, in fact, been
written partly by James Macpherson. On the impact of these poems on nationalism in Britain, see Trumpener (1997).

[31] On the use of experience as a rhetorical trope, see Bellany and Leontis 1993 and Lambropoulos 1997.

a "new German educated language" but also the new national culture "as teachers, clergymen, and middle-rank administrators" carried into the provinces the new ideas on the nation (Elias [1939] 1978: 24).

The case of Germany shows, first, that the university has been a most powerful engine for both the production and transmission of nationalist ideas and, second, that intellectuals portray themselves as drivers of this engine. In the comparisons intellectuals make between their own and other societies, the former seem inferior and hence in need of transformation. Because they find themselves shut out from positions of power, through class distinctions or by colonial regimes, they promote national culture—their area of specialization—in order to gain influence in society. The principal figures of the Sturm und Drang, the literary movement flourishing between 1770 and 1778, Hamann, Herder, Goethe, Lenz, and Schiller, turned to questions of literature, art, and identity as a way of criticizing the social hierarchies of their time. Culture had for them a reconstructive function. It was a social movement, rather than a political party, aiming at the "transformation of society" (Elias 1978: 18).[32]

Its success lay not in bringing about the political unification of Germany but in providing the discursive means to imagine such a reality. By making Kultur[33] an indispensable topic for public discussion, German writers of the later eighteenth century could not only criticize the social order but also pose a burning question that only they could answer: "What does it mean to be German?" In this, the role of intellectuals has not changed in the past two centuries. They are usually first to conceive of how a person can be a Hellene, a Filipino/a, a Mexican American. Be they in preindependence Greece, postcolonial Philippines, or multicultural America, intellectuals have gained prestige by politicizing identity.

Although German intellectuals became influential in their society, needless to say they did not create the conditions in which they operated. Their political critique as well as their conception of national culture emerged in the space that had been opening up since the early eighteenth century between the public and private realms, as has been explored by Jürgen Habermas (1989).[34] This space would come to be known as civil society,

[32] See Dülmen 1986.

[33] While Kultur connoted national difference, the French civilisation indicated level of technology, evolution of science, and manners. Our nationalist age has jettisoned the neoclassical "civilization" in favor of the romantic "culture," with its emphasis on ethnic and racial differences.

[34] Habermas's thesis is well known. It has been subjected to criticism, not least for its idealization of the public sphere. Whereas Habermas claimed that the public sphere was opened to all, it was accessible chiefly to those with the requisite financial resources and schooling. Nancy Fraser objects to his emphasis on the bourgeois sphere at the expense of "a host of competing counterpublics, including nationalist publics, popular peasant publics, elite women's publics and working class publics" (1990: 61). See also DeJean 1997.

an overlapping network of social practices belonging neither to the realm of government nor to the family, but somewhere in between. What is important about these elites in the latter part of the eighteenth century is the belief that national unity and a better future would be achieved in the realm of the imagination. As August Wilhelm Schlegel declared to his audience in Vienna in 1808, "the mental dominion of thought and poetry" was "inaccessible to worldly power" (1846: 5–6). The function of this national culture was not just to preserve authentic identities but to set the nation on its path toward the future. The goal of a national literature, his brother Friedrich Schlegel argued, was to record a "nation's intellectual capacity and progress" (1882: 9).[35] This faith in progress perhaps differentiates the nationalism of the nineteenth century from that of the twentieth. For we, as heirs to two centuries of nationalist secession, are not as sanguine of the future as the Schlegels.

THE PERILS OF COMPARISONS

Although recent nationalism is not propelled by a confident doctrine of progress, it is still motivated by the necessity of comparisons that "reveal" the belatedness of the society in question. The prominence given to culture in projects of nation building stems from the analogies people make between their own society and an aggressive neighbor or colonial power. In the German case, these evaluations exposed in the eyes of the elites the backwardness of Germany, a situation that compelled them to copy the achievements of France and England. Germany shows that the making of national culture has always involved the urgency of copying the powerful Other and the consequent attempt of overcoming this imitation.

When German intellectuals likened their own society to that of their neighbors, they discovered that Germany fell short in all respects—it lacked a state, an identity, a literature. In their opinion, the backwardness of the Germans imposed on them the inferior role of desiring the "greatness" of others. Fichte recognized the unfavorable situation of Germany. In the past, he insisted, the originality of the Germans had enabled them to influence other countries, as in the reformation of the church. Yet in more recent times Germany had lagged behind. "By means of this influ-

[35] One cannot exaggerate the personal ties binding these writers. A. W. Schlegel knew Schiller and Goethe, worked with his brother, Friedrich, in Jena, and collaborated with the poets Tieck and Novalis. In 1805 he met Madame de Staël, became a tutor to her children, introduced her to German culture, and assisted her in writing *De l'Allemagne*, which presented German thought and literature to France and England. Theirs must count as one of the most influential interpretive communities of modern Europe. On these networks of collaboration, see Collins 1987.

ence Germany once more made other countries its forerunners and its instigators to new creations" (1979: 99).

His concern over the belated nature of German society was shared by the writers of the Enlightenment. In his famous essay on drama, G. E. Lessing bemoaned the lack of a German stage. "We have actors," he wrote in his *Hamburg Dramaturgy* (1767), "but no mimetic art" ([1767] 1962:261). More glaring than a nonexistent stage was, of course, the want of a German nation. Sharing the Enlightenment belief in education as a way of changing reality, writers like Lessing faced a peculiar problem. If the purpose of literature was to transform society, how could it do this in the absence of German nationhood? A "national theater," he argued, would be unthinkable without its milieu, that is, an overarching German identity. Yet the latter proved impossible since the Germans were still following the examples of others. "We are still the sworn copyists of all that is foreign; especially are we still the obedient admirers of the never sufficiently admired French" (1962: 261).

Herder himself reacted to the felt backwardness of the Germans vis-à-vis the English and the French, wondering whether the German people were fated to be mere translators and imitators.[36] Imitation constituted the most grievous error in romantic thought for it meant that a nation could not be itself. The best German authors, he complained, were unknown in both home and school, and ridiculed in the courts. "Which of you, young people, knows Uz and Haller, Kleist and Klopstock, Lessing and Winckelmann as the Italians know and revere their Ariosto and Tasso, the British their Milton and Shakespeare, the French so many of their writers" (1877–99: 30:222). Herder's lament has been echoed by a host of writers: Georgios Theotokas in Greece, Herman Melville in the United States, Antonio Gramsci in Italy, Margaret Atwood in Canada. They have all voiced distress at the lack of a national literature and the necessity this imposed on the nation to search for foreign originals.[37]

To copy others is humiliating. Madame de Staël herself recognized this when she characterized eighteenth-century Germany as lacking originality. A literature "that develops later than that of neighboring nations is at

---

[36] There was a difference, however, between the two generations. Whereas Lessing and his contemporaries were striving for a national literature, Herder sought a fatherland. Enlightenment thinkers yearned for an educated, urbane public but the romantics expanded this public to embrace all Germans. Herder devoted himself to exploring the attributes and metaphysical meaning of the *Volk*. Each *Volk*, he wrote, "has its own national culture [*Bildung*] as well as its own language" (1887–99: 13:258).

[37] Even foreign commentators on Germany had brought attention to its belated nature. David Hume, for instance, noted that "the multitude of productions in the French language, dispersed all over Germany and the North, hinder these nations from cultivating their own language, and keep them still dependent on their neighbors" (1826: 154).

a real disadvantage; for the imitation of already existing literatures often takes the place of national genius" (1959: 243). In *De l'Allemagne* she concluded that "the delay in the progress"[38] of German writing imposed on the Germans the role of following "an already trodden path" (1956: 115). The lack of authenticity and the state of belatedness are connected in a knot of double estrangement which renders a nation foreign to itself but always reaching for the achievements of others.

Traditionally students of Germany, either of the present or the past, have interpreted the prominent place given to national culture in German thought as a response to the disconnectedness of German society. They have regarded the drive to fashion an all-encompassing identity as a reaction to the physical, linguistic, and ethnic fragmentation of the Germans, seeing an ecumenical culture as the needed plaster to hold the pieces together. Culture, as the creation and expression of all Germans, would unify segregated polities, transcend unsettling linguistic cleavages, and integrate dispersed peoples. Undoubtedly the notion of fragmentation was of profound concern to German intellectuals of the eighteenth century.

But it is wrong to regard this sense of fragmentation as the most important factor in explaining the enormous investment German intellectuals made in culture. This interpretation of German history ignores the tendency of Enlightenment authors to regard imperial federalism as a mode of political organization most suitable to the German soul. It also portrays culture as a derivative phenomenon, reacting to a social, physical, economic, and political reality. More important, however, it overlooks the comparisons Germans had been making between themselves and other nations out of which their society appeared inferior and backward. Although the depiction of Germany as a delayed nation may seem preposterous today, a look at the eighteenth century shows a country regarding itself as late in comparison to the cultural and political advances of both England and France. Rather than heralding hopeful beginnings, modernity represented for the Germans the epoch of their decline, that is, the decomposition of the Holy Roman Empire and their dependence on other countries for models of modernization. Moreover, the consolidation of the nation-state in the nineteenth century was felt by most Germans as

---

[38] It is instructive that she speaks of "progrès" with reference to culture rather than the more quantitative disciplines of science and technology. Earlier in her study, Staël affirmed the indispensability of literary advance for the promotion of political freedom. "The progress of literature, that is, the perfection of the art of thought and expression, is necessary for the establishment and maintenance of liberty" (1959: 30). In this she was faithful to the Enlightenment belief in the significance of education for social development. But her sentiments also manifest a faith—which had emerged in the Battle of the Books—that culture itself can progress.

having come rather late by at least one century in comparison to other European powers (Plessner 1959: 22, 70).[39]

I propose that culture was given a prominent place in the nationalist project because Germany, like other nations since, had been placed in an ideological tension between belatedness and progress. I am not reproducing here the *Sonderweg* reading of Germany. That is, I am arguing neither that backwardness determined German history nor that culture served as a compensatory agent for delayed modernization. Rather I am suggesting that intellectuals reacted to the condition of tardiness by accentuating the role of culture in modernization. Even though the rhetoric of these intellectuals was hyperbolic, exaggerating for their own class interests the extent of German imitation of others, they brought attention to the need for models. The Germans, like all nations perceiving themselves to be late-comers, self-consciously had to formulate what they felt was missing. Harold James argues that France, classical Greece, England, the Netherlands, and the United States all provided suitable ideals at various times. France offered blueprints for culture and, briefly, for political revolution. To England Germans looked for political and economic success. Greece provided an idealized image of the past and of community. The modern Greeks inspired liberal Germans as an ancient nation reasserting itself against foreign oppression. In the United States Germans saw a source of inspiration for national revival and a rational constitution (James 1989).

The search for foreign paradigms persisted in the nineteenth century. Imitation informed many of the formulations about the "nation." Germans, James contends, relentlessly sought the national images and ideals of other peoples "as a set of variegated and diverse building blocks from which German identity could be constructed, synthesized, or manufactured." Even though by then they could boast a distinguished cultural heritage, they needed a way of understanding that tradition as an alternative to French and British power. They sought, in short, "a model for national thought" (James 1989: 11). The predilection for cultural protocols was superseded by the quest of political and then economic plans for modernization.

At its core, nationalism constitutes an acknowledgment of and a reaction to the need to copy the institutions of hegemonic powers. Paradoxically this demonstrates that, despite its exterior ethnocentrism, nationalism is inherently a global discourse. For in conceding the necessity to borrow, it shows that nation building, like identity, is a synthetic process.

---

[39] While Plessner in his *Die Verspätete Nation* calls attention to the implications of belatedness on Germany, his argument often becomes metaphysical inasmuch as he sees developments in German history as compensations for internalized feelings of lack. See also Schulze 1991.

At the same time, the acceptance of models compels modernizers to iden- tify a realm, culture, in which the distinctive qualities and strengths of the nation are preserved. Some may dismiss the involvement of culture in modernization as insignificant, the flutter of a butterfly in comparison to the power of the machine, the efficiency of the factory, and the violence of the gun. Perhaps in these quantifiable measurements, culture is destined to lose always. But the effort to conceive of an integrated society is far from inconsequential. For the enterprise to imagine a nation was done not for art's sake but for establishing a political community.

NATIONAL INTELLECTUALS

The German example illustrates the extraordinary authority poets, writ- ers, teachers, and philosophers have had in nationalist enterprises. The place and function of intellectuals in society has a long tradition in philo- sophical discourse. As we reflect on their social significance today, it is useful to keep in mind that the history of nationalism over the past two hundred years demonstrates the capacity of intellectuals to have an im- pact outside their realm of expertise.

Intellectuals are prominent in the modernization of their societies be- cause they are often the first to encounter modernity abroad or through colonialism at home. They find, John H. Kautsky has pointed out in his analysis of postcolonial nationalism, that "in their old societies their newly acquired skills and knowledge [acquired in the West] are out of place" (1962: 46). More often than not they are shut out from positions of influence through prejudice or official policy. By promoting cultural, political, and economic reform they are not only advancing the ameliora- tion of the nation but also creating the public need for their own expertise. Modernization, in this sense, may be seen as a way for these elites to secure slots in the civil service, law, journalism, secondary and postsec- ondary education, and medicine.[40]

Intellectuals are themselves a product of modernity, as can be seen in a recent example of nationalism, that in East Timor. A colony of Portugal, East Timor was invaded by Indonesian troops in 1975, who subjected it to a brutal oppression. Between 1977 and 1979 one-third of the popula- tion had died as a result of massacres, famine, and epidemics. In the

---

[40] Coleridge recognized the importance of intellectuals in the building of nations. This national clerisy would be composed of "the sages and professors of the law and jurispru- dence . . . in short, all the so called liberal arts and sciences . . ." ([1832] 1972: 36). Cole- ridge connected the process of cultivation with the act of governance: "The proper *object* and the end of the National Church is civilization with freedom" (43).

1980s, however, the Suharto regime invested great sums into building infrastructure, including the setting up of schools and a university. Illiteracy was reduced from 90 percent in 1972 to 42 percent in 1990. This development, Benedict Anderson argues, resulted in the creation of a literate educated class of East Timorese who became fluent in Indonesian. Through this language they gained access to the Indonesian intelligentsia and press and through both to the outside world. As in other cases of nationalism, this class helped devise a nationalist discourse and a political program against Indonesian colonialism (1998: 134). Modernization went in tandem with the nationalization of culture as was the case in Indonesia itself whose own nationalism had emerged early in the twentieth century in response to Dutch colonialism.

Intellectuals are most prominent in the first phase of nationalism, which coincides with the effort to imagine the identity of the disparate groups residing within the state's boundaries. Experts in the realm of interpretation and representation, they politicize identity. When successful—and many such efforts are not—this identity is accepted by influential figures in politics, business, and religion, who consolidate and help transmit it and justify the need for independence. At this stage the nationalist movement becomes a mass phenomenon, attracting wide support from people who begin to portray themselves as a distinct national group seeking political autonomy. In later phases intellectuals, disappointed by the appropriation of their movement by politicians, often drop out of the cause.

In many cases, particularly in this century, when political autonomy was attained within one generation, intellectuals became the new political leaders as, for instance, Jawaharlal Nehru (1889–1964) of India, Habib Bourguiba (1903–2000) of Tunisia, Kwame Nkrumah (1909–72) of Ghana. In African anticolonial struggles, the Kenyan intellectual Ngugi Wa Thiong'o writes, the writer and the politician have often been the same person. For them the gun and the pen served the same purpose, the liberation of their countries from colonialism (1981: 73). A similar situation obtained in the United States. Intellectuals contributed to the establishment of the nation, combining scholarship with politics, as was the case of Benjamin Franklin.[41] The leaders *were* intellectuals: John Adams, John Dickinson, Benjamin Franklin, Alexander Hamilton, John Quincy Adams, Thomas Jefferson, James Madison, George Mason, James Wilson, and George Wythe (Hofstadter 1963: 145). The relationship between intellectuals and politics was not seen as problematical in the early history of the country, as has been the case ever since. It is ironic that, although the country was founded by intellectuals, for much of its history

---

[41] See Lipset 1963.

intellectuals have seen themselves and often celebrated their status as outsiders to politics.

The academic institutions of the former Soviet Union billeted future
revolutionaries, many of whom had come to power. The musicologist
Vitautas Landsbergis became president in Lithuania, the orientalist Levon
Ter-Petrossian in Armenia, and the literary critic Zviad Gamsakhurdia in
Georgia (and, of course, the playwright and poet Vaclav Havel in the
Czech Republic). Like countless other scholars in the Soviet Union, having
found intellectual asylum in academies and institutes, they conducted research on politics, religion, folklore, literature, ethnography, and theology
much in the manner of nationalists elsewhere. They may have withdrawn
from politics by necessity, but they appropriated culture, their realm of
expertise.[42]

Many who assumed political posts after Ceausescu's downfall in Romania, Katherine Verdery argues, were cultural figures (1991: 316). They
did not suddenly jump into prominence, however, for intellectuals had
been involved in politics in the past two centuries. To be an intellectual
meant to have a central role in defining the Romanian nation to itself and
the world. Until 1900 those who spoke for the nation did so largely in
opposition to the holders of power; the nation as a "sociosymbolic
construct" was produced in "counterdiscourse" to the exercise of rule
(21, 41).

Intellectuals themselves have become political leaders because, in nation building, culture and politics overlap. Indeed, their true role can be
appreciated only if nationalism is seen as an amalgam of culture and politics rather than as a strictly political movement. As the chief agents in the
politicization of culture, intellectuals delegate themselves as the creators
and interpreters of national identity. Even though they cannot alone bring
about a complex historical transformation as modernization, they are capable of making short-term plans, which in the long term may or may
not work. Specifically they take advantage of prevailing conditions that
call for their domain of expertise—ideas, knowledge, cultural models.
Above all, intellectuals begin the process of comparisons between their
own communities and those which they consider more advanced—the
European, the Western, the modern, the colonial. Comparisons, as I have
argued, often inaugurate the enterprise of nationalism.

This can be seen in the writings of Egyptian elites of the nineteenth
century. In the wake of Napoleon's invasion of Egypt in 1798, Charles

---

[42] In this intellectuals followed a tradition going back to the Russian Revolution when
artists and intellectuals joined, first, revolutionaries and, later, politicians to refashion society. Artists like Vladimir Mayakovsky (1893–1930) and Alexandre Rodchenko (1891–
1956) assumed roles as propagandists, rushing to celebrate the new order by writing political poetry, drawing revolutionary posters, and putting art in the service of the great cause.

Wendell writes, political elites came to recognize "European superiority in matters of material culture and scientific advancement." To be sure, the "*how* and *why* of Western superiority" would "exercise the leaders of Egyptian thought for a century to come" (1972: 116). Even though Egyptians regarded the West as an archenemy, particularly so after the British invasion in 1882, they saw it as a power to emulate. Of particular interest to political and cultural elites was the "world-triumphant national-state" and the political philosophy of nationalism it embodied (117). Typical is the following passage by the popular journalist Abd Allah Al-Nadim (1845–96), which echoes similar sentiments expressed by the Greek scholars a century earlier on Greece's relationship to Europe: "For now they [the Europeans] are the ones who are doing all the inventing and setting the rules." The "peoples of the East," he continued, had to copy European rules and methods "so as to compete with them on their own terms" (in Wendell 1972: 153). The aim of importing European practices and institutions was to create a more powerful Egypt, which could in turn resist Western hegemony. Although the mold was European, the content was to be Egyptian. Their ultimate purpose was to build an Egyptian state fortified by nationalism.

At the very heart of nationalist thought is the recognition among elites that their neighbors or the colonizing power is technically more advanced than their own society. The effect of this comparison becomes clear in the work of José Rizal, a central figure of Filipino nationhood. A poet, novelist, essayist, doctor, and revolutionary, he was born in 1861 and executed in 1896 by the Spanish on charges of sedition. As a young man, Rizal had the best available education in the colony, studied in Spain, and traveled throughout Europe. His novel, *Noli me Tangere*, exemplifies the global aspect of nationalism, having been written in Spanish, the then colonial language of the Philippines, and published in Berlin in 1887.[43] So does Rizal's life. Cosmopolitan yet a fervent nationalist, Rizal is revered as the first Filipino and even the first Asian nationalist.[44] For, as Guerrero notes in the preface to his translation, the novel was published at a time when "Filipinos were only beginning to think of themselves as Filipinos, rather than as members of various tribes scattered among 7,000 islands" (Rizal 1961: ix).

In his travels Rizal came to discover the "backwardness" of his home as well as of Spain itself in relationship to the "centers of progress." In-

---

[43] It was translated into English, the second imperial language of the nation, as *The Lost Eden* in 1961 by another Filipino nationalist, León Ma. Guerrero. See Rizal 1961.

[44] In 1896 the Philippines became the first Asian nation to rebel against a European colonial power. It declared its independence in 1898 only to have it crushed a year later by the United States, which ruled the Philippines until 1946. On the period of American rule, see Stanley 1974 and Wurfel 1988.

deed his generation, a product of the economic expansion in the nineteenth century, represented the first class of Filipinos to travel abroad and send their children to Europe to study. The recognition of the belatedness of their own society and of the imperial power enabled him to undertake a critique of both. Moreover, he encountered what he called "the specter of comparisons," by which he meant that he could not visit Berlin without thinking of Manila and vice versa (Anderson 1998: 229). This process, E. San Juan observes, continues to this very day, for Filipino writers still read Western authors, "but they write their hermeneutic responses with an Eastern signature" (1992a: 11). The history of nationalism shows that intellectuals cannot experience Berlin without Paris, Istanbul without Munich, Toronto without New York, Skopje without Thessaloniki, São Paulo without Lisbon and the other way around.

Although I have been concentrating here on comparisons made by nationalists between their societies and those they consider more advanced, it goes without saying that theirs is not the only society that under-goes change. Nor are they the only ones drawing connections between, say, Lagos and London. The centralized state or colonial power is itself transformed through this encounter. For at the very least it has defined itself against rebellious minorities at home or colonized peoples abroad. More often than not, it has tried to crush such revolutions. Thus change goes both ways. Franco Venturi, for instance, has demonstrated that the numerous rebellions taking place on the periphery of Europe at the latter part of the eighteenth century had an impact on the destruction of the ancient regime in central Europe. Postcolonial studies have shown that colonialism has had as much effect on the colonizers as on the colonized.

Filipino intellectuals who went overseas discovered that they were not inferior to Spaniards (as they had been taught) and that the Hispanic society at home and even in Spain itself were provincial (Corpuz 1965: 61; Stanley 1974: 47). During their stay in the 1880s in Spain, France, Britain, Germany, and Hong Kong, they formulated a discourse of nationalism that criticized the injustices of Spanish civil and clerical authority. Initially they sought to modernize their society through reforms, but when these reforms were thwarted, they fought for outright independence. Their nationalism was a product of the conflict between an exploitative colonial regime and the aspirations of a new creole society—creole both as a mélange of ethnic and racial groups and as a syncretic product of native and Spanish Catholic features. Out of this conflict the slowly coalescing Filipino self-consciousness was politicized. As Emilio Aguinaldo declared in 1898: Let "our innocent blood, and the countless tyrannical acts of our enemy, serve from now on as the insurmountable barrier between Spain and the Philippines" (Agoncillo 1975: 93). The drive to define the distinguishing characteristics of Filipinos was motivated both by the need to preserve indigenous identities from Spanish influences and by the necessity to unite against the oppression of an imperial power. This is what makes nationalism into an interplay between the political and the cultural. Insurgent nationalism defines itself against the overwhelming strength of the foreign, be that Russia in the case of Finland or Spain in the case of the Philippines. For ultimately nationalism is built upon a difference from a hegemonic power. And this difference is always seen in cultural terms, that is, the "traditional" way of life. To protect this domain, however, the local has to borrow from the foreign while it resists it.

We see this in a passage from Rizal's *Noli me Tangere*. A young Filipino named Ibarra, who had just returned from Spain, passed by the Botanical Garden in Manila and began thinking of other such gardens in Europe. Then he began to reminisce the things he had learned from an old Filipino priest, ideas that had guided Ibarra during his time in the "rich" countries of Europe. Particularly memorable is the advice the priest had given the young man before his departure abroad: "They [the Europeans] come here seeking gold; go you to their countries in search of the treasures we lack" (1961: 46).[45] This passage, John N. Schumacher writes, sums up the position of the nationalist discourse of Rizal and *La Liga Filipina*, which was founded in 1892 and which aimed at the unification of the whole archipelago into one nation-state. Namely, nationalists should "cherish the values, ideals, and accomplishments of the Filipino people, while learning from Europe the tools and values of the modern world" (Schumacher 1981: 39). Rather than being passive admirers of modernity, they should oppose it in one domain while borrowing from it in another.

In his classic study of Nigerian nationalism, James S. Coleman demonstrates that Nigerian nationalists had recognized they had to appropriate Western know-how while at the same time fighting for independence from Britain. As in other cases of anticolonial nationalism, the leaders and most active supporters of the nationalist cause came from the ranks of those strongly affected by colonialism: the Western-educated, English-speaking elites who for the most part were excluded from the administrative, technical, and juridical branches of the senior British civil service (Coleman 1971: 141, 154). The policy of white supremacy of the colonial administration and the racism of the Europeans promoted, particularly among the educated Nigerians, an experience of shared problems and the consequent

---

[45] It should be noted that the fictitious priest had been executed by the Spanish authorities in a place where three actual priests had been killed in 1872. In the final years of imperial rule Spain had resorted to a reign of terror against the nationalist movement (Agoncillo 1975: 90).

desire to unite against this oppression. But it was in their studies abroad, especially in Britain and the United States, that they too came to undertake a process of comparisons. For they discovered, Coleman argues, that contrary to the teachings and practices of colonialism, what separated Africans from whites was only technical expertise (247).

In other words, nationalists recognized that their belatedness was technological. Bitter at racial discrimination and political repression, they at the same time were firm believers in progress and the power of technology. Their drive to win independence from Britain was launched to end colonialism and control their own destiny. Removal of inequalities was not enough, because they felt that Nigerians had "a natural right to rule their country" (Coleman 1971: 316). But this drive was cultural as much as political. For nationalists had to answer what this country—made of various ethnic, religious, and linguistic peoples who had never imagined themselves as belonging to one political entity—actually was. This was a particularly challenging process, inasmuch as the land mass of Nigeria encompassed a number of autonomous states and ethnic and religious groups that had been united administratively only by colonialism (Nwankwo 1985: 5).[46] Although there was no clearly defined national entity of Nigeria at the time of independence in the 1960s, the effort to imagine the qualities of a national consciousness had started decades earlier. In short, the acknowledgment of Western material superiority went in tandem with the project to awaken respect for African traditions and to foster a collective national consciousness.

Such an orientation toward modernity is shared by all anticolonial struggles. As Chatterjee has shown, anticolonial nationalists divide the world into two domains, the material and the spiritual, granting the West preeminence in the first while maintaining local sovereignty over the second.[47] That is to say, whereas they acknowledge the need to replicate Western progress, they feel an even more urgent necessity to preserve the uniqueness of their society (Chatterjee 1993). Filipino nationalists, for instance, sought to define the distinctive features of a Filipino identity, which they believed was being destroyed by Spanish colonialism. The revolts were intended not only to end the humiliation and agony of colonialism but also to preserve the enclave of indigenous culture upon which they

[46] M. Adebayo Belo reminds us that there is "not a single African country that came out of colonialism whose diverse peoples have ever been under a central control before colonialism" (1996: 29).

[47] The conception of culture, however, as a bastion of indigenous lifeways is hardly the exclusive feature of anticolonial nationalism, as my examples from Scandinavia and central Europe have shown.

planned to construct a state. This bulwark, of course, included language, myths, history, traditions, the arts, and way of life.[48]

The process of comparisons launched by nationalists takes place in a context of belatedness. They fashion a discourse that both makes sense of an oppressive situation and devises programs to overcome this. We see this very clearly in the appearance of the discourse of Hebraism among European Jews. Although not a nationalism per se, Hebraism appeared as a discourse among Jewish intellectuals in Enlightenment Europe who found ghetto Jewry "backward." As John Murray Cuddihy argues, Jewish intellectuals were among the first to promote the entry of Jews into bourgeois society. At the early stage the project was cultural: intellectuals had to prove that Jews were *Salonsfähig, Gesellschaftsfähig*, and *Romansfähig*—that is, capable of entry into the salon and society and of the reading and writing of novels. They constructed Hebraism to make sense of their perceived belatedness and of the "culture shock" brought about by the confrontation with modernity. "Hebraism is the tactic of admitting one's inferiority in terms of power in order to claim moral superiority in terms of indigenous spirituality and simplicity. It is a standing temptation for the modernizing intellectual" (1974: 171). By emphasizing the eminent place of the Hebrew Bible in the Western tradition, these intellectuals could celebrate their ancient ancestors as the source of that tradition while also surveying a territory of Jewish uniqueness within European society.[49]

The mapping of this distinctive cultural space should not be seen as the response of the defeated, the weak, or the envious to delayed modernization. Rather it constitutes the attempt by elites to participate in modernity while safeguarding their traditions. It is, in fact, the classic strategy of nationalists, be it the Germans vis-à-vis the French, the Indians and Irish vis-à-vis the British, and racial minorities vis-à-vis Euro-Americans in the United States. In their situation we see a double-headed reaction—the tendency to admire and denounce the West. Since the earliest contact with modernity, Daryush Shayegan explains, the Islamic world has revered the West while condemning it (1992: 89). But in order to make sense of this copying, these societies come to see their identities as stronger than guns; not because these identities represent ersatz weapons but because they

---

[48] Like many colonies, the Philippines emerged as a nation-state without a common language. When the first republic was declared, it had necessarily to use Spanish as the official means of communication. The effort to declare Tagalog as the national tongue was complicated with the imposition of English by the American administration. The constitution of 1943 ratified Tagalog as the national language of the country (Gonzalez 1980: 60).

[49] Toward the end of the nineteenth century some Jewish intellectuals, disenchanted with the pace and costs of emancipation and alarmed at the continuing presence of anti-Semitism, embraced the national idea. They played a chief role in the project to found a nation-state. See Keren 1989.

enable a form of resistance outside the realm of politics. Postcolonial intellectuals make the following case: " 'We have high spiritual qualities despite our poverty, but you are soulless materialists' " (Matossian 1962: 256–57).

Nationalists often display an ambivalent attitude toward modernity that is both xenophobic and xenolatric. On the one hand, they have to borrow Western expertise and become modern; on the other, they wish to preserve their distinct way of life. The very act of copying necessitates the disavowal of the model's supremacy and the consequent elevation of the borrower's spiritual goodness and depth. In this process nationalists do not simply consume the fruits of modernity in the way poets were once thought to borrow from their precursors. Rather they are creators of a new type of identity, a nationalized culture. Belatedness, Harold Bloom has argued in the context of poetry, can be an advantage.[50] The recognition of their tardiness, he insists, motivates strong poets to conceive new types of writing. Backwardness may necessitate the copying of models; but in this process originals are born. The comparisons made by intellectuals between their own societies and the West are similarly productive.

No better example of this can be offered than the struggles against Spanish colonialism in South America. D. A. Brading has shown in his exhaustive study of "creole patriotism" among the Spanish colonies that this nationalism emerged in response to economic and political exploitation of the territories and the denigration of creole society by Spanish authorities. Yet, no matter how much these colonies depended on Europe in general and Spain specifically for their technology and high culture, they created a separate identity, a synthesis of the native and conquering cultures (1991: 5). The necessity to import European products and know-how went in tandem with the invention of indigenous forms of identification. What, in fact, became the national identity of each state resulted from the synthetic mediation between the self and the other, hardly, as the detractors of nationalism would have us believe, an introverted and indulgent exercise of parochialism. Moreover, rather than being an aesthetic enterprise—a case say, of *la culture pour la culture*—this identity was implicated in the fight for an independent state. Nationalism is nothing other than a syncretic and cosmopolitan process by which a group differentiates itself from other groups and builds a republic on the basis of this difference.

[50] Taking as his inspiration Bate's work on the burden of the past, Bloom conceives a whole, albeit baroque, theory on the poetic significance of being late, when a poet confronts the "embarrassments of a tradition grown too wealthy to need anything more" (1973: 21).

Chapter Four

PROGRESS AND BELATEDNESS

NATIONALISM emerges out of comparisons people make regarding the relative standing of nations. What David Hume referred to as the "situation of the nation with regard to its neighbors" (1898: 244) becomes a vital source of national culture. Nations differ in the extent of their development and devise strategies to narrow the gap between themselves and their neighbors or colonizers. In modernity, relationships drawn among nations inevitably reveal that most are technologically, culturally, and politically belated with regard to early modernizers. Those considering themselves or seen by others as backward have no choice but to try to search for models to copy. They turn to national culture as a means of catching up.

From one point of view, intergroup comparisons have always been made. Homer, for instance, often refers to a more perfect time when men were stronger than those of his day. He mourned contemporaneous society as a decline from that golden age. In book 1 of the *Iliad* Nestor spoke to the Achaeans about the valor of an older generation of fighters:

> Never yet have I seen nor shall see again such men as they were, men like Peirithoös, and Dryas, shepherd of the people, or Theseus, Aigeus's son, in the likeness of the immortals. These were the strongest generation of earth-born mortals, the strongest, and they fought against the strongest, the beast men living within the mountains, and terribly they destroyed them. (1.262–68; trans. Lattimore)

Roman poets believed that Greek art and literature were superior to their own. In Epistle II Horace confessed that, while Rome may have conquered Greece militarily, Greece vanquished Rome culturally and "introduced the arts to rustic Latium."[1] In the beginning of the *Satyricon* Petronius (d. A.D. 66) denounced the state of decadence in the arts and rhetoric. "Once standards drop, eloquence loses vigor and voice. Who since then has attained the stature of Thucydides or the reputation of Hyperides? Why, not even poetry has shown a spark of life" (1965: 29).

To confront the excellence of one's neighbors or of one's precursors is a humbling experience, undermining one's self-confidence. This is particu-

---

[1] "Graecia capta ferum victorem cepit et artis intulit agresti Latio" (Horace 1929: Epistle II, 155–56).

larly true in the modern age when one stands on a hill of illustrious traditions. A pressing problem of the moderns, W. J. Bate has written, is the rich and intimidating legacy of the past. Although he examined English poetry specifically, Bate concluded that in the past three centuries one of the most anxiety-ridden questions for artists generally has been, "What is there left to do?" (1971: 3). This question became particularly unsettling in the early eighteenth century when the notion of originality entered critical discourse as an absolute artistic ideal.

Modernity, however, has had to encounter another dreadful obstacle, one not considered by Bate, which has to do with the sudden discovery that some of our contemporaries are already ahead of us in a race of perpetual change. The achievement of our peers, rather than of our precursors, is most threatening because it seems that they have beaten us in a contest of social, technological, and political improvement. What intimidates the moderns is not the legacy of the ancients but the possibility of remaining ancient. This issue becomes even more intense when a nation has been colonized by a technologically more advanced state. To the old concern, "Why are the French better and stronger than us?" modernity adds a more alarming one, "Why are we so behind?" The second question differs from the first in presuming a linear conception of time and, above all, the idea of progress.

The concept of progress differentiates modern from previous conceptions of time. Indeed, the very possibility of unending advance into a perfectible future would have been unthinkable, say, in classical Greece when time was conceived as an endless succession of events or as a series of reiterations between rise and fall.[2] People often point to the moving choral ode in Sophocles' *Antigone* as evidence of progress in antiquity. A paean to human skill and ingenuity, the ode begins loftily with the words *Polla ta deina*: "Many are the wonders but none is as wonderful as man." It then recounts the great achievements of humanity in transportation, agriculture, and politics (1994: 331–75). Christian Meier points out, however, that Sophocles praises "man's awesome nature" rather than his progress (1990: 199–200). There is no expectation of future improvements.

Although Greeks expressed a profound faith in human ability, they did not incorporate it into a general theory of historical transformation. They believed that human beings, as opposed to the gods, were masters of their world, that they invented language, domesticated animals, tamed the seas,

---

[2] Aristotle gave expression to this when discussing political change in the *Politics* (V 1316a 1). Referring to Plato's treatment of this topic in the *Republic*, he wrote that "all things change in a certain cycle." A political revolution could not lead to great social transformation because it took place within cycles. For this reason tyranny could lead into another tyranny, or an oligarchy, democracy, or aristocracy (1984: 2089). Political change involved a return to a previous stage rather than a new phase of human development.

and began to write. But they did not connect human ingenuity to a theory of unending social progression. Thus, democracy was not the highest step in the ladder of ever loftier political evolution. Clearly a basic difference between the modern and ancient perspective on time is the belief in change. While for the Greeks change was confined to certain realms, for moderns it is all-pervasive and normal. Not only is everything subject to modification but we expect from this process unlimited amelioration. We resort to change for solutions to social problems and to history's grand disappointments. After Christianity, restitution for human suffering can be located in the future.[3]

Above all, time in modernity is unique. Like the river's waters streaming through one's fingers, it comes by only once. Having no finitude, it is conceived as being of an irreversible succession of events.[4] The theory of progress presumes a connection between the stride of time and the possibility of social improvement. It interprets humanity as irrevocably proceeding ahead (Bury 1932: 5).

This relatively new view of history was itself a product of the great Battle of the Books between the Ancients and the Moderns.[5] Having been first declared in France between the years 1687 and 1715 and then in England, the Quarrel, as it was known in France, became a decisive conflict in Western history. At this time, Foucault observes, the question of modernity was first self-consciously posed: "It had been formulated either in terms of an authority to be accepted or rejected (what authority should be accepted? what model followed? etc.), or else in the comparative evaluation: are the Ancients superior to the Moderns?" (1986: 90).[6] The notion of progress came about in part out of the audacity of the Moderns to question the priority of the Ancients. Although the Quarrel sought to change the course of the future, it really was fought over the authority enjoyed by classical antiquity.

If a burning question today has to do with the fate of literature and culture in postmodernity, it is useful to keep in mind that questions over

---

[3] On Christianity and time, see Gurevich 1985.

[4] In modernity time and space become compressed by technologies that enable people to cruise at great speeds and messages to traverse enormous distances instantly. On this, see Harvey 1985. Georg Simmel argued a hundred years ago in his *The Philosophy of Money* ([1900] 1978) that money has the capacity to connect people located in various parts of the world.

[5] The metaphor of the battle comes from Jonathan Swift's (1667–1745) satire against the moderns in *A Tale of a Tub* (1704] 1972).

[6] I capitalize Ancients and Moderns here when referring specifically to the combatants in the Battle of the Books, but use lowercase when alluding to ancients or moderns generally. On the Battle of the Books, see Jones 1961), Levine 1991. DeJean (1997) makes fascinating comparisons between this battle of the books and the culture wars in our own fin de siècle.

modernity itself were posed and fought over in the arena of literature.[7] It was in "poetry, that the quarrel was most acrimonious, and that the interest of the public was most keenly aroused" (Bury 1932: 78). When the Ancients and Moderns took arms, Joan DeJean notes, they fought over the issue of "human perfectibility exclusively on literary grounds" (1997: 16). The Battle of the Books is illustrative of a case when issues of great social import, such as the theory of progress, were posed in the realm of culture.

In questioning the irreproachability of ancient wisdom, the Moderns began to doubt the prevalent assumption that change leads to corruption and that human history is a descent from a golden age. They thus rejected the idea that humanity was inherently corrupt. If human nature were actually the same, their thinking went, then the Moderns were capable of deeds equal or superior to the Ancients. This insight eventually allowed historicists from Herder to poststructuralists to argue for the incomensurability of cultures.

One of the triumphs of the Battle of the Books was that it allowed the French to claim supremacy in cultural matters. Because culture was considered a leading agent in the improvement of humanity, the French, as the possessors of cultural prestige, could claim that they were further ahead than anyone else. The theory of progress, in other words, had become implicated in the way societies were compared with one another and in the position they occupied in a hierarchy of distinction. Having felt itself behind economic and political development in England and Holland in the seventeenth and eighteenth centuries, France could claim that it was the most civilized country of all. This development was crucial to the subsequent project of nation building and the process of comparison it entailed. The French strategy would be used by other countries in Europe, as we have seen, and by Europe's colonies to differentiate between the material and cultural realms in their nationalist struggles.

Being Late

It had been necessary for these countries to make these distinctions because western Europe had achieved economic, industrial, and political dominance in the seventeenth and eighteenth centuries, even with regard to other European societies. The fact that England, Holland, and France modernized first gave them an exceptional advantage, economically, mili-

---

[7] The most notorious of these battles was thus fought over Homer, specifically over such issues as his description of the shield of Achilles in the *Iliad*.

tarily, and, of course, psychologically.[8] "The economic and political 'breakthrough,' " writes Reinhard Bendix, "which occurred in England and France at the end of the eighteenth century, put every other country of the world in a position of 'backwardness.' " Ever since these transformations "the world has been divided into advanced and follower societies" (1988: 301). The cleavages separating societies became even wider when Europeans began to ransack the planet in search of markets, natural resources, finished goods, land, cultural treasures, and slaves. As the gap between western Europe and other societies kept expanding, it was becoming necessary for the rest to catch up. Modernity became a daunting reality, imposed on other societies through economic or military conquest. Those feeling themselves left behind had now little choice but to copy Western technological and political achievements, which itself necessitated the strengthening of culture. This was the great task facing all modernizers from the Greeks in the late eighteenth century to the Nigerians in the first half of the twentieth century.

What enabled the conceptual separation between advanced and belated societies was not just the political and economic innovations themselves but the very notion of progress. Certain societies could be characterized as pioneering and others as backward only when time was understood as moving linearly forward. The ideology of ongoing development placed a premium on being modern, equating power and well-being with ever-changing technical sophistication. No other epoch had so sacralized novelty, self-propelling change, and time itself.

A major characteristic of the modern age has been its apotheosis of time as opposed to space, of becoming rather than being.[9] Modern Greeks, for instance, sought the trappings of modernity less because they believed themselves abandoned on the topographical extremities of civilization than because they felt they were lagging behind western Europe. National integration was driven by fear of backwardness rather than geographical remoteness. The privileging of time is expressed in the portrayal of modernization as a transition from traditional to modern forms or as a violent revolution by which a society, having shed its old features, becomes a technologically advanced nation.[10] Revolution is change contracted in a single event, the realization of progress through a spasmodic burst of

---

[8] On how western Europe attained this technological preeminence see Abu-Lughod 1989, Braudel [1946] 1973, Hodgson 1993, Wallerstein 1974, 1979.

[9] Even utopia, originally considered a spatial ideal (i.e., a topos), was given temporal form in modernity. The modern longs more for a lost time than a place (Lowe 1982: 40).

[10] Interestingly, literary criticism first spread the idea of revolution through Europe as it employed the word to describe changes in fortune of a character. "Revolution in this sense implied a capacity for novelty and an openness to change that were often seen as the root of the modern Enlightenment" (S. Smith 1990: 222).

energy. Revolution, as Foucault reminds us, "is the guarantee for future history of the continuity of progress" (1986: 95).

The social theory of the nineteenth century, particularly that generated after 1880, subordinated space to time, making the dynamics of modernity almost exclusively temporal (Soja 1989: 31). One need only point to how Marxism has interpreted human history as the evolution from a feudal to a capitalist economy to understand how history has been portrayed as an eschatological procession. The work of Weber and Durkheim shows the great importance given to time in the representation of modernity. They and other thinkers "prioritize time and history over space and geography, and where they treat the latter at all, tend to view them unproblematically as the stable context or site for historical action" (Harvey 1985: 141–43).

Although temporality has been the dominant determinant in modernization, it is not true, as Soja and Harvey claim, that geography was banished from the conceptual landscape. On the contrary, it had become embodied in the very tensions of nationalism.[11] While people advocate the doctrine of progress, they also fear that the infinite ascent upward could sever their links to the past. As they gaze at an unknown future, their knees buckle. Nationalism provides reassurance with promises that their traditions will be safeguarded.

Although territory was ignored by the grand theorists of modernity, it was always there under their shoes, causing great social tremors. Indeed, their rejection of the situational dimension of history was related to their repudiation of nationalism. By seeing nationalism as an atavistic feature of humanity to be abandoned in evolution, these theorists in effect disregarded the significance of land.[12] For, as both discourse and political movement, nationalism is motivated to a large extent by concerns over space—concerns, however, that are related to the need to modernize. The importance given to territory by nationalism goes hand in hand with the emphasis on temporal relationships. In the competitive modern world, where cultures are threatened by extinction, where the challenge is to move forward with quantum speed, territory provides a sense of constancy. People can look into the eye of time-to-come without flinching because they stand on familiar soil.

---

[11] Noteworthy in this endeavor is Frederick Turner's frontier thesis, a form of geographical determinism that contends that the evolution of American political institutions was dependent on the expansion westward. One of the aims of Turner, himself a midwesterner, was to highlight the significance of the frontier in American history vis-à-vis the East Coast (1962).

[12] Marxism particularly, as John Ehrenreich argues, has failed to incorporate the reality of nationalism in its theoretical understanding of the world (1983: 1).

CATCHING UP

If people experience modernization as a process of catching up, goaded by the angst of lagging behind in a technological marathon, it would be instructive to look at how social change was conceived before the doctrine of progress and in societies outside Western Christendom. An illuminating example is the mission begun in 863 by the Byzantine monks Cyril and Methodius (d. 869 and 884) to convert the Slavic peoples to Christianity. As the Slavs came into contact with the Byzantine Empire they confronted a powerful Christian empire. But the Slavs' late entry into Christianity, Dimitry Obolensky affirms, was not taken by them as a sign of their inferiority. They interpreted it, rather, according to Christ's parable of the man who hired laborers for his vineyard (Matthew 20. 1–16). A man found a group of laborers whom he had sent to the vineyard, having agreed to pay them a denarius (a day's wage). After going to the market place in the third hour, he found more laborers and sent them too to the vineyard. He did this until the eleventh hour, promising to pay them also a denarius. "And when evening came, the owner of the vineyard said to his steward, 'Call the laborers and pay them their wages, beginning with the last, up to the first.' "

Just like the laborers of the eleventh hour, who got the same wages as those hired first, Bulgarians and Russians believed that they received the same blessings from Christ. Although "latecomers" to Christianity, they were still Christians (Obolensky 1972: 8–9). As Christ said to his disciples, when it came time to enter the kingdom of heaven "many that are first will be last, and the last first"—a message in contrast with the principles of progress, which award all to the winner of the meet.

That the Slavic peoples sought to append their stories to a more prestigious narrative (Byzantine Orthodoxy) is not surprising. This pattern has happened countless times in history. What is significant in the Slavs' reaction to Byzantium is that they had neither internalized belatedness as a substantial problem nor made it an issue differentiating the pagan latecomers from the established Christians. Their encounter with Christianity was not cast in the same evolutionary terms as it was for another Balkan people, modern Greeks who, in the face of a technologically advanced Europe, felt themselves both subordinate and backward.

The attitude of eighteenth-century Greek modernizers toward the West differs also from that of Patriarch Cyril Loukaris (1572–1638). Like them, Loukaris was cognizant of the West's military superiority. But he never advocated that the Orthodox East copy the Latins. Indeed, he believed that the East's weakness had come as a punishment for its attempt to reach a union with Rome.[13] Defiantly Loukaris asked the Latins to remember two things:

> First, when wisdom reigned in Greece in earlier times, the Greeks held the Latins for barbarians; now it is not unusual that we have become barbarians and they civilized. It is poverty and the lack of empire that have brought this out. . . . Second, let them consider that, although we have no external wisdom, we do by the grace of Christ possess an internal, spiritual wisdom which adorns our Orthodox faith. In this we are superior to the Latins. . . . If the Turk had come to power in the West, there wouldn't have been any Christians left after ten years; even after three hundred years [of Ottoman rule] people in Greece continue to struggle and suffer for their faith; . . . And you tell me that that we have no wisdom? I don't want your wisdom in place of Christ's cross. (Papadopoulos 1939: 56–57)

This remarkable passage has many points of interest. It reveals, for instance, Loukaris's sense of the continuity of Greek civilization, believing the classical Greeks to be ancestors of today's Hellenes. What is most relevant for my examination here is the comparison Patriarch Loukaris was compelled to make between the weak Orthodox East and strong Catholic West. Although Loukaris acknowledged the West's strength and political autonomy, nowhere did he speak, as would the intellectuals of the eighteenth century, of Western progress, which had left Greece behind in the dark ages. Undoubtedly, he referred to qualitative differences between the two Christian worlds, such as the lack of learning in the Ottoman Empire. But once the Greeks were in possession of an empire again, he believed, they would eventually regain it. He explained their current situation as God's punishment rather than as a structural flaw in Greek society or a function of delayed modernization.

Patriarch Loukaris had no anxiety about the Greeks' backwardness for two reasons. The Catholic West represented in his eyes an inimical Christian society rather than a new economic and political order, as was true for later Greek modernizers. Moreover, his point of view was untouched by the theory of progress and its division of the world into advanced and backward nations. Rather than advocating the reproduction of Western models, he insisted on Orthodoxy's opposition to Catholicism, surely one

---

[13] In a desperate attempt to save the empire, Emperor John VIII (reigned 1425–48) and Patriarch Joseph II (1416–39) gave in, during the Council of Florence (1438–39), to most papal demands on doctrinal difference in exchange for military aid. But the agreement proved unacceptable to most clergy. Many Orthodox, including the Russians, viewed the fall of Constantinople as punishment for the signing of the union with Rome in 1439 (Tachios 1989: 293). C. M. Woodhouse argues that the Byzantines had become aware by this time of the West's superiority in arts and scholarship (1986: 154).

of the great repudiations of history.[14] Braudel rightly sees in the Orthodox renunciation of Catholicism a "dramatic refusal," as "deliberate and categorical" as the rejection of the Reformation by Catholicism ([1946] 1973: 768–69).

GREECE: POSTCOLONIAL NARRATIVES

Such a repudiation was not the case with those Greeks who came into contact with Western modernity in European cities of the eighteenth century. Having recognized the Western advances in science and learning, they were alarmed by the expanding technological rift between themselves and western Europeans. Yet, no longer wishing to maintain the walls against the West, they sought to transform their society according to Western prototypes. In their eyes, the nation-state and global capitalism were realities Greeks could no longer ignore. They advocated thus a program by which Greeks would rebel against Ottoman authority and establish an independent republic.

This project of modernization highlights two characteristics shared with other such enterprises. First, it was brought about by the discovery of a technologically and politically advanced West. Second, it put an emphasis on cultural models. I argue in the previous chapter that nationalism appeared in central Europe and Scandinavia partly in response to Napoleon's campaign to dominate the continent. Nationalism was an effort to protect the autochthonous identities from the newly acquired capacity of the centralized, aggressive state to affect them. National culture—the domain of identities, religion, language, traditions, and the arts—served as a space that protected valuable symbols from the aggressors' guns. It was regarded as a ground upon which to erect an independent republic.

Greece differs from these examples as well as from postcolonial nations insofar as the Greeks rebelled against an empire that was neither Western nor capitalist. It is also useful to keep in mind that the Ottoman Empire did not isolate the private identities of the subject peoples for control or indoctrination. Indeed, Greeks, like other religious groups, actually enjoyed a degree of cultural and civil autonomy. They sought freedom in, rather than from, Europe. Moreover, Greek intellectuals, poets, and merchants thought of themselves as culturally superior to their imperial

---

[14] Orthodox suspicions of the West go back to the official schism between the two churches in 1054, a break whose source lay a century earlier. They were reinforced in the violent sack of Constantinople by the Crusaders in 1204 and reached their peak when the Byzantines realized that their coreligionists would not help them ward off the Turks. Some Byzantines, resentful of Western aggression and the pope's imperial claims, actually preferred Ottoman to Catholic rule. See Runciman 1968 and Ware 1963.

masters. Having defined themselves as Europeans and having accepted the latter's Orientalism, they subjected the empire to this discourse, even though they too had been objects of Orientalism.[15] The Greeks thus provide an example of a people striving to become Western and European.

In this they resemble the Jews seeking emancipation within European society. Through the discourse of Hellenism, Greek intellectuals represented Greeks as the heirs of classical antiquity, the first European civilization. They pleaded for acceptance of their communities in the West by tracing a direct relationship between their own modern nation and European culture, taking advantage of the prominent position Hellenism enjoyed in the West. But Greeks did not wish to disappear within Europe. On the contrary, Greek intellectuals politicized culture in order to maintain the Hellenic difference in the new capitalist system of states.

It is important to emphasize that these developments—the recognition of economic, technological, and political belatedness, on the one hand, and the activation of culture, on the other—were intertwined. Thus when I argue that cultural models predominate in cases of purposeful modernization I am not claiming that the nationalization of culture is a function of uneven development, as proposed, say, by Alexander Gerschenkron. Although not specifically dealing with nationalism, in his *Economic Backwardness in Historical Perspective*, (1962) Gerschenkron examined the effect of "economic backwardness" on the formation of civil society, arguing that the more a society feels itself backward the more it tries to promote modernization by centralized planning. This thesis and the modernization theories of the 1960s distinguished between the organic development of western European countries and the inorganic modernization of the rest. Moreover, these theories incorporated a utopian image of Western development, conceiving modernization as an idealized process of social change which never took place even in England and France. At the same time, they posited postcolonial nations as static entities whose official life began with their initial Western contact. These theorists, therefore, disregarded the past of these societies as irrelevant for the future as they also ignored cultural questions in general.

When I argue that the nationalization of culture is related to the perception by intellectuals of their society as belated, I am not claiming that economic conditions of backwardness somehow lead to the emergence of nationalism. This interpretation of reality would be vulgar and empirically false. If anything, the presence of development, rather than its lack,

[15] Questions of postcolonialism are rarely posed by historians of the Ottoman Empire. Yet they would help us understand the complexity of postcolonial struggle. How was the domination of the Bulgarians, Kurds, or Armenians different from that of the Irish, the Algerians, or the Aztecs? See Jusdanis 1998, 1999.

promotes nationalism. The most economically advanced areas are the ones to generate nationalist fervor. In Europe's colonies, it has always been the educated strata that initially supported the struggle against colonial oppression. This is also evident in Europe itself, as the Greek case, one of the earliest examples of modernization, shows. There are many other examples. Bohemia, the center of Czech nationalism in the nineteenth century, was the most highly developed area in the Habsburg Empire. Belgium was one of the most advanced areas of the continent when it separated from the Netherlands in the 1830s (Orridge 1981: 181–82). Catalonia and the Basque country are the most developed parts of Spain. The rise of Quebecois nationalism coincided with the economic development of the province.

In short, culture does not abruptly become nationalized as soon as patriots discover the tardiness of their societies. Nor is it somehow invented upon declaration of independence from a colonial ruler. The process of cultural integration usually occurs decades before independence. Intellectuals simply give political expression to this culture. They do so, however, as a way of making modernization possible and meaningful rather than as an ersatz for uneven development. In other words, their politicization of identity is not a pathology of delayed modernization; rather it is related to the confrontation, symbolic or actual, of their society with the West. While elites recognize the economic, military, and technological superiority of Western nations, they seek to identify a symbolic domain in which autochthonous identities can be preserved and which eventually can serve as a bedrock of statehood.

This task was undertaken by Greek poets, teachers, philosophers, and students beginning with the latter part of the eighteenth century. Although these elites had themselves not created the conditions for the eruption of the rebellions and had little say on the formation and subsequent development of the state, they had a formative impact on the modernization project, for they provided a set of models, discourses, and symbols of a unified nation. They first imagined the idea of a national identity and then politicized this identity, a process that took place in tandem with political efforts to revolt against the Ottoman Empire.

The first and most important task for intellectuals was to create a sense of collective destiny. They set out to fashion a national story that ran like this. Oppressed, humiliated, denied enlightenment, Greeks should rebel against the Turks; they should realize that, rather than the toiling peasants of a decaying Oriental empire, they were the descendants of ancient Hellas, the spring of Europe and modern Enlightenment. No longer subjects of the Ottoman Empire, Greeks should strive to be citizens of an autonomous Greek state, itself an integral part of Europe. In short, the intellectuals began to endow Greeks with a cultural, linguistic, historical, geographical, and ethnic integrity. Although this narrative had initially diverse manifestations, it was eventually transformed into the epic of Greek nationalism. My concern here is to explain why the mission to restructure Greek society was seen as a primarily cultural phenomenon.

A brief historical overview may be in order. With the capture of Constantinople by the Ottomans in 1453, all of the territory of the current geographical area of Greece as well as the vast Greek populations in the Near East and the Balkans came under Ottoman control. The Orthodox Christians, the majority of them peasants, were grouped administratively into an ethnoreligious community known as a millet, a religious but non-territorial form of social organization. They were subject to the rules and regulations of the Orthodox millet regardless of whether they lived in Cairo, Athens, Istanbul, or Sofia. Within the millet they were entitled to religious and cultural autonomy, although, as non-Muslims, they suffered certain legal discriminations and paid higher taxes. Periodically, between the fourteenth and sixteenth centuries, Orthodox peasants were subject to a levy by which young boys were removed from their families for training in the elite military corps. Although they could reach the high echelons of Ottoman administration, they were thus lost forever to their patrimony.

This religious autonomy as well as the administrative separation of the Orthodox from other millets allowed the patriarch to assume greater civil authority than was possible in the Byzantine Empire. For in addition to being the head of the church, he assumed the secular leadership of Orthodox people, responsible for both their pastoral needs and a host of civil practices such as education, marriage, and inheritance.[16]

While on the popular level (cuisine, names, language) Orthodox and Muslim practices were reciprocally affected, the Ottoman state, as I mentioned earlier, had no official interest in them. Like all premodern polities, it did not impose an imperial Ottoman identity on its diverse peoples. There was no feeling of belonging to the Ottoman Empire in the way people belong to a nation-state. Whereas the Ottoman bureaucracy was the only institution to link the various populations, it did not unify them (Todorova 1997: 163). The Greeks of the Ottoman Empire thus faced a different set of economic, political, and social conditions from, say, those of Brazilians, Filipinos, or Nigerians. Their battle for independence, however, brought to the fore many issues that have been relevant for similar struggles ever since. This is especially true for countries in eastern Europe, all eager to join NATO or the European Union.

[16] A similar situation has developed for Greek immigrants in United States, Canada, and Australia. Under conditions of religious and cultural pluralism, the church has evolved into the most influential institution of Greek culture, serving as a place of worship and ethnicity. See Jusdanis 1991.

OF BACKWARDNESS AND CHANGE

First among these issues is the process of comparisons, which is so crucial to the rise of nationalism. Scholars, students, and merchants of the late eighteenth century had a different perception of the West than previous generations and their contemporaries in the church. For instance, the sons of the Phanariots—the Greek aristocracy that had secured favored positions in Ottoman society and administration—had begun to express doubts about the authority of tradition in the late seventeenth and early eighteenth centuries. They started to travel in greater numbers to the cities of Europe, attending there institutions of higher learning. Upon their return, they wrote of their impressions. This was a momentous period, for until the first half of the eighteenth century there was very little contact with or knowledge of the West in the Greek world. There were few translations of literary works, scant interest in foreign writing, and little mastery of foreign languages (Dimaras 1989: 136). The Patriarchate, however, resisted the new teachings. What ensued was a Greek battle of the books, the last quarrel between ancients and moderns in Europe (Kitromilides 1985).[17] The Patriarchate reacted vigorously to the introduction of modern texts and ideas because it saw them as another Latin crusade threatening the existence of Orthodoxy (Makrides 1988: 169).

Chief among early modernizers was Alexandros Mavrokordatos (1636–1709), who studied philosophy and medicine in Rome and Bologna. He wrote his thesis on the circulation of blood, borrowing from William Harvey's theory. This was a daring move because Harvey's ideas were considered heresy in Europe even by the middle of the seventeenth century (Apostolopoulos 1974: 299).[18] His son, Nikolaos (1680–1730)—who was made dragoman in 1698 and later hospodar (prince) of the Danubian provinces of Moldavia and Wallachia (1709–30)—likewise promoted European philosophic and scientific developments. In his *Filotheou*

---

[17] In order to understand the Greek Quarrel of the eighteenth century one has to go back to the revival of humanistic thinking which had taken place a century earlier. Associated with this regeneration was Theophilos Korydaleos (1570–1646), a philosopher trained in Rome (1604) and at the University of Padua (1608), where he was introduced to neo-Aristotelianism by Cesare Cremonini, a colleague of Galileo. Appointed to the directorship of the influential Patriarchal Academy, he was instrumental in the consolidation of neo-Aristotelianism as the dominant form of philosophy and science of the Greek world, one supported by the church. He reintroduced Aristotelian philosophy to the East where a century and a half earlier it had constituted the primary mode of education. Neo-Aristotelianism thus reinforced existing Greek thought, itself heir to classical and Byzantine traditions (Kitromilides 1990: 188). See Henderson 1970 and Tsourkas 1967.

[18] After teaching at the Patriarchal Academy for a number of years, he was appointed dragoman of the Sublime Porte, the equivalent of foreign minister, an action showing that ethnicity was no bar to administrative office.

Parerga, written in 1718 but not published until 1800, he made what is regarded as the first explicit statement in Greek scholarship on the European struggle between the Ancients and Moderns.[19] Although he cherished the writings of Homer, Plato, and Aristotle, Mavrokordatos noted guardedly, he admired and enjoyed the works of the Moderns, particularly their ability to penetrate the secrets of nature. He also observed that if Aristotle were to come back to life, he would be glad to be a student of one of the Moderns (1800: 54).

Mavrokordatos's allusion to Ancients and Moderns pointed to the growing awareness among elite members of the Balkans of science and philosophy in the West. Their travel, business, and study in European cities allowed them to ascertain the tremendous leaps the West had made vis-à-vis its own medieval past, but more important, their own societies back home. Their discovery of the West's advance, as we saw in the passage from Patriarch Loukaris, was not new. But their reaction to the West most certainly was. They began the process of comparison, which ultimately led to the drafting of plans to restructure Greek society. Their desire for social and ultimately political reform according to Western blueprints brought them into conflict with the Patriarchate, which strove to silence them.[20] These individuals, like modernizers of other societies before and after, existed on the periphery of two worlds: the West, which they considered the home of forward-looking ideas, and their own society, which seemed sunk in obscurantism. The original impetus for modernization came from an elite of Western-oriented but marginalized individuals who had discovered the vast gap in learning separating them from the West.

Foreign travelers to the Balkans and the Near East, like Alexander Drummond, the British consul to Aleppo, confirmed this view. On a visit to the Ionian island of Zakinthos in 1744 he made the following observation:

[19] See Kitromilides 1992 and Dimaras 1989: 263–82. Mavrokordatos's text puts Aristotle's authority into doubt for the first time in Greek letters (Psimmenos 1982: 240). The main aim of the work, however, was to offer a sympathetic picture of the Ottoman Empire to Western readers, particularly the peaceful coexistence of its religious communities. For a French translation of the text, see Mavrokordatos 1989.

[20] One such notorious case is that of Methodios Anthrakitis (ca. 1660–1736) who, having been accused of heterodoxy by the Holy Synod in 1723, was condemned for teaching natural philosophers and mathematics and anathematized (Kitromilides 1992: 21; Henderson 1970: 33–37). In a letter written from Istanbul that year Anthrakitis described his inquisition. "I am condemned by the Synod not for being a bad Christian, . . . but for practicing philosophy in a manner different from the Aristotelians" (Angelou 1955: 171). He was allowed to resume teaching in 1725 on the condition that he remain within the neo-Aristotelianism of Korydaleos. See Pelagidis 1983. On the subsequent struggle between the church and those advocating republicanism, see Korais [1798] 1949, the anonymous author of *Eliniki Nomarhia* ([1806] 1957), and Clogg 1969.

I find that in these parts, the mathematics are totally disregarded; whereas, the musty fathers are studied with great reverence and delight. Locke and Clarke they admire; but the chief bent of their study is to moral philosophy: some experimental authors, especially Graavensade, they have read, but do not fully understand; a circumstance not at all surprising when we consider they have never attended a course of experiments, or seen any of the instruments or apparatus except in drawings. When I talked of the specific gravity of bodies, the pressure and resistance of the air . . . they believed what I said . . . ; but still they discovered a sort of dissatisfaction, upon which, I called for a glass of wine and a cruette of water, to entertain them with the experiment of separating the two liquors which had been mixed; and when they saw the purple clouds arising, their eyes sparkled with joy and admiration. (1754: 95)

Drummond saw "darkness" everywhere he went. In Smyrna he found the "Greek clergy scandalously ignorant." Observing an icon of Jesus, he remarked how these people, "who once excelled all the world in those liberal arts, are now sunk to such a degeneracy of taste and execution" (96). His Orientalist depiction of the Greeks, however, underscored how Greek scholars themselves had begun to perceive their own society. The latter had accepted the world view represented by the former. The epistemological and geopolitical reality outside had been so transformed that the Greek intellectuals believed that Greece should no longer resist the West but copy it. They clearly felt that the Greeks were inferior and backward in comparison with their coreligionists in the West.

J. C. Hobhouse, who journeyed through the provinces of the empire in 1809 and 1810, also commented on the lack of "dissemination of knowledge in Greece." The state of the arts he characterized as "most deplorable," adding that it would be difficult to find an architect, sculptor, or painter "equal to the common workmen in the towns of Christendom." Even the books of the great Greek Enlightenment figures such as Korais, Kodrikas, and Philippidis were not available (1813: 2:534, 571–72). Shocking to Hobhouse was how little aware Greeks were about their classical forebears. Of Leonidas "and of the other heroes of antiquity, the generality of the people have but a very confused notion; . . . very few of them trace the period of their former glory farther back than the days of the Greek Emperors" (588).

Because of the dearth of schools, he noted, Greek students went abroad in vast numbers. Significantly Hobhouse brought attention to the alienation these students experienced on their return, which has always been an impetus for reform. Unable to find positions befitting their expertise due to lack of development or colonial policy, these elites strive to transform society in part for their class interests. The greater the advance a Greek made in knowledge, Hobhouse argued, the more "insupportable" he found his "residence in the Levant." If a Greek had undertaken the study of philosophy, "now so generally diffused throughout Christendom," Hobhouse asked, "how could he contemplate the miserable conditions of the country and continuously behold oppression in all its modes—the injuries of his master and (what is more intolerable) the meanness of the slave?" How could he associate with the priest, the most literate "but unenlightened of his countrymen?" Must he not "feel his genius pine within him, and decay like the exotic transplanted to a soil unfit for his encouragement and growth" (1813: 2:560)?[21]

Although Hobhouse took on a condescending tone toward the places and people he visited, he captured in this passage the estrangement these students and scholars felt from their own communities. Many indeed found residence there "insupportable," the conditions "miserable," Ottoman rule "oppressive," and the village priest "intolerable." It is interesting that Hobhouse, a foreign traveler, chose to give his observations a political interpretation, speaking of masters, slaves, and oppression twelve years before the War of Independence. This only goes to show how the impulse to reform Greek science and philosophy along Western paradigms had been transformed into a political struggle for autonomy. This process of comparisons, originally a cultural project, did not, of course, lead directly to actual rebellions. Rather it represented part of the same effort to transform the Greek world.

Hobhouse himself witnessed these first stirrings of nationalism: "It is easy then to see that the Greeks consider their country to belong to them as much as it ever did. . . . Their patriotism is all aflame. . . . The Greeks when in revolt, are therefore to be regarded, not as rebels, but as patriots fighting for the recovery of their birthright" (1813: 2:599).[22] Evidently he condoned a rebellion if it was conducted as a nationalist campaign for independence. It is important to note that in the eighteenth century Hellenism was largely devoid of any racial or nationalistic overtones. Writing on the possibility of a Greek insurrection, Hobhouse himself noted that

[21] This is confirmed by the experience of the most prominent leader of the rebellions of 1821, Theodoros Kolokotronis (1770–1843), who in his memoirs referred to the lack of education. "In my youth . . . there were no schools or academies; only a few schools existed where reading and writing were taught." Moreover, contact with other Greeks beyond his locality was "limited." There was no sense, in other words, of an imagined national community at the time. The War of Independence, he insisted, united the Greeks for the first time. It was nationalism, via "the French Revolution and Napoleon that . . . opened people's eyes" ([1851] 1964: 70). See Kitromilides 1990a on the impact of the French Revolution in Greece.

[22] Interestingly he remarked that the goal was not a unitary nation-state. The hopes of the Greeks "are directed toward the restoration of the Byzantine kingdom" (1813: 2:588). Hobhouse was not off the mark, for revolutionaries like Rigas Velenstinlis envisioned a multinational, pan-Balkan federation, modeled on the Byzantine and Ottoman Empires but united by Hellenism. The political struggles did not represent an organized campaign with clearly defined goals. Some fought for a republic, others for an empire.

the "Greeks taken collectively cannot, in fact, be so properly an individual people." On the Christians of Ioannina, he remarked that, "though inhabiting a part of Albania and governed by Albanian masters, [they] call themselves Greeks. . . . The appellation Romaios or Roman[23] (once so proud a title but now the badge of bondage) is a religious, not a national distinction, and means a Christian of the Greek church, and denominated accordingly." Hobhouse recognized the overlap of ethnicity and religion and the hazard of differentiating one group from another. To avoid "mistakes" he used "Greek and Albanian with a reference, not to the religion, but to the language and the nation of the person of whom I may have occasion to speak" (1813: 1:70). William Martin Leake similarly attested to the ethnic variety of Greece, although he also observed evidence of assimilation (1814: 254). The ethnic homogeneity presumed by nationalist discourse and the future Greek state had not existed at this stage.

Hobhouse, however, had correctly observed that students instructed in the new philosophy, scholars cognizant of republicanism, and merchants partaking in capitalist enterprises could not accept their lot. They fashioned a discourse critical of both empire and the church and supportive of an independent state. Like postcolonial intellectuals elsewhere, they undertook to transform their society. But this mission to modernize society went hand in hand with the drive to nationalize culture. The one, I would argue, is unthinkable without the other. That is to say, the Greeks undertook to reform society and join the new economic order only with a reinforced, confident, and politicized culture. Social, political, and economic renovation would have been impossible without the assertion of the Greek difference. In short, Greeks nationalized culture not because they were backward but because they wanted to become modern. This is why it is impossible to separate the cultural and political aspects of nation building and why struggles for independence are never political acts exclusively, be they in the Peloponnese or the Punjab.

THE GREEK CULTURE WARS

When Hobshouse spoke about a Greek patriotism, he was referring to the situation in the first decade of the nineteenth century. But in the time of Drummond, sixty years earlier, little thought had been given to the idea

---

[23] The citizens of the eastern half of the Roman Empire called themselves "Romaioi." With the adoption of Romaios, the name "Hellene" began to signify a non-Christian, that is, a follower of pagan practices. The modern, but paradoxically more ancient, Ellinas (Hellene) came into general use after the Enlightenment. Both circulate today, although they have separate meanings, as Michael Herzfeld has demonstrated (1982).

that the boundaries of an independent Greek state should contain the Greek people. Scholars were preoccupied, as I mentioned earlier, with cultural models: instituting a "sound philosophy," choosing the proper language for education, clarifying the relationship between the modern Greeks and the ancients. Their goal was pedagogical rather than nationalist, motivated by the process of comparing Greeks and Westerners.

The figure generally regarded as the most influential in this phase was Evgenios Voulgaris (1716–1806), a thinker who advocated the philosophical and scientific ideas of the Moderns. Born and educated on the Ionian island of Kerkyra, he was trained there in ancient and modern philosophy by Antonios Kateforos. After teaching in Ioannina and Kozani, he was appointed by Patriarch Kyrillos V head of the recently established Academy on Mount Athos from 1753 to 1759. Between 1759 and 1761 he taught at the Patriarchal Academy (Knapp 1984: 4).[24] During his tenure as professor Voulgaris had translated and used in his lectures a number of European philosophical works, including Locke's *Essay Concerning Human Understanding*, which he translated around the mid-eighteenth century, five years before its appearance in Germany and sixty-five years in Italy (Angelou 1954: 141–42).[25] His *Logiki* (Logic) constituted the most authoritative text in Greek philosophy for half a century.

One of Voulgaris's major accomplishments was to bring about a new alignment between modern and ancient Greeks that was to become an overriding preoccupation of later cultural and political life. In order to show the significance of European philosophy, he had first to demonstrate its compatibility with ancient Greek thought (1766: 99). By arguing for the indispensability of classical Greek thinking, he was in a better position to promote modern authors such as Bacon and Locke. Unlike the Moderns in France, he could not renounce classical learning because he needed the ancients to make the moderns more palatable. Even though he did not see modern science as an alternative to classical learning, he presented the ancients and moderns as equals, possessing commensurate explanatory power (Kitromilides 1990a: 191). Philosophical authority from now on could no longer lie exclusively with Plato and Aristotle.

The other cultural issue to become the focus of this project was language, particularly the register to be used for writing and education. Language is central in projects of modernization, particularly in the effort to found an independent polity. This question becomes especially acute in

[24] Having come into conflict with the ecclesiastical authorities over his philosophy, he left in 1762 for central Europe. After a stay in Halle and Leipzig, he went to Russia in 1772 as librarian for Catherine II and was later ordained archbishop in the Ukraine.

[25] On his other translations, see Henderson 1970: 46. His pivotal position in Greek learning had been recognized by thinkers of the nineteenth century. See Koumas 1818: 24–25 and Kairis 1851: 37.

colonies created arbitrarily by European powers and containing diverse ethnic and linguistic groups. What would be the language of the newly defined Filipino people? Spanish, English, or Tagalog? In Greece there was never a question of using the imperial language because Greek has a long, unbroken tradition going back to Homer and beyond. But scholars debated which Greek to adopt as the language of culture and then of the state: ancient Greek, that used by the church, the scholarly register, or the demotic?

Vikendios Damodos (1700–1752) was an early figure who proposed the composition of books in the vernacular and the argument that social improvement could be attained through cultural reconstruction. Educated in Venice in the philosophy of Descartes, he began his teaching career inauspiciously in the very year Anthrakitis was condemned for heresy. Although not the first to use the vernacular, he was the first to write philosophy in that register (Bombou-Stamati 1982: 299). He believed that Greek scholars could contribute to the amelioration of their nation by composing texts in everyday speech. The reason he decided to write his *Phisiologia* (1739) in the demotic was to make it more publicly accessible. In this way he "followed the example of so many wise teachers who have written their profound thoughts in French; their aim was to benefit their nation by teaching in its own native tongue." Ancient Greek—once "our shared language"—was no longer acceptable as a medium for education since it was understood only by a few. Through his own study and travel abroad Damodos discovered that Europeans had forsaken Latin for their national vernaculars. He urged Greeks to do the same in the name of the "common good" (in Bombou-Stamati 349–50).[26]

Damodos converted language into an object of scholarly and public concern, making it part of a pedagogical mission. No longer seeking to distance themselves from the peasants by culture, he and other philosophers sought a communion with them. At the very least these scholars had begun identifying a particular "nation," united by language, even though they had not yet posited it in nationalist terms. Equally important, Damodos explicitly proposed Europe as a model, identifying the interests of the Greeks with the West rather than with the empire. Thus if Europeans had abandoned the classical language for the vernacular, it went without saying that the Greeks should follow suit.

Such arguments were put forward by Athanasios Psalidas (1767–1829), a professor at the Academy in Ioannina, in his tellingly titled *Kalokinimata*, "Moves toward Progress" (1795: 18–19). Psalidas promoted the vernacular and implored his "fellow nationals" to "copy" the civilized

---

[26] The preface of *Phisiologia* has been reprinted by Bombou-Stamati (1982). The entire volume, like most of Damodos's works, exists still in manuscript form.

and enlightened nations of Europe. The Greek nation, he argued, kept in ignorance and darkness, marveled at the smallest sign of wisdom. It was the duty of intellectuals to lead it forward. Until when, he asked, would the "unfortunate descendants" of the glorious Greeks be ruled by the Ottomans and "ridiculed" by other nations? "Or have you not seen the results of Wisdom in all of Europe and the results of Ignorance and Barbarism in all of Greece?" (21–24). Psalidas, who had studied in Moscow and Vienna, came to understand abroad that the Greek nation was not only ruled by foreigners but also sinking in ignorance. To escape both predicaments Greeks had no choice, he believed, but to turn their eyes toward European progress and transmit European learning to Greeks through schooling.[27] To him both the empire and Greek society were provincial. His hortatory arguments were destined to become the standard discourse of intellectuals.

They were brought into prominence by Iosipos Moisiodax (ca. 1725–1800), who occupied a towering position in the intellectual developments of the era. Although born a Vlach in a part of northern Bulgaria populated by his Romanian-speaking people, he entered the Greek world of letters by virtue of his Greek education. Greek culture, Kitromilides explains in his biography of Moisiodax, constituted a "common patrimony" to all the Balkan Orthodox Christians of the eighteenth century. The only means by which Orthodox Christians of the region could improve themselves socially, Greek education "acted as a catalyst in assimilating into Greek culture members of the Orthodox but non-Greek speaking groups of Balkan society, whose symbolic boundaries remained quite fluid in the period before the emergence of nationalism" (1992: 20). Along with Moisiodax, Rigas Velenstinlis (he too a Vlach), Nikolaos Zervoulis, Dimitrios Darvaris, Nikolaos Piccolos, and Athanasios Vogoridis had all assimilated into Hellenism at the time.

During much of the eighteenth and first half of the nineteenth centuries, Hellenism served in the Balkans as an ecumenical cultural ideal, very much like the role it played in the eastern Mediterranean of the Hellenistic period and of late antiquity. Although not supported by military might as was the case in Alexander's time, it attained enormous prestige. Indeed, Greek culture along with Orthodoxy and the Ottoman administration[28]

---

[27] Convinced that education could bring both freedom and progress, he devoted his life to pedagogy and exhorted others to do the same. Because much of the work of these scholars has not yet been reissued, little is available in English. Portions of Psalidas's work *Alithis Evdemonia iti Vasis Pasis Thriskias* [1791] have been translated (see Psalidas 1960).

[28] Until recent years the Ottoman legacy had not been studied sufficiently by Balkan historiographers who were engaged in a postcolonial writing of their respective histories. The bias against this legacy has led scholars to "cleanse" their cultures of this patrimony. See Todorova 1997.

served as the three unifying forces in the Balkans. Hellenism expanded throughout the region because Greeks had dominated the four areas—religion, economy, administration, and intellectual life—that constituted the shared substratum of Balkan life (Tsourkas 1967: 212). Ethnic Greeks occupied positions of enormous prestige and influence in the Ottoman administration and served for decades as governors of Wallachia and Moldavia. Greek had become the language of commerce and Hellenism the secular culture of the Balkans (Camariano-Cioran 1974: 15, 311).[29] The economic and political power of the Greeks enabled them to have more contacts with Westerners than their neighbors, which explains in part their earlier attempts at modernization.

This was the multiethnic world of the Balkans and eastern Mediterranean before nation-states. The great short-story writer, Georgios Viziinos, obsessed with divided identity, alluded to this universe in his portrayal of Greeks in the Ottoman Empire in the latter half of the nineteenth century. The Greek narrator of "Who Is My Brother's Murderer?" (1883) was surprised to receive an offer of hospitality from a Turkish upper-class lady. "The Turks," he observed, "especially those in large cities not only do not live with Christians under the same roof but also cannot bear to live with them in the same neighborhood" (1980: 76). In the novella *O Vasilis O Arvanitis* by Stratis Myrivilis, Greeks and the Turks of Asia Minor, although living in the same village, had distinct institutions: "separate cafés, separate entertainment, separate holidays" ([1943] 1997: 33).[30]

THE DISCOVERY OF TARDINESS

Modernizers, such as Moisiodax, emerged out of this polyethnic ecumene of the Balkans in the eighteenth century. Gradually they had become aware of what for them was a devastating truth, namely, that Europe had surpassed their society in cultural, social, and political development. Contemporary Europe, Moisiodax wrote, "due in part to proper administration and in part to the disposition of local notables toward culture, has

[29] When academies were established in Bucharest (1694) and Jassy (1728), the language of instruction and the professors was Greek. See Völkl's study of Greek culture in the Danubian Principalities in the eighteenth century (1967). Stoyanov investigates the large numbers of Bulgarian subscribers to Greek books (1966). Todorova shows how Bulgarian nationalists reacted against the reliance by the elites on Greek (1990).

[30] On the situation of Greeks in the Ottoman Empire after 1821, see Augustinos 1992. Among other things, he examines how a national Greek identity worked its way into the consciousness of an increasing number of Greeks in the empire. Hirschon (1989) investigates the memories of the Greek refugees who settled in Athens after the exchange of populations between Greece and Turkey in 1922.

actually surpassed ancient Greece with respect to wisdom" ([1761] 1985: 330). Overwhelmed by this discovery, they undertook a general project of cultural restructuring, specifically the revitalization of philosophy and science and, more important, the clarification of a relationship between, on the one hand, Greeks and Europeans and, on the other, between Greeks and their classical forebears (Kitromilides 1985: 80). The new philosophy and science in themselves did (and could) not lead to the emergence of sovereign Greece. Rather they enabled scholars to rebuild their society through general education, to imagine Greeks as participants in modernity, and to reconsider the place of Greece in the empire. The later national revival took place on this foundation of reform.[31]

Moisiodax contended that Greece suffered from two faults: it simultaneously neglected and revered antiquity. That is to say, although modern Greeks may have been proud of their ancestors, they were ignorant of their specific achievements. Comparing Greek and European education, Moisiodax discovered that Greeks had at their disposal neither the texts nor the critical tools (grammars and lexica) to understand the classics. At the same time, the exaltation of classical thought had induced in them unquestioned acceptance of the ancients' authority and "cultivated an implacable hatred of all the moderns" (1985: 327–29). In presenting classical antiquity as a dominant problem, Moisiodax made manifest a question that came to preoccupy Greeks and non-Greeks alike around the middle of the eighteenth century: why modern Greeks differed so much from their ancestors.[32]

The sorry lot of the Greeks, he insisted, was due to their neglect of the ancients and their disdain for the moderns, being ignorant of the former and distrustful of the latter. They were, in a sense, incapable of learning from either civilization. Moisiodax set out to change Greece's predicament by realigning the cultural orientation of Greece toward Europe. He began with language. Every European nation, he wrote in the *Theoria tis Geografias* (Theory of geography), had perfected its own vernacular, hav-

---

[31] Another figure in this struggle is Hristodoulos Pamblekis (1733–93), a fellow student of Moisiodax at Mouth Athos, teacher, and author of works that challenged the authority of Christianity. He believed that the Moderns were wiser than the Ancients because the former resided in a more mature stage of humanity whereas the latter were still children (Kondylis 1988: 35).

[32] See Noutsos 1981. About eighty years later Fallmerayer used this difference as a way of denying Greeks their claims to Hellas. In two works (1830–36, 1835) he presented his Slav thesis. Relying on racial (and racist) arguments, he proposed that during the Byzantine period, what is today Greece, underwent a process of "Slavisierung" and "Albanisierung" through invasions of Slavs and Albanians. Although eventually Hellenized, these invaders altered the cultural and genetic makeup of Greece. This thesis struck Greeks like a hammer and historians rushed to prove him wrong. See Veloudis 1970 on the emergence of Greek historiography in the wake of Fallmerayer's provocation.

ing converted it into a useful instrument for the articulation of work in the sciences and philosophy. Having realized that Europeans were standardizing their languages, he proposed that Greeks do the same and that this vernacular be used for scholarly purposes (1781: x). He was appalled, for instance, by the dialectical variety of Greek, finding this heterogeneity unsuitable for a modern society. Every Greek province, he complained, borrowed from the respective region's dominant language, assimilating the foreign expressions, thereby rendering them a natural part of Greek: in Istanbul it was Turkish, in Epirus Albanian, in the Ionian Islands Italian. "Could it ever be possible," he asked, "for such a mongrel and barbarian register to be reformed?" If it were ever renewed, it would become a "complete idiom," appropriate for every usage and worthy of comparison with any of Europe's languages (1985: 335–36). The emphasis lay on comparisons with and imitating Europe.

Not only Europe's extraordinary "progress in philosophy" and language, he remarked in his *Apologia* (1780) but also its overall social and technical advance made him suggest that Greeks should "copy the Europeans." "Only he who has never traveled to and seen Europe can ignore the countless, necessary, and essential benefits that, thanks to Newtonian philosophy, Europe enjoys, benefits, that is, in machines and buildings and numerous other kinds which improve life" (1976: 24–25). This was a shocking admission to make by a Greek about his society whose ancestry was hailed in Europe as the fountainhead of all knowledge and the arts. The irrefutable clarity with which Moisiodax formulated the belatedness of Greece's position meant that the Greeks had to learn from Europe even about their own ancestors (1976: 155–56). Moisiodax brought this point home in the preface to his translation of Muratori, writing that "many if not all of the European nations that the ancient Greeks and Romans called barbarian have now become civilized and wise" (1985: 339).

Greece, by contrast, was for Moisiodax in a wretched state. He provided a catalog of deficiencies: illiteracy, fear of new ideas, distrust of the West, indifference toward scholarship, scarcity of books, teachers, and schools. Such was its state of unenlightenment, he exclaimed, that Europe actually pitied Greece (1985: 339). This condition of backwardness, which for him was less tolerable than that of servitude, could only be overcome if Greek society oriented itself toward Europe. Indeed, the phrase "the copying of Europe" occurred throughout his work. Greeks had no choice but to emulate the West and to acknowledge that, "while Greece is deprived of many things, Europe overflows with them" (1976: 153).

Moisiodax offered the example of Russia, which, before Peter the Great, had found itself in a similarly disadvantageous situation. Thanks to his reforms, Russia had developed a civility and philosophy hailed among the foremost in Europe. He proposed a similar path of revival to Greeks whose ancestors, after all, stood as the "first teachers of propriety and wisdom" (1985: 339). Like Russia, Greece was now on its way toward a renaissance. Philosophy and mathematics were taught again; the number of teachers was increasing, some of whom, like Voulgaris, had achieved a glory equal to the ancients (326). It was time, he urged, that Greek education took part in European "progress" (1976: 25).

The cajoling tone of Moisiodax's style would become standard by the end of the eighteenth century as authors, having enumerated the ills of Greek society, would propose a program of reconstruction. For him, as for his contemporaries, enlightenment implied more than developing a "sound philosophy" and included a broad social, cultural, and political program. At the very least, he believed this project would help alleviate some practical problems faced by Greeks. In a passage from the *Apologia* he proposed that cultural improvement among Greeks could lead to their social amelioration in the empire:

> If we dedicate ourselves diligently to mathematics and physics, it is possible that our erudition will find some respect with our rulers and our Nation will find some relief with them. The ancient Romans claimed about the Greeks, that while Rome conquered Greece by force of arms, Greece conquered Rome by force of wisdom. We cannot hope the same happy outcome from our rulers; the reasons are, I think, very familiar to those who know their manners. In any case, I think that they too are human beings and they too by nature desire to learn and that, born in Greece and breathing the Greek air, they have the same intelligence of other Greeks. (1976: 36)

Moisiodax here referred to the cultural superiority of Greek scholars vis-à-vis the Ottomans as he also recognized the enormous power wielded by culture, even in the hands of the conquered. The examples of ancient Greece and Rome taught him that the colonized could themselves exercise influence over the colonizers. Although not a stepping-stone to independence, culture for him promised to improve the social condition of Greeks by civilizing their rulers.

Other thinkers, of course, disagreed with this particular vision, proposing instead outright seccession. What I have been calling a project for modernization of Greek society was a diverse effort, characterized by opposing opinions. Moisiodax's particular views on the place of Greeks in the empire are less important than his belief in the power of learning to improve their lot. His scheme was cultural insofar as he sought social change through books, pedagogy, philosophy, and linguistic reform. Culture was a way of both criticizing inherited institutions and undertaking an agenda of renewal.

Greek scholars of the eighteenth century, Panagiotis Kondilis explains, aspired to a synthesis of thought and action that was foreign to the metaphysics of neo-Aristotelianism against which they rebelled. They sought knowledge less for its own inherent value than for its practical application to the modernization of the nation. Thus they were more interested in translating foreign books, transmitting into the Greek world previously unknown ideas, and identifying models for emulation than in writing original works of philosophy and science (1988: 11, 45). Having accepted the notion of the social utility of ideas, they tried to fashion a new society, a mission that necessitated, in the eyes of their intellectual and political heirs, the rejection of empire in favor of a centralized nation-state.

What prompted these scholars to adopt a project of social critique and reconstruction? Primarily, it was the comparisons they had begun to make at the beginning of the eighteenth century, between Europe and the Balkans, which revealed to them the backwardness of Greece. Distressed at and dissatisfied with their society, they inaugurated a program of cultural renewal (Kitromilides 1983: 55–56).[33] Intellectuals, however, were not alone in bewailing the ills of Ottoman society. Merchants had made a similar diagnosis. Ioannis Pringos, for instance, who had established himself in Amsterdam between 1755 and 1774, contrasted the favorable conditions for trade in the Netherlands with the appalling conditions back home. He spoke admiringly in his diary of Amsterdam as a "great place to trade" and of its economic institutions. But he mourned their absence under the Ottomans:

> All these cannot be organized under the Turk . . . for he knows no order and justice, and when the capital equals one thousand, he designates it ten times as much, so as to seize it, to impoverish others, not understanding that the wealth of his subjects is the wealth of his empire. They [the Dutch] organize their affairs with justice but he [the Turk] is totally unjust and cannot achieve anything but can only ruin. May the Almighty destroy him, and may Christianity flourish, and may governments be established like the above, like those in Europe, where every one has his own without fear of injustice, where justice prevails. (Pringos 1931: 851)

Although Pringos called for the "liberation of the Christians from the tyranny of the Turks," he did not necessarily wish a democratic state in its place. What is striking about this passage is the convergence of views

[33] We can imagine their reaction to European progress from Galanaki's postmodern novel *O Vios tou Ismail Ferik Pasa: Spina Nel Cuore* (1989), which deals with Ismail Ferik Pasha, a Greek who was abducted as a boy from Crete, raised as a Moslem in Cairo, and became minister of war. For two years he and Ibrahim, the son of the viceroy, Muhammad Ali, traveled through Europe, marveling at the "wonders" of its modernity (49–50).

among Greeks of the diaspora. Indeed, a new type of merchant appeared at this time who took an intense interest in matters of learning and endowed education back home (Dimaras 1989: 28–29).[34] Pringos, for instance, sent books to his native city of Zagora. The merchants left it to the intelligentsia, however, to envision a cultural program and to imagine the new national reality.

Dimitrios Katartzis (1730–1807), a court official in Wallachia and dominant presence in the Enlightenment, exemplified this form of cultural politics. A firm supporter of the vernacular as the medium of science and education, he saw a correlation between the cultivation of language and modernization. In an essay on the Greek language (1783) Katartzis argued that Greek, after reaching its acme in antiquity, entered a period of corruption in the Roman period, which continued to his day (1970: 10). Nevertheless, he argued, this vernacular should be accepted as the language of a modern society because this was done by European nations.

In order for the vernacular to become the national language, Katartzis believed that Greeks had to follow the European example by cleansing it of foreign elements. Each European country, he explained, began to "cultivate its language collectively and to promote the study of arts and sciences in this register; everything became shared and each nation was enlightened collectively and Latin became the language of learned people, as indeed should happen with ancient Greek" (1970: 21). The refinement of demotic was essential for the social improvement of Greece. "The cultivation of [the vernacular], the composition of books in this language constitutes the general education of the nation" (10). This was so because the people would profit from the availability of books they could understand, "as is the case in the northern countries of Europe." Katartzis emphatically argued that the "collective good" and "collective progress" depended on the nationalization of culture—the transmission of a shared language, history, customs to Greeks through public schools. "The complete education of the nation and its shared happiness necessarily follow from the good education of the youth" (41).

The politicization of culture was, of course, a basis for independence. Although Greeks had not yet developed an "autonomous polity," they constituted a nation. Contrary to what certain Westerners believed, according to Katartzis, Greeks had been bound together by an "ecclesiastical administration," a common language, history, and religion. In fact, the Greeks had fulfilled the criteria for political autonomy; what remained

---

[34] The merchants of the eighteenth century had learned modern business techniques, as can be seen in the manual of Athanasios Psalidas, who offered business classes in the Kaplani School. According to Papageorgiou, the editor of the manual, this is one of many works that sought to teach Greek merchants the latest European trade practices (1990).

was the realization of this vision. Because "we constitute a nation and possess a native soil, we should have our own distinctive ideas which are suitable to us and which differ from Turkish, Italian, and French ideas" (1970: 44–46). Katartzis's claim here exemplifies the argument I was making earlier, namely that the nationalization of culture was seen as a prerequisite for modernization. That is to say, for these intellectuals only a self-defined and self-assured Greece could become European.

Over and over again the texts from this period made the same diagnosis of Greek society, belatedness, and proposed the identical cure, the cultural renovation of Greece. Grigorios Paliouritis, for instance, castigated Greeks for having forgotten their ancestors, for treating ancient Greek as almost a foreign language, and for not calling themselves Hellenes.[35] Whereas "we don't teach history to our children," Paliouritis reminded his readers, the English, the French, and Italians and "all the other enlightened nations of Europe teach the history of their nations as the first lesson in school" (1807: 20).[36] K. M. Koumas (1777–1836), a teacher in Smyrna, similarly wrote his philosophical treatise, *Syntagma Filosofias*, in order to make up for a lack of such works in schools. Koumas recognized that much headway had been made in education during the eighteenth century. It came about because "we came to learn about the progress in philosophy made by the Moderns; Evgenios [Voulgaris] taught us that in order for us to get ahead in learning we could do nothing better than study science and literature in European academies" (1818: 10).[37]

That language became the hub of this movement is not surprising given the centrality it had acquired in nationalist thought. As Adamantios Korais (1748–1833) said in a line laden with Herderian influence, "language is one of the most inalienable possessions of a nation. All members of the nation take part in this possession . . . with democratic equality."[38] He

[35] In addition to "Romios" the other name preferred by Greeks was "Graikos," the Hellenized version of the Latin "Graecus." The philosopher Nikolaos Skoufos complained about its widespread currency. "I ask to be excused if from now on I use our ancient, national appellation [Hellene] rather than the improper Graikos" (1816: 12). Katartzis 1970: 49–50 addressed this point.

[36] He also published a history of Greek archaeology (1815) to describe to his readers the customs, ways, and thoughts of their "forefathers."

[37] Greek students went to study in Europe in great numbers, as they still do. Even though the "Academies of Europe," Paliouritis wrote in another book, are very expensive, "the poor Greeks attend them continuously because they have many wise teachers" (1815: 1:15). For Koumas's work in the school at Smyrna, see Vallianatos 1973.

[38] Korais's work on language overflows with organic metaphors. He supported the acceptance of a (purified) vernacular because it was the living speech and the mother tongue of Greeks (1804: 1:58–64). Tziovas has examined the ideological underpinnings of the language debate (1986). For further discussion of Korais in English, see Vallianatos 1887. The first reference to Herder occurs in 1813, in *Ermis o Logios*, an influential periodical for the transmission of Enlightenment ideas (Dimaras 1989: 290–91).

too tied the evolution of language with the possibility of social development. "It is sufficient for someone to observe the progress in the human
spirit made by other nations to understand that nations can be called
enlightened only when they bring the development of their language to
completion." The Italians, English, and French, he wrote, freed themselves from barbarism when scholars began to write in the vernacular
(1804: 1:15).

It was imperative for Greek scholars to prove that Greek was a suitable
medium for scholarship and literature and that it could serve as a unifying
force of the Greek people. In order to achieve this proof, they, as in the
battles inaugurating Western modernity, had to debunk the authority of
both the liturgical and classical idioms. The Greeks, as I stated earlier,
faced a choice of registers and opted for *katharevousa*, a hybrid of the
archaizing language and the vernacular. Its adoption, however, necessitated the removal of Turkish works, for the renewal of culture required
the cultivation of language. It also, of course, made indispensable the
work of intellectuals. As Korais himself acknowledged, the task of "correcting" language fell on its custodians and interpreters. "The learned
men of the nation are naturally the lawgivers of language" (1804: 1:67,
71). The Greek case shows once more that intellectuals place themselves
on the forefront of modernization by associating their own class interests
with those of the greater public good.

The long uninterrupted history of Greek meant that the language problem raised questions about the connection between linguistic and ethnic
survival and the relationship between an ignominious present and a glorious heritage.[39] In returning to the past, however, elites of the late eighteenth century wanted to change the present. They rejected the reigning
identity of Greeks as Orthodox subjects of the Ottoman Empire and
sought to make them participants in modernity, heirs of a glorious tradition, members of the European community, and citizens of an independent nation-state.

This does not mean that the intellectuals actually changed the social
and political conditions accompanying the transformation of identity.
Stathis Gourgouris correctly argues that the "Greek Enlightenment cannot be reduced to a set of programmatic actions taken at the level of elite
decision, whether political, economic or intellectual" (1996: 75). That the
will of intellectuals could not in itself bring about complex social change

[39] The linguistic question was not settled until the late twentieth century. Writing on language in 1863, Ioannou complained of the many dialects still in use. He noted that while
"vulgar Greek" was appropriate for folk poetry, it was unsuitable for high literature. Finding contemporary language "poor and lacking in scholarly and technical terminology," he
proposed, like his predecessors in the Enlightenment, the creation of one national language
along European lines (1863: 110–15).

or that their designs did not succeed as planned, however, does not prove that these designs were without consequence. Whereas one can argue about a top-down conception of history, the role of intellectuals in history is less debatable. The experience of Greek nationalism, like the history of nationalism in general, shows the extensive influence they have had.

Their resuscitation of the past is such an achievement. Of course, this revival was not entirely of their making. The relationship between the ancient Greeks and their descendants had in fact been already posed in Byzantium, especially during the classical revival of the eleventh and twelfth centuries when "Hellene" was restored to mean Greek (Magdalino 1992: 11; Angold 1975). The rehabilitation of Hellenism reached a peak in the fifteenth century with the humanism of Gemistos Plethon (d. 1452), an "anti-Christian Neoplatonist" who planned the creation of a Hellenic "nation" in the Peloponnese.[40] Moreover, there is ample evidence of transmission of ideas and practices from antiquity to the present such as the ritual lament, which, as Margaret Alexiou has shown, exists as an unbroken heritage from Homer until modern times (1974).[41] Numerous folk narratives attest to the knowledge shared by postclassical Greeks of the ancient past (Kakridis 1979).[42] The persistence of these ancient practices shows the continuity between classical and modern forms of identity.

The intellectuals of the latter part of the eighteenth century, however, brought this past to the fore, systematized it, and gave it a sense of political urgency. "The sense of Hellenic ancestry felt by many of the leading figures of the Greek national movement, the feeling that they were capable of matching the feats of their illustrious ancestors, contributed powerfully to the launching in 1821 of an insurrection which to any rational observer must have seemed doomed to failure" (Clogg 1983: 25). These intellectuals, moreover, were also successful in undermining the reigning universalisms of Orthodoxy, Ottoman administration, and the millet, replacing them with a narrower history, shared by only one ethnic and linguistic community. They stressed that even under Ottoman rule, Greeks constituted a separate nationality, as different from the Turks as from the Slavs. They argued that each people, rather than participating in a common

[40] Around this time the term "Hellenism" appeared to describe both classical as well as modern Greek society. Plethon himself believed that modern Greeks were direct descendants of the ancient Hellenes (Woodhouse 1986: 6, 70, 102). Beck argues that this "national humanism" led centuries later to the emergence of a new national Greek self-consciousness (1960: 87, 90, 92).

[41] On these practices, see Fotinopoulos (1959).

[42] One such oral story is the tale of Alexander the Great. Although Alexander died in 323 B.C., legends about his life and exploits were written down at the end of the third century B.C. A version of this circulated up to the sixteenth century upon which a modern Greek romance was based (Holton 1974: 3–13). See also Veloudis 1968, 1977.

patrimony of Christianity, now possessed their own unique past and future. It goes without saying that their visions, programs, and enthusiasm were resisted by certain groups, embraced by some, and ignored by others.

Opposition by the church, aristocrats, and local notables frustrated the realization of their plans. More important, the relevant context for the application of their ideas was missing in the Greek world. The grand dream of reconstruction did not succeed in the forms originally imagined. To be sure, the introduction of European institutions and ideologies in a stratified, noncapitalist, and "Eastern" society largely incapable of integrating them was a long and tortuous process and the results imperfect and incomplete. "No doubt," Thanos Veremis argues, "the peasant warlords, the local notables, and the seafaring islanders who waged the War of Independence against the Ottomans had a far less clear view of their ideal polity than did their intellectual kin of the Greek diaspora. The dedication of these social groups to the Enlightenment was questionable" (1989: 135). Nevertheless, the War of Independence was conducted in the name of the Greek nation (Petmezas 1999: 62).

Although the program of modernization had not triumphed as envisioned, it had not failed either. Far from it. While the principles supported by the intelligentsia, Veremis continues, were "far removed from the experiences of the Christian Orthodox peasant communities, such harbingers of the uprisings as Rigas, Korais, and the anonymous author of the [*Elliniki Nomarhia*] provided the ideal model for future statebuilders. . . . They developed a strong commitment to collective interests and communal solidarity, and continued to exert considerable influence in Greek nationalism" (1989: 136). Even though they had no immediate intellectual heirs to continue their mission after 1821, intellectuals set the terms for debate for the next two centuries. The relationship between modern and ancient Greece and the connection Greece should have with Europe are topics as alive today as they were Moisiodax's time.

Central to Greek cultural and political life is the subject of belatedness. In the twentieth century the preoccupation with tardiness has become even more intense. The modernist author, Nikos Gavriil Pentzikis, captured this state of being in his pathbreaking novel, *O Pethamenos ke i Anastasi* (The dead man and the resurrection) ([1944] 1987: 31): "How heavy is the fate of those who wish to advance with dignity in a land which lags behind." To be sure, modernist authors, who strived to refashion artistic and intellectual life in the 1930s and 1940s, concluded that Greece had not caught up with developments in Europe. In his influential manifesto of the modernist period, Giorgos Theotokas asked still painful questions: "What position does Greece hold in the creative fervent of contemporary Europe? What contribution do we offer to the great strides being made around us?" ([1929] 1979: 10). While Europe had advanced,

Greece still resorted to copying. Greece, he complained, had not been able to offer anything to the European civilization; no Greek author had been able to gain recognition abroad (37). The modernist poet Giorgos Seferis in the famous dialogue on poetry with the philosopher Kostantinos Tsatsos wrote that contemporaneous Greece was still "compelled to import a greater portion of its cultural nourishment than itself produces" (1979: 31). The authors of the modernist period continued to believe in the power of culture to offer Greece international credibility and prestige, a position proposed by Giannis Psycharis decades earlier. In his autobiographical text, *To Taxidi mou* (My Journey, 1888), he argued that Greece would begin to count in Europe only when it developed its own arts and sciences (1988: 191–92).

The goal of Greek elites for the past two hundred years has been exactly to develop those institutions already in existence in Europe which are the measure of success. This is true in all areas of life. One of the most pressing issues in Greek political campaigns, for instance, has to do with Greece's apparent belatedness in industrialization, economics, social policy, and political practice and the consequent need to catch up and become a nation on a par with its European partners. Greeks continue to compare their achievements (or lack thereof) to a set of criteria established in the industrialized West.

Greek nationalism has to be seen in this perennial comparison of Greece and Western countries and the consequent search for models. The obligation on belated or postcolonial societies to copy patterns of success from abroad means that these societies are intensely syncretic in character. In one respect, all national identities and all human groups are synthetic, created through processes of amalgamation. But those societies considering themselves late in comparison to Western nations or those having been conquered by them have to borrow to a greater degree in order to achieve modernity. They have to assimilate the foreign, to see how they measure up, to incorporate the drafts of others in their own national blueprints. They are compelled to merge sometimes incompatible ideas and institutions. At the same time, however, they assert a national difference from these societies, a difference that entails an emphasis on language, social practices, the arts. That is, the more they have to borrow in the realm of technical expertise, the more they affirm their uniqueness.

When I say that the belated, the minor, the postcolonial are syncretic, I do not wish to privilege these concepts epistemologically. My purpose is not to make them exemplary, to argue, as does Spivak, that the "colonized subaltern is irretrievably heterogeneous" (1988: 284). I do not exalt in diversity for its own sake, as do Gilles Deleuze and Félix Guattari when they write that "nothing is revolutionary except the minor" (1986: 26). Nor do I hope to give these groups representative status, as does Paul

Gilroy when he claims that the "suffering of blacks and Jews has a special redemptive power, not for themselves alone but for humanity as a whole" (1993: 208).[43] My aim is simply to show that for these societies to survive, they have to engage in an intense dialogue with other societies. Although nationalism is inspired by and speaks the language of homogeneity, it is part of the will to modernize, which can only take place through comparisons and the merging of different ways of life.

---

[43] In universalizing the black experience, Gilroy follows the example of Deleuze and Guattari, who insisted that the situation of Czech Jews, like Kafka, is "the problem of us all" (1986: 19). Buell makes similar claims for Asian Americans, who act as outsiders and insiders at the same time in American society (1994).

Chapter Five

POLITICAL NATIONS

B ECAUSE OF the overwhelming urge today to denounce nationalism as a disease or a dead end of history, I have attempted to
present nationalism as a positive force in the recent modernization
of societies. Despite its potential to destabilize social life, nationalism has
had a productive role to play in the past two centuries. In this chapter I
turn to the so-called political nations, which are hailed by a number of
political and social theorists as examples of nonethnic forms of political
association. I argue that the concept of the political nation is conceivable
only in an imaginary sense, for it is impossible empirically to disconnect
the cultural from the political dimension of a nation-state. Although the
drive to build states was originally a separate process from the effort to
invent nations, the two have come to interact with one another since the
later eighteenth century.

All nations have a cultural dimension. It is important to make this claim
even though it may seem obvious to literary and cultural critics. Social
and political theorists, often unaware of cultural studies of nationalism,
continue to posit the existence of civic nations and of a civic identity. They
routinely offer the United States, for instance, as the supreme case of a
nonethnic state. Idealizing the history of the United States, they portray
it as a nation that has managed to overcome Old World ethnic strife by
virtue of its civic culture. The idea of civic identity becomes for these
writers a useful way to criticize other forms of nationalism and to propose
American multiculturalism as a panacea for global ethnic conflict.

The attempt to divide the cultural from the political nations constitutes
part of a current morality tale to distinguish between good and evil nationalism. This distinction has a long history, going back to the work of
Friedrich Meinecke, the leading German historian in the first half of the
twentieth century, who differentiated between cultural nations (*Kultur-
nationen*) and political nations (*Staatsnationen*).[1] While he acknowledged
that the two categories overlapped and were difficult always to keep
apart, he defined the former as growing out of a commonly experienced
cultural heritage, which included literature, language, and religion, and

---

[1] The roots of his conceptual opposition are traced to the early nineteenth century,
namely to comparisons first made in 1830 between Germany as a *Kulturnation* and France
as a *Staatsnation* (Bertier de Sauvigny 1970: 156).

the latter as developing through the unifying force of a common political history and institutions such as the constitution (1970: 10–11). Germany belonged to the first category, France and England to the second.

Meinecke's binary opposition formed the basis of Hans Kohn's influential *The Idea of Nationalism: A Study of Its Origins and Background*. Political nationalism, Kohn argued, having first appeared in England and then the United States, France, and Holland, represented an urge toward greater democracy and economic progress. "Nationalism is inconceivable without the ideas of popular sovereignty preceding—without a complete revision of the position of ruler and ruled, of classes and castes" (1956: 3). The cultural version with its roots in Germany and in eastern and central Europe manifested itself first in language, literature, and folklore. Only later did these cultural assertions develop into political demands. Kohn returned to this thesis in his *Prelude to Nation-States: The French and German Experience, 1789–1815* in which he represented German nationalism as a defensive doctrine and as a model for conservative nationalisms in Russia, Latin America, Spain, and India. An "overcompensation for political backwardness" in a modern world, it claims "spiritual" superiority based on legendary glories of premodern traditions (1967: 2). It finds its justification in ethnic unity rather than in a "rational societal conception" (1956: 331).

Liah Greenfeld's notion of civic nationalism is also based on the distinction between cultural and political nations. She believes that as nationalism evolved, particularly in countries like Germany and Russia, it abandoned the original pursuit of sovereignty for the search of uniqueness. Defensive in nature, this brand of nationalism is dangerous because it was susceptible to *ressentiment* (1992: 10). Greenfeld uses this term, coined by Nietzsche and later developed by Max Scheler, to mean the "suppressed feelings of envy . . . and the impossibility of satisfying these feelings." For Greenfeld *ressentiment* renders a nation more aggressive, serving as a "powerful stimulant of national sentiment and collective action, which makes it easier to mobilize collectivistic nations for aggressive warfare than to mobilize individualist nations, in which national commitment is normally dependent on rational calculations" (1992: 16, 488).

Although Maurizio Viroli does not portray nationalism as a pathological, self-destructive phenomenon, he believes in the possibility of "patriotism without nationalism." For Viroli wishes to disconnect the love of the nation from the love of the republic. He strives for a "patriotism of liberty" which promotes the citizen's identification with civic institutions and principles rather than ethnic values. Like Michael Walzer, he points to the example of the United States where patriotism is sustained through politics instead of shared cultural bonds (1995: 179).

This moral and epistemological canonization of political nations is in a sense a Eurocentric attempt to highlight the experience of a handful of northern European states. Hugh Seton-Watson, for instance, contends that in the old nations of Europe (the English, Scottish, French, Dutch, Castilian, Portuguese, Danish, Swedish, Hungarian, and Polish nations) the formation of national consciousness was a "spontaneous, process, not willed by any one" (1977: 7–8). His assumption of the presence of national consciousness among these nations centuries before the appearance of the doctrine of nationalism allows him to claim that such a consciousness has been absent outside northern and central Europe. The example of the Serbs and Greeks, as old nations, easily disproves this hypothesis, not to mention the existence of state structures in Thailand, Japan, China, and the Asante.

The juxtaposition of cultural and political nations idealizes the histories of France, England, and the United States, seeing them as the realization of Enlightenment principles. It portrays them as cosmopolitan societies that gaze toward the future in contrast to the parochial cultural nations, which turn back to the past. Can this comparison hold out, however? Has France, for instance, not imposed political sovereignty on the basis of language? If it has not, what has happened to all the dialects and languages spoken in the French countryside up to the end of the nineteenth century? They were flattened by the steamroller of Frenchness, only to be resurrected today. Eugen Weber does not mince words when he describes this as a process of internal colonization (1976). The United States has also attempted to neutralize cultural differences among its heterogeneous population. This integration did not require such "irrational" concepts as a common language or ethnic uniqueness, though it did rely on the ideal of a white race.

Although ultimately reductive, the contrast between cultural and political nations is useful in reminding us of the divergent paths toward nationhood.[2] It is not that there was one nationalism, as Greenfeld assumes, which went astray in central Europe and elsewhere. The process of state integration was, as I have shown, distinct from the drive to isolate national culture. But in the late eighteenth century the movement for popular sovereignty came to merge with that for national self-determination.[3]

---

[2] This reminder is particularly necessary in humanistic studies that focus exclusively on the nation at the expense of the state. It is a challenge, for instance, to glean the significance of the state from the works of Bhabha, Said, Appadurai, Miyoshi on globalization, postcolonialism, and diaspora. Surprisingly, even within political science, interest in the state reawakened only in the 1970s (Young 1986: 115). See also Dyson 1980: 7. On the neglect of nationalism by sociology, see Smith 1983.

[3] That things were not that clear can be seen in the Greek War of Independence. While France, Russia, and Britain grudgingly came to the aid of the rebellious Greeks, tipping the

It is true, however, that ethnicity was not the motivating factor in creation of the United States. Because the American colonists shared the same cultural background as their government, they did not regard ethnic differences as a reason to secede from Britain. The war against British rule was first and foremost an exercise in popular sovereignty. Similarly the French Revolution was primarily a political occurrence, heralding a contest against despotism rather than a foreign enemy. It was not impelled forward by the need to differentiate one people from another.[4]

That these revolutions represent the struggle for popular sovereignty rather than national distinction does not prove that the subsequent process of state formation in either country constituted purely a political development, devoid of cultural significance. In other words, because ethnicity was not the motivating factor behind nation building in England, France, and the United States, it does not follow that issues of language, tradition, history, and identity were entirely absent from the operation. Such assumptions are widely held today, not just in political theory but also in journalistic accounts of nationalism. Their prevalence indicates, as I outlined in the preface, a profound denigration of culture and nationalism. In the following pages I put into question the possibility of a political nation and of a purely civic nationalism by looking into specific examples of nation building. I argue that ultimately nationalism has become a cultural discourse. If that is the case, our aim is to develop political solutions, such as federalism, to cope with the consequences of nationalism instead of satisfying ourselves in distinguishing good from bad nations.

ENGLAND

England is held as a quintessential political nation, exemplifying a civic, as opposed to an ethnonational, identity.[5] Recent studies have demonstrated, however, that the two types of national identity cannot so readily be distinguished. Philip Corrigan and Derek Sayer show how the political and cultural aspects of nation building are mutually dependent processes in

---

balance in their favor, they installed a Bavarian prince as monarch. These powers did not see a contradiction in imposing a foreign ruler upon a newly independent nation since they probably did not regard the revolution as an exercise in self-determination.

[4] The revolution put into practice Rousseau's notion of sovereignty, which he defined in his *Social Contract* (1762) as "the exercise of the general will," "inalienable," and "indivisible," which was common to all members of the polity (1959: 25–26).

[5] English nationalism has only recently received scholarly attention. A computerized search of 82,000 articles in literature and history, published between 1972 and 1987, retrieved only 2 entries on British or English nationalism. An identical search for German and Ireland revealed 70 sources (Newman 1987: xviii).

English history.[6] The English conception of national identity, they argue, is closely bound with the history of state formation.

Social theorists characterize England as a political nation because it achieved unification much earlier than other continental kingdoms and subsequently imposed its rule on Wales in 1485, Scotland in 1603, and Ireland in 1800. Boasting one of the longest unbroken traditions of statehood, England is also the first country in Europe to have had a written constitution enshrining the rights of citizens.[7] But these theorists forget that the English had existed as a separate ethnic group. Positive feelings of Englishness have their origins in the medieval period and crystallized in the fourteenth and fifteenth centuries (Hilton 1989: 41; Colls 1986: 29).[8] As an early manifestation of English identity, one can point to a statement written by the English representatives at the Council of the Church at Constance in 1414: "Whether a nation be understood as a people marked off from others by blood relationship and habit or unity, or by peculiarities of language (the most sure and positive sign of a nation is divine and human) . . . or whether a nation be understood, as it should be, as a territory equal to that of the French nation, England is a real nation" (in Boyce 1993: 79). The English here are seen as a distinct people, bound to each other by blood and cultural links. In addition to being an old state, England is an old nation.

The national integration of England in the modern period could have been accomplished only with such positive expressions of peoplehood, as recent literary criticism demonstrates. In his investigation of Elizabethan nationalism Richard Helgerson emphasizes this very fact, namely that "the discursive forms of nationhood and the nation's political forms were mutually self-constituting. Each made each other" (1992: 11). He shows how texts, nations, authors, and institutions were produced and how they were productive of each other. In the sixteenth century England became a sovereign country by severing its ties with the Catholic Church and establishing the monarch as the supreme ruler of both state and church. But when Parliament proclaimed England an empire in the 1530s, people began looking for the cultural signs of Englishness (4).

Trepidations over cultural identity came to a pitch not just in response to developments in politics. The poets, for instance, who were involved

[6] While Corrigan and Sayer put forward persuasive arguments, they understand culture as a shared way of life to be laid on the people by a state or powerful class (1985: 195). See chapter 2 for a critique of this position.

[7] The Magna Carta was issued in four versions: 1215, 1216, 1217, 1225. This political nation incorporated only a small portion of the population. It granted women the right to vote in 1918.

[8] A sign of this was the increased use of English, as opposed to French, in the lawcourts and official life at this time (Kohn 1940: 69).

in the "Elizabethan writing of England" were working within a tradition of verse stretching back about two centuries. These poets strived both to create a national poetry—a poetry in service of the state—and a poetry that could rival all others, present or past. When Edmund Spenser and his contemporaries were born in the latter half of the sixteenth century England could boast of not a single poet of "major standing" since Chaucer. By the time this generation had died, however, English poetry was felt to rival that of any other language, ancient or modern (Helgerson 1992: 299).[9] The development of English poetry was to a certain extent a result of comparisons poets made between English writing and that of other nations. Italy and France remained an inspiration to English intellectual life in the sixteenth century and the English strove to "catch up" (Kohn 1940: 71–72). Writers of the time asked themselves whether they should try to produce sophisticated literatures to rival those of Italy and France or whether they should imitate the classical heritage more effectively than the poets of those countries (Hadfield 1994: 19).[10] The accomplishments of other states, as I argue in the previous chapter, provokes a nation to modernize. Comparison is the springboard to nationalism whether in England or the Philippines.

The anxiety provoked by poetic comparisons is expressed in a sentence of Spenser's: "Why a God's name may not we, as else the Greeks, have the kingdom of our own language?" (in Helgerson 1992: 1). This question, as Helgerson explains, indicates the transformation of communal identity from one determined not just by kinship (i.e., "kingdom") but also by culture (i.e., "language"). The poets of Spencer's generation set out to articulate this postdynastic, national identity through chivalric romance, historical narrative, and topographical description. While this nationalism was not concerned with ethnic uniqueness as was to be the case of those in nineteenth-century Europe, it was a self-conscious project of nation building. In the life-span of this generation, Helgerson adds, "England was mapped, described, and chorographically related to its Roman and medieval past, . . . English history was staged, . . . and a national dramatic literature was provided with its most enduring works" (299).

---

[9] The importance of poets as representatives of national consciousness was underscored by Thomas Carlyle about two hundred years later. "Yes, truly, it is a great thing for a nation that it get an articulate voice; that it produce a man who will speak forth melodiously what the heart of it means." Although Italy, he adds, lies scattered and dismembered, "noble Italy is actually one" because it produced its Dante. Italy can therefore speak. "The nation that has a Dante is bound together as no dumb Russia can be" ([1840]: n.d. 119, 135).

[10] In his investigation of the history of the English language Bailey notes that English speakers had discarded their linguistic inferiority and begun to regard their language as an equal of others only around the sixteenth century (1991: 59). Americans themselves launched a similar enterprise in the nineteenth century to invent an American vernacular, sufficiently different from that of Britain (102–51).

Helgerson shows that English nation building was not just a political affair. Cultural and political issues were enmeshed; the attempt to define the nation coincided with the gradual movement toward democracy. The association of the state with its subjects represented part of a new development in which dynastic and feudal allegiances were being displaced. In sixteenth-century England, Liah Greenfeld writes, the word "nation," referring until then to an elite, had begun to be applied to the populace as a whole and made synonymous with "people" (1992: 6).[11] In the period between 1500 and 1650 the words "country," "empire," "commonwealth," and "nation" all were understood as meaning the "sovereign people of England." Englishness was particularly appealing to the lower classes, especially the nascent bourgeoisie, because it treated everyone equally as far as national identity was concerned. England itself connoted a separate polity, a community of free and equal citizens—however much circumscribed this may have been—rather than a royal patrimony (47). Once again culture worked in tandem with politics. The Reformation significantly affected the further spread of nationalism first by its promotion of literacy and then by forming a basis of a religious but, later, cultural distinctiveness.

Because historians are enamored of the liberal and civic dimensions of English nationalism, they disregard its religious origins in the Reformation. The "birth of English nationalism in the Puritan Revolution," Kohn argues, had so determined its character that "it has always been and still is closer than any other nationalism to the religious matrix from which it rose" (1940: 91–92). In the time of Oliver Cromwell (1599–1658), the English came to see themselves as a separate, chosen people in possession of a covenant with God. This nationalism "filled the English people with an entirely new consciousness, a sense that they, the common people of England, were the bearers of history and the builders of a destiny" (Kohn 1940: 89, 79).[12]

The interplay between culture and politics can be seen in the invention of a broader British identity. A feeling of Britishness was forged in the succession of wars between Britain and France in the eighteenth century, a fact that again underscores that people determine who they are by drawing a boundary between themselves and others. In the course of these wars the government was compelled to mobilize large numbers of men from England, Wales, and Scotland. The soldiers as well as the entire

[11] While the word "state" was used politically for the first time in 1538, the preferred terms were "realm," "body politic," or "commonwealth" (Dyson 1980: 36).

[12] Historical events encouraged this confidence. While the Italian states and Spain were in decline and the Holy Roman Empire was devastated by the Thirty Years' War, England was on the rise, its ascent propelled by scientific advance and remarkable discoveries overseas of land and people to exploit.

civilian population were encouraged to define themselves collectively against their hated enemy. These wars, which challenged the religious and political foundations of Britain, came to be seen as a confrontation between Protestantism and Catholicism. Here again Protestantism was crucial in the formation of the umbrella identity of Britain. For after the act of union of England, Wales, and Scotland in 1707, Britons came to imagine themselves as a single people partly in response to the hated Catholic Other (Colley 1992: 53, 6).[13] This blanket of Britishness was laid over previous ethnic and religious allegiances such as the Welsh, Scottish, Irish, and Catholic.[14] Although war enabled the creation of Britain, it would never have lasted without the unifying potential of Protestantism, which allowed the Scots, English, and Welsh to forge shared bonds despite their many cultural differences.

While Protestantism acted as a major force in the creation of Britain, the empire itself, with its amplitude of races, ethnicities, and languages, served as a distant, wild, and racialized Other, against which the British could set themselves. Postcolonial criticism has demonstrated how the empire provided not just a sense of global destiny but also a set of distinctions from which Britons could define themselves. Robinson Crusoe, for instance, clearly distinguished himself from the Moors along West Africa, the Spaniards and Portuguese in South America, and the "savages" who threatened his life on his private island. Political reform, industrialization, overseas trade, a sense of divine destiny, and the (literally) insular nature of the country further promoted Britishness.[15]

I have argued so far that the characterization of England as a political nation is historically insupportable. Gerald Newman, in his study of English nationalism between 1740 to 1830, goes so far as to argue that English nation building had many similarities with the national move-

[13] Colley explains how commitment to Britain coalesced over time. Patriotic societies, which glorified British culture, led to the founding of national institutions such as the British Museum and the Encyclopedia Britannica. Although the existing hierarchy restricted access to the upper classes, these societies encouraged a more comprehensive view of the nation (1992: 3).

[14] See Kearney 1989: 8. Whereas English identity was formed partly through comparisons made with the Irish, Welsh, and Scots, these groups themselves constructed national identities in the late eighteenth and early nineteenth centuries vis-à-vis England. Intellectual and political leaders identified the damage brought on by imperialism upon their societies and pleaded for cultural preservation and reconstruction (Trumpener 1997).

[15] Today in the absence of an empire, with its promise of trade and booty and a hostile Europe, with the tonic and horror of war, this sense of Britishness is being questioned. Internal political reforms and a federal Europe may actually usher in an independent Wales and Scotland. The crisis of identity has been sharpened by the entry of large numbers of nonwhites into Britain since World War II. The internalization of the empire has brought the problem of race, once largely experienced abroad, home.

ments in eastern Europe. He identifies in eighteenth- and nineteenth-century England the same ethnocentric and xenophobic qualities normally ascribed to continental nationalisms. Newman points to a chorus of laments raised first in the 1750s protesting the excessive cultural influence of France. The most noisy declarations came from the artist William Hogarth (1697–1764), who (very much like German intellectuals a generation later) railed against the cosmopolitan aesthetic tastes of aristocratic connoisseurs (1987: 64).

The decades between 1740 to 1780 were crucial, Newman continues, for the consolidation of English nationalism during which it was transformed into a secular, but also, "anti-cosmopolitan, anti-aristocratic, and nativist" movement inspired by the fear of an "alien cultural invasion." Contributing to its emergence were the rise of the novel, growth of print media, and the expansion of reading publics; feelings of collective fate resulting from the Seven Years' War and the American War of Independence; the military, economic, and diplomatic competition with France; and the rising political activity of the middle and lower classes. Newman isolates four interconnected arguments, representative of a defensive, exclusivist nationalism: "the world is pervaded, even neutered or hermaphroditized, by foreign influence; . . . this foreign cultural influence translates itself into ruinous moral influence; . . . it is a fact that ordinary, innocent Englishmen unthinkingly admire and follow the World's lead—they are seduced by the Quality; . . . hence alien cultural influence brings about collective domestic moral ruin" (Newman 1987: 67). The differences between these sentiments and those expressed by Fichte are slight.

As in the case of German bourgeois intellectuals, their English counterparts condemned the dominance of Gaelic taste in English cultural life and the morally corrupt ruling classes enslaved to it. They too launched a *Kulturkampf* against French letters and against imitation while praising the virtues of the authentic English soul (Newman 1987: 130–40). Newman emphatically characterizes this as a "cultural nationalism" with its emphasis on native languages and literary traditions. The anxiety over uniqueness was part of a greater "*national* revolution" whose mainspring lay not only in aesthetics but also "in the human discontents of the alienated and frustrated intellectual, casting around for a cultural identity," resentful of both French dominance as well as of deficiencies in English cultural life (120). In such a climate critics like Thomas Warton (1728–90) and Samuel Johnson (1709–84) compiled their great histories of English poetry, respectively *History of English Poetry* (1774–81) and *The Lives of the Poets* (1779–81). The readers of these histories expected to find in them "a glorious national poetic pantheon" (Lipking 1970: 328–29). English national literature was institutionalized partly as a result of comparisons between England and France made by intellectuals.

The poets, historians, critics could, as in all cases of cultural nationalism, represent themselves as the defenders of native authenticity against
outsiders. Nationalism enabled intellectuals to strengthen their public importance. It goes without saying that English intellectuals alone were not
responsible for the creation and dissemination of nationalism but they
certainly had their part to play in these processes. By the middle of the
Victorian age, the middle classes, the children of the elites, and a significant number of the workers shared a national identity without parallel
in British history. What prevented it from turning into a purely ethnic
movement, however, were the political institutions that were developing
in tandem with the sense of national identity.

Canada

By looking into the genesis of so-called political nations like England, we
can see that, even if their delivery was not cultural, their subsequent
growth was. This observation certainly applies to Canada, a country
boasting an undistinguished, noiseless beginning and a history relatively
free of spilt blood. Like the other former colonies in the Americas, Canada
came to be as an administrative and commercial center, having been created largely through common economic interests rather than a shared
culture. In the monumental work of Canadian historiography, *The Commercial Empire of the St. Lawrence, 1760–1850* (1937), D. G. Creighton
chronicles economic factors exclusively as an explanation of the Canadian union. His discussion of how early Canada grew along the St. Lawrence River deals with commerce, mercantile society, and products rather
than, say, ideology. He writes that the debates about the political and
customs union in 1841 of upper and lower Canada (Ontario and Quebec)
concerned issues of trade. Indeed, this merger was supposed to transcend
the very ethnic differences separating the French and English colonists.[16]
Business forces were seen as uniting the two peoples, while language, ethnicity, and religion divided them.[17]

[16] This is evident in a speech delivered by a member of the Legislative Assembly for whom
the goals of progress would transcend cultural divides: "Give the people of Upper and
Lower Canada a common objective to pursue, and common interest to sustain, and all
questions of origin, and creed, and institutions and language will vanish in the superior end
to be attained" (Zeller 1987: 8).

[17] Also important to the creation of Canada was the American Civil War and the consequent belief on the part of the British colonists and Britain itself that a united Canada could
serve as a bulwark against American manifest destiny. The American Revolution had incited
a large number of loyalists to move to Canada. The War of 1812 also sharpened divisions
between the two societies.

Canada quite clearly had a commercial rather than an ideological raison d'être. But ideology in the form of science had a decisive impact on
Canada's development, providing a shared basis of mythology and communication. The belief system of science, Suzanne Zeller argues, offered
English and French settlers the practical means to dominate the physical
surroundings and the ideological tools with which to understand the act
of domination. Science gave credence to the idea of a transcontinental
Canada and, by means of circular thought, to the very conviction that
only through science could the dream be realized (1987: 6). What was
known as inventory science (geology, terrestrial magnetism, meteorology,
botany, entomology, zoology, and anthropology) received an extraordinary amount of attention in Victorian Canada because the immensity of
its territories and harshness of its environment necessitated exploration,
mapping, inventory, and cataloging of resources. It went hand in hand
with nation building.

Science had insinuated itself into the very metaphors and ways of
thought. Natural history, for instance, offered lessons about the growth
of Canada's political history and pointed to the natural maturation of a
larger British North American nation (Zeller 1987: 7).[18] Science endowed
colonists with principles to organize their thoughts not only about development and progress but also about the nation. For science and technology made possible the "new nationality" in inhospitable territories. What
must have seemed as a hubristic idea of producing a new nation of various
peoples across the vast continent became feasible through scientific developments and the railroad.

In short, although Canadian confederation was a political response to
a perceived economic backwardness and justification for a westward
expansion, it made use of a cultural ideology. The state was established
in 1867 through the British North America Act, which united Upper and
Lower Canada, New Brunswick, and Nova Scotia as the Dominion of
Canada and which served as Canada's constitution. (British Columbia
joined in 1871, followed by four more provinces in 1905 and Newfound-
land in 1949.)[19] This political entity was not a nation nor was there such
a thing as a Canadian nationality. The Anglo- and Franco-Canadian com-

---

[18] In *Imperial Eyes* (1992) Pratt examines how the descriptive apparatuses of natural
history in the eighteenth century enabled northern Europeans, such as Alexander von Humboldt, to gain knowledge of and classify the interior territories of Africa and South America.

[19] This founding document differs from that of its southern neighbor. The cautious
"peace, order, and good government" of the British North America Act contrasts with the
self-assured "life, liberty, and the pursuit of happiness" announcing American independence. The optimism that led the founders of the United States to define their nation as
subject to natural law and their rights as inalienable vanished like northern mist. For more
on these differences, see Careless 1969.

ponents of this deal had not fused into one another, as subsequent history bears out. The signing of the act, however, was followed by a period of affirmative attempts at state building involving the laying out of the trans-continental railway and the setting up of tariff protection in the 1870s, which shielded domestic industries particularly in Ontario and Quebec and crumbled only with the ratification of the North American Free Trade Agreement in 1991. But in 1871 Canada was a "nation projected rather than a nation formed" (Morton 1961: 46).

Although the infrastructure of the state was established relatively early, a sense of nationhood developed gradually over the next hundred years, at least among Anglophones.[20] That Canada had acquired the trappings of statehood before becoming a nation does not mean that it lacked an ideological orientation, as I have shown. After confederation in 1867, it began to develop a sense of national consciousness "primarily based on cultural arguments" (Bashevkin 1991: 6).

Signs of a nationalism per se began to appear with the Canada First movement. Established in 1868 as the first nationalist front, it remained influential in English-speaking Canada for the next two decades. Al-though the supporters of Canada First saw the country as a part of the British Empire, they tried to define the essence of Canada. Interestingly they found its distinctiveness in Canada's very northern location, seeing in its remorseless climate and icy territory the source of spirit. This physi-cal and meteorological orientation of Canadian identity, present from the beginning, has remained central to the Anglo-Canadian world view.

After World War I a new phase of nationalism appeared among the elites, one quite conscious of the threat to and potential of Canadian iden-tity. They looked to higher education, the arts, and journalism as sites where this identity could be fashioned and an ever-perceptible American-ization resisted. Indeed, they came gradually to realize that Canada was becoming a cultural and economic colony of the United States. As a result, they promoted federal intervention in cultural policy, pressing, among other things, for the creation of the Canadian Broadcasting Corporation in 1936 and the National Film Board of Canada three years later.[21]

[20] Canadians were legally recognized citizens of Canada as opposed to "British subjects" only in 1947. On Canadian citizenship, see Gwyn 1995. The maple leaf became the symbol in the flag only in 1965 and a national anthem was authorized by Parliament in the early 1970s. The apron strings were cut with the repatriation of the Constitution from Westmin-ster in 1982. On the whole, Canada has made fewer demands of allegiance from its citizens than any other Western nation (McRae 1973: 174).

[21] Some cultural institutions were already in existence. The National Museum of Man (originally, the Geological and Natural History Survey of the Province of Canada) was founded in 1842, the National Gallery in 1880.

In the wake of World War II nationalists called for the formation of federal inquiries into the state of Canadian identity. The most influential of these was the Massey Commission, established in 1949 and charged with the task of investigating "those institutions which express national feeling, promote common understanding, and add to the variety and richness of Canadian life." It is not without meaning that this commission, whose findings were tabled in 1951 as the Report of the Royal Commission on National Development in Arts, Letters, and Sciences, was popularly known as the "culture commission." It recommended comprehensive federal support in the organization and financing of the arts and scholarship, in response to ever-growing "American influences on Canadian life:" The threat to Canadian identity was real: "We are now spending millions to maintain a national independence which would be nothing but an empty shell without a vigorous and distinctive cultural life" (in Handler 1988: 82).

The position taken by the Massey Commission bears uncanny similarities to those of nineteenth-century nationalists in Europe.[22] It expressed an uneasiness about the very survival of an authentic Canadian identity facing a foreign invasion from the south. Its recommendation of expenditure on culture was accepted and the federal government created new institutions to disseminate a feeling of shared union.[23] To those already in existence were added the Canada Council (1957), the Board of Broadcast Governors (1958), and Telefilm Canada (1967). Moreover, foreign ownership of noncable television was regulated in 1958, the Canadian content of television began to be managed in 1961, and new Canadian editions of American magazines were prohibited in 1965.[24] These measures had been taken because people felt that American television, books, magazines, movies, and music, crossing unimpeded the longest uncontrolled border in the world, could imperil the uniqueness of Canada. They feared not a military inva-

[22] It left open, however, the questions of Canadian identity. An answer was provided by Pierre Trudeau when he declared multiculturalism official state policy in 1971. Because of historical contingencies Canada has had to concoct the implausible policy of official bilingualism (proclaimed through the Official Languages Act in 1969) and multiculturalism. Canada is the postmodern country par excellence—centerless, fraying at the seams, yet hanging on. It is still common today, notes William Lawton, for Canadians to speak of the "Canadian experiment," more than a century after Confederation, with no sense of irony (1992: 141).

[23] The federal government's initiatives in the realm of culture provoked a reaction on the part of Quebec (see Handler 1988). Its response became more intense in the 1970s with the pursuit of multiculturalism, for Quebec saw multiculturalism as a Trojan horse, fearing that a policy declaring all ethnic groups equal would deny Quebec special status. Quebec undertook a host of nationalist projects within a fortress culture to safeguard its identity.

[24] *Time* and *Reader's Digest* were exempted under heavy pressure from the American government. Even by the 1950s American magazines dominated 80 percent of the Canadian market (Bashevkin 1991: 63).

sion from the south, as in 1812, but a cultural and economic one. Because of the overwhelming presence of the United States in the Canadian economy, politics, the mass media, and the arts, it is not surprising that it has served in the second half of the twentieth century as the greatest impetus to Anglo-Canadian nationalism. Comparisons Canadians made between themselves and Americans and their fear of American cultural and economic imperialism motivated them to maintain a Canadian difference. The journalist Richard Gwyn with some justification observes that a "primal definition of Canadianism has to be that we are among the few peoples in the world who, given a chance to become Americans, have chosen not to" (1995: 17). This repudiation has very much to say about the sustaining power of national culture. For, with all other forces pushing Canadians for union with the United States, how else can one explain their historical refusal than by pointing to their belief in a separate cultural and social presence in North America?[25] Social theorists, who dismiss the pull of national culture, have no answer to this question.

By the 1970s Anglo-Canadians became progressively more preoccupied by what they felt as the lack of a national paste so necessary, given American influences, a vocal Quebecois nationalism, and increased immigration from countries beyond the British Isles. The perceived threat to (a still not clearly articulated) national identity motivated not only the government to intercede further in the cultural arena[26] but also more concerted reflection on the nature of Canadian identity.

One realm where the question of Canadian identity had been posed was, of course, literature, as it had been in the United States, Europe, and many of its colonies. Although Canadian writing existed since colonial times, the issue of a national literature was not raised until the mid-twentieth century. Around the 1960s Anglo-Canadians began asking why Canadian writing was not taught, reviewed, or read at home. Significant were the answers delivered by Margaret Atwood.

In her influential treatise, *Survival*, Atwood voiced the disquiet about the lack of a Canadian national culture. Canada, as a state of mind, she wrote, "is an unknown territory for the people who live in it." In the absence of such a cultural Canada, its people feel lost and need maps. "Our literature is one such map, i.e. we can learn to read it as *our* litera-

[25] The growth of the welfare state was so pervasive that it began to stand in part for Anglo-Canadian identity. The idea of being a Canadian came to be associated with a liberal, caring nation. Barlow and Campbell argue that the creation of a "social Canada was the single most important act of nation-building in the last half of the twentieth century" (1995: 151, 237–38).

[26] By all measures this investment has been immense. In 1990–91, itself a period of belt-tightening, the cultural expenditure of all levels of government was $Can 5.9 billion, the federal share of which was 2.9 billion. The Canadian per capita outlay for the arts is three times that of the United States (Corse 1997: 60).

ture. . . . We need such a map desperately, we need to know about here because here is where we live" (1972: 18–19). But this literature was not "even mentioned (except in derision) in the public sphere" (13).[27] To her question "What is Canadian about Canadian literature?" she answered, "hanging on, staying alive." Canadian culture, Atwood explained, is about survival in a heartless territory; survival as a colony of Britain and, more recently, of the United States; survival as a culture threatened with extinction: "the land *was* hard, and we have been (and are) an exploited colony; our literature is rooted in those facts" (41).

It is instructive that Atwood connected the essence of Canadian literature with cultural survival, exactly as Finnish or Indian intellectuals have done. The anxious questions posed by Atwood over the existence of an autochthonous literature have to do with the very essence of being Canadian. They express the fear, as Antonio Gramsci said of Italians, that by ignoring their national literature, "they *undergo* the moral and intellectual hegemony of foreign intellectuals, that they feel more closely related to foreign intellectuals than to 'domestic' ones, that there is no national intellectual or moral bloc." Gramsci was himself troubled by the absence of a "national literature" in Italy. "A national-popular literature, narrative and other kinds, has been lacking in Italy and still is," he complained. "Why," he asked, "does the Italian public read foreign literature, popular and non-popular, instead of reading its own?" (1985: 210–11). Gramsci's questions express the anxiety of a belated modernity, the fears of being overtaken and dominated by others.

The fears voiced by Atwood are not different from those felt by English, German, Scandinavian, and Brazilian authors. They have to do with the possibility of maintaining a national culture, which has come to define the essence of a people in modernity. A country, whose life began as a colony and whose sense of nationhood was a tardy affair, determined eighty years after its birth that it could not survive without strengthening its national identity.

BRAZIL

This connection fashioned in colonies between nation and state can also be seen in Latin America. Many of the countries of that continent had actually proclaimed their political independence before most European states had done and against metropolitan centers not much more industri-

[27] Atwood's study is both a piece of criticism and a nationalist document, participating in the very struggles it examines. The book's appendix, for instance, contains practical information on how readers can find information on Canadian literature and culture.

ally advanced than themselves: Argentina in 1816, Chile in 1818, Mexico 1821, Brazil 1822. Like the United States, they shared the same cultural heritage with the colonial polities they renounced.

These new states corresponded very closely to the boundaries set up by the imperial powers. The original shaping of the American administrative units, Benedict Anderson observes, was to some extent arbitrary. "But over time they developed a firmer reality. . . . To see how administrative units could, over time, come to be conceived as fatherlands . . . one has to look at the ways in which administrative organizations create meaning" (1983: 54–55). As in Canada, the transformation of these administrative domains into a nation-state, required, among other things, cultural labor, which was expended primarily after the colonies had gained political autonomy. Indeed, as Doris Sommer has shown, the South American novel appeared after the colonies had established themselves as nation-states (1991).

A number of reasons explain why these colonies had developed little sense of shared consciousness before independence. Unlike Britain, Spain and Portugal regarded their possessions as sources of gold, silver, and raw materials rather than also as potential markets. Their policies frustrated the creation of a colonial identity. Spain, for instance, set up intermediary centers between the colonies and itself to maintain monopoly over trade and political control. Only Spaniards sent directly from Spain were granted exclusive trading rights and appointed to high political positions. Moreover, print, the necessary medium of the spread of nationalist ideas, had been in control of the church and crown for two centuries. Spain proscribed the publication and importation of any fictional material in the sixteenth century with the result that novels did not appear until the nineteenth century (Sommer 1991: 11). Each colony was relatively isolated, having more contact with the metropolis than with other colonies (Michelena 1973: 237).

Conflicts between the Spanish and local landowners were inevitable. Revolts took place among indigenous peoples and slaves against an exploitative system. The locals eventually launched wars of emancipation.[28] That the various revolutions were fought on economic and political grounds does not mean that an identity had not been forming slowly over the centuries. In a comprehensive book on creole nationalism in South America, D. A. Brading demonstrates that intellectuals and chroniclers succeeded in creating forms of shared consciousness out of the historical experience of the continent. Texts, myths, and symbols of a syncretic cul-

---

[28] The elites, who participated in these revolutions, wanted an independent and decolonized American society, while retaining European values and white supremacy (Pratt 1992: 175).

ture figured prominently in the efforts of the inhabitants to create autonomous republics in response to their political, economic, and social grievances. That is to say, manifestations of a creole culture, centuries in the making, found political resonance in the nationalist struggles (1991: 5).

The wars and subsequent developments differed, of course, according to the historical contingencies of each colony. Brazil, for instance, could claim no full national consciousness when it became an autonomous state in 1822. The Portuguese crown had prohibited printing and higher education in the New World until 1808, thereby precluding any possibility of the formation and dissemination of a shared culture. Moreover, the state developed in the hands of a small stratum of educated men whose familiarity with print allowed them a monopoly over communication and politics. They did not, however, constitute a homogeneous community. One cannot assume that, between 1822 and 1852, the consolidation of the nation-state was seen by the bulk of the population as being in its interest (Barman 1988: 4–6).

Although not regarding themselves upon independence as an identifiable ethnic group, the colonists did have a shared culture. Roland Greene writes that imperialists, clerics, and other observers had produced since the sixteenth century a host of narratives on Brazil "as both an ethnic enclave and a site in the cultural imagination." Indeed, Brazil's situation resembles much more that of the so-called cultural nations than would be allowed for by social theorists seeking neat distinctions between ethnic and civic nationalism. By 1822, the year of its independence, "Brazilians were both the authors and the objects of a three-hundred-year process of self-definition" (Greene 1995: 107–9). Its writers, like those in the rest of Latin America, also believed that literature had the capacity to intervene and help construct history (Sommer 1991: 10). The experience of nation building in Brazil, like that in Canada, demonstrates an interplay between culture and politics.

A "feeling of distinctiveness and a lack of identification with Europe, and a profound realization of the colonial reality," argues Stuart B. Schwartz, began to characterize the mestiço and mulato populations of Brazil in the latter half the eighteenth century (1987: 16). Unlike the white Europeans and their descendants, who wished to reproduce Portugal in South America, they did not feel the intense pull of Portugal and thus began to differentiate themselves from immigrant Portuguese. The growth of this colonial identity began in the poorest and most isolated regions. But these areas, Schwartz explains, being the least developed and lacking "European-style institutions, tended to express their distinctiveness in action rather than in thought, and in them we must seek popular expressions of *mentalité* rather than an intellectual discourse on their sentiments." Instead it was in developed areas, "where capital accumulation was the greatest and the forms of Europe the fullest, that a traceable tradition of colonial distinctiveness or self-awareness ultimately emerges, although belatedly, and eventually grows into a proto-nationalism" (32). The case of Brazil shows once more that nationalism emerges in developed rather than undeveloped regions, it occurs in a context of comparisons, and is associated with progress rather than its rejection.[29]

Throughout the eighteenth century an "increasing growth of Brazilian self-sufficiency and identity" could be detected, whose roots lay in the previous century, despite the fact that writings about Brazil and by Brazilians had to be published in Portugal "under the watchful eye of the crown and the Inquisition" (Schwartz 1987: 38–39). Intellectuals (teachers, doctors, lawyers, bureaucrats) played a leading role in this process and in the eventual call for independence. They understood "through reading, conversation, or travel, about other areas of the world, particularly western Europe, whose progress and achievements they admired, envied, and hoped to emulate. Partial toward the 'progressive' countries, they freely drew their ideas from them" (Burns 1980: 124). As in Greece, intellectuals made comparisons between their own society and that of the West. They criticized the imperial social and political system and undertook a program of reconstruction. The situation in Brazil shows how questions of identity and tradition came to play an important role in a country originally established as an economic zone. Although the conditions differed from those in Greece, they indicate a profound relationship between belatedness and postcoloniality, on the one hand, and cultural nationalism, on the other. At the very least the situation in South America shows that there are no pure civic nations—that is, polities created solely by political institutions.

EGYPT

We see this same interplay between politics and culture in another postcolonial nation, Egypt, which was an Ottoman province but which in the course of the nineteenth century had gained a considerable degree of self-rule from Istanbul. It was invaded by Napoleon in 1798, an act that sparked an uprising against the French troops as the Napoleonic invasions had done throughout Europe.[30] The occupation of Egypt by Napoleon

[29] On the anticolonial nationalism of Portugal's colonies in Africa, Angola and Mozambique, see Bigler 1989.

[30] Napoleon issued a proclamation to the Egyptians from his flagship *L' Orient* that he had arrived with the values of the French Revolution, freedom and equality, and that his intention was to overthrow the Mamluks (who had ruled Egypt since 1250) and secure the rights of the inhabitants from the "hands of the unjust" (Wendell 1972: 86–87). The

from 1798 until 1801 brought to the attention of Egyptian elites the overwhelming strength of Europe in material culture and scientific advancement. To be sure, in the eighteenth century European states had been asserting their military superiority vis-à-vis the two dominant Islamic powers of the time, the Ottoman Empire and Mughal India (Wendell 1972: 78, 116). No longer feared by Europeans, the Islamic world became another area in the globe to be economically exploited.

This confrontation with superior European powers was devastating to political and intellectual leaders, compelling them to make a series of comparisons between their society and the West in order to determine the reasons for the Western advance. This process, as is and has been the case, led to the emergence of nationalist discourse that sought the modernization of Egyptian society and the establishment of a sovereign nation-state.

Chief among the modernizers was Muhhamad Ali (1769?–1848), who had been installed Pasha of Egypt by the Sublime Porte in 1805. Although not strictly speaking a nationalist, he undertook a sequence of reforms in the economy, army, education, and bureaucracy that provided the setting for the subsequent rise of nationalism and of the future state of Egypt (Safran 1961: 31). At this point, however, his chief aim was to use European expertise to build a powerful Egyptian state and enhance his own authority rather than securing the trappings of a nation.

His son Ibrahim promoted the program of rapid modernization launched by Ali. To this effect he inaugurated in 1826 the famous student missions to Europe, which would have far-reaching implications for society. Like the Greeks before them and many others since, these students confronted modernity in European capitals. They had discovered there that Europeans were more prosperous and better educated; above all, they were much more advanced not only in areas of culture but also in industry, trade, the military. As one such student, Fathi Zaghlul, noted in a preface to a French work he had translated into Arabic, "we are weak compared with the nations of the West; weak in agriculture, in industry, commerce, and science."[31] As a solution to this situation he advocated the creation of a nation-state, which, in his opinion, had enabled Europe to achieve its strength and progress (in Ahmed 1960: 45).

The possibility of an autonomous and sovereign Egypt was increasingly taken up by a new class of intellectual and political leaders who had been

---

justification of his invasion in the name of French universalism is similar to the arguments Tolstoy has Napoleon utter outside Moscow (quoted early in chapter 3). His real aim was to establish French power in the region and cut off British trade routes.

[31] It is interesting that this book, *Á quoi tient la superiorité des Anglo-Saxons* by E. R. Demolins, dealt with Anglo-Saxon superiority.

educated abroad or in the foreign schools at home.[32] Initially formulated in the 1870s, the idea had its antecedents in the social, economic, and military developments following Napoleon's invasion and brief occupation. This nationalism had taken a decidedly cultural dimension. Although the occupation brought to the fore a sense of Muslim association against the hated West among elites and ordinary people alike, intellectuals began to imagine an Egypt that was historically, culturally, geographically, and politically distinct (Jankowski 1991: 244). But this reflection on ethnic uniqueness was not an aesthetic exercise, preoccupied in the creation of a national culture as a *Ding an sich*. It aimed, rather, to overcome Egypt's belatedness with regard to Europe and achieve full independence, especially after Britain's invasion of the country.

At this time, resistance to British occupation took two forms: loyalty to the Ottoman Empire and Egyptianism. Although Ottomanism continued to play a role in public life, the leading thinkers of the late nineteenth century began to conceive of the Nile Valley and its inhabitants as a unique ethnic and territorial unit and enjoined Egyptians to feel love for this homeland as opposed to the Ottoman Empire (Gershoni and Jankowski 1986: 11). Devotion to Egypt in their eyes came to overshadow allegiance to the empire. Like Greek intellectuals of the eighteenth century who mined their classical heritage, they sought to unearth the pre-Islamic past in order to prove a continuous Egyptian habitation of the territory from a golden age to a colonial present. At the same time, the glories of the pharaonic period allowed them, as was true of the Greeks, to justify their promotion of European institutions and ideologies like the nation-state and nationalism. They were not ashamed, they argued, to borrow from Europe because Europeans had long before borrowed from ancient Egypt (Wendell 1972: 148). What received emphasis at this time was the uniqueness of Egypt and its people, the unity of its population, and the majesty of its inheritance. After World War I the question of Egypt's distinctiveness became even more pressing, especially following the collapse of the Ottoman Empire. Egyptian nationalism thus became increasingly Egyptianist rather than Arab or Ottoman. At the same time Egyptian elites began to look at the rise of Kemalist Turkey with growing interest and admiration. For they saw in Kemal Atatürk's reforms the possibility of creating a modern, secular, and strong unitary state, capable of withstanding the West. They were persuaded that only as an independent state

---

[32] The establishment of these schools was promoted by Ismail Pasha, Ali's grandson, who ruled Egypt between 1863 and 1879. He continued the program of rapid modernization begun by Ali (Tignor 1966: 42–44). By that time a considerable number of foreign merchants and professionals had established themselves as a comprador bourgeoisie—intermediaries between foreign capital and local society.

could Egypt realize its authentic character and create the conditions for the modernization of the country.

But what they strived for was not just a state but a nation-state, an amalgam of politics and culture. The intellectuals of the 1920s believed that a direct relationship existed between an authentic nation and the attainment of modernity (Gershoni and Jankowski 1986: 82, 130). That is to say, the invention of a national culture, as an aggregate of contemporaneous and ancient features, had as its goal the political and economic autonomy of Egypt because it allowed Egyptians to participate in modernity while maintaining their identity.

A major component in the construction of national culture was, of course, literature. Literature was considered an essential building block because, as a reflection of national values, it was believed to contain the indivisible uniqueness of the Egyptian nation. The creation of this literature, as of national culture in general, must be seen in the context, first, of the struggle against a colonial power and, second, of the struggle between local values and global realities. For literature enabled educated Egyptians to imagine their country as distinct and free from foreign control as it also enabled them to understand the overwhelming presence of Western modernity and their consequent need to imitate Western models. They believed that an authentic national tradition would fortify autonomy in the political and economic realms. As in so many similar projects, intellectuals used Western literary genres and the very institution of literature as a way of resisting Western influences in politics and society.

That culture was seen as an agent of opposition and a vehicle to modernization does not mean that literary texts themselves or that short-story writers somehow magically brought about political sovereignty. I have never argued for such a simplistic and vulgar relationship between the cultural and political spheres. Rather it suggests that sovereignty was justified by political leaders in the name of Egypt's national character, which was formulated first by intellectuals and poets. The nationalist revolution, which took place between 1919 and 1922, had as its goal the complete independence of Egypt from foreign control. It was thoroughly Egyptianist in its goals and activities. Indeed, as Gershoni and Jankowski point out, the revolution illustrated the triumph of Egyptianism: the constitution, Parliament, the bureaucracy, the daily operations of government, the activities of the political parties, and the liberal and secularizing ideologies of the 1920s "all reflected the dominant Egyptian territorial nationalist orientation" (1986: 271).

The case of Egypt shows again the subtle interplay of cultural and political factors in the building of nations. Unlike Brazil and Canada, which had been established originally as economic zones, Egypt had centuries of continuous rule and a prestigious past. But, like these two examples, it became a nation-state in modernity and exploited the resources of culture to reinforce its own political independence.

THE UNITED STATES

I have argued until now that it is impossible to separate culture from politics in the project to build nation-states. I wish to explore this hypothesis further by looking into the United States, celebrated in popular and academic writing as a political nation, a country that grew largely through republican texts and ideas rather than a common ancestry. Alexis de Tocqueville articulated this thesis when he contended that, unlike European nations, the United States is held together by the citizens' "exercise of political rights." That is to say, Americans are patriotic primarily because they partake in the affairs of the republic ([1835] 1969: 235–36). Although Tocqueville elsewhere emphasized the common cultural bonds uniting Americans, he primarily expounded the notion of the United States as a political society.[33] Even today it is widely believed that the United States is not a traditional nation-state but one founded on abstract principles. This position maintains that the United States is unprecedented in world history because, having transcended the tribalism of Old World loyalties and their impulse to homogeneity, it constitutes a sum of its parts—in other words, *e pluribus unum*. Michael Lind in his *The Next American Nation: The New Nationalism and the Fourth American Revolution* (1995) subjects this position to serious scrutiny, proving it to be a fiction. In my discussion I show that American state building had a perceptible cultural aspect, that an abstract political unit cannot exist in practice, and that a national culture is an attribute of every nation-state.

Even early American history reveals a preponderance of social or cultural to state institutions. "Nothing strikes a European traveler in the United States," Tocqueville himself observed, "more than the absence of what we would call government or administration" ([1835] 1969: 72). State building, Cynthia Enloe writes, was "historically slow and ideologically suspect. Institutions of nation-building were more legitimate and vital from the onset." While the enterprise of state building persisted through the eighteenth and nineteenth centuries, it went in an unhurried pace because it reminded Americans of the centralization of European regimes. "The bureaucracies of the individual states and the federal government were skeletal; the state civil service was treated with contempt"

[33] On the idea of civic society and civic culture, see Almond 1980.

(1981: 124). Frank Adler goes so far as to call the then United States "a society without a state," one in which the "centralized, external state" played a minimal role (1995: 71). Even if Adler exaggerates the stateless nature of nineteenth-century American society, in his wish to uncover an authentic, nonstatist and nonbureaucratic "community," it is fitting to ask how appropriate it is to characterize the United States then (and now) as an exclusively political nation. One does not have to romanticize the "original model" of American democracy in order to appreciate the strong sense of national and racial identity that had already developed by that time.

The argument of American exceptionalism rests on the assumption that Americans developed loyalties to their political institutions in the absence of ethnic ties. But is this true? While ethnicity played no perceptible role in the War of Independence, the colonists shared much with each other, from a common colonial experience to similar European origins. John Jay (1745–1829) wrote in the second of the *Federalist Papers* in 1787 that "Providence has been pleased to give this one connected country, to one united people, a people descended from the same ancestors, speaking the same language, professing the same religion, attached to the same principles of government, very similar in their manners and customs" (1992: 7).

Tocqueville himself stressed the cultural similarities between the colonies and metropolis. The thirteen colonies had "the same religion, language, and mores, and almost the same laws; they fought against a common enemy; they must therefore have had strong reasons for uniting with each other and becoming absorbed in one and the same nation" ([1835] 1969: 112). The collective sense of purpose shared by the colonists cannot be denied, especially when compared with the bicultural situation in Canada.

Americans, the historian Kendric Charles Babcock wrote, had striven for a strong sense of unity and national life and had attained by 1819 a definable national consciousness ([1909] 1969: 215). Even the transnationally minded Horace Kallen believed that colonists "were possessed of ethnic and cultural unity; they were homogeneous with respect to ancestry and ideals. . . . They did not, until the economico-political quarrel with the mother country arose, regard themselves as other than Englishmen" (1924: 71–72). And, we should not forget, they rebelled against Britain because they were denied the rights they were entitled to as Englishmen.

The solidarity that had emerged among the colonists was the result of practical interaction (shared geography, economic goals, political organizations) as well as cultural bonds. It is this "cultural nation" that Lind calls "Anglo-America," the first republic in the United States, dating from 1789–1860. Its identity was a compound of three factors: Anglo-Saxon culture, the ethic of Protestantism, and federal-republican political values (1995: 27). Like all identities this was molded as much by what united Americans as by what separated them from others. Thus Americans could differentiate themselves religiously from French and Spanish Catholics, politically from absolutist governments in Europe, and racially from their African slaves and the indigenous peoples. When the framers of the U.S. Constitution and their successors in the first half of the nineteenth century spoke of the American people, they had in mind "white Americans of English descent or immigrants from the British Isles and the German countries" (27).

There is evidence that the settlers began to refer to themselves as a separate race after 1680. That is, in addition to their being Englishmen and free, they were from then on white. Africans were slaves not because they were inferior but because they supposedly had dishonorable descent (Banton 1983: 37). This was the reason why colonists had been unwilling to mate with women of Indian or African origin, as was the case in central and south America.[34] The American colonists had drawn an almost impassable line between white and black, the political and cultural significance of which intensified with each decade.

Because the founding fathers wanted a country built on the British model, they did not actively encourage immigration from other parts of Europe. In fact, the Continental Congress rejected official acknowledgment of the polyethnic nature of the American people. When it adopted the Great Seal of the United States in 1782, it refused the original draft, which referred to the thirteen colonies and "the arms of the several nations from whence America has been peopled" (Adams 1993: 92).

In short, it is not possible to argue that, because Americans rebelled against Britain for political and economic reasons primarily, identity had no function in American nation building; or that American nationalism was of an entirely civic nature. On the contrary, it exhibited many features usually ascribed to Old World nationalism. Lind goes so far as to portray the conflicts of the republic up to the Civil War in 1861—the near decimation of the native peoples, the annexation of the Mexican Northwest, the establishment of whites-only territories—as "tribal struggles" (1995: 43).

Actually, civic and cultural nationalism went hand in hand, as is true of all projects of nation building. The erection of liberal, democratic insti-

---

[34] Their position regarding Indians and slaves stands in contrast to that of the Spanish and Portuguese. The latter's experience of living in close proximity with the Moors, who were often a match for them in battle, better prepared them to live with reds and blacks. "The Portuguese and Spaniards might have been as proud and brutal as the English and Dutch, but they did not see the gap between themselves and the other groups as being so great, and when they mated with women of Indian or African origin they were less troubled about the morality of such unions" (Banton 1983: 19).

tutions took place even as Americans saw themselves culturally and racially superior, destined to rule the entire continent. How could they otherwise justify, first, the near extermination of the indigenous populations and the appropriation of their land and, second, the constitutionally sanctioned enslavement of Africans, other than through an identity which celebrated white Americans as higher beings? Race played a powerful role in the formation of American identity, the consequences of which Tocqueville had sensed. In antiquity, he wrote, the slave could be the same race as his master, even superior to him in education. In modernity, by contrast, "servitude is most fatally combined with the physical and permanent fact of difference in race" (1969: 341). American nation building reveals the very features often ascribed to ethnic nationalism—biological forms of identity and notions of cultural uniqueness.

This can be seen in the zeal with which writers, scholars, and intellectuals strived for the creation of an American identity. In their search for a national culture, one expressing the American experience, they displayed the same strategies as nationalists had done in Germany and Greece. After the revolution "Americans wanted most . . . a culture of their own." The revolution itself activated an era of nationalism that left its imprint on American cultural and political institutions. Indeed, the intellectual and cultural history of the period between 1776 and 1820 can be best understood as motivated by nationalism and a belief in progress (Nye 1960: 239, 53). Kenneth Silverman rightly characterizes this a period of "cultural nationalism" (1987: 492).

The elites of the eighteenth century became progressively engaged in the quest for an authentic American civilization, one not beholden to British models. For in the minds of many Europeans the United States seemed a derivative nation. Made uneasy by these comparisons, Americans felt they had to reply. Responding to Count de Buffon's condescending remarks about the lack of American literature, Thomas Jefferson laid out an argument that would be valid for decades: the United States would in time create its own canon of writing. "When we shall have existed as a people as long as the Greeks did before they produced a Homer, the Romans a Virgil, the French a Racine and Voltaire, the English a Shakespeare and Milton . . . then the United States would produce one of its own" (1787, in Ruland 1972: 48). Here again comparisons between a former colony and Europe motivated the program to create national institutions. Poets and writers of the late eighteenth and early nineteenth centuries themselves became anxious about their literary canon. Some argued that Americans were not fit to create a literature, others insisted that they lacked their own idiom, while others believed that America lacked appropriate subjects for great writing (Hedges 1988: 188–89).

Some sixty years after Jefferson, the writer Cornelius Matthews (1817–89) still complained of the "retarded" state of "literary growth." He argued that, because the colonists had retained the language, letters, and writers of Britain, they had become "mere imitators of English models. Interestingly, Matthews compared this "intellectual servitude" to the "despotic influence" French writers had exercised over German authors in the eighteenth century. To make his point, he cited a passage from a review of Madame de Staël's *De l'Allemagne* in the *Edinburgh Review*. Matthews reminded his readers that after a half century Germany had acquired its own literature, "perhaps the *most characteristic possessed by any European nation*" (Ruland 1972: 295). It is instructive that Matthews saw both countries as suffering from cultural belatedness and drew comfort from the eventual rise of a German literature.

Exemplary in the project to found an American literary canon was an essay, "Hawthorne and His Mosses," published by Herman Melville in 1850.[35] An impassioned call for the creation of an American literature, the essay represented in miniature the American version of the quarrel between Ancients and Moderns, the former represented by Shakespeare and the latter by Hawthorne. The existence of writers like Shakespeare, he explained, should not intimidate latecomers into thinking they are incapable of originality (1987: 246). Far from it, for there were Shakespeares "this day born on the banks of the Ohio" (245). Even if such writers had not yet been born, it would be preferable for America first to "praise mediocrity, even in her own children, before she praises . . . the best excellence in the children of any other land." This was so because the nation needed to produce not "American Goldsmiths" or "American Miltons" but authentic authors. In a Herderian gesture Melville implored his readers to "condemn imitation" and support an autochthonous "national literature."

Melville's plea for Americans to recognize the greatness of their literature had already been heard in Europe and has often been made since.[36] It is based on the assumption that each nation needs its own literary canon. This is what Walt Whitman had in mind when, in a letter to Ralph Waldo Emerson (1856), he asked rhetorically: "America, grandest of lands in the theory of its politics, in popular reading, in hospitality. . . . Where are any mental expressions from you, beyond what you have copied or stolen? Where the born throngs, literats, orators, you promised? Will you but tag after other nations?" (1982: 1328) Being late and being

---

[35] See also Emerson's essay (1837) delivered to the Phi Beta Kappa Society. On Hawthorne's literary nationalism, see Berlant 1991.

[36] For similar arguments in postcolonial writing of the twentieth century, see Harlow 1987 and Lazarus 1990.

forced to copy was as humiliating to Americans of the nineteenth century, as to the Germans of the eighteenth, or Nigerians of the twentieth. What all nations aspired to, as Whitman put it, was "a class of native authors and literatures, far different, far higher in grade than any yet known . . . fit to cope with our occasions, lands, permeating the whole mass of American mentality, taste, belief" (1982: 932).[37] As Noah Webster believed, a *"national language* is a band of *national union.* Every engine should be employed to render the people of this country *national."* However much Americans "may boast of Independence," their *"opinions* are not sufficiently independent"; they still displayed "a blind imitation" for the arts, literature, and manners of their "parent country." This "habitual respect" prevented them from "respecting themselves" and creating their own culture—exactly the characterization of Germans made by Madame de Staël. Nationalism has always been motivated by comparisons and resulting hurt feelings of self-esteem. Webster saw the publication of the *Dissertations on the English Language,* as a part of a greater enterprise to establishing a "national language" ([1789] 1951: 36–37).[38]

In short, nineteenth-century Americans expressed the same sentiments of belatedness and inferiority that resulted from the comparisons they made between themselves and Europeans. They too launched a campaign for the establishment of a national literature (Spencer 1957: 19). The object of this "literary nationalism was a search for a way to use the resources for the American land, the American past, and American society, to produce an art that was indigenous, new, universally beautiful, morally true, expressive of American ideas, and representative of the American spirit" (Nye 1960: 246).

It was at the universities around the turn of the century that the literary nationalism had its more practical consequences.[39] Although American writers had always lamented the lack of a literary tradition, the quest for an authentic American civilization became a more pressing concern in large part because of the dramatic change in the national origins of the new immigrants. While until the latter part of the century immigrants stemmed largely from the British Isles, Scandinavia, and Germany, appreciably greater numbers began to come from southern and eastern Europe. As the sum of immigrants from these regions increased, David Shumway explains, "developing American nationalism became a much more ex-

---

[37] American literature, we should not forget, has been very preoccupied with the creation of identity. When Ralph Ellison was asked by an interviewer whether the "search for identity is primarily an American theme," he answered: "It is *the* American theme" (1964: 177).

[38] In this regard, see Mencken's discussion of Webster's project (1936).

[39] See Hall's study (1982) of how a handful of universities (Harvard, Yale, Princeton, William and Mary) emerged as national institutions after the Civil War.

plicit goal of public education" (1994: 39). American literature was seen as one means of instilling American virtues in children. More generally, literature was regarded as a source of cultural value. It was seen as, first, providing an aesthetic alternative to the rational, commercial realm of work; second, as encouraging solidarity among the dominant classes; and, finally, as one block in the construction of a national identity (31–32). Although American literature was being produced, read, and enjoyed, it was neither taught nor studied at the university in the 1890s (Graff 1987: 1).[40] But the situation changed in the next century as American writing became a bona fide subject, accruing the recognizable attributes of a discipline. This institutionalization, however, was part of a greater national enterprise rather than of a narrow aesthetic or pedagogic process.

Thus American nationalism, rather than being a strictly political phenomenon expressing universalist ideals, was at the same time a cultural discourse manifesting ideas of ethnic and racial inclusivity. Motivated by feelings of inferiority vis-à-vis England, American intellectuals in the nineteenth century undertook a literary program to define the nature of American identity. Even though this identity was not the motivating factor in the Declaration of Independence, it began to assume greater significance in the process of nation making. It also acquired sacred overtones.

Robert Bellah has shown that American civil religion, a national body of meanings, texts, practices, holidays, and images consecrated as holy, acts as the secular identity of the United States (1970, Bellah and Hammond 1980).[41] This civil religion has its own pantheon of saints (Washington, as the new Moses; Lincoln and Kennedy, as martyrs), holidays (Memorial Day for the nation's fallen and Thanksgiving, the quintessentially American nondenominational celebration), and a host of national monuments and memorials.[42] These symbols, heroes, signs, and sites serve as the ecumenical meaning system of the United States, imbuing Americanness with feelings of sacredness. Along with a set of political and legal documents, they represent the national identity of the United States. It has been ordained as sacred and assigned with universal points of reference.

[40] Until that time literature was treated in classes of Greek and Latin and as part of English grammar and rhetoric (Graff 1987: 1). That its institutionalization occurred so late in the United States should not surprise us. In England it happened in the latter part of the nineteenth century (Baldick 1983). The professionalization of modern Greek literature was a product of the latter part of the twentieth century (Jusdanis 1991a).

[41] In his *Social Contract* (1762) Rousseau differentiated between a private and civil religion. The dogmas of the latter were the existence of a powerful, benevolent God; the possibility of life after death; happiness of the just and the sanctity of laws; tolerance of religious faith (1953: 152–53).

[42] See Coleman 1970–71.

The paradox of this identity, however, is that it eludes the definition of the national.[43] In the same way, this identity represents itself as secular despite its having been sacralized. Although the United States constitutes a nation-state like any other, it represents itself as a nonnational state. Its nationalism is seen as civic rather than ethnic, political instead of cultural, pluralist rather than homogeneous. It has produced a nation that cannot be called a nation, certainly not in the sense of old nations in Europe. In short, it gets away with calling itself a civic nation.

Yet American nationalism is not exceptional. The differences between it and Old World nationalism are not absolute. The United States is still a unitary state with strongly assimilative social tendencies. A unitary state, I have argued, cannot exist as merely a summation of its differences despite its official ideology of liberal pluralism. American nationalism has not escaped history to create a completely new phenomenon. Its message is rather much simpler: nonethnic forms of national identity can still have the mystical appeal and integrative function normally ascribed to cultural nationalism.

CIVIC IDENTITY

My aim in this chapter has been to question the historical possibility of a purely political nation and of a purely civic identity. I have shown in various cases that culture and politics interact in the formation of nation-states. This is true even of those colonies, such as Canada or Brazil, which existed as economic and administrative zones before becoming autonomous nations. The Egyptian example highlights, like so many from the postcolonial world, that the assertion of cultural differences was essential in the establishment of an independent state, free from imperial (Ottoman and British) control.

The debate over civic or ethnic nationalism, political or cultural nations is pointless because at the end *all nationalism takes on a cultural dimension*. This does not mean that nationalism is strictly a xenophobic, inward-looking, racist discourse, preoccupied with ethnic inclusivity. Rather it suggests that issues of national identity, literature, tradition, language have served as stimulants in the construction of even the most quintessentially political nations. The histories of France, the United

---

[43] Bellah points out that in the United States legal institutions acquired an ecclesiastical character. The Supreme Court constitutes a "halting, hesitant, but inevitable effort to perform for American society the religious task of providing a common moral understanding" (1970: 149). On the Constitution as sacred text, see Doctorow 1987 and Hart and Stimpson 1993.

States, and England reveal that it is impossible to disconnect the movement to self-government from the project at self-definition, even if originally they constituted separate historical processes.[44] In the past two centuries the two interpretations of national sovereignty, the political and cultural, have actually merged. For this reason it is impossible to speak of a civic identity and understand by that a political entity, devoid of cultural overtones. We understand and support the creation of a new state on the basis of a group's right to determine its own affairs and to protect its own culture. This is the only way today we can rationalize, say, the possible emergence of republics of Quebec, Catalonia, Chechnya, or Kurdistan. A majority of Quebecois may see themselves so culturally different from the rest of Canada that they may wish to form their own independent country. This new state would undoubtedly be a liberal republic but the reason for its birth would be culture rather than democracy. While the Quebecois may indeed be seeking to govern themselves without any interference from Ottawa or other provinces, the real aim of seccession would be a union of Quebecois state mechanisms and Quebecois culture. Or to use the example of the Kurds, the possible creation of a Kurdistan has as its causes the suppression of the Kurds by Turkey, Iraq, and Syria. An object of that political repression, particularly in Turkey, is Kurdish culture. Kurdish nationalism to a certain extent represents the desire of Kurds for political institutions to develop and protect national life. It is in this respect that nationalism is ultimately a cultural phenomenon. The defenders of a civic identity do not address this issue at all. Is it reasonable to ask the Kurds to transform their culture, an object of their repression, into the symbolic ethnicity characteristic of white Euro-Americans? It is this type of ethnic identification, as I show in the following chapter, that civic nationalism allows—a private and apolitical form of identity. But is it workable outside of multicultural North America?

Ultimately, the glorification of civic identity manifests a tendency among social theorists and journalists to draw moral judgments about nationalism, seeking to distinguish a noble from a base conception of nationhood, an Anglo-Saxon from an eastern European and postcolonial view of nationality. It is fair to ask of those associating cultural nationalism with racism, ethnic cleansing, and genocide why a civic identity did not prevent the English from disenfranchising Catholics and women at home and from launching a brutal imperialism overseas. Is this imperialism a lesser evil than an aggressive, cultural nationalism associated with

---

[44] It can be argued that American nationalism and British nationalism were so long conceived as civic in part because their cultural dimension was not really examined. The study of English and American nationalism is a belated affair, in comparison to the study of German, Greek, Russian, or Irish nationalism.

eastern Europe? By the same token, Americans may have been inspired by federalist, republican principles in the establishment of the nation, but their political ideals did not stop them from making a racist distinction a founding principle of the republic. Again, why should the forced removal of indigenous peoples from their land or the enslavement of others—and this a hundred years after the Enlightenment—constitute a less heinous crime than those perpetrated in the name of blood and belonging? Why should this not be seen as a function of American nationalism in the same way that the Holocaust, the Gulag, or the ethnic cleansing of Kosovo are regularly regarded as products of pathological forms of identity. Americans yearned for a racial homogeneity, even if not for an ethnic or linguistic purity. And they did not need the rousing speeches of rabid nationalists. It is a paradox that the colonists' struggle for freedom from British rule coincided with the enslavement of Africans and the dispossession of the native peoples—in the same way that strides toward greater democracy in Britain took place as its imperial grip upon the world stiffened.

I am not making a relativist argument here, namely, that all societies are the same or that we have no right to judge them. Nor am I rejecting American democracy, or the Athenian for that matter, because of slavery.[45] Both of these democracies show that progressive ideologies, participatory politics, egalitarianism, and populism can go hand in hand with barbarism. There is nothing new in that. My question is simple: Have the so-called political nations not had their history of inhumanity? If so, how can we, on the one hand, find cultural nationalism responsible for evil, all the time exempting civic nationalism? Finally, what is the purpose of comparing the scope of these crimes and thus making untenable comparisons between civic and cultural nationalities? Individuals and groups act as they do not solely for reasons of their ethnic or national identities. We have to look to motivational factors beyond nationalism in the political and economic realms to explain British imperialism, German fascism, the Soviet Gulag, or American slavery.

Civic identity does not guarantee that a given state would apply democratic principles to all its citizens or in its actions abroad. Yet we should acknowledge that Britain, France, and the United States had developed civic institutions, democratic documents, practices, and beliefs that could put in check the most extreme expressions of nationalism. This may be the real lesson of political nations. Their experience of a political society has enabled citizens to perceive liberty in forms of civic rights and parliamentary government as well as self-rule. The history of the past two centuries illustrates that the call for freedom *from* colonial masters is as pro-

---

[45] On the contrary, I criticize those who propose such reductive arguments. See my "Acropolis Now?" (Jusdanis 1996).

found as the call for freedom *of* speech, equality for women, protection for minorities. The right to culture should be placed alongside civil and human rights. If all forms of nationalism are ultimately cultural and if nationalism continues to be a prominent force in social life, then the task before us is to devise political systems that incorporate the reality of nationalism without turning the history of the past two hundred years into a Manichaean tale of good and evil.

Chapter Six

THE END OF IDENTITIES?

THAT CULTURAL matters have figured prominently in endeavors to build nation-states is beyond dispute. What remains to be seen is whether national culture will continue to be prominent in the new millennium. What will its future be in an era when the authority of a nation-state is undermined externally by global forces and challenged internally by demands for greater autonomy? This is one of the most burning questions facing the nation today. Will national culture, a modern phenomenon, deteriorate along with the edifice of the nation-state? Is ethnicity itself going to be transformed under conditions of postmodern and postindustrial society into a meaningless symbol? Will we continue to be citizens of nation-states at the end of the century or will we belong to different political configurations? I consider these questions by looking first into cultural identities in the United States; I wish specifically to determine the form they take in a polity of profound cultural mixing. More generally, I want to examine whether America is being disunited today— that is, whether its national culture is being torn down by various ethnic and racial groups. I then extend my argument to other countries by discussing the phenomenon of globalization, considering whether the winds of globalization, seemingly indifferent to national borders, threaten the viability of both national culture and the nation-state.

THE DISCONNECTING OF AMERICA

The question of America's imminent demise has been hotly debated in the culture wars of the 1980s and 1990s. Political, academic, and journalist commentators point to the ethnic divisions endangering the country's unity. The position that the contemporary accentuation of cultural identities will unravel the national fabric has been forcefully expressed by Arthur Schlesinger. In *The Disuniting of America* he contended that multiculturalism undermines the American ideal of ethnic and racial coexistence by promoting the model of the United States as a nation of groups rather than individuals (1992: 19). E. D. Hirsch similarly argued that multilingualism "enormously increases fragmentation, civil antagonism, illiteracy, and economic-technological ineffectualness" (1987: 92). Hirsch published his *Cultural Literacy* to prop up the sagging tent of national culture. Sheldon Hackney sponsored a series of lectures and town hall meetings throughout the country in response to what he saw as the increasing particularism in the United States. In a speech, given to the National Press Club on November 10, 1993, Hackney asked whether the "politics of difference" was leading the country to the same internecine strife that has torn apart Bosnia-Herzegovina and Azerbaijan.

Are these fears justified? Is the United States facing disintegration? Is the canopy of national identity crashing down upon its citizenry? These questions are at the heart of thinking on globalization. Yet seen from another perspective, they are as old as the history of American immigration itself. If we look into this tradition, we will see that the country's identity has been challenged by each successive wave of foreigners. If academics, journalists, or politicians have underestimated the significance these new Americans have attached to their cultural identities, it is because they believed the United States to be a political nation in which ethnic affiliation was a private affair. Social theorists who studied ethnicity of European groups in the 1920s and 1930s expected it to dissolve in the confluence of assimilation and acculturation. In the model of cultural pluralism, ethnic identities were to be checked at home on the way out. Ethnicity was rarely mentioned in the sociology of the 1950s and 1960s (Greeley 1974: 24; Thompson 1989: 1).[1]

But at the turn of the century it was a controversial topic, forced upon the public sphere by the arrival of millions of people from non-Anglo-Saxon and non-Germanic Europe. People were preoccupied with it as they have been in the last two decades of the twentieth century. Until 1880 about 85 percent of immigrants stemmed from Britain, Germany, Holland, Scandinavia, Ireland and Canada. Although between 1860 to 1890 10 million people had come from eastern and southern Europe, by the 1890s their numbers increased dramatically (Jones 1960: 179). Between 1820 and 1950 about 5 million Italians and 3 million Russians (mostly Jews) had entered the United States (Kessler-Harris and Yans-McLaughlin 1978: 107–9). In 1907 alone 1,285,349 legal immigrants were admitted into a country whose population was 87 million.[2] At that time 80 percent were from countries in southern and eastern Europe; in

---

[1] Until the 1960s assimilationist theories held sway that claimed that the vast legions of new immigrants would gradually replace the garments of their national origins with American dress. They were questioned by Glazer and Moynihan's tellingly titled, *Beyond the Melting Pot* (1963), Greeley's *Why Can't They Be Like Us* (1971), and Novak's *The Rise of the Unmeltable Ethnics* (1972).

[2] These numbers should be contrasted with the 804,416 legal immigrants admitted in 1994 when the country's population was 253 million ("Immigration—Just the Facts," *New York Times*, March 25, 1996). Immigrants constituted a greater proportion of the population than they do today. Indeed, in 1815 the population of the United States was 8,419,000, in 1860 it stood at 31,513,000, and in 1890 it was 63,056,000 (Bureau of the Census 1960: 7).

1880 they had constituted only 13 percent of arrivals. In the first decade of this century over 1 million foreigners were landing on the shores of the United States every year. Public opinion was so disturbed by these numbers that Congress set up the Dillingham Commission in 1907 to examine the cultural implications these immigrants posed to the country.[3]

Social scientists themselves began to study the potential impact of mass immigration. Given the large ethnic composition of Chicago,[4] sociologists at the University of Chicago, headed by Robert E. Park, started to investigate these issues in a systematic way. They wanted to study the process of "cultural diffusion" and determine what happens "when people of divergent cultures come into contact and conflict" (Park 1950: 5). Seeing America as a laboratory for the interaction of peoples of various national, religious, and racial backgrounds, they focused on assimilation, which Park and Ernest W. Burgess defined as "a process of interpenetrating and fusion in which persons and groups acquire the memories, sentiments, and attitudes of other persons or groups, and, by sharing their experience and history, are incorporated with them in a common cultural life" (1921: 735).

Their views were opposed by cultural pluralists like Horace Kallen, who in 1914 published his essay "Democracy versus the Melting-Pot," denouncing nativist arguments.[5] Aware of Park's assimilationist theories and quite conscious of the contemporaneous hostility to immigrants, Kallen rejected the creation of a national culture, which, he pointed out, had taken hold in countries of the Old World. A similar effort on American soil would require "the complete nationalization of education, the abolition of every form of parochial and private school, the abolition of instruction in other tongues than English, and the concentration of teaching of history and literature upon the English tradition" (1924: 118–19). The creation of a melting pot "by law," he argued, would do violence to the "ideals of American fundamental law and the spirit of American institutions." His theory of cultural pluralism, in contrast, would provide ethnic groups the conditions "under which each might attain the cultural perfection that is *proper to its kind*" (120–21). He proposed a model of the United States as a nation of nations (rather than a nation-state), "a democracy of nationalities," in which each group could preserve its culture (124).

---

[3] In 1924 it passed the Reed-Johnson Act to restrict the number of newcomers through quotas based on the national distribution of the 1890 census.

[4] In 1910 nearly *three-quarters* of its population was composed of immigrants and their offspring, representing twenty nationalities (Steinberg 1989: 47). By contrast in 1990 only 16.9 percent of Chicago's population was foreign-born (*1996 Country and City Extra, Annual Metro, City, and Country Data Book*).

[5] In 1846 Margaret Fuller spoke of America as a "mixed race," one "continually enriched with new blood from other stocks." This heterogeneity differentiated the United States from Britain. Her view that American identity had had no "sympathy with national unity" is an early expression of cultural pluralism (1846: 123–24).

Kallen's picture of the United States as the first global, cosmopolitan polity is, of course, another version of American exceptionalism, which portrays the United States as a universal political nation. At roughly the same time Randolph Bourne similarly denounced the melting pot as a failure, calling instead for an America founded on ethnic and racial pluralism. In "Trans-Cultural America" (1916) he denied the existence of a "distinctively American culture" and of an American nationality (1956: 272). He rejected entirely the idea of assimilation, believing that Americanization of the immigrants would lead into "a tasteless, colorless fluid of uniformity" (269). The greater part of his essay portrayed the United States as the first self-consciously cosmopolitan nation. Rather than a traditional nation-state, the United States was for him a "cosmopolitan federation of national colonies, of foreign cultures, . . . a world federation in miniature" (276).[6]

If Kallen's and Bourne's arguments seem to have been taken out of the culture wars of the 1990s, it is because they were reacting to similar issues: how to incorporate millions of foreigners from eastern and southern Europe who were seen by Americans as of a different race.[7] Their views, multicultural in today's sense of the word, were pushed to the side, however, by the model of assimilation, which according to the theories of Park and Burgess, saw immigrants adopting attributes of American national culture in the pursuit of "unity of experience and of orientation" (1921: 737). In public schools, for instance, "Americanization was the order of the day and prevailed without a check throughout the 1920s, 1930s, and 1940s" (Glazer 1994: 124). Proponents of assimilation never doubted the existence of an American national culture.[8]

OF TWO MULTICULTURALISMS

The belligerents in today's culture wars seem to have forgotten the heated discussions about immigration and identity in the early part of the century. Critics of immigration in the 1990s, for instance, do not take into

---

[6] Fearful of the nationalism ignited by World War I, Bourne promoted Zionism as a nationalism devoid of chauvinism and proposed it as an authentic form of transnationalism (Clayton 1984: 197–98).

[7] Kallen noted the quantum changes activated by globalization. "In these days of rapid transit and industrial mobility, . . . hardly anybody seems to have been born where he lives, or to live where he has been born" (1924: 84).

[8] Although assimilation was questioned in the 1960s, it received a theoretical articulation in Milton Gordon's influential *Assimilation in American Life*. While Gordon did not subscribe to a straight-line view of assimilation, he spoke of an "identificational assimilation" which entailed the development among immigrants of a sense of American "peoplehood" (1964: 70–71).

account that immigrants constitute a smaller portion of the population in comparison with the situation a hundred years ago. By the same token, multiculturalists ignore that immigrants from southeastern Europe at the turn of the century were as tightly bound to their countries of origin—without the modern benefit of quick communication and transportation—as those of today are. They too were extensions of diasporas. For instance, Greeks preserved close family networks, sponsored relatives to immigrate to the United States, and sent extraordinary amounts of money back home—about $650 million between 1910 and 1930. Above all, many still participated in the political struggles at home, reproducing in the United States the conflicts in Greece. The clash in Greece (1915–22) between the royalist supporters of King Constantine I (1868–1923) and the republican adherents of Eleftherios Venizelos (1864–1936) tore apart the Greeks in the United States as well. Nothing brings more to the fore their strong involvement in the politics of their native land than the return of 45,000 immigrants to Greece to fight in the Greek army during the Balkan Wars of 1912–13 (Moskos 1989: 11, 31).[9] A look into history will tell us that today's multicultural moment is not as exceptional as multiculturalists maintain.

Similarly, it is necessary to disentangle the various theoretical arguments. To the question of whether multiculturalism is disuniting America, one has to ask which multiculturalism? Although it is usually treated as one in academic as well as popular discussions, there are actually two forms of this discourse whose roots, as I have shown, lie in earlier debates about nation and identity: a liberal version, which celebrates American society as an ethnic neighborhood, and a more radical manifestation, which regards it as nation of nations. The former regards culture as symbolic and private, while the latter sees it as political and instrumental. Whatever form it takes, however, the preoccupation with multiculturalism in America shows the continued prominence of culture in public life.

Liberal multiculturalism, the postmodern rendition of Kallen's cultural pluralism, applies primarily to the identities of white Americans of European descent, which it represents in terms of the private-public dichotomy. It believes, for instance, that in exchange for their admittance into the civic public sphere, Americans must renounce loyalties to their cultural identities, rendering them henceforth private and symbolic. While citizens may parade them in ethnic festivals, they must keep them out of politics.

[9] On their participation in the Greek relief effort during World War II, see Kyrou 1991. Basch, Schiler, and Blanc ignore this earlier phase of immigration when they characterize the attempt of today's "transmigrants" to maintain contacts with their home countries as exceptional (1994).

Embracing the belief of the United States as a political nation, liberal multiculturalism acknowledges individual rather than group rights. This discourse has in a sense depoliticized the identities of Euro-Americans, reducing them to colorful glass in the mosaic of diversity. The basic tenet of this doctrine is that individuals are free to choose any ancestral identity as long as its practice has no impact on governance. By removing ethnicity from the public arena, liberal multiculturalism has converted it into a neutral zone. In this respect, it has followed the example of the European states that, having emerged from the ferocious civil wars of the sixteenth century, banished theology from politics. The cultural pluralism of the twentieth century was superimposed on this earlier model of religious coexistence.[10]

The recent roots of liberal multiculturalism, however, lie in the resurgence of white ethnicity in the 1960s. For, contrary to the predictions of assimilationists, these "ethnics" had not disappeared. In that decade they had begun to take an active interest in their heritages. Not ashamed of their backgrounds, they displayed their traditions proudly in festivals. Gyro, bagels, and pizza entered the American kitchen and vocabulary. Ethnic studies programs were established at universities. In time, white ethnicity was commodified as a consumable product in ethnic restaurants, television, the movies, and entertainment parks. In one respect, this self-conscious attempt to be ethnic may indicate another stage of assimilation. Yet it also represents an increase in manifestations of ethnic identification, seen among other ethnic and racial groups, which again points to the continuing importance of cultural models in the United States.[11]

The reasons for the resurgence of ethnicity are varied. In part it had to do with the third generation, the proverbial granddaughters and grandsons who decided to remember what their own parents had deliberately forgotten. It was also a response to the civil rights movement of the 1960s. Whites (like the state) interpreted the "success" of African Americans in using culture for the pursuit of social justice as a manifestation of ethnic pride rather than class politics (Thompson 1989: 93). The white ethnic

---

[10] The history of cultural pluralism goes back to colonial Pennsylvania, which, as Lawrence H. Fuchs explains, became a model for ethnic integration in the United States because it was the first colony where "immigrants of various nationalities and religious backgrounds moved with relative ease into political life." Unlike Massachusetts, which accepted new members only if they were religiously pure, or Virginia, which relied heavily on slave labor, Pennsylvania "sought immigrants who would be good citizens regardless of religious background." The German narrative of "ethnic-Americanization" has been repeated by every other group of immigrants who have arrived in the United States voluntarily (Fuchs 1990: 5, 20, 29). See also Mann 1979: 154.

[11] Not all Americans believe they possess an ethnic identity. In the census of 1980, 13.3 million out of 226.5 million gave the United States as their ancestry (Lieberson 1985: 171).

renaissance paralleled, borrowed from, and also reacted to the black power movement. The government had a significant role as well. Being receptive, as Daniel Bell has argued, to ethnic rather than class claims, it encouraged the formation of ethnicities, now transformed into quasi interest groups (1975).

The form white identity most often takes is what the sociologist Herbert J. Gans calls symbolic. The ethnic role "is today less of an ascriptive than a voluntary role that people assume alongside other roles" (1979: 8–9). With the decline of immigrant organizations and the rise of mixed marriages, fewer ethnic behaviors are prescribed, and, as a result, individuals have some choice as to how to define themselves. Their identity is situational, that is, it "may be of critical relevance in some situations, while in others it may be totally irrelevant" (Okamura 1981: 460). In a postmodern society, white identity is associated no longer with kinship, profession, or place of residence but with efforts of maintaining feelings of being, say, Italian or Greek.

There is a paradox inherent in liberal multiculturalism. The heightened expression of ethnicity coincides with a visible erosion and often disappearance of ethnic institutions.[12] Indeed, many groups face the possibility of cultural extinction in the United States.[13] While multiculturalism endlessly congratulates itself for the persistence of diversity, research presents a loss of ethnic identification among Euro-Americans. Language is usually the first and most significant symbol of cultural distinctiveness to disappear. There has been a perceptible erosion not only in the use of, but also the exposure to, European languages in the United States. For instance, of those individuals born after 1960 9.8 percent spoke a European language as children and only 5.8 percent currently do so (Alba 1990: 11). Language loss through the generations is inexorable, a development all the more sobering in light of the emphasis nationalists have placed on speech as both the expression and protector of cultural uniqueness. Related to language is the decline of the immigrant press. At the turn of the century numerous newspapers and magazines were published in German, Italian, Greek, Swedish, Yiddish, and a host of other languages.[14] Now

[12] The decline of these institutions has profound implications because they enabled both the survival and assimilation of immigrants. Park and Miller with some justification referred to these institutions as transit stations for immigrants passing from the old to the new world (1921: 120).

[13] Lipset and Raab explore the effect of assimilation on Jews. It is reasonable to predict, they argue, "that the Jewish community will be severely reduced by the middle of the next century" (1995: 199).

[14] *Die Abendschule*, a very popular magazine, began publication in 1854 (first in Buffalo and then St. Louis) to serve ethnic Germans, only to fold in 1940 due to low readership (Peterson 1991: 4). In 1910 it had 51,530 subscribers, an astonishing number when one

few exist. Similar signs of assimilation can be seen in the dissolution of ethnic neighborhoods[15] and the precipitous drop in the number of ethnic schools.

In his study of the 1980 census Richard D. Alba found that among whites "three of every four marriages involve some degree of ethnic boundary crossing." Half of all marriages take place between individuals who share no common ancestry. Increasingly such marriages are the rule rather than the exception. This means that a significant number of whites, about 47% according to the 1980 census, are products of ethnic mixing (1990: 12–13). The high rate of interethnic marriage (which can only rise) and the mixed progeny it produces have had a heavy impact on ethnic consciousness. For the more varied the ancestry of individuals, the more blurred their connections with their traditions, and the less likely they are to recognize or express the attributes of their ethnicity.

Under these conditions cultural identities can only be symbolic, as colorful and low maintenance as spring annuals. The ethnicity of assimilated Europeans has little impact on their lives and makes few demands on their everyday behavior. This does not mean, however, that the remnants of old heritages have been abandoned or that identity has lost significance in people's lives. Rather it suggests that identity has changed. Ethnic identification is expressed today in the preparation of traditional foods and enactment of customs and rituals during holidays, the use of words and phrases of the ancestral tongue, the organization of festivals.[16]

The consequent smudging of ethnic boundaries has given people considerable freedom in manipulating suitable cultural symbols for a personal pastiche. When people of mixed ancestry look back into their pasts, they uncover a number of traditions all vying for attention. Because it would be impossible for them to grasp onto all the branches in their family tree, Mary C. Waters has discovered, they quite often choose a few or just one (1990: 19). This choice, however, is not so simple since after many generations people very often have a dim knowledge of their heritage. The genealogical tree actually comes to resemble an attic stuffed with

---

considers that the 1992 circulation of the *New Republic* stood at 101,828 and *Harper's Magazine* at 200,853 (*The National Directory of Magazines*, 1992).

[15] High levels of segregation characterized most new immigrant communities until 1910 (Yancey, Ericksen, and Leon 1985: 96).

[16] Research into native-born whites reveals that over the previous five years 47 percent ate foods of their heritage, 32.8 percent discussed their background, 31.7 percent felt curious about other ethnic traditions, 29.8 percent used words or phrases from an ancestral language, and 27.2 percent attended ethnic festivals. Only 2.2 percent received special help in professional life from someone of the same ethnic background; 4.3 percent claimed to have been discriminated against because of their ethnicity; 9.8 percent visited their ancestral homeland; and a surprising 15 percent taught their children customs or traditions of their birthright (Alba 1990: 79).

memorabilia. As they rummage through it, they cannot always distinguish among their traditions and are not certain about the origins and meanings of their beliefs and customs.

Individuals simplify or modify their ethnic identities in the course of their life, often in response to changes in their life, be they entry into adulthood, marriage, or middle age. Some may actually adjust it in the course of the day. Waters cites the case of a woman with a Greek-Polish mother and a Welsh father, who identified herself as Greek to family and friends, as Polish at work, and as Welsh in the 1980 census (1990: 19).

This self-conscious creation of ethnicity constitutes an extension of the postmodern proclivity to self-invention, the tendency to regard the self as a synthesis of various traditions. The new "enterprising and consuming self" maximizes the value of life by "assembling a lifestyle, or lifestyles, through personal acts of choice in the marketplace" (Bonner and de Gay 1992: 86).[17] The self becomes a reflexive project, fashioned differently at various stages of a person's life. The individual, Giddens observes, faces numerous life-style choices with biography becoming a navigation through diverse options (1991: 5–14). The questions "How shall I live?" and "Who am I?" have to be faced in daily decisions since they are *not* determined by kinship or traditions. These questions have to be answered with regard to fashion, diet, health, profession, the family, and, of course, ethnicity. In other words, the postmodern individual conceives of identity as a reflexively maintained enterprise rather than a set of duties and obligations. The difference between the white immigrants and their great-grandchildren (and between whites today and racial minorities) is that ethnic identification has become largely a life-style choice.[18]

Today's "ethnics" resemble the Poseidonians in Cavafy's eponymous poem, written in 1906 and posthumously published. The poem tells of the town Poseidonia, now known as Paestum, which is located near Naples and the site of two well-preserved archaic temples. Founded as a Greek colony in 600 B.C. in the area called Magna Graecia (Greater Greece), it was captured by the Romans in 273 B.C. Cavafy imagines what happens to the Poseidonians and the Greek way of life over the centuries. The Poseidonians, he tells us, had forgotten their Greek tongue and culture after centuries of mingling with Tyrrhnians, Latins, and other foreigners. The only connection to their ancestors was a Greek festival, at the end of which they always talked about their old customs and repeated their Greek names.

[17] See also Betz 1992.

[18] Although whites enjoy a certain freedom in fashioning their identity, they are limited, Waters observes, by knowledge of their ancestors; family surname, a conspicuous marker of ethnicity; physical appearance; and ranking—people believe that certain ancestries are

And so their festival always ended sadly
because they remembered that they too were Greeks—
they too were citizens of Magna Graecia once;
but now how they had fallen, what they had become,
living and speaking in a barbarian manner,
removed—what a misfortune!—from Hellenism.

(Cavafy 1977)

Their once renowned culture had been transformed to a celebratory event, an invocation of difference from others, a drama performed in a strange dialogue—hence, the festival's elegiac end. Under conditions of globalization, modern Poseidonians have no choice but to create symbolic ethnicities, wrapping them with the ribbon of melancholy.

The nostalgia for the "old country," however, remains on the surface, for the "ethnics" have learned to market their identities. Pleasurable to insiders and outsiders alike, ethnicity today is sold and consumed as a commodity, as food, dances, quaint neighborhoods, atmosphere, and Old World family values. This, in part, explains the persistence of ethnic modes of identification. If one of the greatest challenges for people today is to maintain a sense of distinctiveness in a society sacralizing continuous differentiation, then ethnicity provides a set of symbols for asserting a degree of constancy and uniqueness. The tragedy of modern culture, Georg Simmel argued, is that people feel submerged in a sea of signs and of ceaseless flux, "surrounded by an innumerable number of cultural elements" (1968: 44). In the polysemia of commercialized life, ethnic symbols promise individuals the possibility of enacting their individuality and of providing a sense of history, however tenuous.

The situation of cultural identities today has thus to be understood in the relentless spread of consumer culture into every niche of life by means of advertising, television, radio, billboards, style, the Internet, and World Wide Web. In contemporary post-Fordist capitalism, with its turn toward services, information, and communication, the exchange value of commodities, as Jean Baudrillard has shown, has been transformed to sign value (1981). A shift has taken place in both production and consumption, away from goods to symbols, which flow relentlessly through society. Subjected to the mechanisms of the market, these signs are converted into commodities themselves to be bought and sold. The consequence of this expansion is that everything in our life, "from economic values and state power to practices and the very structure of the psyche itself can be said to have become 'cultural' in some original and as yet untheorized sense" (Jameson 1984: 87).

---

more attractive than others (1990: 57–58). One has to add the very ideology of multiculturalism that encourages the possession of a (symbolic) ethnic identity in the first place.

What is taking place is a culturalization of life, by which each nuance, object, movement is considered aesthetic in some form or other. This phenomenon fosters a degree of leveling and homogenization through its emphasis on the fragmentary and the fleeting, as it turns the unique into the typical, the accidental into the normal, the superficial into the essential. "Our world view," observed Simmel, "turns into aesthetic pantheism. Every point contains within itself the potential of being reduced to absolute aesthetic importance" (1968: 69).[19] Rather than representing the reintegration of art into life, the goal of the historical avant-garde, this transformation shows the overwhelming importance ascribed to culture today. Given the critique of autonomous art that has already been undertaken first by the avant-garde[20] and continued by postmodernism, the colonization of society by culture means that culture, no longer a specialized realm of experience, is becoming once more a way of life. Since any object or experience can now be cultural, and any article of everyday life a work of art, culture truly is everywhere. This scattering of goods and images suggests that culture has lost its theoretical self-sufficiency. Cultural identities both manifest this development and contradict it. On the one hand, the symbolic, surface identity of today represents this aestheticization of life. On the other hand, these expressions of ethnic uniqueness counteract the tendency toward flattening and homogenization.

Ultimately integrationist, this form of ethnic identification does not threaten American society. Will Kymlicka rightly argues that groups have rarely advanced claims for self-government under the rubric of liberal multiculturalism (1998: 185). This is not the case, however, with racialized minorities whose populations have been either enslaved, colonized, or dispossessed in the United States. They too manifest a heightened ethnic consciousness. But theirs is a politicized, rather than symbolic, identity, reminiscent in this way of nascent nationalism. Indeed, visible minorities come close to resembling Old World communities whose identities are structural rather than symbolic. The denial of civil rights to minorities even in the twentieth century has created an ethnicity characteristic of an older, hierarchical order, one certainly inconsistent with the

---

[19] A contemporary version of this aesthetic theory is the ethic of aesthetics, proposed by Michel Maffesoli, which considers everyday life "a work of art." It is no longer possible, he maintains, "to say that any aspect of social life, not cookery, nor attention to appearance, nor small celebration, nor relaxing walks, is frivolous or insignificant" (1991: 8). The aesthetic is that which brings people together, that which takes "on the function of aggregation and reinforcement which I call *sociability*" (19).

[20] I refer here to Peter Bürger who has argued that the historical avant-garde turned against the distribution system on which works of art depend and the very idea of an autonomous art (1984: 22). In showing that a work of art was a thing among things, it sought ultimately to reconcile art back to life.

universalistic principles of the United States. Insofar as it legitimizes distinctions of status and a whole set of inequalities based on race, this usage of identity corresponds to modes of identification in prenational societies.

RACIAL PANETHNICITIES

The private-public dichotomy inherent in the model of liberal multiculturalism cannot be applied to those disenfranchised from American society on grounds of their race. Rather than being a personal matter, identity was and is the reason for their subjection. Culture, in the form of racial identity, has consequences in their lives and their relationship to other groups and to the state. It is their angry criticism of American society that has made multiculturalism such a copious source of national trauma. It is putting into question the ideal of cultural pluralism, the conception of identity as a personal matter, and the claim of national culture to be all-inclusive. By politicizing their own identities, these groups have also challenged the way Americans understand national culture. No longer a cauldron for the dilution of difference, national culture is now seen as stadium for political conflicts.

That the identity of these groups has furiously burst out onto the street in the latter half of the twentieth century shows this identity is a public affair. As the example of gays and lesbians demonstrates, identity is not a shameful stigma to be hidden in the closet or simply kept at home but is an issue of political discourse.[21] To be black, Indian, Latino involves affirming a separateness from the overall society rather than the transcendence of difference. This affirmation also coincides with the political demand for greater justice.

In order to understand the distinction between symbolic and political identities we have to remember that, in addition to the discourse granting people an ethnicity, there has existed another one creating racial identity. "Racialized people," Bonnie Urciuoli explains, "are typified as human matter out of place: dirty, dangerous, unwilling or unable to do their bit for the nation-state. In ethnic discourses, cultural difference is safe, ordered, a contribution to the nation-state offered by striving immigrants making their way up the ladder of class mobility" (1996: 15–16). Race, in other words, defines individuals in biological terms, representing all

---

[21] Although gay identity is grouped in multiculturalism along with other forms of social movements, I am referring here to ethnic or racial identity. My discussion does not include other social movements such as those by women, gay, lesbian, youth, peace, and green activists. Often they are referred to as cultural movements because they cannot be reduced to class struggle.

signs of difference as physical. It transforms "phenotypical variation into concrete systems of differentiation based on color," which has political and social consequences (Gilroy 1987: 38). Ethnicity, on the other hand, portrays people in cultural terms, as products of nation-states. It operates as a mode of inclusion, making difference more acceptable and less threatening, and representing foreign ways and values more acceptable to Americans.

That racializing discourses present identity as unchanging does not mean, of course, that this category itself is permanent. Race may be portrayed as a genetic marker but it is a cultural mode of classifying human beings. Specific individuals have therefore challenged the polarization between white and black in the United States.[22] Despite the ongoing creation of biracial individuals, however, race continues to operate as one of the fates in American society, determining to a certain extent place of residence, kinship networks, education, and profession. Among other things this means that all groups do not have the same ideological and material resources or the same space to perform and market their cultural differences as an authentic, slightly exotic experience imbued with tradition. They are thus not able to exploit their ethnicity as an avenue for class mobility in the way that Europeans have been able to.[23]

The crucial difference between white and racial identity is, as I noted earlier, the politicization of the latter. The radicalization of racial groups, itself the result of cultural, political, and economic factors, encourages the transformation of identities into associations of shared interests—the hallmark of nationalist thought. In one respect, all ethnic groups attempt to increase their share of scarce resources, such as jobs, housing, status, prestigious schools, and political authority. Glazer and Moynihan brought attention to the way ethnic groups mobilize in the pursuit of material or symbolic goods in their *Beyond the Melting Pot* (1963). They argued that immigrants are connected to one another by "ties of family and friendship" and "ties of *interest*. The ethnic groups in New York are also *interest groups*" (1963: 17). Their thesis, seeing ethnic identity in connection with class advantages, departed from other theorists, like Ed-

---

[22] There are people who choose to define themselves as neither black nor white but as multiracial. See Williams 1995, Lazarre 1996, Funderburg 1994. The 1990 census counted 2 million children younger than eighteen whose parents were of different races (*New York Times*, July 20, 1996). By the year 2100 it may be difficult to assign individuals a position "within the white-black-Hispanic-Asian-American Indian framework" (Sanjek 1994: 118, 19, 21).

[23] Many European groups had themselves been subjected to a racializing discourse at the turn of the century. It is unlikely that Americans would have popped into a Greek restaurant for spanakopita in 1910. On how the Jews, Irish, and Greeks became white, see Sacks 1994, Ignatiev 1995, and Anagnostu 1999, respectively. See Allen 1994, 1997 and Lipsitz 1998.

ward Shils (1957) and Clifford Geertz (1963), who regarded it in connection to primordial ties. Glazer and Moynihan rightly considered these ethnic groups "a new social form" rather than "a survival from the age of mass immigration" (1963: 16). It is a "social form" that manifests both cultural categorization and social stratification. Ethnicity has become so salient today because, in the words of Daniel Bell, it combines interest with an affective tie, politics and culture (1975: 145, 169). It functions, in other words, as both clan and club.[24] Ethnic groups can turn into quasi-political organizations as when Jews or Greeks establish organizations to influence foreign policy in favor of Israel and Greece, respectively.

Racialized minorities, however, move beyond this. They unite in the pursuit of greater social justice, manipulating their cultural distinctiveness in order to affirm collective rights, making their identity an expression and source of politics in the manner of insurgent nationalisms. This is particularly true of the phenomenon of panethnicity in the United States—the consolidation of previously unrelated groups, such as Koreans, Filipinos, Chinese, under one category, such as Asian.[25] Panethnicity is a reaction to past and current injustices and the formulation of government policies to allocate resources like welfare, education, and affirmative action on the basis of racial coalitions. It becomes advantageous for groups to address the state as a corporate structure, to employ culture as a tool to redress past and current wrongs.

But these groups are not dependent on the state, although it may encourage their maintenance through policies of affirmative action and welfare. Disenfranchised from the greater civil society, they exist in the spaces between the state and civil society. They thus cannot be reduced to either the state or civil society.[26] Their emergence, however, manifests the continued importance of culture today, for these groups mobilize cultural resources in their activism. But unlike the case of white ethnicity, they express the politicization, rather than privatization, of identity. The affirmation of cultural difference goes hand in hand with demands for justice—an end to racism and discrimination, safer neighborhoods, employment, respect, recognition by the majority of a group's identity (as

---

[24] Simmel noted that whereas individuals initially established relationships with persons within their kin group or with those physically close to them, eventually they formed other connections on the basis of interests, that is, "inclinations, activities, and talents" (1955: 129–30).

[25] We should keep in mind that a number of European groups acquired a generalized ethnicity in the United States. The original Romans, Neapolitans, Piedmontese, Sicilians, for instance, became Italians in their interaction with other immigrants and Americans who grouped them together. On Italian Americans, see di Leonardo 1984.

[26] Hence, as Lloyd and Thomas (1998) argue, they cannot be contained by the state. For a critique of these movements as examples of destructive left-sectarianism, see Gitlin 1995.

Latino, African American, gay). Politics and culture coexist in a dialectical relationship, an interplay characteristic of cultural nationalism from the beginning. All nationalisms, having composed a story of their people as oppressed, enslaved, or humiliated, proclaim the people's right to autonomy on the basis of their cultural distinction from its oppressors.[27]

As in cases of nationalism, crucial to these programs has been the role of intellectuals. This was understood by Robert E. Park and Herbert E. Miller in the 1920s. They located the source of the "nationalist" movements in the United States in the alienated, the "superior" and "cultured" members of a "foreign group," who, comparing their community with that of a larger society, are "humiliated" and thus seek to repudiate it. "The fact that the individual will not be respected unless his group is respected becomes thus, perhaps, the most sincere source of the nationalistic movements in America" (1921: 143–44).[28]

Historically, the case of African Americans represents the most sweeping creation of a panethnicity. Although the slaves, having been seized at various points in West Africa, had their own local identifications, in the colonies they were collectively treated as black in contrast to the whites. The subsequent black culture that emerged as sets of connected institutions and relationships is a product of the American experience.[29] This process continues today with the indigenous peoples, Asians, and Latinos. A look at their formation gives us a sense of not only the state of cultural identities at the dawn of the twenty-first century but also the connection between culture and political struggles.

The most conspicuous formation of panethnicity has been occurring among the aboriginal peoples of North America, as they have been conflating their tribal differences into the common classification as Indians.[30]

---

[27] Panethnicities can be compared with other forms of macronationalism such as pan-Balkanism, pan-Islam, and pan-Africanism. See Snyder 1984. Once a very attractive solution for smaller countries in the pursuit of a more assertive voice in world politics, these movements have collapsed because of the centrifugal pressures of nationalism among member groups.

[28] Park and Miller saw comparisons made by intellectuals between their own group and the larger society as an impetus to nationalism. As I argue in chapter 3, this has been a motivating factor for nationalist movements.

[29] This was a very complex process, difficult to understand in the relative absence of firsthand written accounts of how the slaves saw themselves. In a recent book Gomez points out that African identities survived among the offspring of slaves up to the early nineteenth century (1998).

[30] A fascinating example of a pan-Indianism is the Metis in Canada, created out of Indian-European unions, particularly between Algonquin and French. They had developed a nationalist consciousness in the nineteenth century, which culminated in the rebellions of 1885 led by Louis Riel. Since the 1960s the Metis have been attempting to forge a unity based on their hybrid origins. They see themselves as "the 'true natives' of Canada while Indians and whites are immigrants differing in their time of arrival" (Jarvenpa 1985: 41).

The appellation "Indians" shows that it is as much a result of prejudice and oppression as it is of self-ascription. For the label is obviously a misnomer, imposed upon the inhabitants of the New World by Christopher Columbus, who thought that he had reached India. The peoples of the Americas were culturally very diverse, but what struck the settlers was the difference between themselves and the natives. They contrasted themselves, Stephen Cornell explains, as white, Christian, European, intelligent, and powerful with the Indians as brown, pagan, native, ignorant, and impotent (1988: 106). The residents of the New World had no collective name for themselves not because they were incapable of generalizations or ethnocentric bias, but because they had no sense of continental geography, progress, the civilized-uncivilized dichotomy, and, above all, the category of race, which enabled the Europeans to classify all native peoples in one group.

The policies of the state, the preaching of missionaries, as well as the prejudice and violence of the white population, encouraged Indians to disregard tribal distinctions and develop a supratribal consciousness. This is a clear example of a situational identity, having appeared in response to particular problems and challenges, as native people came to interact with whites in cities.[31] By the 1940s and 1950s a pan-Indian identity evolved, largely adapted from the tribes of the plains, which came to be regarded by aboriginals and Europeans as a manifestation of an Indian identity: ceremonies, dress, dances, and social events (Cornell 1988: 126). A growing number of Indians came to see themselves as a collective body sharing similar experiences, history (victims of prejudice, massacres, land expropriation, broken agreements), social position, and political interest (Jarvenpa 1985: 42).

Rather than being an aesthetic search for traditions and unifying myths, Indian panethnicity serves as a way of pursuing political goals. "A supratribal consciousness represents both a resource and disposition: a basis on which to mobilize diverse peoples and a tendency to view oneself and the world in particular terms, to interpret issues once viewed as local, personal, or tribal as fundamentally Indian and to act accordingly" (Cornell 1988: 146). This identity could become more prominent in the future among those individuals for whom the city, as opposed to the reservation, may constitute the dominant experience of Indianness. Whatever form their identity takes, the indigenous peoples, conceived either as specific tribes or Indians, see themselves as separate nations, resistant to assimilation. Like other forms of nationalism, Indian panethnicity uses cultural

---

[31] It did not come about at the expense of tribal affiliations. Some individuals hold on to both or switch between them, depending on whether they find themselves in a reservation or a city.

and political resources in the pursuit of specific goals and the maintenance of a separate way of life.

This holds true for Latinos as well, a group representing Cubans, Puerto Ricans, Mexican Americans, and immigrants from other parts of Central and South America. What distinguishes Latinos from the rest of the American population is the Spanish language and Latin heritage, but what has motivated the creation of this panethnicity is the American experience, racism, and government policies of welfare and affirmative action. Identity here again is contextual, a specific product of American history, rather than a cultural heritage passed down through generations. This identity, arising when Spanish speakers from the Americas united to further their political interest, constitutes, Felix M. Padilla observes, a "strategic solution" to the conditions in urban America, an attempt to redress their disadvantaged situation through a collective "Latino" consciousness (1985: 7, 141). It is strategic because, along with cultural sentiments, it stresses economic and political concerns. People become Latinos in particular institutions, such as the university, which serve as the settings for the enactment of their collective sentiments and discussion of their material interests.[32]

That a Latino panethnicity is in the process of formation does not mean that it is internally homogeneous. Like all large-scale social clusters, it is differentiated by gender, professions, age, and education (Yinger 1986: 30). While culture unites, class may divide. For instance, language may link Cubans, Mexicans, and Puerto Ricans, but economic status at entry and subsequent social positioning may keep members apart (Nelson and Tienda 1985: 60). In other words, class and ethnicity do not always coincide.[33] What is certain, however, is that in the latter part of the twentieth century ethnicity has gained more visibility both as an expression of group solidarity and as a weapon in the struggle for social justice. While the grand narratives of national culture are indeed being questioned, the mininationalisms of racialized groups have attained a greater purpose and place enormous emphasis on cultural values. Without the cultural ties,

---

[32] A study conducted at the University of California, Berkeley showed that many Latino students first experience their ethnic-racial heritage at the university, not least, in courses of Chicano studies (Skerry 1993: 362–63). This phenomenon reinforces once again the relationship solidified two hundred years ago between nationalism and pedagogy.

[33] Gunther W. Peck shows this in his analysis of the struggle by Greek immigrants to unionize in Bingham, Utah, in the first decade of this century. Greek workers, exploited often by Greek labor agents, were conscious of their common interests with non-Greek laborers. But when the Greek government issued a draft order at the onset of the Balkan Wars (1912), a large number returned to Greece. Faced with a choice between fighting with their fellow workers against their class enemies or fighting the enemies of Greece, a majority opted for the latter (Peck 1991: 89).

Latino panethnicity would have become another interest group; in the absence of external pressures sentimental associations would never have yielded a self-conscious Latino identity. The cultural markers between Latinos and non-Latinos are "suffused with a differentiating value and elevated into an ethnic identity" (Padilla 1985: 151). These differences themselves become politicized.

Latinos may in the future pose serious challenges to the American polity. Will this group, especially given the concentration of Latinos in the Southwest and Florida, claim cultural autonomy (and even political independence) or will it disappear into a new transracial America? That is, will it maintain its political and cultural integrity, or will it dissolve into the mainstream, following the way of the Jews, Greeks, and Italians?[34] The questions about the future of these individual minorities are as open as that of the United States as a unitary state.

The formation of panethnicities in the United States highlights again the relationship between particularity and universalism so characteristic of the history of nationalism. The questioning of the authority of national culture to represent the nation corresponds to the emergence of politicized identities. On the one hand, the millstones of modernity grind away large-scale nation-states, but, on the other, smaller ethnic groups seem to flourish. Even the transformation of Euro-American ethnicity into a symbolic phenomenon does not at all presage the dissolution of ethnicity in general. The experience in North America as well as elsewhere shows the recalcitrance of ethnic affiliations and their capacity to transform themselves constantly.

This is particularly the case of Asian Americans, a complex blend of linguistically, culturally, religiously, and geographically heterogeneous groups. Asians in the United States, Yen Le Esperitu notes, are in the process of creating a common Asian American heritage out of diverse histories without, as in the case of Latinos, the benefit of a shared language. Differences in points of origin, class, and politics, however, have kept them from becoming yet a potent political force (1992: 55, 80). Asian American identity, like other panethnicities, has been fashioned by social and political forces in the United States. Instrumental in its formation is the way Americans have conceptually lumped Asians of divergent geographical, national, and religious origins into one class.

This categorization but also racism and violence against Asian Americans have encouraged Asians to look for common features among them-

---

[34] We should bear in mind that between 13 to 14 million people in the United States use Spanish as a first language (Falcoff 1996: 14). The Latino markets are among the fastest growing in the country (Skerry 1992: 69). Moreover, 80 percent of immigrants are people of color (Knippling 1996: xv).

selves which they would not have sought in, say, the Philippines or Vietnam. The boundaries and markers of this identity are being fashioned by institutions: pan-Asian organizations, Asian American studies programs at universities, the media. For some, especially children of immigrants, this panethnicity is the only form of identity, but for others it overlaps with their own national or religious affiliations. What remains to be seen, however, is whether native-born Asian Americans will continue to relate to these old traditions or to the new ones evolving in the United States. This will depend on a number of factors, most notably the rates of interracial marriage.[35]

In short, while effective distinctions among Euro-Americans have disappeared, racial cleavages remain profound. These racial distinctions have become the foundation for new, comprehensive identities, often quite politicized. When people decry the disuniting of America, they have in mind these visible minorities who have not and do not wish to be assimilated. They point to such phenomena as gambling casinos and fishing rights in Indian reservations, the establishment of Afrocentric schools, and the plebiscite held in Hawaii in the summer of 1996 on the possibility of establishing a "native Hawaiian government."[36] These demands as well as the geographical concentration of Latinos in the Southwest and Florida and Asians in the West may in the future challenge the viability of the United States as a unitary nation-state.

The question concerning me here is less the possible disintegration of the United States than the current and future state of cultural identities. At the beginning of the chapter I had asked whether we are witnessing the finale of national culture and the end of the two-hundred-year-old association of culture and the state. My examination of ethnicity in the United States seems to indicate that, in the quintessentially political nation, cultural values and traditions both express a sense of difference and are used in political struggles for greater justice.[37] Moreover, the exploitation of culture by visible minorities in their struggles indicates that the original nationalist link between power and culture is still effective today,

---

[35] Intermarriage among European immigrants, Sanjek writes, more than any other factor became the vehicle for their general acculturation. In 1990 one in six Asians and Latinos was married to a person of another race in comparison to one in thirty-three for blacks (1994: 106–7, 113). High rates of interracial marriage may eventually destabilize the distinction between race and ethnicity.

[36] See "Native Hawaiians Vote in Ethnic Referendum," *New York Times,* June 23, 1996.

[37] While the ethnicities of Euro-Americans may have been flattened to surface meanings, they have not lost their value either. Indeed, recent research suggests that, in reaction to the already-formed African American and Native American and the newly arising Asian and Latino panethnicities, a new European ethnicity is being shaped among whites primarily in the metropolitan regions of the Northeast and Midwest (Alba 1990: 314).

even if it does not necessarily lead to the pursuit of national sovereignty. Rather than its disappearance, the new millennium witnesses the resurgence of nationalism in the United States and around the world.

CULTURE, CULTURE EVERYWHERE

In its most violent forms this resurgence manifests itself in outbreaks of violence in Kosovo, Kashmir, and Chechnya. While these struggles catch the attention of the media, there are numerous quiet revolutions breaking out, from the revival of Provençal and other languages in France long regarded as comatose, to the formation of the Northern League in Italy, which seeks political autonomy from Rome. The twenty-first century has been ushered in by the drums of nationalism. Increasingly today ethnic affiliations are overriding other social cleavages such as class and religion to become one of the justifications for political mobilization. Social strife, in other words, erupts more and more along the fault lines of culture.

These ethnic struggles have a life and logic of their own and cannot be reduced to market forces. It is impossible to explain the nationalist movements ranging from Quebec to Macedonia, from Spain to the United States, from the West Bank to Abkhazia as a manifestation of economic dissatisfaction among the populace. Indeed, some of these—for example, Quebec and the Basque territory—are taking place in highly industrialized areas. Yet activists use economic exploitation as a ground for secession.[38] Economic motives are not irrelevant, however. Nationalism in Slovenia and Lombardy has economic roots. Slovenia felt encumbered by the southern republics in Yugoslavia, and the Lombard League continues to regard the poorer South as a drain on the North's resources. In Scotland and Wales economic and cultural issues are intertwined, as is also the case among minorities in the United States. Although today's nationalisms are related to conditions of the global economy, they do not correspond directly to them. Rather, they manifest and contribute to these transformations as well as being products of them. These phenomena are cultural when culture is understood to encompass identity, language, tradition, collective beliefs, symbols. Thus the catalyst in ethnic mobilization may be language in Quebec, skin pigmentation among racial minorities in the United States, tribal affiliations in Rwanda, religion in Northern Ireland.

---

[38] We can see this by comparing the positions Quebec and Maine hold in their respective countries. While median income between the two regions is comparable, in real terms the Quebecois "occupy a more favorable position in the economic structure than do Mainers" (Connor 1994: 149–50). Yet citizens of Maine do not give a cultural interpretation to economic discrepancies as do Quebecois nationalists, who see differences between Quebec and Ontario as the result of discrimination.

Although the point of cleavage may differ from case to case, the stimulus and rationalization for mobilization are put in terms of cultural survival, as they always have been in the history of nationalism.

Why are people affirming their identities worldwide? Why is conflict among peoples seen as an expression of culture? I have argued that nationalism is quintessentially a modern phenomenon. Nationalist movements arise in the give-and-take between tradition and modernity, the indigenous and the Western, the particular and universal. The politicization of culture in the past was partly an act of self-defense, a process of piling sandbags to save autochthonous identities from the flood of Westernization. This most certainly holds true at the start of the century. The spread of cultural nationalism today represents a concentration on an ethnic self facing an inscrutable globality, the attempt of ethnicity to find havens of security in a heartless immensity.

Whereas modernization erodes small-scale identities based on the village or the kin group, it enhances the identification along large-scale ethnic blocks like the panethnicities in the United States. Expansive identities, Susan Olzak explains, are better suited to defend their interests (1992: 16–17). Moreover, by bringing groups into greater contact with each other, modernity intensifies competition among them for scarce resources, such as jobs, housing, and cultural capital. This conflict itself serves further to heighten ethnic or racial affiliation because competition promotes internal cohesion by defining boundaries and enlisting members of the group or nation to a particular cause. Conflict, be it economic, political, military, or ideological, has always fostered identities by differentiating the insider from the outsider, friend from foe.[39]

In other words, boundaries of identity become visible when groups interact with one another. This has always been the case, but because modernity enhances the rate and intensity of intergroup communication, it accentuates cultural identities more than in the past. Strife erupts, Olzak found in her study of ethnic and racial confrontations in the United States, when segregation ends and groups begin to compete for valued resources (1992: 3). Contrary to what is commonly believed, the likelihood of such friction is minimized when groups occupy separate habitats. When "members of groups encounter one another in new situations the boundaries between them will be dissolved if they compete as one individual with another; the boundaries between them will be strengthened if they compete as one group with another" (Banton 1983: 12). The source of the conflict lies not in skin color, language, or national origin, as is often assumed by those treating these categories as immutable, but in the politi-

[39] See Simmel 1955 on how competition and conflict enhance group integrity by defining boundaries.

cal significance these attributes assume—to outsiders who wish to discriminate against the group or to insiders who want to mobilize members to their cause. That identity is a social construct does not lessen its impact on people's lives.

Olzak rightly places importance on the competition among groups but leaves unanswered the question as to why this struggle highlights culture as opposed to those of class or occupations. If membership in large-scale coalitions offers competitive advantage, why cannot unions or professions provide this benefit? Whereas she demonstrates that culture and economy overlap and that mobilization takes place through expansive identities, she does not discuss why indeed these identities are ethnic or why identity itself has become so inescapable today that activists for the disabled wish to create an identity drawn from their disabilities. These questions cannot be answered by looking only in the realm of the economy.[40]

The state, as I showed earlier, encourages ethnic mobilization by acknowledging the right of groups as opposed to individuals to receive its resources. In so doing, it transforms ethnicities into interest groups with a political agenda. But these ethnicities are not just lobbying associations. In addition to material resources they compete for status, acceptance, and recognition. What Hobbes said of people certainly holds true for nations and groups, namely, they "are continually in competition for Honor and Dignity" (1991: 119). They seek to maintain their position in the national or international hierarchy and, more important, to protect their distinctiveness. Culture has become so prominent today because nationalist thinking combines interest and affiliation, providing a platform for political mobilization while offering a degree of interpersonal belonging. Indeed, a distinctive feature of ethnic or national identity is that members feel their own sense of self-worth and personal fate tied up directly with that of the larger group. Thus victory of a national team in the Olympics may send individuals to dance in the streets in a way that the success of collective bargaining cannot. Because cultural identity casts itself in terms of the blood and guts of experience, it has the capacity to incite in people emotions stronger than class. Individuals find the sense of solidarity promoted by cultural identities very appealing and comforting. Communal conflict thus awakens the "deepest anxieties about the innermost attachments of people and indeed their survival, evocative of passion that is less likely to pervade than class conflict" (Young 1986: 122).

Ultimately, however, there is no *ontological* difference between the way class or culture can mobilize individuals. People have rushed to arms in the name of class and may do so again in the future. There is nothing

---

[40] Jalali and Lipset criticize Olzak's model of ethnic competition for relying heavily on economic explanations at the expense of state structures (1992–93: 597).

inherently superior to nationalism in this. Under the social, political, economic conditions of the past two hundred years, nationalist discourse has been more successful in addressing people's fears, dreams, and hopes for the future and their place in the world. It continues to do so today, albeit in different forms.

We have seen that in the United States the all-inclusiveness of American identity is being questioned, white ethnicity is flattened, but Latino pan-ethnicity is affirmed. There is a transcendence and assertion of difference at the same time. That the all-inclusiveness of national culture is put into doubt does not mean that it is disappearing completely. By the same token, although white ethnicity may indeed be becoming symbolic among Euro-Americans, it still retains efficacy among them. It manifests the recognition on their part of both the erosion of their traditions and the enhanced worth cultural identities have acquired. Given the heightened use of ethnicity around them, Euro-Americans have learned that it is in their interest to emphasize their own cultural traditions. In short, there is no evidence to support the belief that these identities are disappearing, as was expected. Value is still placed on ethnic identification and this identification is constantly politicized in certain circumstances.

Cultural issues continue to be paramount in the geopolitics of the late twentieth century because the right to sovereignty still resides in the nation, ethnicity is still used as a weapon for attaining social justice, and groups still unite themselves in the name of identity. As Anthony Smith writes, "communities in their struggle for political rights and recognition have drawn upon their cultural resources—music, literature, the arts and crafts, dress, food and so on—to make their mark in the wider political arena, regionally and internationally, and continue to do so by the use of comparative statistics, prestige projects, tourism, and the like" (A. Smith 1990: 184).

A major reason for the lasting significance of nationalist politics is, of course, the ongoing, epic clash between localism and universalism. Globalization, as Roland Robertson has repeatedly shown, has further affirmed these conceptual oppositions. In fact, it has institutionalized the universalization of particularism and the particularization of universalism, making them structuring principles (Robertson 1991b: 73, 77).[41] Insofar as it brings people and ideas together with a fleetness never before imagined, globalization heightens the interaction among groups. De-

[41] Barber has analyzed this face-off in his *Jihad vs. McWorld* (1996) in which he presents Jihad as the traditional forces reacting to the modernizing impulse of McWorld. These ideas are not new. The classic texts of nationalism have seen the emergence of the nation-state in the interplay between particularism and universalism: Meinecke 1970 and Kohn 1956, 1967. The Russian philosopher Vladimir Solovyof noted in 1897 that nationality was determined by a struggle between the "nationalistic" and "cosmopolitan" (1918: 277).

pending on one's point of view, it is either a blessing or a curse because it strengthens certain ethnic sentiments as it destroys others.[42]

For instance, globalization enables previously isolated groups to communicate with one another. New means of communication, for instance, have enabled the Muslim republics of the former Soviet Union, cut off from Pakistan, Iran, and Turkey, to interact across national borders, a development with heightened political and economic implications in an area rich with oil resources. Evidence also shows that immigrant groups make use of multicultural radio and television channels, satellite, videos, and cassettes in order to open channels of communication, previously inconceivable, both with the metropolis or other centers of their diaspora. Greeks abroad, for instance, have access to Greek audio and video cassettes, newspapers, and television news by satellites. Modern technologies in this respect can facilitate the maintenance of cultural differences, helping to delay or suspend assimilation. Various linguistic groups in Europe regard the new technologies of communication (as well as the European Union's federal system) as a means of uniting disparate speakers, thereby giving local languages and cultures a chance of survival.[43]

But globalization functions as a double-edged sword. The rapid transmission of information, ideologies, and life-styles threatens the very existence of small nations. By accentuating the speed of intergroup contact, globalization intensifies the danger of cultural extinction. This is the crux of the matter: if nationalist thought posited the welfare of ethnicity in cultural terms and if it promised societies the possibility of entering modernity while saving autochthonous forms, then the global flows of television programs, films, radio, cassettes, and video intimidate these societies as never before.

The instant dissemination of ideas, images, and goods has the capacity to infiltrate the most inaccessible hamlet in the world.[44] There is no need to reiterate here the creation of a new global culture. Journalistic and academic accounts in the 1990s have fully described such a phenomenon: a technologically created domain of celluloid images, products, and

[42] Mombeshora demonstrates this with respect to Zimbabwe 1990.

[43] See Williams 1992. This is not the first time that a nation requires the aid of transnationalism. The nonaligned movement, for instance, arose from the nationalist desire of Third-World countries to preserve their independence in the competitive global arena. They looked at the interstate association as a way of consolidating themselves as nation-states (Gupta 1992: 67, 71).

[44] The press in the 1990s abounded with stories of how "American products and culture are the rage everywhere," and how "Japanese are learning to eat at McDonalds, shop at Toys 'R' Us." "Yankee Come Back," *New York Times*, December 17, 1995. The *Jerusalem Report* in its cover story on the "Americanization of Israel" asked if this "Americanization will wreck the country's most distinctive values" (May 18, 1995).

ideas—Reebok shoes, Coca-Cola, CNN, the World Wide Web, the Internet, Disney, Michael Jackson, blue jeans, McDonalds, pizza. There is, of course, a touch of hysteria in these descriptions, motivated in part by apocalyptic thinking. Global culture will not become an integrated reality as one homogeneous, imperial commonwealth. First, the drive to unify markets into one agora will never be reproduced culturally. Global culture, as Anthony Smith notes, is contextless and timeless in contrast to national cultures which are particular and time-bound (1990: 176–78). Second, it is transformed as it comes into contact with local cultures all over the world. Societies have always interacted in their own way with global culture, accepting or rejecting features, or creating entirely new combinations. They respond variously to these flows of commodities, images, and ideas.[45]

Nevertheless, people and governments justifiably fear the effect that open markets and borders may have on their local societies. They ask whether globalization is in effect a process in the creation of a Euro-American economic and cultural imperium whose *kerygma* is "The U.S. 'R' Us." This question is legitimate, for globalization presents the practices of capitalism, the values of Western know-how, and the weapons of NATO peace-keepers as self-explanatory, inevitable, and worthy of emulation.[46] The new economic system strives to make the world into one agora fortified by the ideology of borderless exchange. Whereas Constantine proclaimed one law, one church, one emperor, global capitalism declares one world, one market, one card. One thinks back to Origen's gloating arguments on how the army and roads of the Roman Empire enabled the ultimate triumph of Christianity over paganism.

People worry not just about their identities, however. They are anxious about the effects global capitalism has on their jobs, their way of life, and their environment.[47] Fearful of being sucked down by the economic and cultural Charybdis, governments have taken measures to safeguard their identities. Neither are these the anxieties of small nations. Economic giants like the United States can no longer maintain an independent na-

---

[45] Liebes and Katz analyze the different audience reaction to the American television program, *Dallas*, in Israel, the United States, and Japan (1990). On international television programming, see McNeely and Soysal 1989. In the realm of music, see Gross, McMurray, and Swedenborg 1994 and Roberts 1992.

[46] As early as 1948 T. S. Eliot understood that the United States created a demand for its goods while doing business abroad. For Eliot even the "humblest material artifact, which is a product and symbol of a particular civilization, is emissary of the culture out of which it comes" (1948: 92).

[47] This new form of capitalism has been amply studied. It has been defined variously as postindustrialism (Bell 1973), post-Fordism, disorganized capitalism (Lash and Urry 1987), or flexible capitalism (Harvey 1989).

tional economic policy as they once could. Countries like Canada see the danger to their cultures.[48] "It's a matter of identity," argued the Canadian heritage minister to justify the special protection of magazines, movies, television, and radio Canada sought in the bargaining over the North American Free Trade Agreement (NAFTA). The French sought similar measures for their film industry in negotiations over the General Agreement on Tariffs and Trade (GATT).[49]

The fact that technologically advanced states like Canada and France feel it necessary to put up cultural barricades in the wake of economic integration underscores the dangers smaller countries feel. Large systems exchanging information with smaller ones are not affected by the interaction in the same way as small systems. For instance, "in the case of five million Americans having five million contacts with five million Swiss people, only about 2 percent of the population of the United States learn something about Switzerland but about 90 percent of the population of Switzerland learns something about the United States" (Hondrich 1992: 354). This asymmetry in global exchange is not taken into sufficient account by those waxing celebratory on global mixing. Although ideas and people do move from smaller to larger states, this exchange is not equitable. Globalization is and has always been an unequal cultural, economic, and political encounter.[50] A near Western hegemony, for instance, exists in the means of disseminating news. In the early 1980s 80 percent of news in the world circulated through the channels of four transnational agencies: UPI, AP, Reuters, AFP (Mattelart 1983: 59). While people may know more of each other today, they do so largely through these intermediaries.

---

[48] "Canada Puts Up Barriers to American Culture" *Washington Post*, December 22, 1994. In 1977 Canada passed a law regulating Canadian content in television and radio programs as well as magazines. Ten years later the Canadian Broadcasting Corporation decided to remove all American programs from its offerings at prime-time. "CBC Stands on Guard for Canadian Culture in Fall Schedule," *Vancouver Sun*, June 18, 1997. On similar measures taken by other countries, see Hamelink 1983.

[49] In 1994 the French government proposed a law to regulate the use of foreign words in government communications, radio and television broadcasts, and advertising. "Bar English? French Bicker on Barricades," *New York Times*, March 15, 1994. This law was similar to Bill 101 passed by the Parti Quebecois in 1977 to ensure the existence of French in that province.

[50] We can see this in the area of film making, one of the first modern art forms to become transnational. Japan in the 1980s was one of the largest cinematographic producers, making about 400 films a year. Yet the reach of these films rarely extended beyond Asia. India produced at the same period about 500 to 800 films a year in comparison to 150 to 250 in the United States. Although Indian films dominated box offices in East Africa, their global influence (and their generated income) was minimal in comparison to the unparalleled success of the American film industry (Mattelart 1983: 37–39).

The ever-shrinking world makes each place more vulnerable to direct influence through trade, tourism, military action, and communication.[51] We should keep in mind that nations were erected to protect not only indigenous culture but also the economic, political, and social life of particular communities. Nationalism arose originally either as a response to forces seeking world domination, such as Napoleon, or as a reaction to colonial empires. The danger of cultural extinction is real; the junkyard of memory is littered with societies that have disappeared or have been absorbed into other larger ones. Since the eighteenth century nationalism has offered the main instruments for those seeking to outsmart the Scylla of globalization. The situation at the end of the twentieth century, however, is different from the one faced by Rhinelanders in the early nineteenth. At that time the peril was clearly identifiable, the Napoleonic armies. In a globalized world it is ubiquitous and otherworldly, beamed in from the skies.

Yet the challenges facing many nations today are essentially the same as at the beginning of the nineteenth century: how to become modern or global and to remain faithful to traditional ways; how, as Ricoeur put it, "to get on the road to modernization" without necessarily jettisoning the "old cultural past which has been the *raison d'être* of a nation" (1965: 277). This challenge was succinctly expressed by John Turner, the former prime minister of Canada, who, in his address to the graduates of the University of British Columbia in November 1994, tossed out the following: "Go global, because you're going to have to. But, do me a favor. Stay Canadian" (in Gwyn 1995: 13).[52] Turner's acceptance of the inevitability of globalization as well as his nationalist exhortation underscore the double bind *still* constraining all nations: globalization leads to the affirmation and annihilation of ethnicities all the time. This is why culture acts for us both as flood and arc, menacing social life yet saving it.

DOES GLOBALIZATION SPELL THE END?

The real problem in globalization theory lies less in its apocalyptic style than its ahistorical direction. Discussions of globalization both in the academy and the media have taken place largely in a historical void, with-

---

[51] Much has been written about the dark side of globalization: loss of jobs, sweatshops, pollution, prostitution. Perhaps the most disturbing is the appearance of a new form of slavery in the global economy, that created by poverty. See Bales 1999.

[52] Gwyn captures well Canada's situation: "For about a decade now, Canada's national consciousness has been ground down in-between two millstones." The upper one is the global economy, while the lower one represents cleavages of regions, languages, and identity politics (1995: 14).

out any reference to previous globalization systems. Thus it is regarded as an unprecedented occurrence in the experience of humanity. Those enamored of it promise unfolding benefits of free trade and unlimited information, whereas those who fear it prophesy the destruction of the world as we know it. But is globalization really so new? Of course, certain features are novel: the transformation of the relationship between time and space by new technologies of communication and travel, which give rise to a spatial compression and temporal acceleration; the irrevocable integration of markets; heightened interpersonal contact across continents; the emergence of global institutions such as the United Nations, CARE, the Nobel Prize committee. People, ideas, and goods move with speed unimaginable before.[53] Obviously at no other previous historical period has it been possible for people all over the world to observe an event—the bombing of Baghdad, an Olympics race, the vote on President Clinton's impeachment—in "real time." All these developments give the impression that the world is one place. But this in itself is not entirely new. The idea that the world constitutes one society has its origins in Stoicism, medieval Christianity, sixteenth- and seventeenth-century jusnaturalism, eighteenth-century cosmopolitanism, and twentieth-century universalism (Larochelle 1992: 155).

Indeed, a glance into history reveals that our transnational world has been *one* of many *other global systems*. In Europe, for instance, one could point to such transnational phenomena as the aristocracy and the monarchy, Catholicism, Orthodoxy, the Greek and Roman legacies, the Enlightenment and romanticism, French as the lingua franca, the Hanseatic League, and so on. The world religions have to be seen as ecumenical phenomena in their own right, binding an extraordinary range of racial and ethnic groups over entire continents.[54]

Hellenism, between the conquests of Alexander and the period of late antiquity acted as a cosmopolitan cultural agent, allowing educated individuals in urban centers to communicate with one another not only in Greek but also in the myths, symbols, and narratives of their regional traditions. Globalism, however, had become a reality centuries earlier with the creation of the earliest recorded empire, that of the Persians. Achaemenian Persia, insofar as it united "heterogeneous African, Asian, and European communities into a single international society," established a precedent for transnational relations. Already by the second mil-

---

[53] See Robertson 1992 and Waters 1995.

[54] Although ecumenical, these world religions have not led to the creation of one unified society. This is so because the meaning "of each these religions differs significantly from region to region, and . . . the difference is in each case an expression of a people's earlier beliefs and values" (Bozeman 1984: 391). This, as I noted earlier, is happening today with global culture.

lennium B.C. the geographical range of human contact was vastly extended as the Near East and China became indirectly connected to each
other (Bozeman 1960: 35, 44).

In the thirteenth century the connections established between the
Roman and Byzantine empires and the Far East became more direct and
the area between northwestern Europe and China developed into a worldwide network of production and exchange (Abu-Lughod 1989: 8). This
period was a remarkable moment, for never before had so many regions
come into communication with one another. The world had come to experience the first truly global economy composed of eight distinct but interconnected circuits of trade, each possessing equal strength relative to the
others. This epoch, however, also marked the emergence of western European supremacy as cities like Venice, Genoa, and Marseilles began to be
the equal of Constantinople, Cairo, and Baghdad.[55] Capitalism bound
states and regions in a nexus of interrelationships, unleashing an economic dynamism that lassoed far-flung regions to their market system. At
this very time England, France, and Spain began ransacking the world,
founding colonies, drawing arbitrary boundaries in Africa and South
America, establishing European settlers, transporting slaves to the new
world. Each of these developments resulted in a breathtaking mixing of
peoples.

Mass migration, diasporas, creole societies, ecumenical thinking, which
are assumed to be unique to postmodernity, have characterized humanity
for millennia.[56] The real message of globalization is not that travelers in
Africa can post accounts of their journey on the World Wide Web or that
people can buy stocks in their underwear at home. Before e-mail there was
the telephone and before that, the telegraph. To observers in the future the
significance of today's developments will be our recognition that the
world has always been global. For what is taking place today in both
theory and practice is the questioning of the sociological and political idea
that the boundaries of a nation and the state have to overlap. The globally
integrated economy of the later twentieth century as well as the accelerated mingling of peoples are in a sense leading back to the past, to the
way the world had been arranged before nationalism.

---

[55] In contrast to Braudel and Wallerstein, who trace the origins of Western hegemony to
1571 and 1559 respectively, Abu-Lughod points to the thirteenth century, arguing that the
period leading to the sixteenth was transitional for Europe (1989: 29–22). It was not at all
certain then that western Europe would eventually dominate the globe. But the new European approach of "trade-cum-plunder" changed the nature of this economy; and the world
of multiple centers steadily gave way to one of a single center.

[56] War, conquest, the spread of communicable diseases, trade, and environmental disas-
ters have always resulted in the mingling of peoples. Herder understood this when he wrote
that calamities drive people away from their native land. Although they try to "adhere to

From the epic perspective of time, what is unique is not the borderless world heralded by global capitalists and jet-setting intellectuals but the erection of the national system with its grid of rigidly defined boundaries. It is the idea that a culture, conformable exactly to national boundaries and guardian of the people's distinctiveness, that has been an exception in history. The experience of humanity, William H. McNeil writes, has been polyethnicity rather than the (rarely attained) ideal of monoculturalism (1986: 35). The deterritorialization of culture taking place in postmodernity only emphasizes that societies have never been self-enclosed, homogeneous bodies as nationalists, but also historians and sociologists, have assumed.

The end of the twentieth century is witnessing the weakening of the nation-state as its loses authority to transnational economic and political organizations. But, contrary to predictions, it is not dying; rather it is changing in the new transnational system of states and the integrated marketplace. Nationalism itself is being transformed. Today, it is not motivated by the grand doctrine of universal progress as had been the case for the past two centuries. Too many disappointments and massacres have disconnected the link between nationalism and naive optimism. Moreover, high culture is not implicated in nationalist discourse in the same way it was a hundred years ago. The novel, as Sommer (1991) has shown in the context of South America and Anderson (1998) in Southeast Asia, does not figure prominently in the building of new nations. Visual media are undoing the once sacred relationship between the novel and the nation, print and invention. But the dynamic of cultural survival and the justification of new nations on cultural grounds remains the same. The Kosovars and East Timorese have argued for independence not only because they have been oppressed by a hegemonic power but also because they are different from that power. The Kosovar refugees, driven out of their houses by Serbian forces, constituted a population intensely nationalized, one eager to rid Serbs and Gypsies from an independent Kosovo.

The issue of cultural uniqueness has become more poignant in the world of interconnected states and economies. Indeed, the more global the world is becoming, the more people are reaching to safeguard their national, ethnic, religious, or racial identities. The old *gigantomachy* between universalism and particularism continues to play itself out on a grand scale. The resurgence of ethnic sentiment and bloody "tribalism" occurs alongside (or on account of) the ratification of free-trade zones and federal political systems. On the one hand, Europeans have negotiated the

---

the manners of their forefathers . . . , it would be impossible for them to remain eternally the same" (1968: 160).

Maastricht Treaty for European integration and, on the other, Catalonians and Lombardians are calling for greater autonomy. Whereas the Canadian, American, and Mexican governments have ratified the North
American Free Trade Agreement in 1992, Canada came to the brink of
dissolution in the fall of 1995 as a result of a referendum for separation
in Quebec.[57] The global economy has inexorably expanded while areas
were being "ethnically cleansed" in the former Yugoslavia, blood spilled
in the Caucasus, and genocide was perpetrated in Rwanda. Capitalist production may have become disconnected from local places, but people are
dying for these places. The transnational conversations conducted by
e-mail and fax are being disrupted by the trumpet's blare of enmity. This
situation calls neither for celebration of cosmopolitanism nor the condemnation of nationalism but for the creation of new political systems.

[57] New geoeconomic structures may be emerging such as Cascadia, the region encompassing the Yukon and Northwest Territories, British Columbia, Alberta, and the states of
Idaho, Montana, Washington, and Oregon. See Schell and Hamer 1995.

Chapter Seven

FEDERAL UNIONS

ANY DEFENSE of the nation has to acknowledge nationalism's two-sided nature, that it can inspire the best and worst of humanity and bring about freedom and endless ethnic conflict. In certain times and places it can propel groups to attain autonomy, democracy, and justice just as in other instances it can incite in them xenophobic hatred of others and brutish violence. Tom Nairn rightly characterized nationalism as "morally, politically, humanly ambiguous" (1977: 48). The twentieth century has provided much evidence of this ambiguity, having borne witness to the loftiest and basest manifestations of nationalism—struggles against imperialism and oppression but also genocide and ethnic cleansing. Our century has also had to deal with the practical consequences of political autonomy—an increasing number of nationalist conflicts, ethnic strife, instability, hatred. If the doctrine of nationalism proclaims that each people has the right to determine its own affairs on its own territory, then we can expect the map of the world to be divided endlessly as each group strives to arrange a marriage between culture and politics.

The future portends instability because of a sobering truth: there are many fewer states than ethnic groups. Even though not all groups opt for political independence, statehood for all who desire it could be achieved only through more violence. Nationalism and its exalted dream of popular sovereignty can lead to separatism ad absurdum. The current situation resembles Russian babushka dolls, a series of wooden figurines each containing within itself a still smaller figure. Seen globally, there is always one figurine clamoring to break out. One only need look at the former Yugoslavia: while one of its components, Macedonia, has declared itself an independent republic, its Albanian minority seeks greater autonomy or possibly the creation of a greater Illyrian nation. A similar situation existed in Georgia and Abkhazia after Georgia's secession from the Soviet Union. The real autonomy of these small, impoverished states is open to question.

The double-headed nature of nationalism had always been troubling for political theorists. J. S. Mill, for instance, who had argued that the "boundaries of government should coincide in the main with those of nationalities," also recognized that this coincidence between culture and state was almost impossible to achieve.[1] "There are parts even of Europe in which different nationalities are so locally intermingled that it is not practicable for them to be under separate governments." Mill pointed to the population of Hungary, which, "composed of Magyars, Slovaks, Croats, Serbs, Romanians and in some districts Germans," was so mixed "as to be incapable of local separation" ([1860] 1958: 233). He could easily have referred to Europe's many colonies as other examples of over-lapping national groups, each with the potential to claim the entire state and territory as its own.

Lord Acton had expressed similar reservations about the nationalist doctrine. Although he saw the political benefits of national sovereignty, he distrusted its justification on the basis of ethnicity and race. "When political and national boundaries coincide," he argued, "society ceases to advance, and nations relapse into a condition corresponding to that of men who renounce intercourse with their fellow-men" (Dalberg-Acton 1948: 186). He, in fact, rejected ethnic politics, favoring instead a liberal nationalism, one formed by common traditions and political institutions. For him nationalism would be "essential, but not a supreme element in determining the forms of the State" (184). He referred to state structures of medieval Christianity in which political and national borders were not the same. While he passed over the polyethnic polities of pagan antiquity, he highlighted Christianity's capacity to transcend national differences, at least among believers. Its universalism, he noted, enabled nations "to live together under the same authority, without necessarily losing their cherished habits, their customs, or their laws. The new idea of freedom made room for different races in one State. A nation was . . . a moral and political being; not the creation of geographical or physiological unity but developed in the course of history by the action of the State. It is derived from the State, not supreme over it" (187). That the state should precede nationality was in his opinion essential for the maintenance of liberty and prosperity—the opposite of Herder's belief that the state should grow out of the nation.

But nations have arisen and continue to arise before the formation of state structures, a fact that vexes politicians, scholars, and journalists alike. Fearful of nationalism's potential to instigate interethnic violence

---

[1] I cite his argument here again, although I have discussed it in chapter 1. A portion of humanity, he wrote, "may be said to constitute a Nationality if they are united among themselves by common sympathies which do not exist between them and any others" (Mill [1860] 1958: 229). Mill then went on to claim that a shared nationality was the basis of government, noting that "where the sentiment of nationality exists . . . there is a prima facie case for uniting all the members of the nationality under the same government." A shared culture was the basis for self-government since a "united public opinion" was essential "to the working of representative government" (230).

and destroy already existing states, many wish to do away with it completely. Dividing nationalism into its cultural and civic permutations, they keep the latter while discarding the former. I have already demonstrated that it is impossible to separate the two, for the history of even the quintessentially political nations has manifested characteristics of cultural nationalism. I return to the subject here because I wish to show that these theorists end up privatizing ethnicity in their defense of civic nationalism, as commentators have done in the case of ethnicities in the United States. Whereas Lord Acton sought universal political structures that enable peoples to "live together under the same authority, without necessarily losing their cherished habits, their customs, and laws," cultural and political theorists today aspire to an international version of American multiculturalism (originally proposed by Kallen) that cannot tolerate the public function of ethnicity. Insofar as they deny the political consequences of culture, they participate in an exercise of national self-denial and propose solutions no longer feasible.

Alarmed by the explosion of nationalist fervor around the world in the last quarter of the twentieth century, many writers resort to a familiar strategy: they contrast the Dionysian, chthonic, and irrational nature of cultural nationalism to the Apollonian, civilized, and sober character of civic nationalism. Representative is Michael Ignatieff's *Blood and Belonging: Journeys into the New Nationalism*, a book accompanying a television series produced for the BBC. Having witnessed the rise of ethnic sentiments in the former Yugoslavia, Ukraine, Northern Ireland, Kurdistan, Germany, and Canada, he concludes that the "repressed has returned, and its name is nationalism" (1993: 5). In order to understand the situation, he too resorts to the moralistic distinction between good and bad nationalisms. He denounces ethnic nationalism because it places exclusive emphasis on emotional attachments and lends itself to authoritarian rule (5–8). Civic nationalism, by contrast, promotes a sense of belonging through "rational attachment" and the belief that "what holds a society together is not common roots but law." This civic nationalism is for Ignatieff the only "antidote" to ethnic nationalism "because the only guarantee that ethnic groups will live side by side in peace is shared loyalty to a state strong enough, fair enough, equitable enough to command their obedience" (243).

Ignatieff takes this position because he rejects ethnic nationalism as an antediluvian force sucking humanity back into bad history. Nowhere does he countenance, for instance, that nationalism could also be an urge to translate traditional ideologies into modern forms and provide maps to guide communities into the future. Moreover, because nationalist movements are concerned with the self does not mean they are parochial. One of their aims is to adapt inherited belief systems to contemporary life.

Rather than rejecting the modern, they transform the old by borrowing ideas and institutions from others. An important impetus to nationalism, I have argued, is the comparisons groups make between themselves and others. The resulting project of both borrowing and rebellion can lead to creole identities and independent republics, however imperfect these republics may be.

The denunciation of cultural nationalism is based on the wish that it is possible to make ontological distinctions in nationalist thought. Etienne Balibar believes that there "is always a 'good' and a 'bad' nationalism. There is one which tends to construct a state or a community and the one which tends to subjugate, to destroy; the one which refers to right and the one which refers to might; the one which tolerates other nationalisms and which may even argue in their defense and include them within a single perspective (the great dream of the 'Springtime of the Peoples') and the one which radically excludes them in an imperialist and racist perspective" (Balibar and Wallerstein 1991: 47). Are there really any nationalisms that could be considered entirely "good" according to Balibar's value judgments? Is it ever possible to construct a "state or community" without destroying or subjugating another community? If so, which are they? Is there a single nation-state today not born through a dispossession of another people? Because much of the world's population is not conveniently segregated into self-enclosed communities, it is nearly impossible for every group to have its own state without pushing another off its territory. Balibar disregards this reality in his longing for a world without violence and real identities.

The civic nationalism many commentators have in mind is, of course, that of the United States, which, it is widely believed, unites Americans through rational principles. Michael Walzer, for instance, is faithful to this tradition insofar as he sees the United States as a country held together by political institutions rather than blood ties. Citizenship in the United States connotes not "nativity or nationality" but an act of belonging to a political union. "It is a political adjective, and its politics is liberal in the strict sense: generous, tolerant, ample, accommodating—it allows for the survival, even the enhancement and flourishing, of manyness" (1992: 26).

While Walzer's statement is in one respect a fair description of American citizenship, it does not take into account past or current forms of segregation and intolerance of foreigners and minorities. The civic nationalism that, in his view, transcends factional differences has historically reinforced racial and class differences. Walzer also exaggerates the extent to which the American polity actually enhances "manyness" in a real political sense as opposed to a superficial form of multiculturalism. For, as I noted earlier, ethnic differences among Americans of European descent are of no political consequence. But those divisions among the races, especially between whites and blacks, have an enormous impact on the lives of minorities. A balanced evaluation of American nationalism should also take the latter into account. Furthermore, the policy of cultural pluralism has not prevented the United States from pursuing a policy of assimilation with the aim of creating a homogeneous nation, at least among whites. What solace it must be for Greeks, Jews, or Italians, facing intolerably high rates of interethnic marriage, that they may organize ethnic festivals!

PRIVATE IDENTITIES, PUBLIC ASSIMILATION

Civic nationalism, despite its many appeals, does not offer itself as a viable solution to the problem of ethnic strife. It has been severely put into question in the United States. Minorities that have developed historically separate from American society or were already present before the arrival of Europeans demand group rights and may seek self-government in the future. Such a possibility threatens to undo the distinction of American republicanism between the private and the public realms, based, as this has been, on the separation between religion and state.[2] It is no surprise that Sheldon Hackney resorted to the differentiation between public life and private identities as a solution to the culture wars. "In the public sphere only universalistic rules are legitimate and only individual rights are legally protected. In the private sphere, we can give voice and form to our birthright identities without being any less American. This distinction still goes a long way in sorting out the conflicts between the universal and the particular" (1993). Hackney is, of course, right in claiming that the separation of the public and private domains is constitutive of American democracy. But it is this very separation that is being put to the test today. The cultural wars have shown that the privatization of identity has applied only to the symbolic ethnicity of Euro-Americans. For racial minorities identity has always been a public affair, a cause of their marginalization, rather than a means of transcendence.

The culture wars have indirectly demonstrated one of the lessons of nationalism, that culture is implicated in the administration of power and distribution of resources. These wars, as well as the explosion of ethnic conflict worldwide, should lead us to rethink two essential relationships

---

[2] It is useful to remember that limited group privileges, such as exemption from compulsory education, had been granted in the past to, for instance, the Amish and Hasidim in the United States or the Hutterites in Canada—to groups desiring a separate existence from the wider society. Kymlicka differentiates these privileges from, say, those that allow Sikhs and Jews to wear turbans or yarmulkes while serving in the police force as ways of allowing both groups to integrate into society (1995: 178–79).

of the nationalist system: the link, on the one hand, between territory and culture and, on the other, that between state and culture. The challenge before us should be not to neutralize identity but to accept its existence and devise political systems that would allow people to preserve their own way of life while maintaining peace and intergroup communication. Any solutions to today's problems that do not consider the issue of politics end up only tinkering with the system.

This certainly holds true for the ideology of liberal multiculturalism, widely promoted as a panacea to contemporary political ills in North America and abroad. Although preaching the values of diversity, multiculturalism, as I argue in the previous chapter, is ultimately integrationist, based on the belief that groups will accommodate themselves in a society guaranteeing their traditions. Informed by the principle of cultural relativism, it permits the coexistence of all subidentities except those making constitutional demands. It strives for a postnational unity on the basis of a communal culture but conceives this identity paradoxically as the sum of its differences. Ideally it promotes the maintenance of discrete cultures, making the distinction among them a unifying ideology. In reality, however, such cultural autonomy is without practical import, being largely symbolic, because the unitary state cannot be composed of autonomous regions or cultures without breaking apart. Multiculturalists do not recognize this fact. When Christopher Newfield and Avery F. Gordon call for a "postassimilationist America," they continue to see the problem as an issue of ideology—that is, assimilation—rather than of state structures. Despite their radical rhetoric, they still see America as a unitary state but one governed with "*antiessentialist* notions of identity" (1996: 107). A true postassimilationist America can be not a nation-state but a radically transfigured federal system. For only in a federated state can African Americans, Native peoples, and Latinos have cultural autonomy of any consequence. The true pluralism that Newfield, Gordon, and Appadurai call for cannot be achieved within the nation-state. There is a difference between the cultural pluralism of today and the structural heterogeneity characteristic of today's multinational states or the empires of old. In the latter societies culture (as ethnicity, race, or religion) had a role to play in determining one's marriage partner, place of residence in the city, and often occupation, a function absent in modern multicultural societies, which recognize individuals rather than groups.[3]

---

[3] Ganzis makes this point when he compares the situation of Greeks in multicultural Australia with those who lived in Asia Minor and the Near East at the turn of the century (1995–96: 130). The Greeks of Australia face an assimilative and mobile society (despite the latter's commitment to multicultural policy) that daily dilutes their identity. By contrast, the Greeks of Asia Minor, residents there for millennia, or of Egypt, having emigrated to that country in the nineteenth century, maintained the boundaries between themselves and

Multiculturalism, however, conceives of difference primarily as an aesthetic category, taking as its model the voluntary assimilation in the United States. But in order to act universally it reduces social diversity into a MacDifference: spanakopita, sushi, salsa in the international festival; minoras, Christmas trees, and Kwanza cards in the holidays; the transracial colors of fashion photography. Liberal multiculturalism believes justice and equality can be attained through the redemptive powers of culture, which allows the expression of uniqueness. It aestheticizes identity as life-style, terrified by the possibility of struggle, competition, or discord among groups. It is really a palliative to the pain of ethnic conflict. Above all it does not address a fundamental issue of politics. Todd Gitlin is right in criticizing the left for concentrating on identity exclusively in the culture wars (1998: B4–5). But he is wrong in dismissing the importance culture has acquired in modernity and especially in postmodernity. The problem with the cultural left is that it forgot the issues of governance, constitutions, and history.

This unwillingness to take state structures into account also holds true for the cosmopolitanism advocated by a number of philosophers. In "Patriotism and Cosmopolitanism," originally published in *Boston Review* (October–November 1994) along with twenty-nine replies, Martha Nussbaum articulates her vision of world citizenship. Finding patriotic pride "morally dangerous," she proposes a cosmopolitan education based on the following principles: by means of such an education we get to know more about ourselves; we make better headway by solving problems through international cooperation; we recognize moral obligations to the rest of the world. Nussbaum's essay may have caused a stir but basically pleads for tolerance and love of humanity: while we should learn about our own traditions, she argues, we "should also work to make all human beings part of our community of dialogue and concern, base our political deliberations on the interlocking commonality, and give the circle that defines our humanity special attention and concern" (Nussbaum 1996: 9). Who could disagree with this?

Nussbaum's essay shares a number of characteristics with writings on diaspora, multiculturalism, hybridity. First, like many commentators, she focuses solely on the pathologies of nationalism without ever contemplating its benefits, particularly its capacity to formulate alternative values to globalization. She underestimates, for instance, the positive function of ethnic, religious, and regional identification in counteracting the ecumen-

the other groups. Although there was much cultural exchange between them and other peoples, they never confronted the circumstances of high interethnic marriage, geographical mobility, consumerism, and mass communication which are transforming Greek identity in Australia into a symbolic phenomenon.

ism of global culture. This is why her sweeping dismissal of the local can easily be reconciled with the broader ethic of global, technocratic capitalism. To be sure, today's transnational entrepreneurs, the most fervent supporters of the cosmopolitan and multicultural *Weltanschauung,* would endorse Nussbaum's call for the openness of borders. The merger between multinational corporations in the 1990s has shown that there are no longer American, Japanese, French, or German corporations but only successful ones. Second, Nussbaum ignores the functioning of the state. Cosmopolitanism is an apolitical philosophy because it presumes an existence outside of political structures.

While Nussbaum explores the philosophy of world citizenship, she gives no attention to the political institutions enabling it.[4] Would education alone transform the noble ideal of cosmopolitanism into a living practice? How would it be brought about? It cannot, because cosmopolitanism is really reserved for the educated elites who attend the "cosmopolitan schools." The groundless intellectuals of Davos, Bellagio, and Salzburg are the true heroes of the new global order, they alone being able to incorporate and theorize the postnational condition. This is why becoming "a citizen of the world is often a lonely business . . . a kind of exile— from the comforts of local truths, from the warm nesting feeling of patriotism, from the absorbing drama of pride in oneself and one's own" (Nussbaum 1996: 15). How could becoming a citizen, by a definition a public act, ever be a "lonely business?" It is "lonely" only in the breezy, elevated reaches of global culture. Cosmopolitanism is an isolating endeavor because it fears, is disgusted with, and ultimately abandons the local. Yet it needs the local as its conceptual opposite, contrasting its rational, universal, and brave self to the irrational, parochial, and cowardly others.

Kwame Anthony Appiah believes cosmopolitanism is the ideal philosophy for multicultural liberal democracies. He summarizes its principles in "Cosmopolitan Patriots" as follows: "we value the variety of human forms of social and cultural life; we do not want everybody to become part of a homogeneous global culture; and we know that this means that there will be local differences (both within and between states) in moral climate as well" (1997: 621). Toward the end of his essay it becomes obvious that Appiah is really describing the United States as the country most representative of this philosophy. But he does not outline its political consequences, never showing, for instance, how liberal cosmopolitanism

---

[4] Her position should be contrasted with that of Daniele Archibugi who, in a discussion of "cosmopolitan democracy," investigates how the world's inhabitants can be given political representation in institutions beyond their own borders. To do this, she argues, "a theory of world citizenship rights must be formulated" (1995: 133–34). Ideally, this type of transnational representation would allow citizens to have a say on international affairs.

can address issues of governance. Although he sees that the solution lies with the state rather than the nation, he refrains from discussing the polis. He simply affirms the importance for citizens to share one political culture—that is, their commitment to core institutions. But this notion of political culture presumes the continuance of centralized states. Is this really possible, given the far-reaching trends of globalization? The doctrine of cosmopolitanism, noble as it is, like the idea of diaspora, requires reflection on forms of government. Because it avoids the sociopolitical realities of life, cosmopolitanism turns out to be another version of cultural pluralism, urbanely eloquent in its appreciation of social diversity but silent on the civic and legal arrangements supporting its ideology.

Endless Diaspora

The idealization of cosmopolitanism, diaspora, and hybridity had become by the mid-1990s a characteristic feature of cultural studies in general and postcolonialism in particular. It has been most apparent in the work of Arjun Appadurai. Acknowledging the need to "think ourselves beyond the nation," Appadurai proposes that the answer to today's ethnic violence is a new "postnational imaginary." The challenge then for him becomes to find a "language" to capture the new, "non-territorial, postnational forms of allegiance" he sees being created. This is necessary because "many deterritorialized groups" still cannot think "their way out of the imaginary of the nation-state." Hence "many movements of emancipation and identity are forced, in their struggles against existing nation-states, to embrace the very imaginary they seek to escape" (Appadurai 1993: 418).

As proof of this new type of transnationalism Appadurai refers to "recent ethnic movements" of millions of people "spread across vast territories." He points specifically to Serbs living throughout the former Yugoslavia, Sikhs spread out in India, Great Britain, and Canada, the Hutu refugees languishing in Tanzania, and so on. But Appadurai's presentism prevents him from asking how different this situation is from, say, that of the Greeks, scattered throughout the Balkans and the Mediterranean at least since 1453.[5] The lack of historical awareness allows him to celebrate today's multiculturalism as unique. The United States, he claims, is "awash" in "global diasporas."

[5] Of course, today's situation differs in the absolute sense from any in the past. But by how much? Hellenistic Alexandria, the Rome of late antiquity, Byzantine Constantinople, medieval Baghdad, and Ottoman Istanbul were all great centers of ethnic, racial, and cultural heterogeneity.

> For every nation-state that has exported significant numbers of its populations to the United States as refugees, tourists, or students, there is now a delocalized *transnation*, which retains a special ideological link to a putative place of origin but is otherwise a thoroughly diasporic collectivity. No existing conception of Americanness can contain this large variety of transnations. In this scenario, the hyphenated American might have to be twice-hyphenated (Asian-American-Japanese or Native-American-Seneca . . .) as diasporic identities stay mobile and grow more protean. Or perhaps the sides of the hyphen will have to be reversed, and we can become a federation of diasporas, American-Italians, American-Haitians, American-Irish, American-Africans. (Appadurai 1993: 424)[6]

Appadurai sees the United States as a prototype of the new globalism. In today's "postnational, diasporic world," he believes, "America is being invited to weld these two doctrines [of pluralism and democracy] together, to confront the needs of pluralism and immigration, to construct a society *around* diasporic identity" (425). It is surprising that after his critique of nationalism, he should propose that a society be built on, of all things, an identity, the nationalist concept par excellence. One would expect that his transnationalism would have compelled him to sever the union between identity and politics, anointed by nationalism two hundred years ago. Such a separation would indeed be a radical development.

On closer inspection the mission Appadurai assigns to the United States, by which it can become a "cultural laboratory" or a "major player in the cultural politics of a postnational world," is no different from Whitman's "nation of nations" or Kallen's "democracy of nationalities" (Appadurai 1993: 425, 427).[7] Insofar as he posits today's problems and solutions in cultural terms, he simply idealizes (with postnational language) American exceptionalism. According to him diasporic identity promises to free people from the confines of the nation-state, binding them in deterritorialized unions. But how can diaspora do this? More important, how can such a diaspora exist in the absence of requisite political and institutional structures?

Although studies of multiculturalism, globalization, and postcolonialism have shown that identity is political, they have rarely engaged in dis-

---

[6] I have already cautioned in the preceding chapter against the undue celebration of today's moment as exceptional. The United States was at the start of the twentieth century host to a number of immigrants proportionally far higher than today. Moreover, these immigrants were, in fact, members of diasporas and participated in the internal politics of the original countries.

[7] The line, "Here is not merely a nation, but a teeming nation of nations," is from Whitman's poem "By Blue Ontario's Shore," which appeared in various drafts between 1856 and 1891 (Whitman 1982).

cussing governance. For this reason we are left with the mystification of the hybrid, the diasporic, the liminal. Appadurai speaks of patriotism becoming "plural, serial, contextual, and mobile" and then effortlessly writes about populations becoming "deterritorialized and incompletely nationalized," incapable of producing "the people." On the contrary, while large nation-states may indeed be breaking down, smaller ones may be taking their place. They are having no difficulty in producing the Quebecois, the Kashmiris, the Kurds, the Eritreans, the Chechnyans. The dirge that one hears for the passing of the nation-state is premature. It is weakened internally and challenged externally, but it is not dead.

Moreover, it is insufficient to speak of "transnations" as the "most important social sites in which the crises of patriotism are played out" (Appadurai 1993: 428). How can the transnational perform this role? The Macedonians, residing in multicultural societies of Canada and Australia, did not mute their passions in the fight over Macedonian nationhood on account of their diasporic existence. Their struggle was quintessentially nationalist. But were they wrong to support the foundation of a Macedonian state, the only haven for the protection of Macedonian identity? Nation-states, as we have seen, have been created in part to safeguard ethnicity in a hostile world. Is there no need for state structures in a postnational world? The history of the Palestinians, Kurds, Timorese, and Kosovars shows how vital states can be to protect people from persecution by aggressive states. Who would disagree with Michael Walzer's contention that the Jews and Armenians "would have been better off with states (and with bureaucrats, policemen, and soldiers) of their own" (1986: 229)?

Appadurai would claim that the Macedonians are still trapped in the "imaginary" of nationalist thought. But how would a transnational identity have addressed the specific situation in the Balkans? The real problem here may be the unwillingness of global intellectuals to accept the reality of cultural identities and their relationship to states. For the way out of the interethnic mire today will be shown by federations of political associations rather than by a "federation of diasporas," because the former addresses issues of political coexistence of nations.

In "Diaspora: Generation and the Ground of Jewish Identity," Daniel Boyarin and Jonathan Boyarin argue rightly that the "renunciation of sovereignty . . . combined with a fierce tenacity in holding onto cultural identity" might be a solution to today's internecine strife. Using the example of pre-Zionist Judaism, they claim that it is possible for a people to maintain its cultural difference without the possession of land. Yet they end up mystifying the idea of diaspora when they "propose a *privileging* of Diaspora, a dissociation of ethnicities and political hegemonies as the only social structure that even begins to make possible a maintenance of

cultural identity in a world grown thoroughly and inextricably interconnected" (1993: 723; my emphasis). What does this statement possibly
mean? That we can exist outside political structures? That we all live in
diasporas and should abandon our identification with the land? Is one's
relationship to a native soil evil in itself? In the absence of the state, how
can diasporas defend themselves if the need arises? Because they resist
connecting their conception of diaspora to any form of political structure,
the authors reduce it to utopian ideal, marvelous to contemplate in the
air, but unrealizable on the ground. It is unworkable because it refuses to
consider the possibility of political structures that would allow people to
keep their link to the native land and culture while supporting an overarching government.[8]

It also venerates the idea of homelessness and the congruent condition
of homesickness (nostalgia). The authentic life, it seems, is one of perpetual scattering, migration, and exile. In addition to overlooking the state,
the condemnation of nationalism by cultural critics reveals their distrust
of home. In their discourse the home is often portrayed as a parochial,
xenophobic, if not fascist place, a destination that the much-traveled
Odysseus dreads. He would die of boredom because Ithaca, unlike the
journey of displacement, is the site of essentialist identities.[9] The home
becomes bearable only if it is folkloric, exotic, postcolonial, subaltern, or
minor, but never if it is a Normal (Illinois) or Plain City (Ohio).

The priority given to culture in today's discussions of nationalism, diaspora, and diversity presumes that both the igniting and snuffing out of
racial and ethnic strife are discursive. Seeing the nation as primarily a
conceptual entity, scholarly as well as journalistic writings disregard its
political component. The underestimation of the state and the consequent

---

[8] Often critics use "diaspora" when they actually mean ethnic group. Thus when Winland speaks of the "Croatian diaspora" in Canada, she really means the Croatian community (1995). Chow's *Writing Diaspora: Tactics of Intervention in Cultural Studies* (1993)
says next to nothing about diaspora either as a theoretical concept or a social reality. In a
review of cultural writing on diaspora, John Lie reveals some of its shortcomings. He questions, for instance, the extent of the "sea-change" over past scholarship on immigration (Lie
1995: 304).

[9] The deification of hybridity has much to say about the self-imagining of global intellectuals. For they are most conscious of themselves as diasporic and represent their specific
identity as a human condition. In an article on "transnational anthropology" Appadurai
refers to his own family as an example of the new universal system: "In January 1988, my
wife (who is a white American historian of India) and I (a Tamil Brahman male, brought
up in Bombay and turned into *Homo academicus* in the United States), along with our son,
six members of my eldest brother's family . . . decided to visit the Meekaksi Temple in Maru-
rai, one of the great pilgrimage centers of South India" (1991: 200). Linda Hutcheon begins
an essay on ethnicity by discussing how she "went from being a Bortolotti to being a Hutcheon" and cites other similar examples in the academy (1998: 28). Such autobiographical
allusions to one's mongrel (ethnic) life are standard in academic texts.

elevation of the nation as the object of study make these works profoundly Herderian. This can be seen in Homi Bhabha's influential article "DissemiNation." Bhabha admits that he is concerned with "certain traditions of writing that have attempted to construct narratives of the imaginary of the nation-people" rather than with the "history of nationalist movements" (1990b: 303). He locates the problem as well as the solution within the domain of the national. Bhabha points to the misfits of the nation—the "gathering of exiles" and the "gathering of people in the diaspora"—as nodes of resistance to national imaginaries (291). Wishing to demonstrate that the nation is unstable and "ambivalent," he brings attention to the "counter-discourses" that "erase [the nation's] totalizing boundaries—both actual and conceptual—[and] disturb those ideological maneuvers through which 'imagined communities' are given essentialist identities" (300). In his aim to show national culture as a "contentious space," Bhabha highlights "minority discourses" that disturb the national myth. "The aim of cultural difference is to re-articulate the sum of knowledge from the perspective of the signifying *singularity* of the 'other' that resists totalization" (312).

Bhabha's work on the nation oscillates between the two poles of repression and resistance. Against the homogenizing violence of the nation, he points to the liberating potential of cultural difference. Thus the essay ends dramatically when Bhabha gives way to the "*vox populi*: to a relatively unspoken tradition of the people of the pagus—colonials, postcolonials, migrants, minorities—wandering peoples who will not be contained within the *Heim* of the national culture and its unisonant discourse, but are themselves the marks of a shifting boundary that alienates the frontiers of the modern nation" (1990b: 315). That they should speak and that we should listen is beyond doubt. But should we not also consider how these people can actually live together harmoniously in political communities? Once the overbearing hand of the conductor is subdued and the old score thrown out, can we really expect the voices to sing peacefully together?

Because so much work on national culture is confined within the repression-resistance opposition, it is not surprising that cultural critics see their task as keeping the borders of the nation open. For this reason they give priority to concepts such as diaspora, migration, hybridity, border crossing, and multiculturalism. By the mid-1990s these words had become the slogans of the time, all usually preceded with the word "politics." Their understanding of the political, however, rarely implies issues of governance. The absence of historical reflection allows critics to lionize the contemporary situation, and themselves,[10] as unique and exceptional.

---

[10] We should remember that one of the strategies of intellectuals has been understandably to support their own social positions as intellectuals. This was true of German poets and scholars in the eighteenth century and it is true today. The scattering of culture in postmo-

Ulf Hannerz, for instance, sees the global world as a "world in creoliza-tion" (1987: 551–52). His characterization is indeed true but it can be applied to every "world" in history. All societies are creole at birth and continue to interact with other societies. Michael Kearney similarly argues that current transnationalism is a new phenomenon. As an example, he points to the Mixtecs, those who migrate in large numbers to the Mexi-can-American border area from their Oaxaca, a state in southern Mexico. These migrants "construct a new identity out of the bricolage of their transnational existence. What form does this transnational identity take? It coalesces as *ethnicity*, as an ethnic consciousness, which is the su-premely appropriate form for collective identity to take in the age of trans-nationalism" (1991: 62). For Kearney Mixtec identity appears as an "al-ternative" to national consciousness. The border area between the two countries becomes a "liminal" zone where signs and identities are born "outside of the national projects of the two nations which presume to control identities in this zone" (70). That this area is indeed "blurred" is undeniable; but will it remain so for long? Does it have innate features to frustrate the American and Mexican national cultures perennially? Will its inhabitants never assimilate into either society? Will they seek greater autonomy within the United States or outright independence? If the latter proves true, will this group not strive for its own homogeneity?

In the need to panegyrize these new hybrid identities, critics rarely men-tion the dark side of minority nationalism. History has shown that the minor can become major. Because the state is usually ignored in these studies, the idea that a minority might desire political independence rarely seems a possibility. E. San Juan Jr. writes that we are witnessing today a "profound revitalization of organized cultural projects for the affirmation of dignity and the fundamental right of self-determination for peoples of color" (1992a: 9). This is, no doubt, true. But in order to achieve the goal of "self-determination," these projects, like all such nationalisms, have to devise a political program that would have implications on neighboring communities, large or small.

Frederick Buell claims that "experience in this [global] world is not what it used to be. . . . Unitary subjects are dramatically denaturalized and dispersed. . . . No longer unitary subjects, inhabitants of this post-modern global system reemerge as baroque, syncretic constructions, each

---

dernity has witnessed an astronomic rise in the number of specialists engaged in the produc-tion, dissemination, and interpretation of cultural goods and situated in universities, adver-tising, and the mass media. Their aim in academia has been the introduction and validation of new methods and objects of study. The proliferation of cultural studies, the analysis of the signs and products of consumer culture, has been the most spectacular success of this class. On the new information class, see Ehrenreich and Ehrenreich 1979, Gouldner 1979, Bourdieu 1984, Featherstone 1991, and Guilory 1993.

in him- or herself embodying some always-eccentric version of the cultural, social, economic, heterogeneity of the whole system" (1994: 319). Ignoring a body of sociological research on Asian panethnicity and on Asian assimilation in the United States, Buell offers Asian Americans as the practitioners of the new ethnicity. A hybrid group, caught between black and white and "deficient in identity in a nationalist mold," Asian Americans can "racially deconstruct and decenter American culture" (188). Like Kearney's Mixtecs, Appadurai's "twice-hyphenated" Americans, and Bhabha's "people of the pagus," Asian Americans are important because they frustrate the essentialism of national culture. The minor is again co-opted into the discourse on the major, having been given stature because it has something to say about the Western subject.

What is not discussed is the impact this "new" baroque ethnicity can have on people's lives. Do Asian American activists who fight against prejudice believe that their identity is somehow decentered? Can the new identities not become oppressive to others? Are they not essentialist themselves? Is it possible, in other words, for minorities to struggle for social justice if they believe that their identity is a social fiction? Identity can be felt as real and visceral in the same way that bigotry and racism are felt in the heart and the body. Moreover, that identity results from a process of mixing does not mean that the widespread recognition of its synthetic nature will make people more tolerant of ethnic differences. If so, one wants to ask, what are the implications of the incessant glorification of difference today?[11] What does it say about social institutions, the state, and the way people live? Cultural critics rarely consider these questions. Their only recourse is the liberal argument of pluralism, namely, that the existence of many identities will baffle the homogenizing tendencies of national culture. Like all pluralists, they keep the melting pot but set the temperature low.

LIBERAL NATIONALISM

Not all contemporary judgments of nationalism have been harsh. In response to the overwhelming condemnation of nationalism as a maniacal, destructive force, a few writers see its benefits. They acknowledge that, while nationalism has fueled some of the most devastating regimes of the

[11] This apotheosis of difference seems to take place everywhere from the bumper stickers, which enjoin other drivers to "celebrate diversity," to the op-ed pieces in the newspaper, which applaud "fluidity and self-invention." Writing in the *New York Times* (September 22, 1996) the novelist Bharati Mukherjee, notes that "my books have often been read as unapologetic (and in some quarters overenthusiastic) texts for cultural and psychological 'mongrelization.' It is a word I celebrate."

century, it has also inspired epic struggles against colonialism. Rather than discarding outright the entire movement, they wish to maintain its productive potential. They propose a brand of liberal nationalism that attempts to blend the best of both liberal philosophy and nationalist thought. Yael Tamir, for instance, wants to accommodate the liberal admiration of personal freedom, reflection, and choice with the nationalist emphasis on belonging, loyalty, and solidarity. While denouncing fascism, racism, and Nazism, Tamir draws from liberalism's commitment to personal autonomy and individual rights as well as nationalism's respect for membership in human communities (1993: 4–9, 35).

In *Multicultural Citizenship: A Liberal Theory of Minority Rights* Will Kymlicka pursues a similar strategy. He begins with the reasonable assumption that the most serious challenge to the state today is that of cultural diversity. He notes that, since the Cold War, ethnocultural conflicts serve as the most pervasive source of political violence in the world (1995: 1). As he sees no signs of these struggles abating, Kymlicka supports a liberal theory of minority rights that would promote "*freedom within* minority groups and *equality between* minority and majority groups" (152). Among other things, Kymlicka investigates the issues of group rights, proportional representation on the basis of cultural difference, self-government, and ultimate secession. His discussion is wideranging and never flinches from difficult cases; he is willing to accept the limitations of his theory.

Unlike many liberals, who defend the homogeneity of the nation, who blur the distinction between ethnic and minority groups, or who propose a civic identity as a solution to today's struggles, Kymlicka tackles the prevalence of cultural difference in today's polity. He rightly argues, for instance, that minority rights should be subsumed under the category of human rights because the latter does not deal with the important questions of today: whether minorities should have publicly funded education in their own language, whether political integration of minorities should be brought about by redrawing constituency boundaries or by proportional representation, or whether groups should be entitled to a certain cultural autonomy or outright secession (1995: 5). In contrast to the silence of liberalism on nationalism, Kymlicka devises a theory that recognizes the significance people give to their identities, seeing these identities as participants in politics rather than an expression of private life.

This significance has been criticized as being a product of Kymlicka's own liberal theory. For in order to justify cultural rights in a liberal society Kymlicka has to argue that these rights are essential to freedom and personal autonomy, even in groups that do not value the latter. That is to say, he defends the idea of group rights in a multicultural society on the basis of respect for individual autonomy. Culture is fundamental to Kymlicka's conception of freedom because it supplies individuals with a set of options to evaluate and determine their lives. And such a freedom would be impossible if individuals were denied access to their culture. But, as Chandran Kukathas points out, many cultures that Kymlicka wishes to defend are profoundly illiberal in their subordination of individuals to the interests of the community and their restriction of personal freedom. Rather than argue that human flourishing requires that individuals have a choice of options, Kukathas proposes that "what matters most when assessing whether a way of life is legitimate is whether the individuals taking part in it are prepared to acquiesce in it" (1992: 124). Avishai Margalit and Moshe Halbertal point to Ultra-Orthodox Jews in Israel as one group that limits the range of personal choice. Culture in this case really is a way of life for it "affects everything people do: cooking, architectural style, common language, literary and artistic traditions, music, customs, dress, festivals, ceremonies" (1994: 498). In arguing for the right of Ultra-Orthodox Jews to their own way of life, the authors claim that "members of a particular culture consider it [culture] important because the particular content of the culture gives their lives meaning on a variety of levels" (505).

People emphasize their own traditions, language, native land not out of a commitment to liberalism but out of their belief that they would lose their personal and social bearings without them. They are attached to them in a symbolic but powerful way. An individual's own private identity is tied to the identity of her group. Belonging to such a group has been and continues to be of utmost importance and is manifested in her participation in a communal culture. Although the effects of this culture are experienced individually, its political consequences are public. A person's ethnic-racial identity may, along with other factors, determine her access to valuable resources and her standing in the social order. Moreover, cultural identities may become the foundation on which to launch political movements. Personal self-respect in this way is related to the dignity of the ethnic group.

The preservation of inherited identities and pursuit of national distinction have been, along with the fight against oppression, the principal motivating factors behind the nationalist projects of the past two centuries. There is, of course, no ontological reason for a modern state to be national. In an address delivered in South Korea, Habermas correctly pointed out that democracy theoretically does not need to be backed up by a national consciousness (1996b: 10). But in the past two centuries the right to citizenship has been guaranteed by national states. As Habermas argued in an earlier text, the democratic transformation of the *Adelsnation* (nation of the nobility) to the *Volksnation* in Europe required "a deep mental change" on the part of the general population brought about by nationalist thought. The nationalist discourse disseminated by intellectuals brought about a "political mobilization" in the urban, middle classes that transfigured the modern state into "a democratic republic." The idea of a national identity, then, inspired people, previously ruled by authoritarian governments, to see themselves as a community of citizens, sharing the same culture, state, and territory. The "cultural identity" provided the socially "integrating substrate for the political identity of the republic" (1996a: 284–86). This union of citizenship and nation solidified two centuries ago may be in a process of slow dissolution for reasons outlined earlier. But it will continue to hold for some time because groups regard a national identity as vital to their existence in the international system. Although such a union between nation and state may seem unnecessary, even dangerous, to those already in nation-states, it is essential to those groups oppressed by authoritarian regimes. We have to recognize that this reality will not go away.[12] It would be difficult to conceive of a workable polity in the twenty-first century that does not recognize cultural rights along with political rights.

Moreover, there is no evidence at all that universalism will transcend ethnic factionalism, binding the peoples of the world in a new fraternity. The global world, as I have argued, continues to create conditions for ethnic and national differentiation. The more people are forced to look and act alike, the more they will emphasize distinctions among themselves. While borders crumble in one place, they seem to be erected in another; while member states in the European Union may be forfeiting political authority, subnational groups, such as the Catalans, are enhancing their control over civic and cultural life.

The continuing public import of ethnicity, the ongoing erosion of the state's power to determine fiscal and social policy, and the growing strength of transnational organizations and multinational corporations demonstrate the need for us to reflect on forms of government. Rather than exalt hybridity as an example of boundary crossing or decry national culture for its procrustean tactics, it is time to draft practical solutions to contemporary dilemmas. While the liberal and multicultural plea for respect of others is noble, it is insufficient. Given the challenges posed to traditional polities from globalization and internal fragmentation, we have to consider new political arrangements that recognize the interest of groups—particularly minorities—to protect their identities while at the same time allowing for neighborly cooperation among them.

---

[12] That it should go away is a wish shared by many commentators. Typical is Alexander Star, who would like to imagine what "life without cultural or racial identities would look like" (1997: 83).

Federalism, I believe, provides such a possibility. It is a system best suited to cope with the Janus-nature of nationalism. On the one hand, nationalism is a means by which a group can take hold of its political affairs on the basis of a shared culture and territory. On the other hand, nationalism has an inherently destabilizing potential because the world is not discretely divided into nations—whether we are talking about Bosnia-Herzegovina, Quebec, Texas, Kashmir, or Rwanda, the boundaries of ethnicity, religion, or race overlap. Hence, the call by one group for national sovereignty usually imposes on the similar right of others.

FEDERALISM

The pursuit of cultural homogeneity within national borders is, as I have argued, of recent invention. In classical antiquity a different model was posed. Aristotle, for instance, argued that the city was founded on difference rather than sameness (*ex anomoion he polis*; *Politics* 3.1277a 5–6). Greek philosophers, argues Nicole Loraux, saw discord (*stasis*) at the origins of the polis, a view that had political consequences: "to regard *stasis* as an innate force requires the courage to conceive of a city founded in conflict in its origins" (1991: 48). Turning to a vastly different example, the polyethnic empires of the past maintained order while preserving linguistic, ethnic, racial (and, in many cases, religious) variation. This does not mean that they elevated tolerance—as we understand it—into an ethical ideal. Social conflict and discrimination were always present, inequality being tattooed upon the social body. Moreover, they were not democratic structures. But neither did they make culture a source of the state's authority. Even when the Holy Roman Empire had a political role to play, Sheehan notes, "this role involved guaranteeing diversity rather than imposing cohesion. The empire worked best where it unified least" (1981: 6).[13]

The survival of the Holy Roman Empire into the morning of modernity highlights the divergent ways states and empires conceived of diversity. It and other entities show that it was possible to achieve a nonterritorial unity that accommodated people's sense of collective difference to the necessity of cohabitation. Because the ruler's claim to authority did not depend on ethnicity, as is the case today, cultural identities were politically inconsequential beyond each state. Although the Christian universalism of the Holy Roman Empire could not permit religious heterodoxy, it pre-

---

[13] The empire existed by virtue of legal ties. Its constitution, which developed into a "cumulative product of a centuries-long history," stood not for the acquisition and concentration of power but for its check and dispersal (Gagliardo 1980: 16, 290).

served the constitutional autonomy of its various states and estates in a federated system. It is not surprising that social and political theorists at the preceding turn of the century, who lived through the gradual demise of the Austro-Hungarian Empire, had themselves turned to federalism as a solution to ethnic strife.

Karl Renner, a social Democrat writing in Vienna who published under the pseudonym Rudolf Springer, was one of these influential theorists. In *Das Selbstbestimmungsrecht der Nationen in besonderer Anwendung auf Oesterreich* (1918), he outlined a type of political association in which each national group would enjoy cultural autonomy while at the same time participating in a federal administration. Each group thus would have complete jurisdiction over cultural matters while ceding other types of authority (defense, customs, commerce, transportation) to the federal body. For Renner the answer to the century-old "national question" of the empire was a multinational state (resembling very much the Ottoman millet system) that guaranteed cultural rights of component nations. The closest models in his time, he argued, were the United States and Switzerland, even though both were still organized as territorial states. The polity of the future, he believed, would be built on two forms of government, the national with jurisdiction in civil and cultural affairs, and the federal with authority in military, economic, and intergovernmental matters (1918: 146). Renner thus reconceived the unitary state by divorcing ethnicity from politics. In his system they would once again constitute different spheres, each with specialized functions. The right to self-determination (*das Selbstbestimmungsrecht*) would henceforth entail a different type of political autonomy, the self-government of a unit itself integrated in the affairs of a supranational structure (24–25). Renner's federal constitution separated culture not only from administration but also from territory, a union bequeathed to modernity by the Treaty of Augsburg.

Reducing the consequences territory has on governance would make it possible for people to coexist with those different from themselves since they would all belong to separate national bodies but one overarching government. Such a federalism might be a possible solution for those societies where ethnic and racial groups are in fact intermingled. Federalism has had a long history, going back to the various leagues (amphichtyonies, symmachies, and sympolities) formed in ancient Greece among the disparate city-states to protect themselves from tyrants and empires. Federalist associations existed throughout the medieval world, most notably in the Holy Roman Empire.[14]

Federalism has been a recurring idea in history because of its capacity to reconcile the pull between the universal and the particular, between the

---

[14] Davis (1978) provides a comprehensive historical survey of federalism.

need for political union with the reality of ethnic diversity, between the urgency for amicable coexistence and the demands for cultural rights. Because it can accommodate these conflicting forces, federalism has been again proposed to deal with the cultural and political problems of our postcolonial and global world. Federalism, as Michael Burgess observes, presumes the worth and validity of diversity (1993: 3). But unlike contemporary multiculturalism and cultural studies, which only glorify cultural difference while giving lip service to politics, federalism institutionalizes it in state structures. It presents a political solution to the issue of cultural heterogeneity through constitutional guarantees for autonomy.

Because the word "federalism" has been applied historically to varied forms of government, it is impossible to offer one definition of the term.[15] The oldest usage of federalism connotes the linking of sovereign states for military or economic ends. In modernity it has come to mean the existence of a state with two levels of government, as in the United States after 1787 (Watts 1966: 9–10).[16] In its most basic form federalism provides the means for communities, each aware of its own separate cultural identity, to preserve this difference while at the same time participating in a larger aggregate of other communities for the pursuit of common interests, such as defense or foreign policy. It is possible, however, to differentiate between federalism as a political ideology and a political system (Smith 1995: 4). The former maintains that federalism is an ideal way of organizing human affairs because it can best adjudicate between the mutually exclusive demands for unity and diversity. The second connotes the actual institutional arrangements, such as the Canadian confederation of 1867, which gave birth to Canada, or the European Union, which is taking on the guise of a federalist association.

Today the resurgence of ethnic nationalism throughout the world, the devolution of power away from existing unitary states, large-scale migration, and formation of new diasporas give added urgency to federal structures. Federalism is best suited for the challenges of polyethnic societies because, without the need of an all-encompassing national culture, it re-

[15] There is no general definition of federalism among scholars and constitutional lawyers. Because my intent here is to investigate the broad issues implicated in federalist forms of government, I do not evaluate different manifestations of federalism, such as corporate federalism, consociation, confederation, common markets, defensive alliances. These are discussed in Duchacek 1986, Forsyth 1989, Friedrich 1968, and Watts 1966.

[16] The 1787 American model has exercised considerable influence on the subsequent formation of federations in Canada (1867), Germany (1871), Switzerland (1874), and Australia (1901). Interestingly, after the federal system of 1871 was discarded and especially after the Civil War, the American solution came to resemble less a true federation than a unitary nation-state. The federal government grew at the expense of the states. This development perhaps was inevitable inasmuch as the American founding fathers saw the federal union "composed of individual persons as well as of states" (Friedrich 1968: 13).

moves from politics this apple of discord. The question of whose ethnic culture is to become nationalized would no longer serve as such a divisive issue. At the same time, however, federalism, in contrast to cosmopolitanism or civic nationalism, recognizes that citizens have ethnic, racial, national, and religious garments. It does not require that citizens hang them up in their home or place of worship before they enter the agora. Unlike American pluralism, which assigns ethnicity to the private realm, it accepts its public impact. It neither rejoices in culture, as does multiculturalism, nor does it deny its political significance, as does liberalism.

Federalism can transform the way we have understood the idea of national sovereignty over the past few centuries. Or, rather, federalism can allow us to come to terms with the changing nature of national sovereignty. The Treaty of Westphalia conferred upon Europe and then the rest of the world a political system that recognized the authority of states to exercise absolute jurisdiction over their territory and citizens. This treaty marked the beginning of a process of what Duchacek calls "territorial socialization," by which values and feelings of the population were directed toward their native land. This process is being undone by internal as well as external forces. The nation-state will not disappear abruptly, of course, but its unquestioned power within its borders is being checked.[17] Given the waning of the state's authority, federalism can prevent endless territorial fragmentation by allowing various groups to exist in a corporate political structure that does not threaten their ethnic, racial, linguistic, or religious values. In practical terms this means that groups, states, or nations would govern themselves while participating in supranational political institutions. These individual units would enter this arrangement in order to solve common problems. There would be two levels of government, the one local, the other federal. For true federalism to flourish, however, the various communities must coexist and interact as autonomous entities (Friedrich 1968: 7). These federal bodies should be accompanied by transnational organizations which could monitor and restrain the abuse by individual states of their citizens.[18]

---

[17] Its authority is increasingly restricted not only by the market but also by international bodies such as the UN General Assembly, the Security Council, the International Court of Justice, and organizations like NATO. An interesting example is the European Commission on Human Rights, which receives petitions from citizens who feel aggrieved by their governments. The effect is that in Europe states no longer have exclusive authority over their citizens because the latter may "initiate proceedings against their own governments" (Held 1991: 219).

[18] The nature of such organizations, which extend the principles and structures of federalism internationally, is explored in a collections of papers on cosmopolitan democracy (Archibugi and Held 1995).

It is not that federalism eliminates all interethnic conflict. Rather, it provides mechanisms by which this type of conflict can be checked by groups committed to maintaining an interconnected system without necessarily trampling on the interests of minorities. In fact, federalism acknowledges that conflicts are an "inherent component of all federal societies" (Gagnon and Erk 1998: 24). But it also demonstrates that different ethnic groups may live alongside one another because they will simultaneously belong to their own cultural community and the collective federal administration. In short, matters of local, particularly cultural, interest would be vested in the local institutions, whereas issues of general concern would be handled by the federal government. The essence of this arrangement, John McClaughry writes, is the division of political tasks among a caretaker central government and the various ethnic groups. Based on the assumption that "nobody much cares who manages the sewer system, but everyone cares whose cultural values are taught in the schools," federalism might work when geographical partition is not possible. Technical services of the state, such as the postal system, transportation, sanitation, defense, economic policy and so on, would be taken care of by a federal or national government and paid for by general taxation. "But the social and cultural 'people centered' collective functions—education, health care, museums, recreation, social services etc.—are supervised for each ethnic group by a government chosen by that group's self-identified membership wherever situated, and paid for with revenues raised from that group alone" (1996: 5).

This proposition may seem outlandish and unworkable, given the long history of nationalism and statism. But we should not forget that the millet system of the Ottoman Empire operated in such a manner, allowing the empire to govern a vast number of ethnic, racial, and religious groups spread over two continents. The Ottoman Empire, as I explained in chapter 4, was organized into nonterritorial, ethnoreligious groupings known as millets, such as the Orthodox, Muslim, Jewish millets, which had jurisdiction over cultural and civil matters relating to their respective subjects. Orthodox subjects of the empire, for instance, were members of the Orthodox millet regardless of where they lived. It should be obvious that I am not offering the Ottoman or Holy Roman Empires as models for emulation.[19] These empires, built on inequality, are not systems of government for the twenty-first century. My aim is simply to bring attention to nonnational modes of social and political organization that our statist prejudices disregard.

---

[19] The nation grew out of and rejected the empire, seeing it, in the words of Verlaine's poem "Langueur," as "la fin de la décadence." Although Verlaine was describing the aes-

A nonterritorial means of organizing people may similarly allow territorially dispersed groups, such as African Americans, to gain greater control of social and cultural policy while participating in a federal American union. Federalism can accomplish this because it does not demand that groups forsake their particular affiliations for the sake of a national universality. While the unitary state guarantees the right of individuals to political representation, it cannot do so in case of collectivities. Despite the claims of American pluralism, the United States cannot be a "nation of nations" because this would imply the recognition of minority groups as autonomous, subnational units. This, of course, is to a certain extent taking place as the federal government recognizes groups in terms of affirmative action, thus further enhancing the formation of ethnic-racial coalitions.

In a truly federal system it would be possible to protect the rights of regions or minorities to be culturally different, to maintain their way of life. Federalism, Graham Smith argues, broadens the category of social justice because it constitutionally enshrines the rights of groups to representation according to regions and/or cultures (1995: 3). Thus to liberalism's list of civil and political rights would be added the right to culture that nationalist thought proposed two centuries ago.

Whatever form it takes specifically, federalism provides an alternative to the idea that each nation is entitled to its own state. A voluntary association among self-governing entities would diffuse the ultimately unwinnable conflict over land by allowing people of the same ethnicity or religion a sense of belonging and the exercise of political rights outside of their states. A sort of federalism, for instance, may permit a union among the ethnic Albanians of Kosovo, Albania, and Macedonia without changing actual borders.[20] It could be applied now or in the future to any number of places from Jerusalem to Montreal, from the American Southwest to Nigeria, from Chechnya to Wales.

This development is in fact taking place. Canada, for instance, which has for its entire history tried to accommodate within a loose state the divergent interests of provinces and groups, represents a laboratory for experiments in federalism. Pierre Trudeau's efforts in the 1970s to placate Quebec's nationalist claims through the policies of bilingualism and multiculturalism have not succeeded.[21] Moreover, Quebec's calls for au-

---

thetic disposition of ennui and decadence, his line illustrates the way the nation portrays the empire as the end of a political tradition (1948: 192).

[20] See Gottlieb 1994: 110–11.

[21] Although a proponent of Canadian federalism, Trudeau has been a fierce opponent of the nationalist policies of any group, particularly of the Quebecois. In an essay "Against Nationalism" he cites with approval of Lord Acton's position that nationalism is a "retrograde step in history." Seeing nationalism as the source of violence in the world today,

tonomy have been echoed by the native peoples who have entered the constitutional debates, seeking collective rights and recognition of their status as *first nations*. "Acceptance of a pre-existing inherent right to aboriginal self-government within the constitution of Canada has become for them a *sine qua non*, the basis for their claims to legislative powers as an *order of government*" (Milne 1993: 205).[22] These discussions may lead to a reconsideration of Canadian federalism.

Similar developments are occurring in Spain. The new constitution of 1978 rejected Francoist centralism and put in place one based on federalist principles. While acknowledging the unity of Spain, the constitution guaranteed the right to autonomy of the nationalities and regions. The effect of this, Montserrat Guibernau points out, is that the autonomous governments of Catalonia and the Basque country act as states. They provide services in education, health, culture, housing, local transportation, and agriculture, while the central government retains jurisdiction over defense, administration of justice, foreign policy, and overall economic planning (1995: 245). In order to avoid the enormous political, social, and human consequences of independence, these two nations have chosen thus far to remain within the Spanish state.

In the 1980s there emerged in Lombardy a locally oriented movement called the Lombard League, which seeks more autonomy, if not outright secession from Italy. The reasons usually cited for its demands are hostility toward the poor south of Italy; resentment of the central state, which it sees as bureaucratically inefficient, fiscally irresponsible, and morally corrupt; aspiration toward more effective local, self-government; and disillusionment with traditional parties. "According to the Lega, Northern Italy is already a fully European (Central European) area, in economic, social, and cultural terms" (Strassoldo 1992: 51).

The European Union is gradually becoming a federated structure and in fact encourages various subnational groups such as the Catalonians, Scots, and Lombardians to assert their autonomy. They in turn promote the idea of a "Europe of Regions" or a "Europe of Peoples." Evidence shows that these groups would enhance their autonomy in a federated Europe while the authority of traditional states would erode. It is with much justification that James Anderson speaks of Europe heading to a new medievalism, a system of "overlapping authorities and multiple loy-

---

Trudeau argues that wars between nations will not end until "the 'nation' in ethnic terms ceases to be the basis of a state" (1990: 60).

[22] Williams summarizes the various attempts both to undermine and to fix the Canadian versions of federalism over the past twenty-five years (1995). On August 4, 1998, a landmark treaty was signed between the federal government and the Nisga'a nation, a tribe in northwestern British Columbia, ceding to the Nisga'a considerable degree of self-rule (*New York Times*, August 5, 1998).

alties" reminiscent of medieval polities. The nation-state will not disappear overnight, to be replaced by other institutions. Rather, it will change slowly as pressure from above and below, from outside and inside, gradually shifts political authority away from traditional territorial units to overarching federal systems and smaller, self-governing units (1995: 289–90). In other words, the state will coexist with other structures, all sharing varying degrees of power. This new medievalism, however, which was foreseen by Hedley Bull twenty years ago (1977, 1984), is perhaps already here. For two developments are taking place in the international arena, Walzer points out: a devolution of sovereignty, which creates autonomous units within states, and the formation of alliances, which establishes federations and economic unions among states (1986: 231). Federalism would push the simultaneously downward and outward division of sovereignty even further, leading to a transformation of the world system, rather than, as Walzer would like, its reform.

Federalism, however, should be seen not as a panacea to contemporary problems. Although it presents a practical means of handling intergroup conflict, of accommodating the clashing demands of autonomy and unity, of reconciling the ongoing struggle between particular identities and global structures, federalism leaves many issues unresolved. One such crucial topic is the very definition of the local. What constitutes a community? Although theoretically the conceptual boundaries seem simple to determine, in practice they are not. How should the federal system or member units react if one community becomes oppressive to its citizens, practices genital mutilation, institutes slavery, or commits genocide? Should these acts not lead to the intervention in the internal workings of an autonomous state? This question, confronting today's multicultural societies, becomes even more troubling for a federal system because it not only prizes diversity but constitutionally guarantees it. Moreover, we should keep in mind that federalism in itself does not imply democracy. The examples of Yugoslavia and Russia show that federalist institutions can coexist with dictatorships that can brutalize secessionist movements in Kosovo and Chechnya, respectively. It is imperative, therefore, that the discourse on federalism, the proper association of various polities, be accompanied by a reflection on freedom, democracy, and citizenship. Equally important is the creation of transnational organizations that would restrict the power of individual states, federated or not, to coerce their citizens. Federalism in the absence of democratic institutions could lead to repressive governments, trampling on the rights of minorities and individuals.

If the challenge facing us today is to devise political systems that allow a people to affirm its uniqueness and make claims to self-rule while sharing with others the same land, an equally crucial duty is to ensure that these systems be democratic. The creation of national culture and the questions of sovereignty this process poses have been two of the most urgent political issues of the past two centuries. Federalism allows us to deal with the question of national culture without idealizing, privatizing, or disregarding it. The most hopeful defense of the nation lies in politics.

REFERENCES

Abercrombie, Nicholas, Stephen Hill, and Bryan S. Turner. 1980. *The Dominant Ideology Thesis*. London: George Allen.

Abraham, Gary A. 1992. "Within the Weber Circle." *Theory, Culture and Society* 9, no. 2: 134–37.

Abu-Lughod, Janet L. 1989. *Before European Hegemony: The World System, A.D. 1250–1350*. New York: Oxford University Press.

———. 1991. "Going Beyond the Global Babble." In *Culture, Globalization and the World System: Contemporary Conditions for the Representation of Identity. Current Art History* 3.

Ádám, Magda. 1993. "Ethnicity and Nationalism in the Successor States." In *Ethnicity and Nationalism: Case Studies In their Intrinsic Tension and Political Dynamics*, edited by Peter Krüger, 35–46. Marburg: Hitzeroth.

Adams, Willi Paul. 1993. "Nation over Ethnic Groups: A European Look at the American Experience." In *Ethnicity and Nationalism: Case Studies in their Intrinsic Tension and Political Dynamics*, edited by Peter Krüger, 91–96. Marburg: Hitzeroth.

Adler, Frank. 1995. "The Original Model of American Democracy and the Turn to Statism." *Telos* 104: 68–76.

Agoncillo, Theodoro A. 1975. *A Short History of the Philippines*. New York: New American Library.

Ahmad, Aijaz. 1992. *In Theory*. London: Verso.

Ahmed, Jamal Mohammed. 1960. *The Intellectual Origins of Egyptian Nationalism*. London: Oxford University Press.

Ake, Claude. 1967. *A Theory of Political Integration*. Homewood, Ill.: Dorsey Press.

Akzin, Benjamin. 1964. *State and Nation*. London: Hutchinson.

Alba, Richard D. 1990. *Ethnic Identity: The Transformation of White America*. New Haven: Yale University Press.

Alexander, Jeffrey C. 1988. "Culture and Political Crisis: Watergate and Durkheimian Sociology." In *Durkheimian Sociology: Cultural Studies*, edited by Jeffrey Alexander, 187–224. Cambridge: Cambridge University Press.

Alexiou, Margaret. 1974. *The Ritual Lament in Greek Tradition*. Cambridge: Cambridge University Press.

———. 1982. "Diglossia in Greece." In *Standard Languages: Spoken and Written*, edited by W. Hass, 156–92. Manchester: Manchester University Press.

Allen, Theodore W. 1994. *The Invention of the White Race*. Vol. 1, *The Origin of Racial Oppression in Anglo-America*. New York: Verso.

———. 1997. *The Invention of the White Race*. Vol. 2, *Racial Oppression and Social Control*. New York: Verso.

Almond, Gabriel A. 1980. "The Intellectual History of the Civic Culture Concept." In *The Civic Culture Revisited*, edited by Gabriel A. Almond and Sidney Verba, 1–36. Newbery Park, Calif: Sage.

Althusser, Louis. 1971. *Lenin and Philosophy and Other Essays*. Translated by Ben Brewster. New York: Monthly Review Press.

Anagnostu, Georgios. 1999. "Negotiating Identity, Connecting through Culture: Hellenism and Neohellenism in Greek America." Ph.D. diss., The Ohio State University.

Anderson, Benedict. 1983. *Imagined Communities: Reflections on the Origin and Spread of Nationalism*. London: Verso.

———. 1998. *Spectre of Comparisons: Nationalism, Southeast Asia, and the World*. London: Verso.

Anderson, James. 1995. "Arrested Federalization? Europe, Britain, Ireland." In *Federalism: The Multiethnic Challenge*, edited by Graham Smith. London: Longman.

Andreiomenos, Giorgos. 1997. "I Gali, ta Ionia Nisia kai I strofi tis Eptanisiakis Logotehnias: Me aformi ta diakosia xronia apo tin elevsi ton Gallon sta Eptanisa (1797–1997)." Kerkyra.

Angelou, Alkis. 1954. "Pos i neoelliniki Skepsi Egnorise to Dokomio tou John Locke." *Angloelliniki Epitheorisi* 5: 128–49.

———. 1955. "I Diki tou Methodiou Anthrakiti." Athens. Reprinted from *Afieroma eis tin Ipiron. Eis Mnimin Christon Souli*.

Angold, Michael. 1975. "Byzantine 'Nationalism' and the Nicaean Empire." *Byzantine and Modern Greek Studies* 1: 49–70.

Anonymous. [1806] 1957. *Elliniki Nomarhia*. Athens: Vivlioekdotiki.

Apostolopoulos, D. G. 1974. "Yia tin Proistoria tou Neoellinikou Diafotismou." *O Eranistis* 11: 296–310.

Appadurai, Arjun. 1990. "Disjuncture and Difference in the Global Cultural Economy." In *Global Culture: Nationalism, Globalization, and Modernity*, edited by Mike Featherstone, 295–310. London: Sage.

———. 1991. "Global Ethnoscapes: Notes and Queries for a Transnational Anthropology." In *Recapturing Anthropology: Working in the Present*, edited by Richard G. Fox, 192–210. Santa Fe: School of American Research Press.

———. 1993. "Patriotism and its Futures." *Public Culture 5*, no. 3: 411–29.

———. 1996. *Modernity at Large: Cultural Dimensions of Globalization*. Minneapolis: University of Minnesota Press.

Appiah, Kwame Anthony. 1997. "Cosmopolitan Patriots." *Critical Inquiry* 23, no. 3: 617–39.

Applegate, Celia. 1990. *A Nation of Provincials: The German Idea of Heimat*. Berkeley: University of California Press.

Archer, Margaret S. 1988. *Culture and Agency: The Place of Culture in Social Theory*. Cambridge: Cambridge University Press.

Archibugi, Daniele. 1995. "From the United Nations to Cosmopolitan Democracy." In *Cosmopolitan Democracy: An Agenda for the New World Order*, edited by Daniele Archibugi and David Held, 121–62. Cambridge: Polity Press.

Archibugi, Daniele, and David Held, eds. 1995. *Cosmopolitan Democracy: An Agenda for the New World Order*. Cambridge: Polity Press.

Aristotle. 1984. *The Complete Works of Aristotle*. Vol. 2, *The Politics*. Translated by Benjamin Jowett. Edited by Jonathan Barnes. Princeton: Princeton University Press.

Armstrong, John A. 1982. *Nations before Nationalism.* Chapel Hill: University of North Carolina Press.

Arnold, Matthew. 1971. *Culture and Anarchy.* New York: Bobbs-Merrill.

Ashcroft, Bill, Gareth Griffiths, and Helen Tiffin. 1989. *The Empire Writes Back: Theory and Practice in Post-Colonial Literatures.* London: Routledge.

Atlas, James. 1987. "Chicago's Grumpy Guru: Best-Selling Professor Allan Bloom." *New York Times Magazine*, January 31.

Atwood, Margaret. 1972. *Survival: A Thematic Guide to Canadian Literature.* Toronto: Anansi.

Augustinos, Gerasimos. 1992. *The Greeks of Asia Minor: Confession, Community, and Ethnicity in the Nineteenth Century.* Kent, Ohio: Kent State University Press.

Austen, Jane. 1966. *Pride and Prejudice.* Edited by Donald J. Gray. New York: W. W. Norton.

Babcock, Kendric Charles. [1909] 1969. *The Rise of American Nationality, 1811–1819.* New York: Haskell.

Bailey, Richard W. 1991. *Images of English: A Cultural History of the Language.* Ann Arbor: University of Michigan Press.

Baldick, Chris. 1983. *The Social Mission of English Criticism, 1848–1932.* Oxford: Oxford University Press.

Bales, Kevin. 1999. *Disposable People: New Slavery in the Global Economy.* Berkeley: University of California Press.

Balibar, Etienne, and Immanuel Wallerstein. 1991. *Race, Nation, Class: Ambiguous Identities.* London: Verso.

Balsdon, J.P.V.D. 1979. *Romans and Aliens.* Chapel Hill: University of North Carolina Press.

Banton, Michael. 1983. *Racial and Ethnic Competition.* Cambridge: Cambridge University Press.

Barber, Benjamin. 1996. *Jihad vs. McWorld.* New York: Ballantine Books.

Barlow, Maude, and Bruce Campbell. 1995. *Straight through the Heart: How the Liberals Abandoned the Just Society.* Toronto: HarperCollins.

Barman, Roderick J. 1988. *Brazil: The Forging of a Nation, 1798–1852.* Stanford, Calif.: Stanford University Press.

Barth, Frederik, ed. 1969. *Ethnic Groups and Boundaries: The Social Organization of Cultural Difference.* London: George Allen and Unwin.

Basch, Linda, Nina Glick Schiller, and Christina Szanton Blanc. 1994. *Nations Unbound: Transnational Projects, Postcolonial Predicaments, and Deterritorialized Nation-States.* Langhorne Pa.: Gordon and Breach.

Bashevkin, Sylvia B. 1991. *True Patriot Love: The Politics of Canadian Nationalism.* Toronto: Oxford University Press.

Batatu, Hanna. 1978. *The Old Social Classes and the Revolutionary Movements of Iraq.* Princeton: Princeton University Press.

Bate, W. J. 1971. *The Burden of the Past and the English Poet.* London: Chatto and Windus.

Baudrillard, Jean. 1981. *For a Critique of the Political Economy of the Sign.* Translated by Charles Levin. St. Louis: Telos Press.

Beck, H. G. 1960. "Reichsidee und Nationale Politik im spätbyzantinischen Staat." *Byzantinische Zeitschrift* 53, no. 1: 86–94.

Beissinger, Mark R. 1993. "Demise of an Empire-State: Identity, Legitimacy, and the Deconstruction of Soviet Politics." In *The Rising Tide of Cultural Pluralism: The Nation-State at Bay?*, edited by Crawford Young, 93–115. Madison: University of Wisconsin Press.

Bell, Daniel. 1973. *The Coming of Post-Industrial Society.* New York: Basic Books.

———. 1975. "Ethnicity and Social Change." In *Ethnicity: Theory and Experience*, edited by Nathan Glazer and Daniel P. Moynihan, 141–74. Cambridge, Mass.: Harvard University Press.

Bell, Wendel, and Walter E. Freeman, eds. 1974. *Ethnicity and Nation-Building: Comparative, International and Historical Perspectives.* London: Sage.

Bellah, Robert N. 1970. *Beyond Belief: Essays on Religion in a Post Traditional World.* New York: Harper and Row.

Bellah, Robert N., and Philip E. Hammond. 1980. *Varieties of Civil Religion.* San Francisco: Harper and Row.

Bellamy, Elizabeth J., and Artemis Leontis. 1993. "A Geneology of Experience: From Epistemology to Politics." *Yale Journal of Criticism* 6: 163–84.

Belo, M. Adebayo. 1996. *Nigeria and Multi-Nationalism.* Lagos: Malthouse Press.

Benda, Harry J. 1962. "Non-Western Intelligentsias as Political Elites." In *Political Change in Underdeveloped Countries: Nationalism and Communism*, edited by John H. Kautsky, 235–51. New York: John Wiley and Sons.

Bendix, Reinhard. 1988. *Embattled Reason: Essays on Social Knowledge.* New Brunswick, N.J.: Transaction Books.

Bénéton, Philippe. 1975. *Histoire de mots: Culture et civilisation.* Paris: Presses de la foundation nationale des sciences politiques.

Berlant, Lauren. 1991. *The Anatomy of National Fantasy: Hawthorne, Utopia, and Everyday Life.* Chicago: University of Chicago Press.

Berlin, Isaiah. 1976. *Vico and Herder: Two Studies in the History of Ideas.* New York: Viking Press.

Bernal, Martin. 1987. *Black Athena: The Afroasiatic Roots of Classical Civilization.* London: Free Association Press.

Bernheimer, Charles, ed. 1995. *Comparative Literature in the Age of Multiculturalism.* Baltimore: Johns Hopkins University Press.

Bertier de Sauvigny, G. de 1970. "Liberalism, Nationalism, Socialism: The Birth of Three Words." *Review of Politics* 2, no. 32: 147–66.

Betz, Hans-Georg. 1992. "Postmodernism and the New Middle Class." *Theory, Culture and Society* 9, no. 2: 93–114.

Bhabha, Homi. 1990a. Introduction to *Nation and Narration*, edited by Homi Bhabha, 1–7. London: Routledge.

———. 1990b. "Dissemination: Time, Narrative, and the Margins of the Modern Nation." In *Nation and Narration*, edited by Homi Bhabha, 291–322. London: Routledge.

Bigler, Robert M. 1989. "Problems of Development and Nation Building: A Comparative Study of Angola and Mozambique." *International Journal of Contemporary Sociology* 26, nos. 1–2: 93–105.

Blackbourn, David. 1991. "The German Bourgeoisie: An Introduction." In *The German Bourgeoisie*, edited by David Blackbourn and Richard J. Evans, 1–45. London: Routledge.

Blanning, T.C.W. 1983. *The French Revolution in Germany: Occupation and Resistance in the Rhineland, 1792–1802*. Oxford: Clarendon Press.

Blaut, James. M. 1987. *The National Question: Decolonizing the Theory of Nationalism*. London: Zed Books.

Bloom, Harold. 1973. *The Anxiety of Influence: A Theory of Poetry*. New York: Oxford University Press.

Bloom, William. 1990. *Personal Identity, National Identity and International Relations*. Cambridge: Cambridge University Press.

Blumenberg, Hans. 1983. *The Legitimacy of the Modern Age*. Translated by Robert M. Wallace. Cambridge, Mass.: MIT Press.

Bombou-Stamati, Vasiliki. 1982. "O Vikendios Damodos: Viografia—Ergografia 1700–1752." Ph.D. diss., University of Thessaloniki.

Bonner Frances, and Paul de Gay. 1992. "Representing the Enterprising Self: *thirtysomething* and Contemporary Consumer Culture." *Theory, Culture and Society* 2, no. 9: 67–92.

Borchardt, Frank L. 1971. *German Antiquity in Renaissance Myth*. Baltimore: Johns Hopkins Press.

Boulding, K. E. 1959. "National Images and International Systems." *Journal of Conflict Resolution* 3: 120–31.

Bourdieu, Pierre. 1984. *Distinction: A Social Critique of the Judgment of Taste*. Translated by R. Nice. London: Routledge.

Bourne, Randolph. 1956. *The History of a Literary Radical and Other Papers* New York: S. A. Russell.

Bowersock, G. W. 1990. *Hellenism in Late Antiquity*. Ann Arbor: University of Michigan Press.

———. 1994. *Fiction as History: Nero to Julian*. Berkeley: University of California Press.

Boyarin, Daniel, and Jonathan Boyarin. 1993. "Diaspora: Generation and the Ground of Jewish Identity." *Critical Inquiry* 19, no. 4: 693–725.

Boyce, George. 1993. "Ethnicity versus Nationalism in Britain and Ireland." In *Ethnicity and Nationalism: Case Studies in Their Intrinsic Tension and Political Dynamics*, edited by Peter Krüger, 75–89. Marburg: Hitzeroth.

Boyne, Roy. 1990. "Culture and the World-System." In *Global Culture: Nationalism, Globalization, Modernity*, edited by Mike Featherstone, 57–62. London: Sage.

Bozemann, Adda B. 1960. *Politics and Culture in International History*. Princeton: Princeton University Press.

———. 1984. "The International Order in a Multicultural World." In *The Expansion of International Society*, edited by Hedley Bull and Adam Watson, 387–406. Oxford: Clarendon Press.

Brading, D. A. 1991. *The First America: The Spanish Monarchy, Creole Patriots, and the Liberal State, 1492–1867*. Cambridge: Cambridge University Press.

Braudel, Fernand. [1946] 1973. *The Mediterranean and the Mediterranean World in the Age of Philip II*. Vol. 2. Translated by Sian Reynolds. New York: Harper and Row.

Bredvold, Louis I. 1962. *The Natural History of Sensibility*. Detroit: Wayne State University Press.

Brennan, Timothy. 1997. *At Home in the World: Cosmopolitanism Now*. Cambridge, Mass.: Harvard University Press.

Breuilly, John. 1982. *Nationalism and the State*. Chicago: Chicago University Press.

Brown, Peter. 1992. *Power and Persuasion in Late Antiquity: Towards a Christian Empire*. Madison: University of Wisconsin Press.

Browning, Robert. 1983. *Medieval and Modern Greek*. 2nd ed. Cambridge: Cambridge University Press.

Brubaker, Rogers. 1992. *Citizenship and Nationhood in France and Germany*. Cambridge, Mass.: Harvard University Press.

Buell, Frederick. 1994. *National Culture and the New Global System*. Baltimore: Johns Hopkins University Press.

Bull, Hedley. 1977. *The Anarchical Society: A Study of Order in World Politics*. New York: Columbia University Press.

———. 1984. "The Emergence of a Universal International Society." In *The Expansion of International Society*, edited by Hedley Bull and Adam Watson, 117–26. Oxford: Clarendon Press.

Bureau of the Census. 1960. *Historical Statistics of the United States: Colonial Times to 1957*. Washington, D.C.

Bürger, Peter. 1984. *Theory of the Avant-Garde*. Translated by Michael Shaw. Minneapolis: University of Minnesota Press.

Burgess, Michael. 1993. "Federalism and Federation: A Reappraisal." In *Comparative Federalism and Federation: Competing Traditions and Future Dimensions*, edited by Michael Burgess and Alain-G. Gagnon. Toronto: University of Toronto Press.

Burke, Edmund. 1910. *Reflections on the French Revolution and Other Essays*. London: J. M. Dent.

Burke, Peter. 1978. *Popular Culture in Early Modern Europe*. New York: New York University Press.

———. 1991. "Reflections on the Origins of Cultural History." In *Interpretation and Cultural History*, edited by Joan H. Pittock and Andrew Wear, 3–14. New York: St. Martin's Press.

Burns, E. Bradford. 1980. *A History of Brazil*. 2nd ed. New York: Columbia University Press.

Bury, J. B. 1932. *The Idea of Progress: An Inquiry into Its Origins and Growth*. New York: Macmillan.

Camariano-Cioran, Adiadna. 1974. *Les académies princières de Bucarest et de Jassy et leurs professeurs*. Thessaloniki: Institute for Balkan Studies.

Cameron, Averil. 1993. *The Mediterranean World in Late Antiquity, A.D. 395–600*. London: Routledge.

————. 1997. "Hellenism and the Emergence of Islam." *Dialogos* 4: 4–18.

Campbell, Colin. 1987. *The Romantic Ethic and the Spirit of Modern Consumerism*. Oxford: Basil Blackwell.

Careless, J.M.S. 1969. " 'Limited Identities' in Canada." *Canadian Historical Review* 50: 1–10.

Cavafy, Constantine P. 1977. *Anekdota Piimata 1882–1923*. Edited by G. P. Savidis. Athens: Ikaros.

Chadwick, Owen. 1975. *The Secularization of the European Mind*. Cambridge: Cambridge University Press.

Carlyle, Thomas. n.d. *Heroes and Hero Worship and the Heroic in History*. New York: A. L. Burt.

Chambers, Ian. 1994. *Migrancy, Culture, Identity*. London: Routledge.

Chatterjee, Partha. 1986. *Nationalist Thought and the Colonial World: A Derivative Discourse*. Minneapolis: University of Minnesota Press.

————. 1993. *The Nation and Its Fragments: Colonial and Postcolonial Histories*. Princeton: Princeton University Press.

Chinweizu, Jemie Onwuchekwa, and Madubuike Imechukwu. 1983. *Toward the Decolonization of African Literature*. Washington, D.C.: Howard University Press.

Chow, Rey. 1993. *Writing Diaspora: Tactics of Intervention in Contemporary Cultural Studies*. Bloomington: Indiana University Press.

Clayton, Bruce. 1984. *Forgotten Prophet: The Life of Randolph Bourne*. Baton Rouge: Louisianna State University Press.

Clogg, Richard. 1969. "The 'Didaskalia Patriki' (1789): An Orthodox Reaction to French Revolutionary Propaganda." *Middle Eastern Studies* 5: 87–115.

————. 1983. "Sense of the Past in Pre-Independence Greece." In *Culture and Nationalism in Nineteenth-Century Eastern Europe*, edited by Roland Sussex and J. C. Eade, 7–30. Columbus: Slavica.

Cobban, Alfred. 1964. *Rousseau and the Modern State*. Camden, Conn: Archon Books.

Cochran, Terry. 1990. "Culture against the State." *Boundary 2* 17, no. 3: 1–68.

Cohn, Bernard S., and Nicholas B. Dirks. 1988. "Beyond the Fringe: The Nation-State, Colonialism and the Technologies of Power." *Journal of Historical Sociology* 1, no. 2: 224–29.

Coleman, James S. 1971. *Nigeria: Background to Nationalism*. Berkeley: University of California Press.

Coleman, John A. 1970–71. "Civil Religion." *Sociological Analysis* 31, no. 1: 67–77.

Coleridge, Samuel Taylor. [1830] 1972. *On the Constitution of the Church and State According to the Idea of Each*. London: J. M. Dent and Sons.

Colley, Linda. 1992. *Britons: Forging the Nation, 1707–1837*. New Haven: Yale University Press.

Collins, Randall. 1987. "A Micro-Macro Theory of Intellectual Creativity: The Case of German Idealist Philosophy." *Sociological Theory* 5: 47–69.

Collins, Richard, James Curran, Nicholas Garnham, Paddy Scannell, Philip Schlesinger, and Colin Sparks, eds. 1986. *Media, Culture and Society*. London: Sage.

Colls, Robert. 1986. "Englishness and the Political Culture." In *Englishness: Politics and Culture, 1880–1920*, edited by Robert Colls and Philip Dodd, 29–61. London: Croom Helm.

Comaroff, Jean, and John Comaroff. 1993. Introduction to *Modernity and Its Malcontents*, edited by Jean Comaroff and John Comaroff, xl–xxxvii. Chicago: University of Chicago Press.

Comaroff, John. 1987. "Of Totemism and Ethnicity: Consciousness, Practice, and the Signs of Inequality." *Ethnos* 52, nos. 3–4: 301–23.

Connor, Walker. 1973. "The Politics of Ethnonationalism." *Journal of International Affairs* 27, no. 1: 1–21.

———. 1976. "The Political Significance of Ethnonationalism within Western Europe." In *Ethnicity in an International Context*, edited by Abdul Said and Luiz R. Simmons, 110–33. New Brunswick, N.J.: Transaction Books.

———. 1978. "A Nation Is a Nation, Is a State, Is an Ethnic Group Is a . . ." *Ethnic and Racial Studies* 1, no. 4: 377–99.

———. 1994. *Ethnonationalism: The Quest for Understanding*. Princeton: Princeton University Press.

Cornell, Stephen. 1988. *The Return of the Native American: Indian Political Resurgence*. New York: Oxford University Press.

Corpuz, Onofre D. 1965. *The Philippines*. Englewood Cliffs, N.J.: Prentice-Hall.

Corrigan, Philip, and Derek Sayer. 1985. *The Great Arch: English State Formation as Cultural Revolution*. Oxford: Basil Blackwell.

Corse, Sarah M. 1997. *Nationalism and Literature: The Politics of Culture in Canada and the United States*. Cambridge: Cambridge University Press.

Creighton, D. G. 1937. *The Commercial Empire of the St. Lawrence, 1760–1850*. Toronto: Ryerson Press.

Cuddihy, John Murray. 1974. *The Ordeal of Civility: Freud, Marx, Lévi-Strauss, and the Jewish Struggle with Modernity*. New York: Basic Books.

Cunliffe, Barry. 1988. *Greeks, Romans, and Barbarians: Spheres of Interaction*. New York: Methuen.

Daadler, Hans. 1973. "Building Consociational Nations." In *Building States and Nations*, vol. 2, edited by S. N. Eisenstadt and Stein Rokkan, 14–31. London: Sage.

Dalberg-Acton, John Emerich Edward. 1948. *Essays on Freedom and Power*. Edited by Gertrude Himmelfarb. Boston: Beacon Press.

Danforth, Loring M. 1995. *The Macedonian Conflict: Ethnic Nationalism in a Transnational World*. Princeton: Princeton University Press.

Davidson, Basil. 1992. *The Black Man's Burden: Africa and the Curse of the Nation-State*. New York: Times Books.

Davis, S. Rufus. 1978. *The Federal Principle: A Journey through Time in Quest of a Meaning*. Berkeley: University of California Press.

Dean, Seamus. 1997. *Strange Country: Modernity and Nationhood in Irish Writing since 1790*. Oxford: Oxford University Press.

Defoe, Daniel. 1982. *The Life and Adventures of Robinson Crusoe*. Edited by Angus Ross. New York: Greenwich House.

DeJean, Joan. 1997. *Ancients against Moderns: Culture Wars and the Making of a Fin de Siècle*. Chicago: University of Chicago Press.

Deleuze, Gilles, and Félix Guattari. 1986. *Kafka: Toward a Theory of Minor Literature*. Translated by Dana Polan. Minneapolis: University of Minnesota Press.

di Leonardo, Micaela. 1984. *The Varieties of Ethnic Experience: Kinship, Class, and Gender among California Italian-Americans*. Ithaca, N.Y.: Cornell University Press.

Dimaras, K. Th. 1989. *Neoellinikos Diafotismos*. 5th ed. Athens: Ermis.

Dirlik, Arif. 1994. "The Postcolonial Aura: Third World Criticism in the Age of Global Capitalism." *Critical Inquiry* 20, no. 2: 328–56.

Doctorow, E. L. 1987. "A Citizen Reads the Constitution." *Nation*, February 21, 208–17.

Drummond, Alexander. 1754. *Travels through different Cities of Germany, Italy, Greece, and several Parts of Asia, as far as the Banks of the Euphrates: In a Series of Letters*. London: W. Strahan.

Dülmen, Richard van. 1986. *Die Gesellschaft der Aufklärer: Zur bürgerlichen Emanzipation und aufklärerischen Kultur in Deutschland*. Frankfurt am Main: Fischer Taschenbuch Verlag.

Duchacek, Ivo D. 1986. *The Territorial Dimension of Politics: Within, among and across Nations*. Boulder, Colo.: Westview Press.

Düding, Dieter. 1987. "The Nineteenth-Century German Nationalist Movement as a Movement of Societies." In *Nation-Building in Central Europe*. Edited by Hagen Schulze. New York: Berg Publishers.

Duri, A. A. 1987. *The Historical Formation of the Arab Nation: A Study in Identity and Consciousness*. Translated by Lawrence I. Conrad. London: Croom Helm.

Durkheim, Emile. 1915. *The Elementary Forms of Religious Life*. Translated by Joseph Ward Swain. London: Allen and Unwin.

———. 1957. *Professional Ethics and Civic Morals*. Translated by Cornelia Brookfield. London: Routledge.

———. 1972. *Emile Durkheim: Selected Writings*. Edited and translated by Anthony Giddens. Cambridge: Cambridge University Press.

———. 1984. *The Division of Labor in Society*. Edited by W. D. Halls. New York: Free Press.

Dyson, H. F. Kenneth. 1980. *The State Tradition in Western Europe: A Study of an Idea and Institution*. New York: Oxford University Press.

Eagleton, Terry. 1990. *The Ideology of the Aesthetic*. Oxford: Basil Blackwell.

Ehrenberg, Victor. 1960. *The Greek State*. Oxford: Basil Blackwell.

Ehrenreich, Barbara, and John H. Ehrenreich. 1979 "The Professional-Managerial Class." In *Between Labor and Capital*, edited by Pat Walker, 5–45. Boston: South End Press.

Ehrenreich, John H. 1983. "Socialism, Nationalism, and Capitalist Development." *Review of Radical Political Economics* 15, no. 1: 1–42.

Eisenstadt, S. N., and Stein Rokkan, eds. 1973. *Building States and Nations*. Vol. 2. London: Sage.

Eley, Geoff. 1982. "State Formation, Nationalism and Political Culture in Nineteenth-Century Germany." In *Culture, Ideology and Politics*, edited by Raphael Samuel and Gareth S. Jones, 277–301. London: Routledge.

Elias, Norbert. [1939] 1978. *The Civilizing Process: The History of Manners.* Translated by Edmund Jephcott. New York: Pantheon.

Eliot, T. S. 1948. *Notes towards the Definition of Culture.* London: Faber.

Ellison, Ralph. 1964. *Shadow and Act.* New York: Random House.

Emerson, Ralph Waldo. 1837. "An Oration, Delivered before the Phi Beta Kappa Society." Boston: James Munroe.

Emerson, Rupert. 1962. *From Empire to Nation: The Rise of Self-Assertion of Asian and African Peoples.* Cambridge, Mass.: Harvard University Press.

Enloe, Cynthia. 1981. "The Growth of the State and Ethnic Mobilization: The American Experience." *Ethnic and Racial Studies* 4, no. 2: 123–36.

Ergang, Robert Reinhold. 1966. *Herder and the Foundations of German Nationalism.* New York: Octagon Books.

Espiritu, Yen Le. 1992. *Asian American Panethnicity: Bridging Institutions and Identities.* Philadelphia: Temple University Press.

Falcoff, Mark. 1996. "North of the Border: Origins and Falacies of the 'Hispanic' Threat in the United States." *TLS,* May 17, 14–17.

Fallmerayer, Jakob Phillip. 1830–36. *Geschichte der Halbinsel Morea währed des Mittelalters.* 2 vols. Stuttgart.

———. 1835. *Welchen Einfluß hatte die Besetzung Griechenlands durch die Slaven auf das Schicksal der Stadt Athen und der Landschaft Attika?* Stuttgart.

Fanon, Frantz. 1963. *The Wretched of the Earth.* Translated by Constance Farrington. New York: Grove Press.

Featherstone, Mike. 1991. *Consumer, Culture and Postmodernism.* London: Sage.

Fichte, Johann Gottlieb. 1835. *Nachgelassene Werke.* Vol. 3. Edited by F. H. Fichte. Bonn: Adolph Marcus.

———. 1979. *Addresses to the German Nation.* Translated by R. F. Jones and G. H. Turnbull. Westport, Conn.: Greenwood Press.

Finley, M. I. 1986. *The Use and Abuse of History.* 2nd ed. New York: Penguin Books.

Fischer, Berndt. 1995. *Das Eigene und das Eigentliche: Klopstock, Herder, Fichte, Kleist. Episoden aus der Konstruktionsgeschichte nationaler Intentionalitäten.* Berlin: Erich Schmidt.

Fiske, John. 1989. *Understanding Popular Culture.* Boston: Unwin and Hyman.

Fitzgerald, Penelope. 1995. *The Blue Flower.* Boston: Houghton Mifflin.

Forsyth, Murray, ed. 1989. *Federalism and Nationalism.* Leicester: Leicester University Press.

Foster, John. 1989. "Nationality, Social Change, and Class: Transformations of National Identity in Scotland." In *The Making of Scotland: Nation, Culture and Social Change,* edited by David McCrone, Stephen Kendricks, and Pat Straw, 31–52. Edinburgh: Edinburgh University Press.

Fotinopoulos, Mihail. 1959. *Nomikon Prohiron.* Edited by P. I. Zepos, Athens: Arhion Idiotikou Dikeou.

Foucault, Michel. 1979. *Discipline and Punish: The Birth of the Prison.* Translated by Alan Sheridan. New York: Vintage Books.

———. 1986. "Kant on Enlightenment and Revolution." *Economy and Society.* 15, no. 1: 88–96.

Fowden, Garth. 1993. *Empire to Commonwealth: Consequences of Monotheism in Late Antiquity.* Princeton: Princeton University Press.

Frank, Manfred. 1993. "Nationality and Democracy: Defining Terms in Germany." *Common Knowledge* 2, no. 3: 65–78.

Fraser, Nancy. 1990. "Rethinking the Public Sphere: A Contribution to the Critique of Actually Existing Democracy." *Social Text* 25, no. 6: 56–80.

Friedman, Jonathan. 1994. *Cultural Identity and Global Process.* London: Sage.

Friedrich, Carl J. 1968. *Trends of Federalism in Theory and Practice.* New York: Praeger.

Fuchs, Lawrence H. 1990. *The American Kaleidoscope: Race, Ethnicity, and the Civic Culture.* Hanover, N.H.: University Press of New England.

Fuller, S. Margaret. 1846. *Papers on Literature and Art.* New York: Putnam.

Funderburg, Lise. 1994. *Black, White, Other: Biracial Americans Talk about Race and Identity.* New York: W. Morrow.

Gagliardo, John G. 1980. *Reich and Nation: The Holy Roman Empire as Idea and Reality, 1763–1806.* Bloomington: Indiana University Press.

Gagnon, Alain-G., and Can Erk. 1998. "A Compact Theory of Federalism: Can the Canadian Federal Experience Provide Lessons for Cyprus?" *Cyprus Review* 10, no. 1: 19–31.

Galanaki, Rea. 1989. *O Vios tou Ismail Ferik Pasa: Spina Nel Cuore.* Athens: Agra.

———. 1996. *The Life of Ismail Ferik Pasha: Spina Nel Cuore.* Translated by Kay Cicellis. London: UNESCO Publishing.

Gans, Herbert J. 1979. "Symbolic Ethnicity: The Future of Ethnic Groups and Cultures in America." *Ethnic and Racial Studies* 2, no. 1: 1–20.

Ganzis, Nicholas. 1995–96. "The Structural Imperatives of Ethnic Identity: Greek Ethnic Consciousness and the Greek Community of South Australia." *Journal of Modern Hellenism* 12–13: 115–54.

Geertz, Clifford. 1963. "The Integrated Revolution." In *Old Societies and New States: The Quest for Modernity in Asia and Africa:* New York: Free Press of Glencoe.

———. 1993. " 'Ethnic Conflict': Three Alternative Terms." *Common Knowledge* 2, no. 3: 54–65.

Gellner, Ernest. 1983. *Nations and Nationalism.* Oxford: Basil Blackwell.

Georgakas, Dan. 1991. "Demosthenes Nikas: Labor Radical." *New Directions in Greek American Studies.* Edited by Dan Georgakas and Chales C. Moskos, 95–110. New York: Pella.

Gerschenkron, Alexander. 1962. *Economic Backwardness in Historical Perspective.* Cambridge, Mass.: Harvard University Press.

Gershoni, Israel, and James P. Jankowski. 1986. *Egypt, Islam, and the Arabs: The Search for Egyptian Nationhood, 1900–1930.* New York: Oxford University Press.

Giddens, Anthony. 1985. *The Nation-State and Violence.* Cambridge: Polity Press.

———. 1991. *Modernity and Self-Identity: Self and Society in the Late Modern Age.* Cambridge: Cambridge University Press.

Gilbert, W. S. [1878] N.d. *H.M.S. Pinafore or The Lass That Loved a Sailor.* New York: G. Schirmer.

Gilroy, Paul. 1987. *There Ain't No Black in the Union Jack: The Cultural Politics of Race and Nation.* London: Hutchinson.

———. 1993. *The Black Atlantic: Modernity and Double Consciousness.* Cambridge, Mass.: Harvard University Press.

Gitlin, Todd. 1995. *The Twilight of Common Dreams: How America Is Wracked by Culture Wars.* New York: Metropolitan Books.

———. 1998. "A Truce Prevails; for the Left, Many Victories are Pyrrhic." *Chronicle of Higher Education,* March 6, B4–5.

Glazer, Nathan. 1994. "Multiculturalism and Public Policy." In *Values and Public Policy,* edited by Henry J. Aaron, Thomas E. Mann, and Timothy Taylor, 113–145. Washington, D.C.: Brookings Institution.

Glazer, Nathan, and Daniel P. Moynihan. 1963. *Beyond the Melting Pot: The Negroes, Puerto Ricans, Jews, Italians, and the Irish of New York City.* Cambridge, Mass.: Harvard University Press.

Goethe, Johann Wolfgang von. 1929. *The Sorrows of Young Werther.* Translated by William Rose. London: Scholartis Press.

Gomez, Michael A. 1998. *Exchanging Our Country Marks: The Transformation of African Identities in the Colonial and Antebellum South.* Chapell Hill: University of North Carolina Press.

Gonzalez, Andrew B. 1980. *Language and Nationalism: The Philippine Experience Thus Far.* Manila: Ateneo de Manila University Press.

Gordon, Milton M. 1964. *Assimilation in American Life: The Role of Race, Religion, and National Origins.* New York: Oxford University Press.

Gottlieb, Gidon. 1994. "Nations without States." *Foreign Affairs* 73, no. 3: 100–112.

Goulbourne, Harry. 1991. *Ethnicity and Nationalism in Post-Imperial Britain.* Cambridge: Cambridge University Press.

Gouldner, Alvin W. 1979. *The Future of Intellectuals and the Rise of the New Class.* New York: Continuum.

Gourgouris, Stathis. 1996. *Dream Nation: Enlightenment, Colonization, and the Institution of Modern Greece.* Stanford, Calif.: Stanford University Press.

Graff, Gerald. 1987. *Professing Literature: An Institutional History.* Chicago: University of Chicago Press.

Gramsci, Antonio. 1985. *Selections from Cultural Writings.* Edited by David Forgacs and Geoffrey Nowell-Smith. Translated by William Boelhower. Cambridge, Mass.: Harvard University Press.

Greeley, Andrew M. 1971. *Why Can't They Be Like Us: America's White Ethnic Groups.* New York: E. P. Dutton.

———. 1974. *Ethnicity in the United States: A Preliminary Reconnaissance.* New York: John Wiley and Sons.

Greene, Roland. 1995. "Nation-Building by Anthology." *Diaspora* 4, no. 1: 105–20.

Greenfeld, Liah. 1992. *Nationalism: Five Roads in Modernity.* Cambridge, Mass.: Harvard University Press.

Greenfield, Jeanette. 1989. *The Return of Cultural Treasures*. Cambridge: Cambridge University Press.

Griswold, Wendy. 1987. "The Fabrication of Meaning: Literary Interpretation in the United States, Great Britain, and the West Indies." *American Journal of Sociology* 92, no. 5: 1077–1117.

Gross, Joan, David McMurray, and Ted Swedenborg. 1994. "Arab Noise and Ramadan Nights: Rai, Rap, and Franco-Maghrebi Identity." *Diaspora* 3, no. 1: 3–40.

Grossberg, Lawrence. 1988. "Putting the Pop Back into Postmodernism." In *Universal Abandon*, edited by Andrew Ross, 167–190. Minneapolis: University of Minnesota Press.

Grossberg, Lawrence, Cary Nelson, and Paula A. Treichler, eds. 1992. *Cultural Studies*. New York: Routledge.

Guibernau, Montserrat. 1995. "Spain: A Federation in the Making?" In *Federalism: The Multiethnic Challenge*, edited by Graham Smith, 239–54. London: Longman.

———. 1996. *Nationalisms: The Nation-State and Nationalism in the Twentieth Century*. Cambridge: Polity Press.

Guillory, John. 1993. *Cultural Capital: The Problem of Literary Canon Formation*. Chicago: University of Chicago Press.

Guilmartin, John F., Jr. 1991. "The Cutting Edge: An Analysis of the Spanish Invasion and Overthrow of the Inca Empire, 1532–1539." In *Transatlantic Encounters: Europeans and Andeans in the Sixteenth Century*, edited by Kenneth J. Andrien and Rolena Adorno, 40–72. Berkeley: University of California Press.

Gupta, Akhil. 1992. "The Song of the Nonaligned World: Transnational Identities and the Reinscription of Space in Late Capitalism." *Cultural Anthropology* 7, no. 1: 6–23.

Gupta, Akhil, and James Ferguson. 1992. "Beyond 'Culture': Space, Identity, and the Politics of Difference." *Cultural Anthropology* 7, no. 1: 6–23.

Gurevich, A. J. 1985. *Categories of Medieval Culture*. Translated by G. L. Campbell. London: Routledge and Kegan Paul.

Gwyn, Richard. 1995. *Nationalism without Walls: The Unbearable Lightness of Being Canadian*. Toronto: McLelland and Stewart.

Habermas, Jürgen. 1981. "Modernity vs Postmodernity." *New German Critique* 22: 3–14.

———. 1984. "Questions and Counterquestions." *Praxis International* 4, no. 3: 229–49.

———. 1996a. "The European Nation-state—Its Achievements and Its Limits." In *Mapping the Nation*, editing by Gopal Balakrishnan, 281–94. London: Verso.

———. 1996b. "National Unification and Popular Sovereignty." *New Left Review* 219: 3–13.

Hackney, Sheldon. 1993. "Remarks of Sheldon Hackney at the National Press Club." November 10. National Endowment for the Humanities, Washington, D.C. Unpublished manuscript.

Hadfield, Andrew. 1994. *Literature, Politics, and National Identity: Reformation to Renaissance*. Cambridge: Cambridge University Press.

Hall, Peter Dubkin. 1982. *Organization of American Culture: Private Institutions, Elite, and the Origins of American Nationality*. New York: New York University Press.

Hall, Stuart. 1985. "Cultural Studies: Two Paradigms." In *Media, Culture, and Society: A Critical Reader*. Edited by Richard Collins, James Curran, Nicholas Garnham, Paddy Scannell, Philip Schlesinger, and Colin Sparks. London: Sage.

Hamelink, Cees. J. 1983. *Cultural Autonomy in Global Communications*. New York: Longman.

Handler, Richard. 1988. *Nationalism and the Politics of Culture in Quebec*. Madison: University of Wisconsin Press.

Hannerz, Ulf. 1987. "The World in Creolisation." *Africa* 57, no. 4: 546–59.

Hansen, Mogens Herman. 1991. *The Athenian Democracy in the Age of Demosthenes: Structure, Principles and Ideology*. Translated by J. A. Cook. Oxford: Blackwell.

Harlow, Barbara. 1987. *Resistance Literature*. New York: Methuen.

Hart, Vivien, and Shannon C. Stimson, eds. 1993. *Writing a National Identity: Political, Economic, and Cultural Perspectives on the Written Constitution*. Manchester: Manchester University Press.

Hartog, François. 1988. *The Mirror of Herodotus: The Representation of the Other in the Writing of History*. Translated by Janet Lloyd. Berkeley: University of California Press.

Harvey, David. 1985. "The Geopolitics of Capitalism." In *Social Relations and Spatial Structures*, edited by Derek Gregory and John Urry. New York: St. Martin's Press.

———. 1989. *The Conditions of Postmodernity: An Inquiry into the Origins of Cultural Change*. Oxford: Basil Blackwell.

Haugen, Einar. 1966. *Language Conflict and Language Planning: The Case of Modern Norwegian*. Cambridge, Mass.: Harvard University Press.

Heater, Derek. 1990. *Citizenship: The Civic Ideal in World History, Politics, and Education*. London: Longman.

Hedges, William L. 1988. "Toward a National Literature." In *Columbia Literary History of the United States*, edited by Emory Elliott, 187–202. New York: Columbia University Press.

Held, David. 1991. "Democracy, the Nation-State and the Global System." In *Political Theory Today*, edited by David Held, 197–235. Stanford, Calif.: Stanford University Press.

Helgerson, Richard. 1992. *Forms of Nationhood: The Elizabethan Writing of England*. Chicago: University of Chicago Press.

Henderson, G. P. 1970. *The Revival of Greek Thought, 1620–1830*. Albany: State University of New York Press.

Herbert, Christopher. 1991. *Culture and Anomie: Ethnographic Imagination in the Nineteenth Century*. Chicago: University of Chicago Press.

Herder, Johann Gottfried von. 1877–99. *Sämmtliche Werke*. 32 vols. Edited by Bernhard Suphan. Berlin: Beidmannische Buchhandlung.

———. 1968. *Reflections on the Philosophy of the History of Mankind*. Chicago: University of Chicago Press.

———. 1989a. *Against Pure Reason: Writings on Religion, Language, and History*. Translated and edited by Marcia Bunge. Minneapolis: Fortress Press.

———. 1989b. *Ideen zur Philosophie der Geschichte der Menschheit*. Frankfurt: Deutscher Klassiker Verlag.

———. 1992. *Gottfried Herder: Selected Early Works, 1764–1767*. Edited by Ernest A. Menze and Michael Palma. University Park: Pennsylvania State University Press.

Herodotus. 1987. *The Histories*. Translated by David Grene. Chicago: University of Chicago Press.

Herzfeld, Michael. 1982. *Ours Once More: Folklore, Ideology, and the Making of Modern Greece*. Austin: University of Texas Press.

Hicks, Emily D. 1991. *Border Writing: The Multidimensional Text*. Minneapolis: University of Minnesota Press.

Hilton, Rodney. 1989. "Were the English English?" In *Patriotism: The Making and Unmaking of British National Identity*, vol. 1, edited by Raphael Samuel, 39–43. New York: Routledge.

Hinsley, F. H. 1973. *Nationalism and the International System*. London: Hodder and Stoughton.

Hirsch, E. D. 1987. *Cultural Literacy: What Every American Needs to Know*. Boston: Houghton Mifflin.

Hirschon, Renée. 1989. *Heirs of the Greek Catastrophe: The Social Life of Asia Minor Refugees in Piraeus*. Oxford: Clarendon Press.

Hobbes, Thomas. [1651] 1991. *Leviathan*. Edited by Richard Tuck. Cambridge: Cambridge University Press.

Hobhouse, J. C. 1813. *A Journey through Albania and other Provinces of Turkey, in Europe and Asia, to Constantinople during the years 1808 and 1810*. 2nd ed. 2 vols. London: Lames Cawthorn.

Hobsbawm, Eric. 1990. *Nations and Nationalism since 1870: Programme, Myth, Reality*. Cambridge: Cambridge University Press.

Hobsbawm, Eric, and Terence Ranger, eds. 1983. *The Invention of Tradition*. Cambridge: Cambridge University Press.

Hodgson, Marshall. 1993. *Rethinking World History: Essays on Europe, Islam, and World History*. Edited by Edmund Burke III. Cambridge: Cambridge University Press.

Hofstadter, Richard. 1963. *Anti-Intellectualism in American Life*. New York: Knopf.

Hoggart, Richard. 1957. *The Uses of Literacy*. London: Chatto and Windus.

Hohendahl, Peter Uwe. 1989. *Building a National Literature: The Case of Germany, 1830–1870*. Translated by Renate B. Franciscono. Ithaca, N.Y.: Cornell University Press.

Homer. 1951. *The Iliad*. Translated by Richmond Lattimore. Chicago: University of Chicago Press.

Holquist, Michael. 1996. "A New Tower of Babel: Recent Trends Linking Comparative Literature Departments, Foreign Language Departments, and Area Studies Programs." In *Profession 1996*, 103–14. New York: MLA.

Holton, David, ed. 1974. *The Tale of Alexander: The Rhymed Version*. Thessaloniki: Bizantini ke Neoelliniki Vivliothiki.

Hondrich, Karl Otto. 1992. "World Society versus Niche Societies." *Social Change and Modernity*, edited by Hans Haferkamp and Neil Smelser, 350–68. Berkeley: University of California Press.

Horace. 1929. *Satires, Epistles, and Ars Poetica*. Edited and translated by H. Rushton Fairclough. New York: Putnam's.

Howe, Nicholas. 1997. "The Figural Presence of Erich Auerbach." *Yale Review* 85, no. 1: 136–43.

Hroch, Miroslav. 1985. *Social Preconditions of National Revival in Europe: A Comparative Analysis of Social Composition of Patriotic Groups among the Smaller European Countries*. Translated by Ben Fawkes. Cambridge: Cambridge Univesity Press.

Hughes, Michael. 1988. *Nationalism and Society: Germany, 1800–1945*. London: Edward Arnold.

Huizinga, Johan. 1972. "Nationalism in the Middle Ages." In *Nationalism in the Middle Ages*, edited by C. Leon Tipton, 14–24. New York. Rinehart and Winston.

Hume, David. [1742] 1898. *Essays: Moral, Political, and Literary*. Volume 1. Edited by T. H. Green and T. H. Grose. London: Longmans Green.

———. 1826. *The Philosophical Works*. Vol. 3. Edinburgh: Adam Black, William Tait, Charles Tait.

Hunter, Ian. 1992. "Aesthetics and Cultural Studies." In *Cultural Studies*, edited by Lawrence Grossberg, Cary Nelson, and Paula Treichler. New York: Routledge.

———. 1996. "Literary Theory in Civil Life." *South Atlantic Quarterly* 95, no. 4: 1099–1134.

Huntington, Samuel P. 1993. "The Clash of Civilizations." *Foreign Affairs* 77: 22–49.

Hutcheon, Linda. 1998. "Crypto-Ethnicity." *PMLA* 113, no. 1: 28–33.

Hutchinson, John. 1987. *The Dynamics of Cultural Nationalism: The Gaelic Revival and the Creation of the Irish Nation State*. London: Allen and Unwin.

Iggers, Georg G. 1968. *The German Conception of History: The National Tradition of Historical Thought from Herder to the Present*. Middletown, Conn.: Wesleyan University Press.

Ignatieff, Michael. 1993. *Blood and Belonging: Journeys into the New Nationalism*. New York: Farrar Straus, & Giroux.

Ignatiev, Noel. 1995. *How the Irish Became White*. New York: Routledge.

Ioannou, Filippos. 1863. "Peri tis Neoteras Ellinikis Glossis." *Ethnikon Imerologion*.

Jalali, Rita, and Seymour Martin Lipset. 1992–93. "Racial and Ethnic Conflicts: A Global Perspective." *Political Science Quarterly* 107, no. 4: 585–606.

James, Harold. 1989. *A German Identity: 1770–1990*. London: Weidenfeld and Nicolson.

Jameson, Fredric. 1984. "Postmodernism, or the Cultural Logic of Late Capitalism." *New Left Review* 146: 53–92.

Jankowski, James. 1991. "Egypt and Early Arab Nationalism, 1908–1922." In *The Origins of Arab Nationalism*, edited by Rashid Khalidi, Lisa Anderson,

Muhammad Muslih, and Reeva S. Simon, 243–70. New York: Columbia University Press.

Jarvenpa, Robert. 1985. "The Political Economy and Political Ethnicity of American Indian Adaptions and Identities." *Ethnic and Racial Studies* 8, no. 1: 29–48.

Jay, John. 1992. *The Federalist Papers*. Cutchogue, N.Y.: Buccaneer Books.

Jones, Maldwyn Allen. 1960. *American Immigration*. Chicago: University of Chicago Press.

Jones, Richard Foster. 1961. *Ancients and Moderns: A Study of the Rise of the Scientific Movement in Seventeenth-Century England*. 2nd ed. St. Louis: Washington University Press.

Jusdanis, Gregory. 1987. "Is Postmodernism Possible Outside the West? The Case of Greece." *Byzantine and Modern Greek Studies* 11: 69–92.

———. 1991a. *Belated Modernity and Aesthetic Culture: Inventing National Literature*. Theory and History of Literature, 81. Minneapolis: University of Minnesota Press.

———. 1991b. "Greek Americans and the Disapora." *Diaspora* 1, no. 2: 209–23.

———. 1996. "Acropolis Now?" *boundary 2* 23, no. 1: 185–93.

———. 1998. Review of *Imagining the Balkans* by Maria Todorova. *Journal of Modern Greek Studies* 16, no. 2: 375–77.

———. 1999. Review of *Bardic Nationalism: The Romantic Novel and the British Empire* by Katie Trumpener. *Research in African Literatures* 30, no. 2: 229–32.

Kairis, Theofilos. 1851. *Stihia Filosofias, i, ton peri ta onta genikoteron theoroumenon ta stihiodestera*. Athens: D. Irinidou.

Kakridis, Ioannis Th. 1979. *I Arhei Ellines stin neoelliniki Laïki Paradosi*. 2nd ed. Athens: National Bank of Greece.

Kalka, Iris. 1990. "Attachment to the Mother Country—Image and Reality." *Ethnic Groups* 8, no. 4: 249–65.

Kallen, Horace M. 1924. *Culture and Democracy in the United States: Studies in the Group Psychology of the American Peoples*. New York: Boni and Liveright.

Kalyvas, Stathis N., David D. Laitin, and Carlota Solé. 1994. "Language and the Construction of States: The Case of Catalonia in Spain." *Politics and Society* 22, no. 1: 5–29.

Kamenka, Eugene. 1976. "Political Nationalism—The Evolution of the Idea." In *Nationalism: The Nature and Evolution of an Idea*. Edited by C. Leon Tipton. New York: St. Martin's Press.

Kaschuba, Wolfgang. 1988. "Deutsche Bürgerlichkeit nach 1800. Kultur als symbolische Praxis." In *Bürgertum im 19. Jahrhundert, Deutschland im europäischen vergleich*. Edited by Jürgen Kocka, 9–44. Munich: D.T.V.

Katartzis, Dimitrios. 1970. *Ta Evriskomena*. Edited by K. Th. Dimaras. Athens: Ermis.

Kautsky, John H. 1962. "Nationalism." In *Political Change in Underdeveloped Countries: Nationalism and Communism*, edited by John H. Kautsky. New York: John Wiley and Sons.

Keane, John, ed. 1988. *Civil Society and the State: New European Perspectives*. London: Verso.

Kearney, Hugh. 1989. *The British Isles: A History of Four Nations*. Cambridge: Cambridge University Press.

Kearney, Michael. 1991. "Borders and Boundaries of State and Self at the End of Empire." *Journal of Historical Sociology* 4, no. 1: 52–74.

Kedourie, Elie, ed. 1970. *Nationalism in Asia and Africa*. New York: New American Library.

———. 1993. *Nationalism*. 4th ed. Oxford: Blackwell.

Keren, Michael. 1989. *The Pen and the Sword: Israeli Intellectuals and the Making of the Nation-State*. Boulder, Colo.: Westview Press.

Kessler-Harris, Alice, and Virginia Yans-McLaughlin. 1978. "European Immigrant Groups." In *American Ethnic Groups*, edited by Thomas Sowell, 107–38. Urban Institute.

Kiberd, Declan. 1996. *Inventing Ireland*. Cambridge, Mass.: Harvard University Press.

Kitromilides, Paschalis M. 1983. "The Enlightenment East and West: A Comparative Perspective on the Ideological Origins of the Balkan Political Tradition." *Canadian Review of Studies in Nationalism* 10, no. 1: 51–70.

———. 1985. "The Last Battle of the Ancients and Moderns: Ancient Greece and Modern Europe in the Neohellenic Revival." *Modern Greek Studies Yearbook* 1: 79–91.

———. 1990a. "The Idea of Science in the Modern Greek Enlightenment." In *Greek Studies in the Philosophy of History and Science*, edited by Pantelis Nicolacopoulos, 187–200. Dordrecht: Kluwer.

———. 1990b. *I Galliki Epanastasi ke i Notioanatoliki Evropi*. Athens: Diatton.

———. 1992. *The Enlightenment as Social Criticism: Iosipos Moisiodax and Greek Culture in the Eighteenth Century*. Princeton: Princeton University Press.

Knapp, Martin. 1984. *Evjenios Vulgaris im Einfluss der Aufklärung. Der Begriff der Toleranz bei Vulgaris und Voltaire*. Amsterdam: Hakkert.

Knippling, Alpana Sharma, ed. 1996. *New Immigrant Literatures in the United States: A Sourcebook to Our Multicultural Literary Heritage*. Westport, Conn.: Greenwood Press.

Kohn, Hans. 1940. "The Genesis and Character of English Nationalism." *Journal of the History of Ideas* 1, no. 1: 69–94.

———. 1949. "The Paradox of Fichte's Nationalism." *Journal of the History of Ideas* 10, no. 3: 319–43.

———. 1956. *The Idea of Nationalism: A Study in Its Origins and Background*. New York: Macmillan.

———. 1967. *Prelude to Nation-States: The French and German Experience, 1789–1815*. Princeton: D. Van Nostrand.

Kolokotronis, Theodoros. [1851] 1964. *Apomnimonevmata*. Athens: Drakopoulos.

Kondylis, Panagiotis. 1988. *O Neoellinikos Diafotismos: I Filosofikes Idees*. Athens: Themelio.

Korais, Adamantios. 1804. *Iliodorou Ethiopikon*. 2 vols. Paris.

———. [1798] 1949. *Adelfiki Didaskalia*. Edited by G. Valetas. Athens: Pigis.

Kosseleck, Reinhart. 1988. *Critique and Crisis: Enlightenment and the Pathogenesis of Modern Society.* Cambridge, Mass.: MIT Press.

Koukou, Eleni E. 1983. *Istoria ton Eptanison apo to 1797 mehri tin Anglokratia.* Athens: Papadimas.

Koumas, K. M. 1818. *Syntagma Filosofias.* Vol. 1. Vienna.

Krasner, Stephen D. 1989. "Sovereignty: An Institutional Perspective." In *The Elusive State: International and Comparative Perspectives*, edited by James A. Caporaso, 69–96. London: Sage.

Kremmidas, Vasilis. 1976. *Eisagogi stin Istoria tis Neoellinikis Koinonias 1700–1821.* Athens: Exantas.

Kroeber, A. L., and Clyde Kluckhohn. 1952. *Culture: A Critical Review of Concepts and Definitions.* New York: Vintage Books.

Kukathas, Chandran. 1992. "Are There Any Cultural Rights?" *Political Theory* 20, no. 1: 105–39.

Kymlicka, Will. 1995. *Multicultural Citizenship: A Liberal Theory of Minority Rights.* Oxford: Clarendon Press.

———. 1998. "Ethnic Association and Democratic Citizenship." In *Freedom of Association*, edited by Amy Gutman, 177–213. Princeton: Princeton University Press.

Kyrou, Alexandros K. 1991. "Ethnicity as Humanitarianism: The Greek-American Relief Campaign for Occupied Greece, 1941–1944." In *New Directions in Greek American Studies*, edited by Dan Georgakas and Charles C. Moskos, 111–28. New York: Pella.

Lal, Barbara Ballis. 1983. "Perspectives on Ethnicity: Old Wine in New Bottles." *Ethnic and Racial Studies* 6, no. 2: 154–73.

Lambropoulos, Vassilis. 1988. *Literature as National Institution: Studies in the Politics of Modern Greek Criticism.* Princeton: Princeton University Press.

———. 1993. *The Rise of Eurocentrism: Anatomy of Interpretation.* Princeton: Princeton University Press.

———. 1996a. "Introduction: Approaches to Ethnic Politics." *South Atlantic Quarterly* 95, no. 4: 851–54.

———. 1996b. "Nomoscopic Analysis." *South Atlantic Quarterly* 95, no. 4: 855–79.

———. 1997. "Modern Greek Studies in the Age of Ethnography." *Journal of Modern Greek Studies* 15, no. 2: 197–208.

Larochelle, Gilbert. 1992. "Interdependence, Globalization, and Fragmentation." In *Globalization and Territorial Identities*, edited by Sdravko Mlinar, 150–64. Aldershot: Avebury.

Larsen, Neil. 1995. *Reading North by South: On Latin American Literature, Culture, and Politics.* Minneapolis: University of Minnesota Press.

Lasch, Christopher. 1991. *The One and Only Heaven: Progress and Its Critics.* New York: Norton.

Lash, Scott, and John Urry. 1987. *The End of Organized Capitalism.* Cambridge: Cambridge University Press.

Latham, Edward. 1970. *Famous Sayings and Their Authors.* Detroit: Gale Research.

Lawton, William. 1992. "The Crisis of the Nation-State: A Post-Modernist Canada?" *Acadiensis* 22, no. 1: 134–45.

Lazarre, Jean. 1996. *Beyond the Whiteness of Whiteness: A Memoir of a White Mother of Black Sons*. Durham, N.C.: Duke University Press.

Lazarus, Neil. 1990. *Resistance in Postcolonial African Fiction*. New Haven: Yale University Press.

Leake, William Martin. 1814. *Researches in Greece*. London: John Booth.

Lechner, Frank J. 1984. "Ethnicity and Revitalization in the Modern World System." *Sociological Focus* 17, no. 3: 243–56.

Lenin, V. I. 1964. *Collected Works*. Vol. 20. Moscow: Progress Publishers.

Leontis, Artemis. 1995. *Topographies of Hellenism: Mapping the Homeland*. Ithaca, N.Y.: Cornell University Press.

Lessing, G. E. [1767] 1962. *Hamburg Dramaturgy*. Translated by Helen Zimmern. New York: Dover.

Levine, Joseph M. 1991. *The Battle of the Books, History, and Literature in the Augustan Age*. Ithaca, N.Y.: Cornell University Press.

Lévi-Strauss, Claude. 1963. *Structural Anthropology*. Translated by Claire Jacobson and Brooke Grundfest Schoept. New York: Basic Books.

Lewis, Bernard. 1975. *History: Remembered, Recovered, Invented*. Princeton: Princeton University Press.

Lie, John. 1995. "From International Migration to Transnational Diaspora," *Contemporary Sociology* 24, no. 4: 303–6.

Lieberson, Stanley. 1985. "Unhyphenated Whites in the United States." *Ethnic and Racial Studies* 8, no. 1: 159–80.

Liebes, Tamar, and Elihu Katz. 1990. *The Export of Meaning: Cross-Cultural Readings of "Dallas."* New York: Oxford University Press.

Lind, Michael. 1995. *The Next American Nation: The New Nationalism and the Fourth American Revolution*. New York: Free Press.

Linz, Juan. 1973. "Early State-Building and Late Peripheral Nationalism against the State: The Case of Spain." In *Building States and Nations*, vol. 2, edited by S. N. Eisenstadt and Stein Rokkan, 32–116. London: Sage.

Lipking, Lawrence. 1970. *The Ordering of the Arts in Eighteenth-Century England*. Princeton: Princeton University Press.

Lipset, Seymour Martin. 1963. *The First New Nation: The United States in Historical and Comparative Perspective*. New York: Basic Books.

Lipset, Seymour Martin, and Earl Raab. 1995. *Jews and the New American Scene*. Cambridge, Mass.: Harvard University Press.

Lipsitz, George. 1998. *The Possessive Investment in Whiteness: How White People Profit from Identity Politics*. Philadelphia: Temple University Press.

Lloyd, David. 1993. *Anamolous States: Irish Writing and the Post-Colonial Moment*. Dublin: Lilliput Press.

Lloyd, David, and Paul Thomas. 1998. *Culture and the State*. New York: Routledge.

Loraux, Nicole. 1991. "Reflections of the Greek City on Unity and Division." In *City States in Classical Antiquity and Medieval Italy: Athens and Rome, Florence and Venice*, edited by Anthony Molho, Kurt Raaflaub, and Julia Emlen, 33–52. Stuttgart: Franz Steiner.

Lovejoy, Arthur O., Gilbert Chinard, George Boas, and Ronald S. Crane, eds. 1935. *A Documentary History of Primitivism and Related Ideas*. Baltimore: Johns Hopkins Press.

Lowe, Donald M. 1982. *History of Bourgeois Perception*. Chicago: University of Chicago Press.

Macfie, A. L. 1967. *The Individual in Society: Papers on Adam Smith*. London: Allen and Unwin.

Mackridge, Peter. 1985. *The Modern Greek Language*. Oxford: Oxford University Press.

Maffesoli. Michel. 1991. "The End of Aesthetics." *Theory, Culture and Society* 8, no. 1: 7–20.

Magdalino, Paul. 1992. "Hellenism and Nationalism in Byzantium." In *Neohellenism*, edited by John Burke and Stathis Gauntlett, 1–30. Canberra: Australian National University.

Makrides, Vassilios N. 1988. "Science and the Orthodox Church in Eighteenth- and Early Nineteenth-Century Greece: Sociological Considerations." *Balkan Studies* 29, no. 2: 165–82.

Malinowski, Bronislaw. 1944. *A Scientific Theory of Culture*. Chapel Hill: University of North Carolina Press.

Mann, Arthur. 1979. *The One and the Many: Reflections on the American Identity*. Chicago: University of Chicago Press.

Mann, Michael. 1986. *The Sources of Social Power*. Vol. 1, *A History of Power from the Beginning to A.D. 1760*. Cambridge: Cambridge University Press.

Manville, Philip Brooke. 1990. *The Origins of Citizenship in Ancient Athens*. Princeton: Princeton University Press.

Margalit, Avishai, and Moshe Halbertal. 1994. "Liberalism and the Right to Culture." *Social Research* 61, no. 3: 491–510.

Mariátegui, José Carlos. 1971. *Seven Interpretive Essays*. Translated by M. Urquidi. Austin: University of Texas Press.

Mathiopoulos, Margarita. 1989. *History and Progress: In Search of the European and American Mind*. New York: Praeger.

Mattelart, Armand. 1983. *Transnational and the Third World: The Struggle for Culture*. South Hadley, Mass.: Bergin and Harvey.

Matossian, Mary. 1962. "Ideologies of Delayed Industrialization: Some Tensions and Ambiguities." In *Political Change in Underdeveloped Countries: Nationalism and Communism*, edited by John H. Kautsky, 252–65. New York: John Wiley and Sons.

Mauriac, Henry M. de 1949. "Alexander the Great and the Politics of 'Homonoia.' " *Journal of the History of Ideas* 10, no. 1: 104–14.

Mavrokordatos, Nikolaos. 1800. *Filotheou Parerga*. Edited by Grigorios I. Kostantas. Vienna.

Mavrokordatos, Nikolaos. 1989. *Les loisirs de Philothée*. Translated by Jacques Bouchard. Montreal: Les Presses de l'Université de Montréal.

Mayall, James. 1990. *Nationalism and International Society*. Cambridge: Cambridge University Press.

McClaughry, John. 1996. "Secession Now (Maybe)." *Good Society* 6, no. 3: 1–5.

McNeely, Connie, and Yasemin Nuhoglu Soysal. 1989. "International Flows of Television Programming: A Revisionist Research Orientation." *Public Culture* 2, no. 1: 136–44.

McNeil, William H. 1986. *Polyethnicity and National Unity in World History.* Toronto: University of Toronto Press.

McRae, Kenneth D. 1973. "Empire, Language, and Nation: The Canadian Case." In *Building States and Nations*, vol. 2, edited by S. N. Eisenstadt and Stein Rokkan, 14–76. London: Sage.

Meier, Christian. 1990. *The Greek Discovery of Politics.* Translated by David McLintock. Cambridge: Cambridge University Press.

Meinecke, Friedrich. 1970. *Cosmopolitanism and the National State.* Translated by Robert B. Kimber. Princeton: Princeton University Press.

Mejer, Jan. 1993. "Les événements de mai-juin 1968 as a Modernity Crisis." *Theory Culture and Society* 10, no. 1: 53–74.

Melville, Herman. 1987. *The Piazza Tales and Other Prose Pieces, 1839–1860.* Evanston, Ill.: Northwestern University Press.

Mencken, H. L. 1936. *The American Spelling: An Inquiry into the Development of English in the United States.* New York: Knopf.

Mendels, Doron. 1992. *The Rise and Fall of Jewish Nationalism.* New York: Doubleday.

Michelena, José A. Silva. 1973. "Diversities among Dependent Nations: An Overview of Latin American Developments." In *Building States and Nations*, vol. 2, edited by S. N. Eisenstadt and Stein Rokkan, 232–49. London: Sage.

Mill, J. S. [1860] 1958. *Considerations on Representative Government.* Indianapolis: Bobbs-Merrill.

———. [1838] 1980. *Mill on Bentham and Coleridge.* Cambridge: Cambridge University Press.

Miller, David, ed. 1991. *The Blackwell Encyclopaedia of Political Thought.* Oxford: Basil Blackwell.

———. 1993. "In Defence of Nationality." *Society for Applied Philosophy* 10, no. 1: 3–16.

———. 1995. *On Nationality.* New York: Clarendon Press.

Milne, David. 1993. "Whither Canadian Federalism? Alternative Constitutional Futures." In *Comparative Federalism and Federation: Competing Traditions and Future Dimensions*, edited by Michael Burgess and Alain-G. Gagnon, 203–26. Toronto: University of Toronto Press.

Milner, Andrew. 1994. "Cultural Materialism, Culturalism, and Post-Culturalism: The Legacy of Raymond Williams." *Theory, Culture and Society* 11, no. 1: 43–73.

Minogue, K. R. 1967. *Nationalism.* New York: Basic Books.

Moisiodax, Iosipos. 1781. *Theoria tis Geografias.* Vienna.

———. 1976. *Apologia.* Edited by Alkis Angelou. Athens: Ermis.

———. 1985. "Proïmion" (1761). In *Iosipos Moisiodax: I Syntetagmenes tis Balkanikis Skepsis ton 18o eona*, edited by Paschalis M. Kitromilides. Athens: Morfotiko Idrima Ethnikis Trapezis.

Mombeshora, Solomon. 1990. "The Salience of Ethnicity in Political Development: The Case of Zimbabwe." *International Sociology* 4, no. 5: 427–44.

Moran, Daniel. 1990. *Towards the Century of Words: Johann Cotta and the Politics of the Public Realm in Germany, 1795–1832.* Berkeley: University of California Press.

Morton, W. L. 1961. *The Canadian Identity.* Toronto: University of Toronto Press.

Moskos, Charles C. 1989. *Greek Americans: Struggle and Success.* 2nd ed. New Brunswick, N.J.: Transaction Publishers.

Mosse, George L. 1975. *The Nationalization of the Masses: Political Symbolism and Mass Movements in Germany from the Napoleonic Wars through the Third Reich.* New York: Howard Fertig.

Murphy, Peter. 1997. "The Roars of Whispers: Cosmopolitanism and Neohellenism." *Journal of Modern Greek Studies* 15, no. 2: 274–81.

Musil, Robert. [1951] 1995. *The Man without Qualities.* Translated by Sophie Wilkins. New York: Knopf.

Myrivilis, Stratis. [1943] 1997. *O Vasilis O Arvanitis.* Athens: Estia.

Nagel, Joanne. 1986. "The Political Construction of Ethnicity." In *Competitive Ethnic Relations,* edited by Suzan Olzak and Joanne Nagel, 93–112. Orlando, Fla.: Academic Press.

Nairn, Tom. 1977. *The Break-Up of Britain: Crisis and Neo-Nationalism.* London: NLB.

Nash, Manning. 1989. *The Cauldron of Ethnicity in the Modern World.* Chicago: University of Chicago Press.

Nelson, Candace, and Marta Tienda. 1985. "The Structuring of Hispanic Ethnicity: Historical and Contemporary Perspectives." *Ethnic and Racial Studies* 8, no. 1: 49–74.

Neokessareos, Nathanail. 1802. *Antifonisis.* Triest.

Newfield, Christopher, and Avery F. Gordon. 1996. "Multiculturalism's Unfinished Business." In *Mapping Multiculturalism,* edited by Avery F. Gordon and Christopher Newfield, Minneapolis: University of Minnesota Press.

Newman, Gerald. 1987. *The Rise of English Nationalism: A Cultural History, 1740–1830.* New York: St. Martin's Press.

Ngugi Wa Thiong'o. 1981. *Writers in Politics.* London: Heinemann.

Nisbet, H. B., ed. 1985. *German Aesthetic and Literary Criticism: Winckelmann, Lessing, Hamann, Herder, Schiller, Goethe.* Cambridge: Cambridge University Press.

Norton, Robert E. 1991. *Herder's Aesthetics and the European Enlightenment.* Ithaca, N.Y.: Cornell University Press.

Noutsos, Panagiotis. 1980. "Evgenios Voulgaris ke Francis Bacon." *Ipirotika Hronika* 22: 151–61.

———. 1981. *Neoelliniki Filosofia: I Ideologikes Diastaseis ton Evropaikon tis Prosengisseon.* Athens: Kedros.

Novak, Michael, 1972. *TheRise of the Unmeltable Ethics Politics and Culture in the Seventies.* New York: Macmillan.

Nussbaum, Martha C. 1996. *For Love of Country: Debating the Limits of Patriotism.* Boston: Beacon Press.

Nwankwo, Arthur A. 1985. *National Concsiousness in Nigeria.* Enugu: Fourth Dimension Publishing.

Nye, Russel Blaire. 1960. *The Cultural Life of the New Nation, 1776–1830.* New York: Harper Brothers.

Obolensky, Dimitri. 1972. "Nationalism in Eastern Europe in the Middle Ages." *Transactions of the Royal Historical Society* 22, 5th ser, 1–16. London: Royal Historical Society.

Okamura, Jonathan Y. 1981. "Situational Ethnicity." *Ethnic and Racial Studies* 4, no. 4: 452–65.

Olzak, Susan. 1992. *The Dynamics of Ethnic Competition and Conflict.* Stanford, Calif.: Stanford University Press.

Origen. 1980. *Contra Celsum.* Translated by Henry Chadwick. Cambridge: Cambridge University Press.

Orridge, A. W. 1981. "Uneven Development and Nationalism: 2." *Political Studies* 29, no. 2: 181–90.

Padilla, Felix M. 1985. *Latino Ethnic Consciousness: The Case of Mexican Americans and Puerto Ricans in Chicago.* Notre Dame, Ind.: University of Notre Dame Press.

Paliouritis, Grigorios. 1807. *Epitomi Istoria tis Ellados.* Venice.

———. 1815. *Arheologia Elliniki, iti, Filosofiki Istoria.* 2 vols. Venice: Glikis.

Pantazopoulos, N. J. 1967. *Church and Law in the Balkan Peninsula during the Ottoman Rule.* Thessaloniki: Institute for Balkan Studies.

Papadopoulos, Chrisostomos. 1939. "O Kyrillos Loukaris os Patriarchis Alexandreias." In *Kyrillos Loukaris 1572–1638.* Athens: Eteria Kritikon Spoudon.

Papadopoulos, Thanasis. 1982. *I Filosofikes ke Kinoniko-Politikes Antilipseis tou Veniamin Lesviou.* Athens: Kedros.

Papageorgiou, Georgios. 1990. *O Eksinghronismos tou Ellina Pragmatefti simfona me ta Evropaïka Protipa (teli 18ou–arhes 19ou eona).* Athens: Adelfi Tolidi.

Park, Robert E. 1950. *Race and Culture.* New York: Free Press.

Park, Robert E., and Ernest W. Burgess. 1921. *Introduction to the Science of Sociology.* Chicago: University of Chicago Press.

Park, Robert E., and Herbert A. Miller. 1921. *Old World Traits Transplanted.* New York: Harper Brothers.

Parsons, Talcott. 1975. "Some Theoretical Considerations on the Nature and Trends of Change of Ethnicity." In *Ethnicity: Theory and Practice*, edited by Nathan Glazer and Daniel P. Moynihan, 52–83. Cambridge, Mass.: Harvard University Press.

Pascal, Roy. 1953. *The German Sturm und Drang.* New York: Philosophical Library.

Peck, Gunther W. 1991. "Crisis in the Family: Padrones and Radicals in Utah, 1908–1912." In *New Directions in Greek American Studies*, edited by Dan Georgakas and Chales C. Moskos, 73–94. New York: Pella.

Pelagidis, Eustathios. 1983. "I Synodiki Apofasi gia tin Oristiki 'Apokatastasi' tou Methodiou Anthrakiti." *Makedonika* 23: 134–46.

Pentzikis, Nikos. G. [1944] 1987. *O Pethamenos ke i Anastasi.* Athens: Agra.

Perlman, S. 1976. "Panhellism, the Polis and Imperialism." *Historia* 25, no. 1: 1–30.

Peterson, Brent O. 1991. *Popular Narratives and Ethnic Identity: Literature and Community in Die Abendschule*. Ithaca, N.Y.: Cornell University Press.

Petmezas, Socrates D. 1999. "The Formation of Early Hellenic Nationalism and the Special Symbolic and Material Interests of the New Radical Republican Intelligentsia (1730–1830)." *Historein* 1: 51–74.

Petronius. 1965. *The Satyricon and Other Fragments*. Translated by J. P. Sullivan. Harmondsworth: Penguin.

Pinson, Koppel S. 1934. *Pietism as a Factor in the Rise of German Nationalism*. New York: Columbia University Press.

Plamenatz, John. 1976. "Two Types of Nationalism." In *Nationalism: The Nature and Evolution of an Idea*, edited by Eugene Kamenka, 22–37. New York: St. Martin's Press.

Plano, Jack C., and Roy Olton. 1982. *The International Relations Dictionary*. 3rd ed. Santa Barbara: ABC-Clio.

Plessner, Helmuth. 1959. *Die Verspätete Nation. Über Die Politische Verführbarkeit Bürgerlicher Geistes*. Stuttgart: W. Kohlhammer.

Poggi, Gianfranco. 1978. *The Development of the Modern State: A Sociological Introduction*. Stanford, Calif.: Stanford University Press.

———. 1990. *The State: Its Nature, Development, and Prospects*. Stanford, Calif.: Stanford University Press.

Pratt, Mary Louise. 1992. *Imperial Eyes: Travel Writing and Transculturation*. London: Routledge.

Pringos, Ioannis. 1931. "To Hroniko tou Amsterdam." *Nea Estia* 10: 846–53.

Psalidas, Athanasios P. 1795. *Kalokinimata, iti Enghiridion kata Fthonou ke kata tis Logikis tou Evgeniou*. Vienna.

———. 1960. "True Happiness, or the Basis of all Religion." Translated by Raphael Demos. *Journal of the History of Ideas* 21, no. 4: 481–96.

Psimmenos, Nikos K. 1982. "I 'Epitetmimeni Eparithmisi' tou Dimitriou Prokopiou as Pigi Gnosis tis Neoellinikis Philosophias." *Ipirotika Hronika* 24: 204–48.

Psycharis, G. 1988. *To Taxidi mou*. Athens: Nefeli.

Radhakrishnan, R. 1992. "Nationalism, Gender, and the Narrative of Identity." In *Nationalisms and Sexualities*, edited by Andrew Parker, Mary Russo, Doris Sommer, and Patricia Yaeger, 77–95. London: Routledge.

Rahe, Paul A. 1984. "The Primacy of Politics in Classical Greece." *American Historical Association* 89, no. 2: 265–93.

Readings, Bill. 1996. *The University in Ruins*. Cambridge, Mass.: Harvard University Press.

Renan, Ernest. 1990. "What Is a Nation?" (1882). In *Nation and Narration*, edited by Homi K. Bhabha, ed. New York: Routledge.

Renner, Karl. 1918. *Das Selstbestimmungsrecht der Nationen in besonderer Anwendung auf Oesterreich*. Leipzig: Franz Deuticke.

Ricoeur, Paul. 1965. *History and Truth*. Translated by Charles A. Kelbley. Evanston, Ill.: Northwestern University Press.

Riggs, Fred W. 1992. "Ethnicity, Nationalism, Race, Minority: A Semantic/Onomantic Exercise (Part One)." *International Sociology* 6, no. 3: 281–305.

Rizal, José. 1961. *The Lost Eden*. Translated by León Ma. Guerrero. Blooming-ton: Indiana University Press.

Roberts, Martin. 1992. " 'World Music' and the Global Cultural Economy." *Di-aspora* 2, no. 2: 229–42.

Robertson, Roland. 1991a. "Mapping the Global Condition: Globalization as the Central Concept." In *Global Culture: Nationalism, Globalization, and Moder-nity*, edited by Mike Featherstone, 15–30. London: Sage.

———. 1991b. "Social Theory, Cultural Relativity, and the Problem of Glob-ality." *Current Debates in Art History* 3: 69–90.

———. 1992. *Globalization: Social Theory and Global Culture*. London: Sage.

Rosaldo, Renato I. 1994. "Whose Cultural Studies?" *American Anthropologist* 96: 524–29.

Rosecrance, Richard. 1996. "The Rise of the Virtual State." *Foreign Affairs* 75, no. 4: 45–61.

Rousseau, Jean Jacques. 1915. *The Political Writings*. Edited by C. E. Vaughan. Cambridge: Cambridge University Press.

———. 1953. *Political Writings*. Translated by Frederick Watkins. Edinburgh: Nelson.

Roxborough, Ian. 1979. *Theories of Underdevelopment*. London: Macmillan.

Rudolph, Lloyd I, and Susanne Hoeker Rudolph. 1967. *The Modernity of Tradi-tion in India*. Chicago: University of Chicago Press.

Ruland, Richard, ed. 1972. *The Native Muse: Theories of American Literature*. Vol. 1. New York: Dutton.

Runciman, Steven. 1968. *The Great Church in Captivity*. Cambridge: Cambridge University Press.

Runciman, W. G. 1982. "Origins of States: The Case of Archaic Greece." *Com-parative Studies in Society and History* 24, 3: 351–77.

Runte, Roseann, ed. 1979. *Studies in Eighteenth-Century Culture*. Vol. 8. Madi-son: University of Wisconsin Press.

Ryan, Michael. 1989. *Politics and Culture: Working Hypotheses for a Post-Revo-lutionary Society*. London: Macmillan.

Sacks, Karen Brodkin. 1994. "How Did Jews Become White Folks?" In *Race*, edited by Steven Gregory and Roger Sanjek, 78–102. New Brunswick, N.J.: Rutgers University Press.

Safran, Nadav. 1961. *Egypt in Search of a Political Community: An Analysis of the Intellectual and Political Evolution of Egypt, 1804–1952*. Cambridge, Mass.: Harvard University Press.

Said, Edward. 1979. *Orientalism*. New York: Vintage Books.

———. 1993. *Culture and Imperialism*. New York: Knopf.

———. 1999. "Restoring Intellectual Coherence." *MLA Newsletter*, Spring.

San Juan, E. Jr. 1992a. *Reading the West/Writing the East: Studies in Comparative Literature and Culture*. New York: Peter Lang.

———. 1992b. *Racial Formations/Critical Transformations: Articulations of Power in Ethnic and Racial Studies in the United States*. Atlantic Highlands, N.J.: Humanities Press.

Sanjek, Roger. 1994. "Intermarriage and the Future of the Races in the United States." In *Race*, edited by Steven Gregory and Roger Sanjek, 103–30. New Brunswick, N.J.: Rutgers University Press.

Sawyer, Jeffrey K. 1990. *Printed Poison: Pamphlet Propaganda, Faction Politics, and the Public Sphere in Early Seventeenth-Century France*. Berkeley: University of California Press.

Schell, Paul, and John Hamer. 1995. "Cascadia: The New Binationalism of Western Canada and the U. S. Pacific Northwest." In *Identities in North America: The Search for Community*, edited by Robert L. Earle and John D. Wirth, 140–56. Stanford, Calif.: Stanford University Press.

Schiller, Frederick. 1844. *Sämtliche Werke*. Vol. 2. Stuttgart: I. G. Cotta'sche Buchhandlung.

———. 1985. "Theater Considered as a Moral Institution" 1784. In *Poet of Freedom*. Translated by John Sigerson and John Chambless. New York: Benjamin Franklin House.

Schlegel, August Wilhelm. 1846. *A Course of Lectures on Dramatic Art and Literature*. Translated by John N. Black. London: Henry G. Bohn.

Schlegel, Friedrich. 1882. *Lectures on the History of Literature, Ancient and Modern*. London: George Bell and Sons.

Schlesinger, Arthur. 1992. *The Disuniting of America*. New York: Norton.

Schluchter, Wolfgang. 1996. *Paradoxes of Modernity: Culture and Conduct in the Theory of Max Weber*. Translated by Neil Solomon. Stanford, Calif.: Stanford University Press.

Schmitt, Carl. 1993. "The Age of Neutralizations and Depoliticizations." *Telos* 96: 130–42.

Schneider, David M. 1969. "Kinship, Nationality and Religion in American Culture: Toward a Definition of Kinship." In *Forms of Symbolic Action*, edited by Robert F. Spencer, 116–25. Seattle, Wash.: American Ethnological Society.

———. 1980. *American Kinship: A Cultural Account*. 2nd ed. Chicago: University of Chicago Press.

Schroeder, Ralph. 1992. *Max Weber and the Sociology of Culture*. London: Sage.

Schulte-Sasse, Jochen. 1989. "The Prestige of the Artist under Conditions of Modernity." *Cultural Critique* 12: 83–100.

Schulze, Hagen. 1991. *The Course of German Nationalism from Frederick the Great to Bismarck, 1763–1867*. Translated by Sarah Hanburg-Tenison. Cambridge: Cambridge University Press.

———, ed. 1987. *Nation-Building in Central Europe*. New York: Berg Publishers.

Schumacher, John N. 1981. *Revolutionary Clergy: The Filipino Clergy and the Nationalist Movement, 1859–1903*. Manila: Ateneo de Manila University Press.

Schwartz, Stuart B. 1987. "The Formation of a Colonial Identity in Brazil." In *Colonial Identity in the Atlantic, 1500–1800*, edited by Nicholas Canny and Anthony Pagden, 15–50. Princeton: Princeton University Press.

Seferis, Giorgos. 1979. *Enas Dialogos gia tin Piisi*. Edited by Loukas Kousoulas. Athens: Ermis.

Seton-Watson, Hugh. 1977. *Nations and States: An Enquiry into the Origins of Nations and the Politics of Nationalism*. London: Methuen.

Shafer, Boyd C. 1972. *Faces of Nationalism: New Realities and Old Myths.* New York: Harcourt Brace Jovanovich.

Shayegan, Daryush. 1992. *Cultural Schizophrenia: Islamic Societies Confronting the West.* Translated by John Howe. London: Saqi Books.

Sheehan, James J. 1981. "What is German History? Reflections on the Role of the *Nation* in German History and Historiography." *Journal of Modern History* 53, no. 1: 1–23.

———. 1989. *German History: 1770–1866.* Oxford: Clarendon Press.

Shils, Edward. 1957. "Primordial, Personal, Sacred, and Civil Ties." *British Journal of Sociology* 8: 130–45.

———. 1962. "The Intellectuals in the Political Development of the New States." In *Political Change in Underdeveloped Countries: Nationalism and Communism,* edited by John H. Kautsky, 195–234. New York: John Wiley and Sons.

Shumway, David R. 1994. *Creating American Civilization: A Genealogy of American Literature as an Academic Discipline.* Minneapolis: University of Minnesota Press.

Silberman, Neil Asher. 1989. *Between Past and Present: Archaeology, Ideology and Nationalism in the Modern Middle East.* New York: Henry Holt.

Silverman, Kenneth. 1987. *A Cultural History of the American Revolution.* New York: Columbia University Press.

Simmel, Georg. 1955. *Conflict.* Translated by Kurt H. Wolff. *The Web of Group-Affiliations.* Translated by Reinhard Bendix. Glencoe, Il.: Free Press.

———. 1968. *The Conflict in Modern Culture and Other Essays.* Translated by K. Peter Etzkorn. New York: Teachers College Press.

———. [1900] 1978. *The Philosophy of Money* 2nd ed. Translated by Tom Bottomore and David Frisby. London: Routledge.

Skerry, Peter. 1992. "E Pluribus Hispanic?" *Wilson Quarterly,* Summer, 62–73.

———. 1993. *Mexican Americans: The Ambivalent Minority.* New York: Free Press.

Skoufos, Nikolaos. 1816. *Sinoptiki Istoria tis Ellinikis Filologias.* 2 vols. Vienna.

———. 1817. *Dokimion peri Patriotismou.* 2nd ed. Philadelphia.

Slack, Jennifer Daryl, and Laurie Anne White. 1992. "Ethics and Cultural Studies." In *Cultural Studies,* edited by Lawrence Grossberg, Cary Nelson and Paula A. Treichler, 571–96. New York: Routledge.

Smith, Adam. [1759] 1982. *The Theory of Moral Sentiments.* Edited by D. D. Raphael and A. L. Macfie. Indianapolis: Liberty Classics.

Smith, Anthony D. 1983. "Nationalism and Classical Social Theory." *British Journal of Sociology* 34, no. 1: 19–38.

———. 1984. "Ethnic Myths and Ethnic Revivals." *Archives européenes de sociologie* 25: 283–305.

———. 1986. *The Ethnic Origins of Nations.* Oxford: Basil Blackwell.

———. 1990. "Towards a Global Culture?" In *Global Culture: Nationalism, Globalization, and Modernity,* edited by Mike Featherstone, 171–192. London: Sage.

———. 1994. "The Problem of National Identity: Ancient, Medieval, and Modern?" *Ethnic and Racial Studies* 17, no. 3: 375–99.

Smith, Graham. 1995. "Mapping the Federal Condition: Ideology, Political Practice, and Social Justice." In *Federalism: The Multiethnic Challenge*, edited by Graham Smith, 1–28. London: Longman.

Smith, Stephen. 1990. "Hegel and the French Revolution: An Epitaph for Republicanism." In *The French Revolution and the Birth of Modernity*, edited by Ferenc Fehér, 219–39. Berkeley: University of California Press.

Snodgrass, Anthony. 1980. *Archaic Greece: The Age of Experiment*. Berkeley: University of California Press.

Snyder, Louis L. 1984. *Macro-Nationalisms: A History of the Pan-Movements*. Westport, Conn.: Greenwood Press.

Soja, Edward W. 1989. *Postmodern Geographies: The Reassertion of Space in Critical Social Theory*. London: Verso.

Sokolis, K. S. 1993. *Aftokratoria*. Athens: Roes.

Solovyof, Vladimir. [1897] 1918. *The Justification of the Good: An Essay on Moral Philosophy*. Translated by Nathalie A. Duddington. London: Constable.

Sommer, Doris. 1991. *Foundational Fictions: The National Romances of Latin America*. Berkeley: University of California Press.

Sontag, Deborah. 1993. "Oy Gevalt! New Yawkese An Endangered Dialect?" *New York Times*, February 14, A1, A18.

———. 1993. "A Fervent 'No' to Assimilation in New America." *New York Times*, June 29, A6.

Sophocles. 1994. *Antigone, The Women of Trachis, Philoctetes, Oedipus at Colonus*. Edited and translated by Hugh Lloyd-Jones. Cambridge, Mass.: Harvard University Press.

Souza, Anthony R., de, and Philip W. Porter. 1974. *The Underdevelopment and Modernization of the Third World*. Washington, D.C.: Association of American Geographers.

Spencer, Benjamin T. 1957. *The Quest for Nationality: An American Literary Campaign*. Syracuse: Syracuse University Press.

Spivak, Gayatri Chakravorty. 1988. "Can the Subaltern Speak?" In *Marxism and the Interpretation of Culture*, edited by Cary Nelson and Lawrence Grossberg. Chicago: University of Illinois Press.

Staël, Madame de. 1956. *De l' Allemagne*. Edited by André Monchoux. Paris: Librairie Marcel Didier.

———. 1959. *De la littérature: Considérée dans ses rapports avec les institutions sociales*. Edited by Paul Van Tieghem. Geneva: Librairie Droz.

Stanley, Peter A. 1974. *A Nation in the Making: The Philippines and the United States, 1899–1921*. Cambridge, Mass.: Harvard University Press.

Star, Alexander. 1997. "Don't Look Back: A Proposal for Our Roots-Obsessed Culture." *New Yorker*, February 3, 81–83.

Steinberg, Stephen. 1989. *The Ethnic Myth: Race, Ethnicity, and Class in America*. Boston: Beacon Press.

Stoyanov, Manio. 1966. "Les 'syndromites' Bulgares de livres Grecs au cours de la première moitie du XIXe siècle." *Byzantinisch-neugriechische Jarhbücher* 19: 373–405.

Strassoldo, Raimondo. 1992. "Globalism and Localism: Theoretical Reflections and Some Evidence." In *Globalization and Territorial Identities*, edited by Sdravko Mlinar, 35–59. Aldershot: Avebury.

Strauss, Barry S. 1994. "The Melting Pot, the Mosaic, and the Agora." In *Athenian Political Thought and the Reconstruction of American Democracy*, edited by J. Peter Euben, John R. Wallach, and Josiah Ober, 252–64. Ithaca, N.Y.: Cornell University Press.

Strayer, R. Joseph. 1972. "Laicization and Nationalism in the Thirteenth Century." In *Nationalism in the Middle Ages*, edited by C. Leon Tipton, 30–39. New York: Rinehart and Winston.

Suleri, Sara. 1992. *The Rhetoric of British India*. Chicago. University of Chicago Press.

Suro, Roberto. 1992. "Poll Finds Hispanic Desire to Assimilate." *New York Times*, December 15, A1, A18.

Swift, Jonathan. [1704] 1972. *A Tale of a Tub*. New York: Garland Publishing.

Tachios, A.E.N. 1989. "The National Regeneration of the Greeks as Seen by the Russian Intelligentsia." *Balkan Studies* 30, no. 2: 291–310.

Tambiah, Stanley J. 1989. "Ethnic Conflict in the World Today." *American Ethnologist* 16, no. 2: 335–49.

Tamir, Yael. 1993. *Liberal Nationalism*. Princeton: Princeton University Press.

Tcherikover, Victor. 1959. *Hellenistic Civilization and the Jews*. Translated by S. Applebaum. Philadelphia: Jewish Publication Society of America.

Tenbruck, Friedrich. 1994. "Internal History of Society or Universal History?" *Theory, Culture, and Society* 11, no. 1: 75–93.

Theotokas, Giorgos. [1929] 1979. *Eleftrho Pnevma*. Athens: Nea Elliniki Vivliothiki.

Thompson, John B. 1990. *Ideology and Modern Culture: Critical Social Theory in the Era of Mass Communication*. Stanford, Calif.: Stanford University Press.

Thompson, Richard H. 1989. *Theories of Ethnicity: A Critical Appraisal*. New York: Greenwood Press.

Tignor, Robert L. 1966. *Modernization and British Colonial Rule in Egypt, 1882–1914*. Princeton: Princeton University Press.

Tilly, Charles. 1975. "Reflections on the History of European State-Making." *The Formation of National States in Europe*, edited by Charles Tilly, 3–83. Princeton: Princeton University Press.

Tipps, Dean C. 1973. "Modernization Theory and the Comparative Study of Societies: A 'Critical Perspective.' " *Comparative Studies in Society and History* 15, no. 1: 199–226.

Tocqueville, Alexis de. [1835] 1969. *Democracy in America*. Translated by George Lawrence. New York: Harper Perennial.

Todorova, Maria. 1990. "Language as Cultural Unifier in a Multilingual Setting: The Bulgarian Case during the Nineteenth Century." *East European Politics and Societies* 4, no. 3: 439–50.

———. 1997. *Imagining the Balkans*. New York: Oxford University Press.

Tolstoy, Leo. N.d. *War and Peace*. Translated by Constance Garnett. New York: Modern Library.

Trudeau, Pierre. 1990. "Against Nationalism." *New Perspectives Quarterly* 7, no. 3: 60–61.

Trumpener, Katie. 1997. *Bardic Nationalism: The Romantic Novel and the British Empire*. Princeton: Princeton University Press.

Tsoukalas, Konstantinos. 1977. *Exartisi ke Anaparagogi: O Kinonikos Rolos ton Ekpedeftikon Mihanismon stin Ellada*. Athens: Themelio.

Tsourkas, Cléobule. 1967. *Les débuts de l'enseignement philosophique et de la libre pensée dans les Balkans. La vie et l'oeuvre de Théophile Corydalée (1570–1646)*. 2nd ed. Thessaloniki: Institute for Balkan Studies.

Turner, Frederick Jackson. 1962. *The Frontier in American History*. New York: Holt, Rinehart and Winston.

Tylor, Edward Burnett. 1958. *The Origins of Culture*. New York: Harper and Row.

Tziovas, Dimitris. 1986. *The Nationism of the Demoticists and Its Impact on Their Literary Theory (1888–1930)*. Amsterdam: Adolf M. Hakkert.

Urciuoli, Bonnie. 2000. "Whose Quincentenary Is It? Puerto Rican and Italian-American Class Identity in the U.S. in 1992." Unpublished manuscript.

———. 1996. *Exposing Prejudice: Puerto Rican Experience of Language, Race, and Class*. Boulder, Colo.: Westview Press.

Usher, S., ed. 1990. *Isocrates: Panegyricus and To Nicoles*. Warminster: Aris and Phillips.

Vallianatos, E. G. 1973. "Constantine Koumas and the Philological Gymnasium of Smyrna, 1810–1819." *East European Quarterly* 6, no. 4: 419–43.

———. 1987. *From Graikos to Hellene: Adamantios Koraes and the Greek Revolution*. Athens: Academy of Athens.

Veloudis, Georg. 1968. *Der neugriechische Alexander: Tradition in Bewahrung und Wandel*. Munich: Institüt für Byzantinistik und neugriechische Philologie.

———. 1970. "Jakob Phillip Fallmerayer und die Enstehung des neugriechischen Historismus." *Südostforschungen* 29: 43–90.

———. 1977. *Diigisis tou Alexandrou tou Makedonos*. Athens: Nea Elliniki Vivliothiki.

Venturi, Franco. 1989. *The End of the Old Regime, 1768–1776*. Translated R. Burr Litchfield. Princeton: Princeton University Press.

Verdery, Katherine. 1991. *National Ideology under Socialism: Identity and Cultural Politics in Ceausescu's Romania*. Berkeley: University of California Press.

Veremis, Thanos. 1989. "From National State to the Stateless Nation, 1821–1910." *European History Quarterly* 19: 135–49.

Verlaine, Paul. 1948. *Selected Poems*. Translated by C. F. MacIntyre. Berkeley: University of California Press.

Viroli, Maurizio. 1995. *For Love of Country: An Essay on Patriotism and Nationalism*. Oxford: Clarendon Press.

Viziinos, Georgios M. 1980. *Neoellinika Diigimata*. Edited by Panagiotis Moullas. Athens: Ermis.

Völkl, Ekkehard. 1967. "Die griechische Kultur in der Moldau während der Phanariotenzeit (1711–1821)." *Sudostforschungen* 26: 102–39.

Voulgaris, Evgenios. 1766. *I Logiki*. Leipzig.

Walbank, Frank W. 1985. *Selected Papers: Studies in Greek and Roman History and Historiography*. Cambridge: Cambridge University Press.

Waldman, Marilyn Robinson. 1991–92. "Tradition as a Modality of Change: Islamic Examples." *History of Religions*. 25, no. 4: 318–40.

Wallerstein, Immanuel. 1961. *Africa: The Politics of Independence*. New York: Random House.

Wallerstein, Immanuel. 1974. *The Modern World-System: Capitalist Agriculture and the Origins of the European World-Economy in the 16th Century*. New York: Academic Press.

———. 1979. *The Capitalist World-Economy*. Cambridge: Cambridge University Press.

———. 1990. "Culture as an Ideological Battleground of the Modern World-System." In *Global Culture: Nationalism, Globalization, and Modernity*, edited by Mike Featherstone, 31–56. London: Sage.

Walzer, Michael. 1986. "The Reform of the International System." In *Studies in War and Peace*, edited by Øyvind Østerud, 227–50. Oslo: Norwegian University Press.

———. 1992 *What It Means to Be an American: Essays on the American Experience*. New York: Marsilio.

Ware, Timothy. 1963. *The Orthodox Church*. London: Penguin.

Waters, Malcolm. 1995. *Globalization*. London: Routledge.

Waters, Mary C. 1990. *Ethnic Options: Choosing Identities in America*. Berkeley: University of California Press.

Watkins, Susan Scott. 1991. *From Provinces into Nations: Demographic Integration in Western Europe, 1870–1960*. Princeton: Princeton University Press.

Watts, R. L. 1966. *New Federations: Experiments in the Commonwealth*. Oxford: Clarendon Press.

Weber, Eugen. 1976. *Peasants into Frenchmen: The Modernization of Rural France, 1870–1914*. Stanford, Calif.: Stanford University Press.

Weber, Max. 1946. *From Max Weber: Essays in Sociology*. Translated by H. H. Gerth and C. Wright Mills. Oxford: Oxford University Press.

———. 1958. *The Protestant Ethic and the Spirit of Capitalism*. Translated by Talcott Parsons. New York: Scribner's.

———. 1968. *Economy and Society*. Vol. 1. Edited by Guenther Roth and Claus Wittich. New York: Bedminister Press.

Webster, Noah. [1789] 1951. *Dissertations on the English Language*. Gainesville, Fla.: Scholars' Facsimiles and Reprints.

Wendell, Charles. 1972. *The Evolution of the Egyptian National Image: From Its Origins to Ahmad Lutfi al-Sayyid*. Berkeley: University of California Press.

Werblowsky, R. J. Zwi. 1976. *Beyond Tradition and Modernity: Changing Religions in a Changing World*. London: Athlone Press.

West, Lois A., ed. 1997. *Feminist Nationalism*. New York: Routledge.

West, M. L. 1997. *The East Face of Helicon: West Asiatic Elements in Greek Poetry and Myth*. Oxford: Clarendon Press.

Wharton, Edith. [1920] 1966. *The Age of Innocence*. London: Constable.

Whitman, Walt. 1982. *Complete Poetry and Collected Prose*. New York: Library of America.

Williams, Colin H. 1992. "Identity, Autonomy, and the Ambiguity of Technological Development." In *Globalization and Territorial Identities*, edited by Sdravko Mlinar, 115–28. Aldershot: Avebury.

———. 1995. "A Requiem for Canada?" In *Federalism: The Multiethnic Challenge*, edited by Graham Smith, 31–72. London: Longman.

Williams, Gregory Howard. 1995. *Life on the Color Line: The True Story of a White Boy Who Discovered He Was Black*. New York: Dutton.

Williams, Raymond. 1958. *Culture and Society, 1780–1950*. New York: Columbia University Press.

———. 1961. *The Long Revolution*. New York: Columbia.

Winland, Daphne N. 1995. " 'We Are Now an Actual Nation': The Impact of National Independence on the Croatian Diaspora in Canada." *Diaspora* 4, no. 1: 3–29.

Wolff, Janet. 1991. "The Global and Specific: Reconciling Conflicting Theories of Culture." *Current Debates in Art History* 3: 160–73.

Woodhouse, C. M. 1986. *George Gemistos Plethon: The Last of the Hellenes*. Oxford: Clarendon Press.

Wuorinen, John H. 1931. *Nationalism in Modern Finland*. New York: Columbia University Press.

———. 1950. "Scandinavia and the Rise of Modern National Consciousness." In *Nationalism and Internationalism*, edited by Edward Mead Earle, 455–79. New York: Columbia University Press.

Wurfel, David. 1988. *Filipino Politics: Development and Decay*. Ithaca, N.Y.: Cornell University Press.

Wuthnow, Robert. 1992. "Cultural Change and Sociological Theory." In *Social Change and Modernity*, edited by Hans Haferkamp and Neil J. Smelser. Berkeley: University of California Press.

Yancey, William L., Eugene P. Ericksen, and George H. Leon. 1985. "The Structure of Pluralism." *Ethnic and Racial Studies* 8, no. 1: 994–116.

Yinger, J. Milton. 1986. "Intersecting Strands in the Theorization of Race and Ethnic Relations." In *Theories of Race and Ethnic Relations*, edited by John Rex and David Mason, 20–41. Cambridge: Cambridge University Press.

Young, M. Crawford. 1986. "Cultural Pluralism in the Third World." In *Competitive Ethnic Relations*, edited by Suzan Olzak and Joanne Nagel, 113–36. Orlando, Fla.: Academic Press.

———. 1993. "The Dialectics of Cultural Pluralism: Concept and Reality." In *The Rising Tide of Cultural Pluralism: The Nation-State at Bay?*, edited by Crawford M. Young, 3–35. Madison: University of Wisconsin Press.

Zeller, Suzanne. 1987. *Inventing Canada: Early Victorian Science and the Idea of a Transcontinental Nation*. Toronto: University of Toronto Press.

Zernatto, Guido. 1944. "Nation: The History of a Word." *Review of Politics* 6, no. 3: 351–66.

Zubaida, Sami. 1989. "Nations: Old and New. Comments on Anthony D. Smith's 'The Myth of the Modern Nation and the Myths of Nations.' " *Ethnic and Racial Studies* 12, no. 3: 329–39.

INDEX

Abu-Lughod, Janet L., 194
Alba, Richard D., 172–73
ancients and moderns, 104–5; in Greece, 114–15, 118–22; in the United States, 159. *See also* culture wars; multiculturalism
Anderson, Benedict, 36
Appadurai, Arjun, 19, 205–7
Appiah, Kwame Anthony, 204–5
Archer, Margaret S., 50–51
assimilation theory, 168–69
Atwood, Margaret, 147–48
Augsburg, Peace of, 52–53

Balibar, Etienne, 200
Bate, W. J., 103
Battle of the Books, 104–5. *See also* culture wars
Bellah, Robert N., 161–62
Bhabha, Homi, 26–27, 209
Blanning, T.C.W., 74
Blaut, James M. , 60–61
Bourne, Randolph, 169
Boyarin, Daniel and Jonathan Boyarin, 207–8
Brading, D. A. , 149–50
Brazil, 148–51
Brubaker, Rogers, 25–26
Buell, Frederick, 210–11
Burke, Edmund, 47

Campbell, Colin, 66
Canada, 192, 143–48; identity of, 29
Cavafy, Constantine, 174–75
Chatterjee, Partha, 8, 9, 72, 99
civic identity, 162–65. *See also* ethnicity
Comaroff, John, 63–66
comparisons, 102–4; and American nationalism, 158–59; and Canadian nationalism, 147–48; and Egyptian nationalism, 152–54; and English nationalism, 139–43; and German nationalism, 89–93; and Greek nationalism, 108–10, 114
Connor, Walker, 20
Cornell, Stephen, 181
Corrigan, Philip, 137–38

cosmopolitanism, 203–5. *See also* diaspora; universalism
Cuddihy, John Murray, 100
cultural determinism, 65–70
culture: and autonomy, 69–70; and belatedness, 59–60; as compensatory agent, 56–58; and homogeneity, 61–63; and imperialism, 60–61; and modernization, 61–63; and social change, 11–12; and state, 76–77; theory of, 44–45
culture wars, 166–67. *See also* ancients and moderns; multiculturalism
Cyril and Methodius, 108

Dalberg-Acton (Lord Acton), 3, 198–99
Damodos, Vikendios, 120
diaspora, 205–11. *See also* cosmopolitanism; universalism
Drummond, Alexander, 115–16
Duchacek, Ivo D., 218
Durkheim, Emile, 12, 32–33, 50

Eagleton, Terry, 47
East Timor, 93–94
Egypt, 8, 95–96, 151–55
England, 137–43
ethnicity: in antiquity, 21–23; and class interest, 63–66, 178–79, 186–89; and competition, 186–88; politicization of 53, 71–72; symbolic, 172–75; white, 171–72. *See also* multiculturalism; race

Fallmerayer, Jakob Phillip, 123
Fanon, Frantz, 9–10
Federalism: in Canada, 220; and democracy, 222; and ethnic competition, 219–20; and European Union, 221–22; history of, 215–17; in Spain, 221; theories of, 217–18
Fichte, Johann Gottlieb, 82–83
Finland, 77–78
France, 40. *See also* Napoleon
French Revolution, 72–73

Galanaki, Rea, 126
Gans, Herbert J., 172
Gellner, Ernest, 62–63

Novalis, 73
Nussbaum, Martha C., 203–4

Olzak, Susan, 186–87
Origen, 42–43
Ottoman Empire, 113, 219

Paliouritis, Grigorios, 128
panethnicity: Asian, 183–84; Indian, 180–
   82; Latino, 182–83. *See also* ethnicity
Park, Robert E., 168
Pentzikis, Nikos, 131
Petronius, 102
Philippines, 96–98
Pietism, 31. *See also* German nationalism
Pringos, Ioannis, 126–27
Psalidas, Athanasios, 120–21
Psycharis, G., 132

race, 177–80. *See also* ethnicity; multicul-
   turalism
Renner, Karl, 216
Rhineland, 74–75. *See also* German Na-
   tionalism; Germany; Napoleon
Rizal, José, 96–97. *See also* Philippines
Robertson, Roland, 65–66, 188

Sayer, Derek, 137–38
Schiller, Frederick, 80–81
Schlegel, August Wilhelm, 89
Schlegel, Friedrich, 86
Schlesinger, Arthur, 166
Simmel, Georg, 175, 179

Smith, Adam, 46–47
Soja, Edward W., 107
Sophocles, 103–4
South America, 101, 148–49, 151
Staël, Madame de, 83–84, 89, 90–91

Tocqueville, Alexis de, 155
Tolstoy, Leo, 75
tradition, invention of 37–39. *See also*
   nationalism
Tylor, Edward Burnett, 49

United States: ancients and moderns in,
   159; and belatedness, 157–61; and civil
   religion, 161–62; culture wars in, 166–
   67; ethnicity in, 205–7; identity of, 156–
   57; immigration to, 167–68; nationalism
   in, 160–61
universalism, 42–43, 193–95. *See also* globalization

Verlaine, Paul, 219–20
Viroli, Maurizio, 135
Viziinos, Georgios, 122

Wallerstein, Immanuel, 58–59
Walzer, Michael, 135, 200–201
Waters, Mary C., 174–75
Weber, Max, 67–69
Westphalia, Peace of, 54–55
Williams, Raymond, 45, 57–58

Zeller, Suzanne, 144